KU-504-027

Jack Fishman

# And the Walls Came Tumbling Down

Pan Books London and Sydney

First published 1982 by Souvenir Press Ltd
This edition published 1983 by Pan Books Ltd,
Cavaye Place, London SW10 9PG
© Jack Fishman and John Hill Productions Ltd 1982
ISBN 0 330 26920 8
Photoset by Parker Typesetting Service, Leicester
Printed and bound in Great Britain by
Collins, Glasgow

# And the Walls Came Tumbling Down

Jack Fishman has already achieved worldwide acclaim as the author of two non-fiction bestselling books. *The Seven Men of Spandau*, about the Hitler lieutenants who escaped the gallows at Nuremberg and were sentenced to be the sole inmates of Berlin's Spandau prison, was translated into almost every language; *My Darling Clementine*, his biography of Lady Churchill, became number one on the bestseller lists of both Britain and the United States and went into seventeen translations. It was Fishman's investigative ability as a journalist that exposed Philby as the 'third man', and more recently, under the pseudonym of J. D. Gilman, he was co-author of *KG 200*, the factually based No. 1 bestselling novel on the astounding stories he had uncovered about Luftwaffe squadrons that masqueraded as Allied airmen flying B17s and Liberator bombers.

In his research for *And the Walls Came Tumbling Down* Jack Fishman received the cooperation of the intelligence services of four countries and the statements of hundreds of surviving participants in Operation 'Jericho', the name given to one of the most secret operations of the Second World War.

By the same author in Pan Books
(co-authored under the pseudonym J. D. Gilman)

KG 200: The Force with No Face

# Contents

Preface                                          11

1   The man who sold people                       15
2   No.23 Herrengasse                             22
3   The pint-sized giant                          35
4   A job for a Joshua                            43
5   The melting pot                               53
6   Best laid plans                               70
7   Courvoisier the pimp                          93
8   'New boy'                                    112
9   Opportunity knocks at noon                   142
10  The madame and the maid                      169
11  Visibility zero                              178
12  Nobody got soup                              206
13  A burglar's lot                              222
14  Of brothels and men                         243
15  Pick-a-back nightmare                        275
16  It's safer in gaol                           302
17  Requiem mass                                 335
18  The cycling assassin                         365

Postscript                                       375
Author's notes and acknowledgements              386
Bibliography                                     391
Illustrations                                    392
Dedication                                       393
Index                                            395

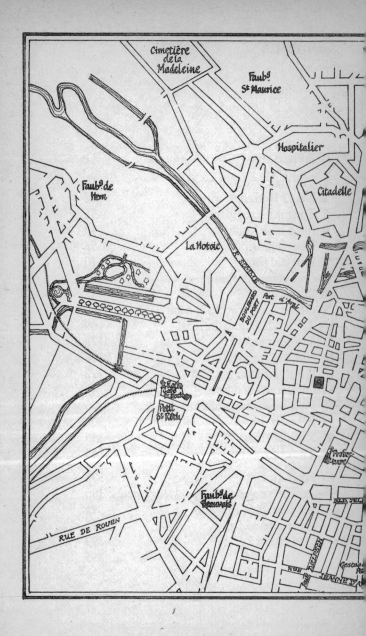

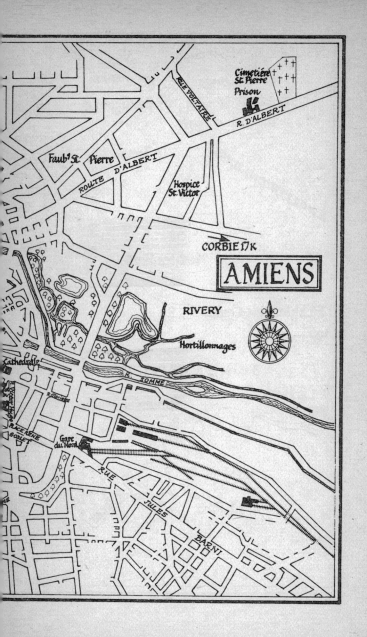

# Preface

An official communiqué published on 22 October 1944 announced:

*Mosquitos* attacked the prison at Amiens in an attempt to assist 120 prisoners, condemned to death for assisting the Allies, to escape.

This was one of the most spectacular operations of the war, and it is not until now that the full account of this exploit may be revealed. This exacting task was carried out even at the risk of killing some of those we wished to rescue ...

The raid had actually taken place on February 18th of that year, but had to remain secret for security reasons.

The epic event has been argued about ever since. Every anniversary of the attack revived controversy as to whether it should have taken place at all, but the arguments were based on generally known and officially recorded war history accounts.

All were inaccurate and significantly incomplete.

Only a handful of people knew the motives for the attack and what was actually at stake – an American in Berne, Switzerland, another in Washington, a Frenchman in Geneva, and two Englishmen in London.

Not even those who planned and carried out the operation realised its complete purpose. The main stakes were not, as was widely believed, the freeing or mercy killing of prisoners who, if they had to die, preferred Allied to Gestapo executioners. Far more depended on the attack.

*At risk was postponement for at least a year of the June 1944 Allied invasion and liberation of Europe; millions more lives, and even the outcome of the war itself*, had Hitler gained sufficient breathing space to further strengthen and regroup his forces and increase the devastation of his V-weapon rocket missiles.

This book is not simply a fresh account of a raid, nor merely its behind-the-scenes secrets. It is, above all, a mosaic of the ordinary and extraordinary people this incident threw together as allies and enemies ... convicted spies, burglars, saboteurs, pickpockets, Resistance fighters, confidence tricksters, clandestine radio operators, murderers and forgers, shot-down pilots and prostitutes, pimps and Black Marketeers.

What happened before, on and after 18 February 1944 encapsulates in one single incident a complete picture of virtually every facet of the struggle, endurance, deceit, treachery and courage of war.

Not only did prison walls come tumbling down on that February day, but also walls of indifference to the sufferings and enslavement of others, walls of selfishness, and walls that too often divide us from each other.

Amiens, capital of the Somme region, at the centre of northern France and the junction of its rail and canal communications, had so often been at the heart of tragedy, for Amiens and its neighbouring towns of Cambrai, St. Quentin, Albert, Abbeville and Arras were the old World War I battlefields. The slaughter, resolution and heroism endured and witnessed, were prodigious. Infantrymen who slogged over the cobbled roads of the Somme and Pas de Calais and spent winters in the mud and ice of the trenches, writing their names in blood on the villages, didn't call the area 'picturesque'. Farmer and villager of toughened fibre loved their land, their barns, their drab, often primitive homes with sagging rooftops and cracked and peeling walls. Some collaborated with the German invaders, but the majority worked effectively against them.

The people of the Somme were no strangers to battles for survival. They saw the encirclement of the Belgian, British and French armies, and in 1940, the terrible retreat to Dunkirk. No wonder so many Amienois never stopped secretly or openly fighting back.

The bombing of Amiens prison wrote another page of the town's history, and my involvement with this story started during the war. It resumed a few years ago when I was investigating a totally different matter and examining freshly declassified secret war documents. There was a misplaced file amongst them. I would have ignored it but for the folder's label: 'Amiens, Feb. 1944'. I opened the file because in March 1944, when I was a newspaper war reporter, I had unofficially learned details of the bombing attack that had taken place weeks earlier at Amiens prison. I wrote the story, but on submission to the censor for security checking, it was instantly 'killed' and I was warned that nothing whatsoever could be cleared for publication on this subject as it was still too sensitive.

Even those involved were unaware of the outcome of their efforts, nor had the whereabouts of personnel reported missing during the raid been ascertained. I wasn't allowed to publish a word about it for eight months, and then the front page lead story of my newspaper, reprinted in many countries, detailed the exploit which cost the life of one of the greatest airmen of World War II – Percy Charles Pickard.

This misplaced file I accidentally came across a few years ago, and the hitherto secret correspondence it contained indicated that previously published and historically recorded 'facts' concerning the raid were substantially incorrect and completely inadequate.

Curious events almost propelled me into writing the story. When I went to check some general material at the RAF Museum's library, I picked up a book lying on a table. As I glanced at it casually, a business card fell from its pages. Printed in the centre of the card were the words: 'With compliments of Walter J. Pickard', and in the bottom left hand corner, the name of his company – Mecca Ltd. Typed at the top of the card was a message – 'Please see Chapter 10 – Page 167'. I opened the book to the suggested pages and found myself reading about Percy Charles Pickard.

I telephoned the company named on the card, asked for Walter Pickard and was informed that he had died several years ago. When I inquired whether the Personnel department happened to have his family's address, a voice replied: 'Would you like to speak to his nephew, Mr. Michael Woods? – he's still here.'

Walter J. Pickard, O.B.E. was Percy Pickard's elder brother. He was Group Captain in charge of the famous RAF Transport Command station at Lyneham, in Wiltshire, during the war, and commanded a base in Russia for a time to organise air transport services for the historic Roosevelt-Churchill-Stalin conference at Yalta.

His nephew, Michael, invited me to his home where I was introduced to a cousin who had unexpectedly arrived from abroad that day. This was Nicholas Pickard, the son of Percy Charles Pickard.

I was due to leave for France the following day. Nicholas Pickard, Michael Woods and his wife, and Charles Pickard's sister were also departing for France. We were all going to the same place – to Amiens for the service held annually on 18 February, or the Sunday closest to it, in commemoration of those who died in the raid on the prison. I therefore felt, with some justification, that I was somehow meant to investigate and tell this story.

So, by a strange sequence of accidents (although people who believe in pre-ordained events wouldn't call them accidental) my wife Lilian and I found ourselves marching with members of the Pickard family, accompanied by a military band, in a procession of some two hundred people – uniformed and civilian – along the Route d'Albert, heading for Amiens prison.

We read the tablet set in the wall beside the main gate, inscribed:

Aux Patriotes Français tués le 18
Février 1944 dans cette prison où
les barbares Nazis martyrisaient

Also, at the base of a stone bowl of flowers set in the wall, a second tablet read:

Deportés et Internés Patriotes D'Amiens

The commemoration proceedings outside the gaol itself had been preceded by a service in the local church.

After the prison gate ceremony, the procession marched a brief distance to the little St. Pierre cemetery to pay homage at the graves of Percy Charles Pickard, and his navigator, Alan Broadley – by his side even in death – within sight of the prison that put them there.

As we walked away from the graves, I turned to a silver-haired distinguished-looking man who had stood beside us with tears in his eyes as the buglers sounded the final salute.

'Were you involved in the affair?' I asked.

'Yes. I was in the prison when it was bombed, so I come to Amiens sometimes to pay my respects to the men who set me free.'

'Were you one of the patriots who escaped?'

'No, one of the criminals. I was a thief – retired now, you understand,' he said reassuringly, with a hint of a smile, then added bitterly, 'But whatever I was then, no insect on earth could crawl lower than the man who put in that gaol so many whom the bombers came to get out . . .'

# 1 The man who sold people

Lucien Pieri had two profitable businesses. Behind the counter of his modest shop in Amiens' Place René Goblet, facing the pleasant restful little public garden, the tall, nattily dressed hosier with the curly receding hair sold shirts, ties, and socks until a black Citroen car, with one man at the wheel and two in the back, called for him.

Attending to someone when the car drew up outside, he courteously finished serving before disappearing into the back room to reappear within minutes in grey riding breeches, black leather jackboots, and wearing a navy-blue jacket, with swastika armband: attired to take care of his other business – selling people.

Relatives, friends, anyone – he wasn't particular who he sold to the Reich Central Security Office and the Gestapo. He was paid by the head, like old-time bounty hunters, except that those he sought were not simply outlaws wanted by the authorities, but men and women fighting to regain freedom for themselves and others.

Customers of his shop knew the round-faced muscular shirt-maker with the prominent jaw and boxer's nose as a very amiable personality. Unfortunately, you can't tell a traitor by looking at him. Pieri was a born predator, and 'clients' of his sideline business were more familiar with the not-so-friendly Lucien.

It was said that in 1940, when in the air force, he had been arrested for treason and espionage, but been saved by the invading Germans, and you could believe anything of Pieri, a man who organised treachery into a lucrative commercial operation covering all northern France.

His best customer – inside and outside his Amiens shop – was stocky red-faced Braumann, the local Gestapo chief. Braumann loved smart clothes, even smarter information and repeating his favourite quip that another place you could always tell a man by his clothes was in prison.

'There's nothing wrong with anyone that execution can't cure', Braumann's second favourite remark, was guaranteed to make him shake with rare laughter at hearing himself restate his own little joke.

Privileged Pieri sped around town and countryside on his motor cycle or at the wheel of his own black Citroen car, with all the rationed petrol he needed, usually accompanied by personal or Gestapo bodyguards.

'I saw our old world going to the dogs, so I started selling dog food,' was how he casually explained his main source of income. He was paid a minimum of 10,000 Francs for each person denounced, and sometimes considerably more. He was also allowed generous expenses.

The entire coastal area of northern France was a 'Prohibited Zone', patrolled day and night by soldiers and military police making snap-checks and putting up instant road blocks. The importance of maintaining the secrecy of coastal defences was ceaselessly rammed home with the warning that the fate of any Allied invasion forces could depend on it. But no zone was prohibited to Pieri. He could go at will wherever he liked. He had earned his ticket.

As soon as he first instigated arrests of fellow countrymen in 1941, he recognised the potential of the new trade. Desperately needing short-supply goods for his hosiery shop, he realised the Gestapo and the German High Command's espionage and counter-espionage service, the Abwehr, could get him anything he wanted through the Black Market they had organised for their own benefit.

At first, he worked closest to the Abwehr, when it ruled the power roost. Counter-espionage, penetrating and misleading hostile organisations, was the military Abwehr's responsibility, and espionage cases in areas allotted to the Gestapo had to be passed to appropriate Abwehr stations. But as the Abwehr hadn't a police force of its own, when police-style actions had to be undertaken, a Gestapo agent was inevitably around.

Abwehr appreciated Pieri's style because he made them look 'respectable' by employing the psychological ploy of informing prisoners under interrogation that he would 'regret the necessity of having to hand them over to the Gestapo if they refused to co-operate'. Exploiting the reputation of the Gestapo often paid off, demoralising individuals and groups through the fear of the unknown, and seemingly keeping Abwehr hands clean of brutal tactics. Pieri's shrewd approach heightened him in their estimation.

As the tide of war began to flow against Germany, and Pieri saw influence slip from the army into Gestapo hands, he concentrated on keeping the Gestapo happy by offering them 'chain-store' treachery – a network covering every town and village in northern France, with links in many other areas of the country.

'You have created a regional service for every district which in turn operates posts in each of the main towns, and I guarantee to feed all your posts with information,' Pieri offered Gestapo chief Braumann. 'I can recruit "experts" for you from among convicted criminals, to do things you and the Abwehr would prefer not to be publicly associated with – assassinations, kidnappings, anything. All it will involve, in return, is allowing my people licenced crime, such as robbery during authorised house searches, blackmail, and any kind of trafficking that takes their fancy.

'To recruit the expertise of criminals as well as collaborationists to our counter forces, we need to legalise a wide area of crime. Don't forget resistance also often depends on the skills of professional criminals – especially forgers and smugglers – for manufacturing cover identities and false travel passes, as well as for contact with the outside world.'

The Abwehr detested the idea, disagreeing with the increasingly ruthless and repressive measures of Himmler's S.D. (Sicherheitsdienst – the Security Service), especially in its attitude towards the execution of hostages. Considering this a contravention of international law, the Abwehr asserted that far from achieving its object of terrorising people, it would have the reverse effect. The Gestapo nevertheless gave Pieri the go-ahead, for by now, Hitler had granted Himmler's men absolute jurisdiction over every civilian. They could arrest, torture, interrogate, and determine through summary courts whether a death sentence was desirable or not. If it wasn't, victims were deported to concentration camps. Power on a plate was handed to criminals, psychopaths, and unscrupulous opportunists such as Lucien Pieri.

The cornerstones of Pieri's success were cafés and restaurants. He had friends listening and working for him – infiltrating for him everywhere.

'A little gossip goes a long way,' he told all his recruits. 'Even when people don't believe it all, they tell it all. Ninety per cent of those arrested are caught simply because friends are incapable of keeping their mouths shut. Fortunately for us, the French are generally not very good at hiding, or staying silent. Whatever you try to keep dark eventually comes to light.'

When there were air raid alerts, he, and his army of ears, moved among people in shelters listening to gossip, and for any clues to anti-German or underground army activities or personnel.

'When bombs fall and people are crowded together, or when they drink too much in cafés and restaurants, they usually talk too much,' Pieri advised those working for him, and his reputation grew to such an extent that even German officers were often seen to salute him. He recognised that total security meant total inactivity.

'Security is only care and common sense,' he calculated. 'With well-trained agents, security is second nature, so danger is not from themselves but in the people they have to contact, which is where I, and my local knowledge come in.'

Pieri enjoyed power.

From time to time, Braumann would summon him to his headquarters in the five-storey house on the corner of rue Jeanne d'Arc and rue Dhavernas in Amiens, to inspect possible new recruits for the informer army, or to assist in interrogation of prisoners arrested on his information.

Smooth-looking, outwardly mild-mannered Lucien Pieri was often worse than the worst of the Milice – the 250,000-strong army of scum scoured from the prisons and gutters of France by Nice brothel owner Joseph Darnand to work for their conquerors.

Pieri's technique was to keep victims waiting for days after arrest, ensuring they missed meals and remained in unheated cells, if it was winter, 'because', he pointed out, 'frozen hungry prisoners break more easily, and if we delay questioning, leaving them on their own in complete solitude, they're liable to be swiftly overcome by despair, doubts, depression – all nicely softened up for us.'

But he didn't always go in for the torture and degradation to get a prisoner to talk. He enjoyed heightening the certainty in them that they were due for physical torture, then letting them down so lightly that their defences weakened. This, he believed, could make the toughest most unflinching captive vulnerable.

When a prisoner made no reply, he admonished:

'There are only two sides to every question – are you guilty or not guilty? Silence isn't always golden, sometimes it's guilt.'

Although never specifically trained as an interrogator, he knew instinctively when to use psychology and when violence, and Gestapo chief Braumann let him have his way because his success rate was so high.

'Give him to me,' he boasted in front of a prisoner, 'and I promise to turn the key and unlock him without toothpicks under the fingernails.' He liked to put a case report on the desk before him and watch a prisoner's eyes furtively straining to read the report upside down.

Pieri had a thing about eyes, believing that the pupils of a person's eyes give away more secrets than they realise, which is why whenever he grilled someone, he noted the slightest contraction of the eye pupils, then concentrated on questions which caused this.

He frequently favoured freeing prisoners after declaring there was no evidence, then permitting them unsuspectingly to rejoin friends, and having them followed and watched. He was adept at scooping up as informers and collaborators the selfish, greedy, embittered, ambitious, religious bigots – people whose only concern was themselves. Many of those working for him would otherwise have found themselves in prison or condemned to death for other crimes. Granted life-or-death power over so many by his paymasters, Pieri could save the neck of anyone who agreed to join his Gestapo-linked network. Such powerful recruiting inducements were irresistible.

Pieri, and his organisation, sent an ever-increasing stream of men and women into cells of the 'political wing' of Amiens prison, and sometimes to Germany where the penalty for spying was beheading, with head strapped to a block, face up, so the victim could see the axe fall. On Pieri's information, arrests, and executions, also took place in regions far from Picardy.

The thousands of eyes and ears, watching and listening to everything, trying to tell the Allies all they needed to know for invasion, had to be blinded and deafened. German counter-espionage couldn't handle the job alone – it was too big. They needed an army of counter spies, particularly in northern France where Hitler's High Command were convinced invasion would hit the Calais and Somme area first, as this was clearly the shortest route in.

The Commander-in-Chief Western Front – Oberbefehlshaber West – in Paris, and the Nord and Pas de Calais departments administered by the security authorities in Brussels, gave Pieri his biggest get-rich opportunity:

'If we can discover whether the invasion spearhead will be in Normandy, the Pas de Calais, or Brittany, we can counter-attack fast in the right place and at the right time,' he was informed at a joint Abwehr-Gestapo meeting in Amiens. 'If we can massacre resistance forces before invasion day, there will be no secret armies left to harass or sabotage us, leaving us free to throw our full weight against the enemy.'

Pieri was given an open cheque book to get results, and did. Successes increased among Resistance groups which his informers and double agents penetrated, sometimes even obtaining control. Unable to wipe out resistance, the main fresh tactic was to infiltrate and, where possible, feed misleading information to London.

By the winter of 1943–44, German security effectiveness had reached the point where any active Resistance fighter was estimated to have only a maximum of six months more freedom before arrest and execution. If they couldn't hold out long enough to help the

Allied invasion, and Hitler's forces repelled it, the Allies would be unable to try again for a very long time ('Overlord' took almost two years' preparation). Morale in Europe, in exhausted Russia, and among Allied forces would be wrecked. And Hitler would have time to complete his new high-speed under-water endurance submarines and effectively employ his *Me-163* jet planes, and rocket warfare, offering the chance of victory instead of defeat.

Although hundreds of consignments of arms, materials, special invasion advance agents, and combat teams, were being air-dropped into France by the Allies at every phase of the moon, German security services captured a high proportion of them. They were aided by the fact that seven of the ten secret radio transmitters reporting to London from the Paris area were in Gestapo hands and being used for deception operations.

Using his vast team of collaborators, Pieri pierced one covert resistance group after another, piecing together the web of communications until he hit a jackpot and obtained key Allied invasion code phrases the BBC were scheduled to broadcast before and during the invasion. Phrases in the 'A' list were to alert groups and secret armies for invasion readiness: the 'B' list indicated its imminence, whilst other phrases were 'Go' signals for specific pre-planned sabotage and guerilla activities. Pieri reported that each resistance group had code messages. Knowing in advance the action area of a message could point at invasion beaches.

Advantageously for him, most Resistance Intelligence groups were really untrained for the work and, through inexperience, died in terrible numbers.

In French, British and American intelligence centres in London and Washington, and even at General Eisenhower's Supreme Headquarters of the Allied Expeditionary Force, the name of Lucien Pieri eventually became identified as a dangerous threat to invasion support plans. As the controlling shadow behind the wave of wholesale arrests he was on the brink of destroying years of underground preparations for the final push for Europe's liberation. Arrest after arrest, made at his prompting, endangered all France, Holland, Belgium, and freedom itself. The insignificant little hosier, in a position to jeopardise so much, was an enemy to be eliminated, but Gestapo escorts accompanied him almost everywhere he went. This nothing of a man had made himself one of their most valuable anti-invasion weapons. Hundreds were in cells in Amiens and other gaols, awaiting execution because of him.

'Chop the main heads' was the priority issued to all Gestapo and Abwehr Intelligence throughout Northern France. It was logical.

'Don't arrest everyone suspected. There isn't enough room in the prisons – they're already full,' the German High Command order continued. 'If we get the chiefs, the others will be scared, neutralised, and nervous of using contacts. In this manner we will annihilate their effectiveness.'

Amiens Gestapo Chief Braumann had an alternative:

'If the prisons are too full, the best thing we can do is shoot more of them to make room in the cells,' he ordered, and arranged for fresh batches to face firing squads.

Whenever Braumann needed hostages for a public demonstration of discipline and force, he simply collected extra inmates from both the German and French sections of Amiens prison to make up the numbers he felt necessary to make official retaliation for 'misbehaviour' more publicly impressive.

Assuming Supreme Command of the Allied forces in January 1944, Eisenhower told Commanders:

In no previous war and in no other theatre during this war, have resistance forces been so closely harnessed to the main military effort.

I consider that the disruption of enemy rail communications, the harassing of German road moves and the continual and increasing strain placed on the German war economy and internal security services throughout occupied Europe by the organised forces of resistance, must play a very considerable part in our complete and final victory.

Discussing the intriguing subject of conscience with the Amiens' officer responsible for Gendarmerie liaison with German forces and services in the area, Lucien Pieri observed:

'As for myself, I have no conscience at all. Only a good person can have a bad conscience. In any case, the most infallible cure for a guilty conscience is success.'

But there were two factors the usually well-informed Pieri didn't know about when he uttered that comment: the crucial factors which were liable to halt his run of success.

Marceau Laverdure, the police lieutenant to whom he made the remark, also happened to be chief of Resistance group Zero France – an Intelligence section with its own radio transmitter link to London; and far from Amiens, across the border in neutral Switzerland, someone in an apartment in the city of Berne's picturesque cobblestoned Herengasse, was also interested in Lucien Pieri's activities.

# 2 No.23 Herrengasse

Sole occupant of the apartment in the medieval house, complete with courtyard and creaking gate, on the ancient arcaded street running along the ridge high above the Swiss capital's river Aare, close to Berne's Cathedral, was a big broad-shouldered man with tousled hair, high forehead and full grey moustache, who looked and talked more like a school headmaster than a spymaster.

The inconspicuous sign on the front door of 23 Herrengasse declared it to be the home of 'Allen W. Dulles, Special Assistant to the Minister.' The official title screened the real job which was to gather information on Hitler and Mussolini's War and quietly render support and encouragement to Resistance forces in Germany, Italy and conquered territories.

Dulles, America's first career spy, whose cloak-and-dagger activities spanned two world wars, arrived in Berne in November 1942 as one of the first members of the newly established Office of Strategic Services. This office had been created by former New York lawyer, Colonel, later General William J. Donovan, and modelled on Britain's MI6. Donovan was convinced that victory strategy would depend on Intelligence as never before.

Answerable only to the President himself, Donovan, fearing nothing and no one, rigidly adhered to his policy of: 'What do you want? When do you want it? I'll get it for you.'

To President Roosevelt he confessed: 'Britain has been the shield behind which we could pull up our socks, tie our shoelaces, and get ready – and also our laboratory.'

Possessing the power to visualise an oak when he saw an acorn, Donovan rose rapidly through the ranks in World War I, to become a Colonel in the famous Irish 69th Division, in which he earned the Congressional Medal of Honour, America's highest award for courage. Despite his mild blue eyes and soft Irish voice, he had the unshakeable nickname of 'Wild Bill', although he was everything but wild. Some people counted time. He made time count.

Donovan was desperate for anyone with potential talents for OSS. There was no time to indulge in Intelligence tradecraft apprenticeships before starting work, so he dragooned military personnel, bankers, businessmen, lawyers, librarians, writers, publishers, ball-players, missionaries, reformed safecrackers, bartenders, tugboat operators – grabbing specialist experience wherever he could. 'Every man or woman who can hurt the enemy is okay with me,' said Donovan.

'In espionage, you've got to *know* the traffic laws, not learn them by accident,' he insisted, 'or you can lose your head through sticking your neck out too far.'

Nevertheless, urgency necessitated calculated risks, and green, freshly-enlisted OSS officers were instantly despatched to the neutral information hunting grounds of Sweden, Spain, Portugal, Tangier, Switzerland – some assigned to diplomatic posts, others with cover jobs.

Invaluable past espionage and diplomatic experience in Germany, Austria, Hungary and Switzerland made Allen Dulles an OSS 'must' recruitment. It was said he had such a brilliant mind that the day he graduated from law school, he sued the college, won the case, and got his tuition fees back.

'You know how to handle porcupines without disturbing the quills, so you're perfect for us,' Donovan complimented Dulles when they met to discuss his joining the OSS, soon after the Japanese attack on Pearl Harbor. They knew each other well from Dulles' Department of Justice days in Washington, and as New York lawyers.

'You're the kind of diplomat we need because you speak several languages including doubletalk, and can cut a neighbour's throat without him noticing it, which is why I want you to head our London office,' Donovan proposed.

Dulles was intrigued by the fresh challenge offered, although, as ever, he calmly and impassively hid his enthusiasm. He removed from his mouth the cheap-looking briar pipe that was as much a part of him as the tweeds he almost always wore, and in his matching slightly English accent replied:

'We can learn more from our enemies than we can from our friends. I'd be better employed on Hitler's doorstep, in Switzerland, where I lived and worked twenty-four years ago. You can't beat the place as a base for our kind of activities. I learned in World War I how valuable it was for information.'

Usually, when stocky, soft-spoken Bill Donovan asked someone working for him to do something, he expected them to do it, no matter what, and didn't say how. But at the same time, he despised 'yes' men.

'I'd rather have a young lieutenant with guts enough to disobey an order than a Colonel too regimented to think for himself,' he admitted. Insubordination became almost a way of life for OSS officers.

Respecting Allen Dulles' disagreement with his own judgement, Donovan accepted the counter-suggestion and posted him to the American Legation in Berne, appointing David Bruce – son of a senator, millionaire in his own right, and son-in-law of steel magnate Andrew J. Mellon – to take over the OSS London bureau. Urbane, easy-smiling Bruce, a man of mannered and meticulous thoughtfulness, was an excellent counter to Donovan's impulsiveness and helped him nurse the OSS baby from birth, although it was Donovan alone who became known as the 'Wizard of OSS'.

As 'Intelligence' and 'Espionage' are by no means synonymous, both being part of the whole necessary for making decisions and estimating consequences, Dulles immediately began organising separate Intelligence and Espionage operations – one for processing raw knowledge into finished intelligence; the second to undertake actual espionage plus liaison with Resistance groups in the conquered countries and among people inside Germany itself willing to help undermine Hitler and the Nazis.

Speedily Dulles wove a network across Europe, deep into Hitler's Third Reich, and within days of re-establishing himself in Switzerland, was utilising American officials whose original work had more or less become obsolete through the war. He also recruited other Americans who had been stranded in the country, or lived there, for health reasons.

Briefing new, inexperienced staff after screening out the romantics, he emphasised:

'Don't try to do everything today – save some mistakes for tomorrow. Above all, be careful not to stretch the truth too far, or it may snap back.'

Only weeks after his arrival, a newspaper labelled him: 'Personal representative of President Roosevelt, with a special duty assignment.'

'What's the point in trying to deny it?' Dulles counselled Donovan. 'Anyway, the story has done us a good turn because since it was published, adventurers, professional and amateur spies and informants, have been beating a path to my door. Conveniently, between my apartment and the river below, vineyards afford an ideal covered approach for visitors who prefer not to be seen entering my front door on the Herrengasse.'

Donovan agreed to ignore journalistic speculation as to Dulles's true task. He didn't believe in senior representatives going deep underground, on the reasonable premises that it was futile.

'Better to let people know you're in the business of Intelligence and tell them where they can find you,' he asserted.

Making sure whoever wanted him could find him, Dulles let it be known he was prepared to meet, talk, and listen to anybody, for as he said with good reason: 'You never know where or when lightning will strike.'

The depth of feeling with which he said this originated through the lesson learned from avoiding an appointment with a strange little journalist in Switzerland in the final months of World War I. The man he never found time enough to meet, who left the country shortly afterwards for Russia, was Lenin. Remembering that lost opportunity, Allen Dulles was now ever-ready to talk to anyone anytime, insisting: 'Everyone has some useful purpose in life, even if it's only to serve as a terrible example.'

Seated before the fireplace of his spacious lounge room, looking more like an English country gentleman than controller of an army of agents, he discreetly received Resistance leaders and contacts from other Intelligence services.

An Intelligence post in a neutral country is a delicate matter, of necessity even involving dealing with enemy informants, but he took care to observe and preserve the neutrality of the country from which he functioned so effectively.

The official Swiss policy towards his mission observed the proper decorum of benevolent neutrality. By maintaining contact with both the Germans and the Allies, the Swiss could thus never be accused of favouring one belligerent over the other. Colonel Roger Masson of the Swiss General Staff was in direct touch with porno-graphy-loving Walter Schellenberg, head of Himmler's Intelligence Service, whilst Max Waibel and close associates in Swiss Intelligence consulted Dulles and British representatives.

Although largely dependent on coded diplomatic messages sent by Swiss commercial radio facilities, Dulles also had a transatlantic radio-telephone connection to Washington for which the Swiss provided a speech-scrambling device, which he knew they inter-cepted and unscrambled, so he took to including items he wanted overheard.

Everyone in the OSS had an individual code number for secret communications, so that if messages were intercepted, at least the identity of the persons mentioned therein wouldn't be exposed. Since the code numbers had to be used daily for incoming and outgoing messages, they became attached, like a name. Dulles was 110, Donovan 109.

Because in all of their actions, the Swiss usually strove to serve the interests of peace, to avoid embarrassing them Allen Dulles made a point of developing the art of diving into trouble without making a splash, despite the fact that from his apartment he directed agents in Germany, Austria, Hungary, Yugoslavia, Roumania, Czechoslovakia, Spain, Portugal, North Africa, Bulgaria, and Greece. He filtered information – military, political, economic, sociological, anything which would increase Allied intimacy with enemy thinking and planning.

Sedate, mature Dulles, constantly wary of working too closely with Washington, maintained:

'Only a man on the spot can really pass judgement on operational details as contrasted with the policy decisions which, of course, belong to the boss at headquarters. It has always amazed me how desk personnel thousands of miles away seem to acquire wisdom and special knowledge about local field conditions which they assume goes deeper than that available to the man on the spot. Nobody should try to stand between a dog and a tree.'

Like many of his agents, Dulles had ways of slipping in and out of the country to question informants in occupied Europe. The city of Basle, touching France on the West and Germany on the East, was particularly handy for crossings, with its countless exits and entrances creating a nightmare for even the most watchful of border patrols. If on the run, an obliging barge captain could drop you north in Little Basle, or south in Great Basle.

For information from inside Germany, Dulles's closest collaborator was Gero von Schulze Gaevernitz – a naturalised American, German by birth, with extensive Swiss business interests. Tall, handsome, in his early forties, Gaevernitz's father had been a well-known professor and political scientist, and a member of the old German Reichstag liberal wing. Gero's excellent connections with members of the underground opposition to Hitler in Germany picked up first hints from Berlin and from the headquarters of Colonel Giskes (in charge of German counter-espionage in Holland, Belgium and northern France), that Allied underground forces and information networks were about to be bled almost to death, largely as a result of treachery stemming from the Amiens area.

Confirmation came from other sources controlled from the Dulles apartment, which also happened to be 'bank' and 'exchange centre' for locating and trading in the vast volume of Reichsmarks and Continental currencies essential to the financing of espionage and Resistance activities. Dispersal of the currencies was mainly the responsibility of the Special Funds Officer – Robert Haydon Alcorn, Executive Officer to David Bruce in London. OSS-supplied money was parachuted to Maquis and others. Alternatively,

Dulles sent cash into occupied territories via regular frontier-crossing messengers.

Funding for the dossier compiled by Gendarme Lieutenant Marceau Laverdure's Réseau Zèro France on the escalating threat of Lucien Pieri to Allied invasion preparations, came from the Dulles 'bank' in Berne.

Early in 1943, Dulles learned of the existence of the experimental laboratory at Peenemunde for testing rocket bombs, and subsequently of the construction of rocket installations in the Pas de Calais – another zone covered by Pieri and his increasingly successful Gestapo auxiliary.

Unable to conceal the massive build-up of coastal fortifications and missile sites from the gaze of armies of amateur and professional spies, the enemy began to put out their eyes, with the assistance of Pieri's organisation. Counter-measures were at last succeeding beyond the German's wildest hopes. Through the effective help of traitors, the Germans were destroying or, at the very least, extensively contaminating sabotage, guerilla and espionage units organised by the British, American, and French in north and north-western France.

Mounting disasters overtaking underground forces were daily more and more concerning Allen Dulles in Berne; Bill Donovan in Washington; a Colonel 'Gilbert' in Geneva; a man called 'C' in London, and the phenomenal brothers Dominique and Pierre Ponchardier in France. Dominique decided to discuss the crisis almost overwhelming him and his comrades, with Colonel 'Gilbert', his link with Washington and London – whom he visited monthly to exchange information personally and to review tactics. The formidable fact that to do so necessitated crossing forbidden zones and evading border patrols, didn't worry him. There was an accommodating way round the problem.

It was literally a standing joke, for there it stood – straddling the border so that you went in the French front door of the house, and came out the Swiss back door. A pre-war laugh, but a wartime gift from heaven protected by international neutrality law. Trust Dominique Ponchardier to be aware of such unique attractions, as he was of similar properties along other stretches of the Franco-Swiss boundary. But then it was natural for him to be knowledgeable about these desirous residences as his identity papers declared him to be in the building and estate agency trades.

At times Dominique used the boarding school at Ville-la-Grand, run by Father Favre. Part of the school building was right on the Swiss frontier, making it a valuable jumping off point to freedom, and enabling it to double as a transmission centre for letters and military information.

The youthful, brilliantly daring brothers Ponchardier headed the Resistance network known as the 'Sosies', which was, in fact, two organisations, one concentrating on intelligence, the second on sabotage and guerilla action. Short, thick-set Dominique, with his bushy eyebrows and hair that wouldn't stay combed, entered the Resistance in 1940. Three years later, when only twenty-six, he and his elder brother Pierre, a former navy pilot, headed one of the largest, most successful undercover operations. Pierre concentrated on Vichy country; Dominique on northern France.

The Amiens area was significantly designated 'Priority 1' by the Allies. This strategically vital zone stretched along the Channel coast covering Dunkirk, Calais, Boulogne, Pas de Calais, Abbeville, Beauvais, Lille, Arras, Cambrai, St. Quentin, Soissons, Reims, the Somme, Ardennes and Marne.

'How are we going to achieve everything expected of us during the invasion if the enemy continues massive executions and arrests?' Dominique impatiently demanded of Colonel 'Gilbert' on arriving in Geneva towards the end of 1943.

'Liberation day is probably just months away, but the Gestapo and their friends are annihilating us to such an extent that unless we counter-attack spectacularly, free comrades in Amiens and St. Quentin gaols, and boost morale, it'll be miraculous if there are enough of us left to matter by the time invasion comes.

'Apart from a handful who escaped, most of the Amiens OCM Intelligence organisation have just been arrested – betrayed by a traitor – and our Sosies, and other groups, are being terribly mauled too. *Something* needs to be done – and quickly!'

Colonel 'Gilbert' was accustomed to outbursts from the Ponchardiers who, when difficulties arose and they couldn't get either their own way or the assistance required, often lost their tempers, but the seriousness of the situation was plain. To back his assertions Dominique had brought lists of men and women recently gaoled, and the charges against them. He even had preliminary details and sketches of Amiens and St. Quentin prison buildings.

Although masters at reconstructing destroyed networks, and disdainful of danger to themselves, the Ponchardiers were always concerned for the security, spirit and discipline of those who served with them. In turn, they expected unwavering support from Allen Dulles. They accepted orders from him via Colonel 'Gilbert', who promised to discuss forthwith Dominique's report with Dulles.

'Gilbert' was the cover name of Colonel Groussard, a former

Commandant of France's famous Saint-Cyr military academy, and also code name of the network he ran from Geneva, assisted by Colonel Paul Paillole, in charge of clandestine activities, and backed by America and Britain. Originally Groussard travelled to London from Vichy France to offer his services to the Free French, but General de Gaulle declined to see him, and even de Gaulle's deceptively gentle Intelligence chief, Andre Dewavrin, then known as Passy, avoided meeting him, suspicious of anyone from Vichy. Frustrated by his own countrymen, but nevertheless determined to put his experience to Allied use, he contacted Winston Churchill, Anthony Eden, and American Ambassador in London John Winant. All agreed Switzerland ideal for Groussard to establish an Intelligence service watching all France. He was also empowered to organise action forces and liaison lines between members of the Vichy, British and American governments.

Knowing 'Gilbert's' true identity, and having complete confidence in him, Dominique Ponchardier returned to France, certain the warning wouldn't be quietly filed away.

The fate of secret armies and action units in the 'Priority 1' key Amiens zone was of equal importance to Hitler and the Allies.

At a meeting at his headquarters, Hitler warned Commanders:

'The issue of this war and the fate of the Reich depend on the Western Front, the number one theatre of operations.'

The same point was forcefully brought home to Donovan on his arrival in London from one of his regular round-the-world 'keeping in touch' trips. Awaiting him was a dossier from Berne. Allen Dulles had despatched a copy of the Ponchardier report to him, care of David Bruce, with the suggestion that it be urgently discussed personally with 'C' and 'Uncle Claude'.

*

Within hours of checking into his usual suite at Claridges Hotel, conveniently situated within a few hundred yards of David Bruce's OSS bureau at 68, 70 and 72 Grosvenor Square, Bill Donovan was on the phone to the London offices of the Minimax fire extinguisher company, at Broadway Buildings, opposite St. James's Park underground station in Westminster.

On being put through to the executive he sought, Donovan explained: 'I'd like to see you immediately regarding a particular fire problem requiring attention.'

The company's shiny brass nameplate at the main door didn't somehow go with the uniformed despatch riders scurrying in and out, and the military cars constantly pulling up beside the building. The spacious entrance hall was big enough to hold some twenty waiting people, but none could pass the reception desk with its two middle-aged uniformed commissionaires, without stating business and being officially passed through.

Ushered through an outer office with two secretaries – one like a middle-aged hospital matron; the other young, provocatively pretty – into a carpeted, modestly-furnished executive office with a large mahogany desk and bright green telephone on it, Donovan greeted, with his surprisingly soft handshake, a good-looking, six-foot-two Guards Officer type who wouldn't stand out in any crowd. He had an academic sensitive face, and silver-hair, thin on top. Wearing a soberly plain grey suit with neat coloured breast pocket handkerchief, white shirt, and sporting a favourite white spotted tie, he looked more like a Harley Street doctor or university professor. Yet this was 'C' – Major-General Sir Stewart Menzies – chief of Britain's Secret Service since 1936.

Normally, to see Menzies you had to go through Captain Howard, his Chief of Staff. This protocol hadn't applied to Bill Donovan since 1940 when, asked by President Roosevelt to report on the determination and ability of the European countries, including Britain, to resist the Nazis, he had been briefed by Menzies who had arranged for him an MI6-conducted tour of France, Belgium, the Netherlands, Yugoslavia and the Balkans.

Menzies' precise but gentle voice was, as Donovan well knew, deceptive. Only the eyes gave some indication of the razor-sharp personality beneath, who liked to repeat his predecessor's words:

'If you can listen to someone important telling someone else important about some event of importance and, knowing the story to be quite inaccurate, you can keep your mouth shut, you may in due course make a good intelligence officer.'

Detailing the Dulles Amiens-zone disasters report, and pointing out how far beyond Dominique Ponchardier's problems the potential damage could extend, Donovan, with his customary calm approach to danger, said in a voice almost modulated to a whisper:

'For a start, Bill Maddox is concerned about his SI team's future effectiveness and security.'

David Bruce's SI chief, Dr. William Maddox, former Professor of Political Science at Harvard and Princeton Universities, assisted by Russell D'Oench, grandson of the founder of the Grace Shipping Lines, was responsible for espionage and collecting intelligence information. Maximum priority pre-invasion assignments, closely co-operating with MI6, were in the laps of the Maddox team. This was headed by Norman Holmes Pearson, a

Yale professor of English, assisted by Robert Blum, a Yale instructor in international relations, and Chicago attorney Hubert Will.

'The Jedburghs and Sussex are at risk too,' Donovan continued, 'unless the situation in the Amiens area can be swiftly repaired and reasonably stabilised.'

'Jedburghs', comprising one American, one British, and one French officer – all in uniform – were to be dropped at strategic points to officer sabotage and guerilla units, and many teams were in position well ahead of the invasion. Equipment, including arms caches, were being dropped for them by USAAF bombers, and a vast range of sabotage 'aides' stored in special depots. The OSS, for example, had produced and shipped across sacks of flour with a difference – an ingenious explosive that looked like flour could therefore be stored right under the enemy's nose, and when required, be kneaded and baked into bread or biscuits. OSS called it their 'Aunt Jemima' pancake mix.

Suggested by former stockbroker Sir Claude Dansey – Menzies' MI6 'vice-chairman and Managing Director' – 'Sussex' called for Anglo-American-French collaboration in the despatch of fifty two-man teams throughout northern France in advance of 'Overlord' invasion landings. Agents were to be parachuted forty to sixty miles inland from the Channel coast, covering an area from Brittany to Belgium, collecting military information of value to Allied Command.

To ensure complete co-ordination, a tripartite 'Sussex' Anglo-Franco-American committee was set up under the chairmanship of Menzies' top aide, lanky naval Commander Kenneth Cohen – ideally suited because of his virtually unrivalled intimacy with overall Continental Intelligence activities. Kentucky-born Colonel Francis Pickens Miller, Oxford Rhodes Scholar and chairman of the World Student Christian Federation in Geneva, would speak for the OSS, whilst Free France's BCRA – Bureau Central de Renseignments et d'Action – de Gaulle's Intelligence arm, chose one of their most brilliant agents, Colonel Gilbert Renault-Roulier, known as Remy.

As liaison officer and a member himself of the enormously effective Alliance network, which operated independently of de Gaulle, Kenneth Cohen already had tragic personal experience of the appalling losses being inflicted by the Gestapo's Winter 1943 offensive. Alliance, known as 'Noah's Ark' because all its members bore animal code names – Cohen was 'Crane' – had been savagely mauled, with overwhelming indications that treachery was at the root of the disaster. The Alliance organisation, which was led by the incredible young Marie-Madeleine Fourcade, only serviced American and British Intelligence, and the Halberts of Amiens, who worked with Marie-Madeleine, were unknown to Dominique Ponchardier. They were arrested in the evening of 18 November 1943.

Forty-six-year-old Gabrielle Halbert and her thirty-six-year-old garage mechanic husband, René, jointly in charge of Alliance's Amiens 'mail box', were caught as a radio operator was transmitting a message to London from their home. Tipped off by Lucien Pieri, Gestapo encircled the house in rue Claudius Sbocassaint; arrested Gabrielle and her ten-year-old daughter, Renée, then afterwards the father who was at work at the nearby Garage Eteve. The radio operator escaped.

Husband and wife were thrown into Amiens prison the same night. Separating the child from the parents, Gestapo chief Braumann let them know he was taking her to his headquarters in rue Jeanne d'Arc. Using the threat to the child, as well as physical torture, didn't succeed in making the Halberts talk.

Attempting instead to break the child, Braumann arranged a mock hanging of both parents, callously showing their limp unconscious bodies to the terrified child.

Seeing little Renée uncontrollably trembling, Braumann sneered:

'You are afraid now.'

'I'm not frightened,' she insisted, 'I'm cold,' and courageously continued to refuse information.

Although the parents remained in Amiens gaol, they didn't figure among prisoners named by Dominique Ponchardier who, unconnected and unfamiliar with Alliance as well as other innumerable réseaux, had, in fact, innocently supplied Allen Dulles and Bill Donovan with an inadequate picture of the true scale of current Gestapo captures and imprisonments. The Halberts appeared on prison lists reaching Broadway Buildings, Westminster, from American and British agents active in the Somme area.

Most people working in Broadway Buildings never saw 'C' at all. It was commanding, yet benign-looking 'Uncle Claude', as he was widely known – Menzies' deputy, with an office directly above 'C' – whom everyone recognised as the man in charge of day-to-day decisions and the real MI6 power. Colonel Sir Claude Edward Marjoribanks Dansey personally briefed and questioned agents, usually at the Westminster offices of 'the firm', as MI6 was respectfully and affectionately called by its employees. Dansey also used his personal apartment in Albemarle Street, Piccadilly, or his permanently reserved suite in the nearby Mayfair Hotel, for 'business appointments'. The hotel accommodation was for nights when Luftwaffe bombers made the concrete and steel hotel securer than the frailer bricks-and-mortar Albemarle Street quarters. Both the apartment and hotel were conveniently close to Claridges Hotel, a few hundred yards away across Berkeley Square. Claridges, another favourite Dansey rendezvous, also happened to be the war-time home of a close friend whom he employed from time to time for MI6 'jobs' – legendary Hungarian film producer Alexander Korda. Laurence Olivier, Leslie Howard, Charles Laughton, Ralph Richardson, Vivien Leigh and Merle Oberon, whom Korda married, were among the many he fashioned into world stars. His Hollywood, Washington and New York film, political and commercial connections were immensely valuable to Dansey who highly regarded the shrewd Hungarian starmaker's assessments of people and events. Dansey was almost fanatical about gathering every item of information concerning everything and everyone of possible use to him. Similarly, there was nothing white-haired, blue-eyed 'Uncle Claude' didn't know about his staff, including who they slept with.

'I can't have sex interfering with our work', he'd grunt.

As for the general air of benevolence, one might as well have tried dissolving iron in boiling water as melt him. In the Boer war, just before the relief of Mafeking, he filled stockings with sand then went out at night to slug Boer sentries. You needed courage to face up to 'Uncle', who could reduce staff to jelly, scan you sharply up and down, and bark:

'Surely I make myself plain?'

Although an habitual sender of barbed memos, he was far kinder than he would ever allow himself to appear in front of subordinates. Opposed to rough interrogation, he insisted:

'Kindness and sympathy gets better results.'

He spent a considerable period in Washington between the two World Wars teaching international espionage ropes to Intelligence-green Defence and State Department senior officials, who for too long entirely depended on ambassadors for information on other countries' visible and hidden activities. Even the United States' only centralised Intelligence unit – the War Department's cryptography division – was obliterated at the instigation of Secretary of State Henry Stimson, who declared that 'Gentleman do not read other gentlemen's mail' – a remark that made realist Claude Dansey almost explode with disgust. Stimson's tune changed when he became Secretary of War and found himself thankfully at the receiving end of copies of reports by Dansey and his MI6 team on Hitler's war preparations. It was Bill Donovan's appreciation of how extensively and effectively Dansey's Washington advisory role contributed towards the foundation of America's first world-wide Intelligence network that resulted in MI6 becoming the inspiration and model for his OSS dreams. Donovan always openly acknowledged that he faithfully followed the footsteps of the Master – 'Uncle Claude'.

Espionage had largely been Dansey's career and life since World War I. Ever keen on commercial enterprise covers for clandestine work, horses camouflaged his secret manipulations when, in harness with world-renowned Irish trainer 'Atty' Persse, he managed eight racehorses based at the famous Chattis Hill stables in Stockbridge, Hampshire. For some five years, racing provided Dansey with excellent entrée into well-informed influential international circles.

In Mussolini's Italy he set up a spying organisation essentially aimed at penetrating Hitler's Germany. Also, behind a variety of business fronts, he built Organisation 'Z' in Switzerland. 'Z' security was so effective that many branches were unaware of each other, which is how 'Uncle Claude' liked things, on the principle that:

'The less you know, the less you can give away.'

'Z' initiated the 'Jens Dons' ring in Copenhagen for collecting intelligence from Germany, and sabotage. The 'Z' centre at the Hague was his particular pride and joy, not only for espionage efficiency, but also for its significant participation in Germany's own anti-Nazi underground.

Sarcastically critical of frequent waste of valuable agents by what he termed 'amateur departments', he was consequently deeply disturbed on hearing Donovan's news when called to 'C's' office.

Listening carefully, impassive-faced, as the situation was explained, the rarely talkative Dansey didn't interrupt or comment until all the facts had been given, then, turning to Donovan he said brusquely:

'My job and that of my agents is to collect information about enemy intentions and activities, not to act as nursemaids to people. I have very definite inhibitions about working with unfamiliar networks in an emergency, preferring to remain in complete control of my own operations. I don't like bloody amateurs forcing decisions where I'm involved.'

Momentarily pausing to settle himself more comfortably in his chair, he continued:

'War sharpens one's sixth sense, and in France, as the French say, the wood hides the trees, but clearly, with the enemy stepping up his drive against the underground – and we need them all for the future – remedial counter-measures of some kind are urgently required. Imponderables are nevertheless a major factor, so before we can decide what to do, we need to know more – a lot more – about the networks, prisoners, and prisons concerned.'

Bill Donovan accepted the advice without question, recognising that 'Uncle Claude' was ruthless, but usually right.

Dansey never wasted time in getting down to business. Returning to his office, he pressed the bell for his secretary.

'Miss Reade, get me the file on Amiens prison.'

'Yes, sir,' the attractive red-headed girl replied.

Also summoning a secretary, Menzies demanded:

'The Cabinet Offices on the scrambler, please.'

Donovan stayed silent as Menzies, who always scrawled his famous 'C' signature in green ink, lifted the green telephone on his desk.

'This is Zero C speaking,' he announced, and, on making a priority appointment to convey the Dulles report to the Prime Minister, replaced the green phone.

It was Winston Churchill who dropped the problem in Basil Embry's lap.


# 3  The pint-sized giant


When Air Vice Marshal Basil Embry spoke, you listened, memorised, noted, and understood instructions. It was inevitable that Charles Pickard should become 'Basilised', as Embry's magnetic spell was affectionately termed among his closest staff.

Energetic Embry, wearing more decorations for bravery than anyone serving under him, continuously left a trail of shattered enemies in his wake. Succeeding in a sensational escape from the Germans by killing his guards and getting away over the Pyrenees mountains, he commanded a bomber squadron and a station sector of Fighter Command; became a Desert Air Force leader; then Air Officer Commanding No. 2 Group of the 2nd Tactical Air Force, and still persisted in flying as often as possible on raids. The German High Command badly wanted him back behind barbed wire.

His near pint size belied the giant dynamic character. Born in

Gloucester in February 1902, this son of an Irish clergyman was a real son-of-a-devil when it came to fighting and leading men.

Being a very Irish Englishman, he was charming and rude, prejudiced and broad-minded, pliable and obstinate, overpowering and modest, dedicated and human. It was undoubtedly fated for Basil Embry and Percy Charles Pickard to team up, for towering, six-feet-four pilot Pickard was also no slouch.

Soft-voiced, basically shy, powerfully built yet always boyish, Sheffield-born 'Pick' was already famous as 'F' for Freddie to millions all over the world as the reluctant star of an official bomber raid propaganda film entitled 'Target for Tonight', made to boost public morale. The hefty blue-eyed pipe-smoking Yorkshireman – perfectly cast for the part made his feelings clear in emphatically plain language, on being lumbered with the film assignment, but he had to do it – orders were to be obeyed, or else. His family never called him Percy – only 'Boy' because his little sister couldn't say 'Percy'.

By the time he teamed with Basil Embry he had bombed almost every big target in the RAF book, starting on ops in 1940 when the Germans invaded Norway. Time and again he returned with his machine almost shot to pieces. He went on to head a Czech squadron with such skill and patriotic fervour that the Czechs awarded him their own Military Medal, yet he was a very kind, gentle person, who never wanted to hurt anyone, let alone bomb them. Fighting was actually against his nature.

The six feet four-and-a-half blond-haired giant of a man dwarfed his five-feet-nothing mother and five-feet-four-high Pickard senior who was terrified of planes – even of driving a car – whereas Pickard junior had become one of the war's most daring flying characters.

Between raids his favourite off-duty relaxation was rabbit hunting with Ming, his wife Dorothy's English sheep dog. Outstanding at chasing, and eating rabbit, Ming frequently accompanied her master on test flights and became renowned as the most famous pet of the Allied Air Forces, and also for an uncanny instinct defying explanation.

'That bugger can say more with her tail in minutes than most people can say in hours,' Pick proudly boasted. 'What's more, she's the finest sentry we've got on this base. You know, no intruder can get through without her warning us.'

'What does she do? – Bark her head off?' a voice asked.

'Oh, no. Dives straight for my quarters and hides under my bed.'

Pick also claimed with pride: 'You can talk to Ming, and whatever you tell her to do, she immediately does.'

One of his new orderlies disputed this after taking the dog out for a pee. On returning, he complained:

'I walked her for ages, but she didn't do a thing – not a drop.'

'Oh, I forgot to tell you,' Pick apologised. 'You have to say "Good girl" to her when you want her to spend a penny.'

Orderly and dog disappeared outside again, and the instant the magic 'Open Sesame' words 'Good girl' were uttered, Ming obliged. Enthusiastically, the orderly kept repeating the two words at brief intervals, and Ming did her stuff every time.

Dorothy Hodgkin, daughter of a former mayor of Belfast, met Charles Pickard before the war. She provided secretarial help to his elder sister Helena, who was married to actor Sir Cedric Hardwicke and lived in Avenue Road, off London's Regent's Park. Dorothy married pilot Pickard in a London registry office in November 1939. Soon after, Ming joined the family and Dorothy began to notice the dog's restlessness when Pick took off on a raid, and also how between take-off and return, Ming would settle down and go to sleep. Whenever Dorothy said goodbye to Pick she knew if Ming trotted outside, that he was going on a mission.

On 19 June 1940, at the controls of *Wellington* bomber 'O for Orange', Pick, together with Sergeant Alan Broadley, who became his regular navigator, took off with five other aircraft to bomb a Ruhr factory. In early war days, wives were housed in air station married quarters, so Ming was conveniently on hand to watch Pick's departure on ops.

That June Ruhr attack night, 'O for Orange' was so seriously flak-damaged that, making for home on one engine, it crashed into the North Sea, but the crew of five managed to scramble into their rubber dinghy.

It was 3.20 a.m. when Ming tugged violently at Dorothy's bed clothes. Assuming the usual, she opened the front door to let Ming do the necessary. Ming hurried out but sat down, and simply went on scanning the sky from right to left. Dorothy rang base Operations Room.

'Any news?' she inquired, striving to disguise anxiety.

'Yes, Mrs. Pickard. "O for Orange" is missing.'

Ming had followed her into the house to watch her make the call. A couple of hours later, Dorothy walked to the end of the runway, and throughout the day she sat on a tree stump watching planes returning from searches for Pick and his crew. Beside her, continuing to stare at the sky, sat Ming. Late that afternoon, the dog suddenly went to sleep. At six Dorothy phoned Ops Room again.

'We found them this afternoon – in the middle of a minefield –

and have had to wait for their dinghy to drift out,' the Duty Officer dutifully assured her. 'They should be ashore between seven and eight.'

Tying a large red ribbon on Ming's head, Dorothy headed for the Mess with set of dry clothes for Pick. An Air Sea Rescue launch picked them up fourteen hours after they had ditched.

Celebrating the following night at a Vera Lynn show in London's West End, Dorothy asked whether Pick could remember exactly when his bomber had ditched.

'Easy,' he answered. 'My watch glass was shattered when I was thrown against the instrument panel, and the watch stopped at 3.20.'

In 1942, he commanded the carrying force of bombers that ferried paratroopers to Bruneval to land and capture secrets of the devastating new German radar detection system threatening night bombers. The same year he was given command of 161 Squadron at Tempsford – base of the 'Moon Men' and the 161 and 138 'Moon Squadrons' – so called because, using little, *Lysander*s and *Whitley*, *Halifax*, *Havoc* and *Hudson* bombers, these two squadrons delivered by night thousands of containers, packages, underground agents and spies to Europe and Scandinavia. Tempsford was air base of the shadow war, and the very versatile *Lysander* aircraft, on moon period nights in particular, were used to shuttle agents back and forth to enemy territory like a bus service.

*Lysander*s continually took off from England to fly deep into the heart of the Continent to land in fields, carrying important men and women to and from London, but on the night of 24 February 1943, Pick needed a bigger plane to carry a full load going to France, as well as the return load he was scheduled to bring back – seven agents pursued by the Gestapo.

Heading for the Tournais/Cuisery area, he ran into fog and was forced to circle the rendezvous position for a dangerously long period until, after many abortive attempts, he finally managed to land, only to find himself bogged down with wheels stuck firmly in the ground.

The few people on the spot couldn't budge the plane, so one of them ran to the nearby village, and although German troops and security forces were everywhere and must have heard the sound of an aircraft circling to land, the entire village – including the police, and farm horses – turned out to help free Pick's *Hudson* bomber. It took all night, and dawn was breaking at 5.30 a.m. when, with two Gestapo-filled cars bearing down on them, Pick was finally able to get away.

Choosing the return route carefully to avoid flak concentrations and Luftwaffe fighters, he flew across France with one of his passengers at the ready with a Sten gun – the only armament aboard. The return flight was in broad daylight most of the way.

Although they reached base at 08.00 hours, Dorothy Pickard had known from 1.30 a.m. that Pick had been in great danger when Ming yanked the blankets off her. As before, she let the dog out and, ignoring cold and snow, Ming simple gazed up at the sky, moving her head from right to left, sometimes whimpering, sometimes howling. Nothing would budge her.

When Dorothy telephoned the Ops Room, there was no news.

At precisely 5.30 a.m. – the time Pick had taken off from France – she heard Ming scratching at the door and opened it to see the dog, tail wagging, head straight for the fireplace. When Ming immediately fell asleep, Dorothy was certain Pick was safe. At about 8.00 a.m., she was again woken by Ming who, instantly the front door was unlocked, scurried towards the runway and a *Hudson* which was coming in to land.

The legend of Ming, to whom Pick had issued a personal flying log book, marked 'Honorary Observer', in recognition of her many hours in the air with him, spread from base to base.

'That dog has friends everywhere because she wags her tail instead of her tongue,' asserted Pick.

Transferred to a Fighter Command ground job, Pick loathed it, fretted, and was irritably restless. He had to fly. Night after night he fretted about not being allowed to take part in bombing raids over Germany, although he had done more than his share with hundreds of hours of ops.

'God, how I wish I were with those boys,' he moaned with restlessness loud and clear in his voice.

'Don't worry,' Dorothy comforted him, 'you'll be back in action soon.'

Pessimistically he insisted:

'I have the feeling that when my ship comes in, I'll be at the airport,' then determinedly: 'I'm not staying on this bloody station! There's no operational flying here, so I've had it!'

Unable to tolerate inaction, living for risk-taking, and seeming to possess a charmed existence, Pick nagged at higher ups until, two months later, he was posted to Sculthorpe and the aircraft that was so much to influence his future – the *Mosquito*. The man and plane were born for each other. Alan Broadley, from whom he had been separated much of the time whilst shuttling *Lysander*s to the Continent from Tempsford, rejoined him at Sculthorpe.

It was Sculthorpe which brought him to Basil Embry's 2 Group team. Embry pulled strings to have Pickard posted there. He sympathised with Pick's frustration at being given all kinds of important jobs to keep him out of the air.

When Embry took over 2 Group and found morale low, he inveigled a promise of *Mosquito* re-equipment from the Air Ministry, toured Squadrons, pep-talked crews, personally tested aircraft, and ordered sweeping changes. When Pick first joined him he explained:

'I want you to help me drive home by example the principle that those who direct operations should fly on operations from time to time, and thereby be able to speak on level terms with fighting personnel.'

Pick could have kissed him for the words.

Embry forecast that the Group's best effectiveness would be operating day and night. Being able to locate and hit any target, down to a single building, would compensate for lack of numbers.

Neither could have foreseen that the tactics they were about to employ would be the basis of their involvement with a prison in France that winter.

Basil Embry rammed his idea and ideals home to Pick because, although he knew Pickard was unquestionably one of the finest and most versatile pilots flying for the Allies, he was also aware that self-discipline was not his strongest point. It was normal to find him standing beneath fully armed and refuelled aircraft, happily puffing his pipe. If they were to work effectively together, they had to understand how each other ticked.

Pick was only too willing to accept his advice.

Embry's rigid rule was:

'During an attack the leader must be more than human; mustn't worry about enemy fighters or anti-aircraft fire; must keep only one thing in mind – the target.'

Pick nodded pensively then promised:

'I intend to get through to my crews that you can be the best and most accurate pilot in the world, but if you're a bad shot you'll never shoot down the enemy. On the other hand, if you are the best shot in the world and not a good pilot, the enemy will shoot you down.'

Agreeing, Embry summarised with a single sentence:

'War doesn't always decide who's right – only who's left.'

During the first six months of 1943, *Mosquito*s were almost solely used on low-level daylight operations over north west Europe. Their strength was surprise and speed. Cruising speed on these ops ranged from 260 m.p.h. to 300 m.p.h. They kept a stand-by list of small selected difficult targets to attack whenever the opportunity arose.

After only two hours familiarisation test flying, Pick got the hang of the *Mosquito* and, with Alan Broadley, piled up daily experience, including regular flights and landings on one engine. It was fortunate they had rehearsed single-engine landings for on their first operational sortie in a *Mosquito*, they had to return on one engine after the other had been shot up and set ablaze.

Again Ming kept sentinel watch outside until they safely forced-landed at another aerodrome in Southern England, at which precise moment Ming, as usual, trotted back inside and fell contentedly asleep.

Coming under new management with Basil Embry, 2 Group – long the Cinderella of Bomber Command – finally discovered its niche and commenced establishing its importance in the largely Anglo-American controlled 2nd Tactical Air Force which had been created in readiness for its invasion role. Fighting strength of the Group was raised from eight to twelve squadrons by addition of French, British, Dutch and Polish units, and Embry's immense courage, resourcefulness, persistence and genius made him an admirable and loved leader for them all, although these qualities didn't always endear him to those outside his command. He was nevertheless swiftly becoming one of the Allies' greatest war winners, and from the outset of association with 2 Group, mainly concentrated on preparing for invasion of Europe. Little wonder German High Command set a reward of 70,000 Marks for him – dead or alive – thereby compelling him to fly raids as 'Wing Commander Smith' with a tag around his neck bearing the number of a genuine Smith of that rank. He had false identification discs, false markings on all clothes in which he flew, and even arranged for rank badges to be switched at will. Although recognising such elementary precautions wouldn't have long resisted Gestapo or German Intelligence investigation, he hoped they would provide time enough for an escape opportunity, if he fell into enemy hands.

The one occasion he was shot down, he killed his guards to escape, then arrived from Spain dressed in a smart lounge suit and Panama hat.

Arriving for a raid flight, he invariably appeared with a revolver in his boot, Commando dagger attached to his braces, a variety of metal files hidden about his person – always fully prepared for a fight or escape on the ground, as well as in the air.

'If necessary, I'll bash their heads in with my boots. It's just like cracking an egg – it makes the same noise.'

Reorganisation of planning and tactics couldn't have been more timely with overwhelming information being received of a massive offensive by long-range rockets, pilotless aeroplanes and very long-range guns against London and southern England, with other launching sites in the Cherbourg area aimed at Bristol. Unless those sites could be destroyed or heavily reduced, London might have to be evacuated, and preparations for operation 'Overlord' – the invasion of Europe – rethought. Rocket and flying bomb sites and their storage and manufacturing centres were code-named 'No Ball' targets.

Astutely, the United States built a number of replica launching sites at an experimental establishment at Eglin Air Base in Florida to test attacking them with the complete weapon range available to American and British air forces based in Britain. United States Air Force experts concluded that minimum-altitude bombing, if properly delivered by *Thunderbolts* and fighter bombers, would be the most effective and economical counter to 'No Ball' targets.

'There's only one thing more contagious than measles, and that's a good example,' Embry smiled broadly at David Atcherley, 'and that Florida dummy rocket pad bug has got to me too. I want our own model VI site built to scale on one of the practice ranges.'

Knocked together by tacking hessian on a wooden frame, the model helped achieve better results by rehearsing tactics and familiarising crews with target layouts. Approaching low and hitting them from twenty feet, the sites appeared very fast, particularly if located in a wood or orchard, as they often were, so it was essential to come in straight at the correct angle to aiming points, and for the pilot to have a clear mind picture of the look of a site, thereby aiding him to spot unhesitatingly the objective and decide the best aiming point instantly.

Under the code heading of 'Crossbow', combined forces of the United States 8th and 9th Air Forces, the 2nd Tactical Air Force and British Bomber Command began thousands of sorties against 'No Ball' targets from November 1943, and simultaneously, the 8th and 15th U.S. Air Forces were assigned the task of 'Operation Argument' – destruction of the enemy's aircraft industry, and particularly factories engaged in fighter production. The task was formidable. The Luftwaffe had substantially increased fighter strength during the winter, and the first 'Operation Argument' raid showed the Luftwaffe capable of opposing with unprecedented ferocity thousand-plus Allied bombers aiming at supply life-lines.

Eisenhower pointed out in a letter to General Arnold that the Germans might conceivably finish their full V-weapons offensive preparations before the invasion was ready, and stressed that the Allies must prevent this.

The Americans anticipated tough opposition and correspondingly heavy losses, but were now committed to launch the biggest strategic air offensive in history. The success of a vast percentage of this, and the V1-V2 attacks, depended on the flow of accurate Intelligence information getting through from the Continent. More than ever, full-strength uninterrupted help was needed from every friend and agent there, if the Allies were to smash the threat of rocket bases and aircraft supply centres, then invade, and liberate.

The gaolbreak jigsaw was fitting into place.

# 4 A job for a Joshua

'Do you play the trumpet, John?' Bill Donovan asked his personal aide, John Haskell.

'Trumpet?' puzzled Haskell queried.

'What we need are some great trumpeters to do for us what they did for Joshua and the walls of Jericho.'

Before elaborating, Donovan re-read the report freshly arrived on his Washington desk from Allen Dulles in Berne, smiling as he again reached the final page footnote where Dulles had written in ink:

'The clever may say it can't be done, but the fool will simply do it.'

To general's son John Haskell, Donovan explained:

'When we were last in London, I saw "C" about this same problem to explore how they, or any of us, could come up with an answer to it, and none of us have to date.

'The Gestapo are winning in northern France and our networks are being wiped out or falling apart in the very areas where we can least afford to lose them.

'Hitler's playing for time for his V1s and V2s to paralyse southern England, knowing we'll invade from there between Ostend and the Cherbourg peninsula because we're limited to where we can provide adequate fighter cover. Consequently he's massively stepping up the drive to smash and demoralise our underground to prevent them giving us effective invasion support.

'One of our most important outfits in the area – the Sosies, run by the Ponchardier brothers who work for us through Groussard and Dulles – are in deep trouble. Far too many of their men are already inside Amiens gaol, due for almost certain execution, alongside a load of others from different networks, and Dominique Ponchardier wants to organise a mass escape and get either our air force or the RAF to knock down the outer prison walls.'

Picking up the Dulles documents from his desk and waving them at Haskell, he added:

'It's all here. They've sent layouts of the gaol, even old architectural blueprints of the place filched from Amiens Prefecture, as well as supplied names of people inside they want out.'

'Do they accept how easy it would be for it all to go wrong and end with us slaughtering their own friends?' Haskell questioned.

Deep in thought, Donovan didn't reply for an instant, then answered:

'Yes.'

To Bill Donovan, each day, never sufficient unto itself, was always teeming with the seeds of a boundless future, and every completed project bred a host of new ones, but he wasn't too happy about this one from Dulles. Bombing the enemy was one thing, but bombing your own people was a very different plate of soup you could fall into. There were always more problems than solutions, but this was one problem he could do without.

'Ponchardier says it should be done, not only to help the gaoled men who worked for him and us, but also so everyone will know that if they go to prison, someone will try to get them out,' Donovan continued, sounding out points the Dulles documents raised on his assistant, but in reality, drumming them further into his own head.

Ponchardier, he said, had asserted to Dulles that such a symbolic attack was vital to prepare the minds and spirits of everyone for the invasion. It would be a galvanic morale booster, – a fact which registered heavily with Donovan who believed intensely in the importance of morale, agreeing with his friend Winston Churchill that there are many kinds of manoeuvres in war, only some of which take place on the battlefield. There are manoeuvres in time, in diplomacy, in mechanics, in psychology; all of which are removed from the battlefield, but often react decisively upon it, the object of all being to find easier ways, other than sheer slaughter, of achieving the main purpose.

Clandestine sabotage, particularly in northern France, was scheduled to provide a continuing threat which would supplement invasion attacks by making the enemy deploy an undue number of protective troops and maintenance personnel. Support was essential if this threat was to be maintained, as it was also expected to prevent the enemy from bringing reinforcement and supplies to invasion battle areas by rail, and compelling detrainment further and further from the battlefields. Continued aid of this kind would give crucial direct assistance to 'Overlord', so the force of Dominique Ponchardier's morale-boosting argument was inescapable.

'Maybe he's got the right idea!' Donovan the irrepressible optimist suddenly exclaimed.

'We are dealing with life or death situations, and are using adults whom we assume to be adult enough to recognise the real meaning of self-sacrifice. Self-sacrifice presupposes a readiness and courage to sacrifice oneself by one's own hand for the protection of co-workers in a network or to insure the success of a mission. It's that simple.

'There are good things even in war. You see self-effacement, resourcefulness, daring, plain guts – there just aren't enough words to cover the things you see some men and women do in the name of patriotism.'

Suddenly grinning at Haskell, Donovan, who refused to consider anything impossible, said determinedly:

'Anyway, who says the idea won't work? Where there's a won't there's a way.'

Haskell grinned too, knowing that, as far as his chief was concerned, nothing was too ridiculous to be dismissed. Even cautious David Bruce, in London, warned:

'Woe to the officer who turns down a project because on its face, it seems ridiculous, or at least unusual!'

Every eccentric schemer with a hare-brained plan for secret operations, from phosphorescent foxes to incendiary bats, could find a sympathetic ear in Donovan's office, because he insisted:

'I ignore nothing – you never can tell.'

Haskell remembered the man from San Francisco who didn't know a thing about Intelligence work, but wanted to get into OSS and personally reached Donovan with an idea.

'I have German ancestors,' he told Donovan. 'As inflation ruined Germany after the first World War, I have a deathly hatred of inflation. Why not print millions of German marks, drop them instead of bombs onto Germany, then there'll be inflation and the country will collapse by itself?'

'A wonderful idea!' Donovan cried. 'You're hired!'

As one of nine children from a humble home in Buffalo, Bill Donovan, son of an Irish railway worker, cared most of all about people. Individuals meant a lot to him, and he would never let them, or himself, get lost in the machinery. Some men always recognised duty in time to side-step it, but Bill Donovan wasn't like that. Once something got his backing, it had it right down the line, but on the transatlantic scrambler phone connection to Allen Dulles in Berne, he admitted:

'I'm not crazy about the sound of this Amiens business. There's a big difference between reasons that sound good and good sound reasons.'

He never turned down an idea before turning it over, so he had methodically gone over all the possibilities he could envisage, and considered options.

'It's got me really worried, Allen.'

There was a pause at the other end of the phone, then Dulles observed:

'I set aside a little time every day to do most of my worrying, then take a nap during this period.'

Both laughed, and it helped.

'I'm going to throw it at the Joint Chiefs of Staff with a recommendation for a top priority feasibility study,' Donovan said.

'That's the best direction,' Dulles agreed.

Whilst Donovan often tangled with top brass about the role of Intelligence and the conduct of unconventional operations, he held their respect. They would listen to him about Amiens because his words usually had a sense of urgency encouraging everyone to attempt the seemingly impossible, and he was sure they believed as fervently as he did in unstinted support for those in the firing line.

*

Usually the best way to kill a good idea is to get a committee to work on it. But this didn't apply to the Joint Chiefs of Staff to whom Bill Donovan submitted the Amiens proposal, nor to another committee to whom it was forwarded, which regularly met in the main room of a large mansion known as Bentley Priory, at Stanmore, on the outskirts of London.

The elegant room had French windows which opened on to a balcony, and a flight of stone steps which led to spacious grounds. This was the office of the Commander-in-Chief of RAF Fighter Command, also appointed by General Eisenhower in December 1943, C-in-C of all Allied Expeditionary Forces.

From this room, with the somewhat magisterial manner that was his custom, forceful Air Chief Marshal Sir Trafford Leigh Mallory, KCB, DSO, controlled a command the like of which the world had never seen before. As head of both American and British Tactical

Forces, he was responsible for co-ordinating the efforts of heavy bombers placed at his disposal by the Chiefs of Staff.

Like Embry and so many other top fighting men of action, moustached, Cheshire-born Leigh Mallory was the son of a clergyman – youngest son of the rector of the parish of Mobberly. Although from comparatively humble beginnings, he loved affecting magnificence and rushing about issuing orders in his deceptively pompous voice.

Fighter Command had given him unrivalled experience of controlling aircraft – medium and light bombers, fighter bombers and fighters – operating over mainland Europe, and he launched into planning air co-operation essential to the invasion of Europe as soon as he took up his appointment under Eisenhower.

'Impossible' was a challenge to him. It was his instinct to look for things that were difficult to do, and then do them, so he was undeterred by the formidable difficulty of effecting a blissful marriage between the two strategic bomber commanders – Lt. General Carl Spaatz of the United States Strategic Air Forces, and Air Chief Marshal Sir Arthur 'Bomber' Harris of the RAF. Ike had assigned Leigh Mallory the sensitive matchmaking task of getting the two bristly bomber force commanders happily, or unhappily, hand in hand in order to direct bombers where most necessary for Basil Embry's invasion-spearheading Tactical Air Force squadrons.

The main article of furniture in the Bentley Priory room was a large desk facing a large-scale wall map of France and Belgium. A long table, with a dozen chairs beside it, was set between the windows for use at the C-in-C's conferences. Opposite the windows was a large board indicating the number of American and British squadrons available.

On the mantelpiece behind the desk were photographs of the Allied Commanders, with Eisenhower in the central place of honour, and one of the opposition – Luftwaffe commander General Sperrle.

The carpet was standard-patterned RAF pink and blue, as were most of the chairs. Outside, through the tall French windows, rhododendron bushes and trees in the garden gave an evergreen setting to the bleak wintry day. Beyond them could be seen the landing strip for the puddle jumpers – the light aircraft used for short journeys.

It was cold and overcast and even the news was gloomy. The only bright spot at the conference that morning was the fire burning in the grate. Adverse flying conditions were favouring the enemy, giving them too many days free from counter-attack and therefore too much time to complete construction of further batteries of V1 and V2 sites. It was all the more galling because by the end of 1943, the Americans had not only increased the range of the fighter escorts, but also considerably stepped up operational strength of their bombers. In addition to which the Eighth American Air Force had at last reached its intended size, and could now comfortably launch 500 and 600 bomber attacks with more than adequate P-47 *Thunderbolt* and P-38 *Lightning* fighter escorts. The allies had the means to smash Hitler's rockets, but not the weather.

'I'm feeling a bit depressed today – you know the kind of feeling when your instinct is to go out and have several drinks,' Leigh Mallory unhappily confessed to the top brass assembled at his daily conferences.

'I'm experiencing a certain sense of frustration because it's maddening to think that if we hadn't this bad weather we could have clobbered them already.' The C-in-C paused for effect. 'If we break the crust, there may not be an awful lot to the other side. The weather's been so damnable that I sometimes think the Powers above may have Fascist tendencies.'

Hopefully, he tapped the portable barometer beside him, but frowned on seeing it fall.

American bombers were managing to fly over the worst of the weather, in radiant sunshine, high above snow or the icing-up danger zone, completing effective raids with navigational aids and bombsights. The thought clearly pleased the C-in-C.

'The Luftwaffe will be beaten – I'm sure of that,' Leigh Mallory snapped. 'They have to be forced to a point where they must decide to fight it out till they win or are destroyed, or refuse to take that risk and adopt the course of preserving strength for some future effort to be made at a time when they judge the situation to be most suitable, or possibly most desperate.'

Obstinately blunt in presenting views and hot tempered when crossed, he forever voiced strong opinions about air power use, and more often than not his original ideas were proved correct.

Day-to-day matters were dealt with at the Stanmore meetings he chaired, and there he always had the final say. But it was Basil Embry's immediate chief – Air Marshal Sir Arthur Coningham, KCB, DSO, MC, DFC, AFC, shortly to command Allied Expeditionary Air Forces in the first phase of the invasion – who was about to bear major responsibility for the Amiens attack and to become closer acquainted with its innermost background than either the C-in-C or Embry.

48

The American liaison Colonel attending the Fighter Command HQ conference on that particular morning didn't realise the full topicality of his contribution to the discussion.

'The standstill of low-level "No Ball" attacks is even more serious now than perhaps some of you realise,' he advised, 'because land counter-measures, including sabotage of V-site and rocket storage caverns, as well as sources of up to date information on them, are drying up due to recent Gestapo arrests of scores of people they've thrown into Amiens gaol. Our Resistance support in northern France is in danger of complete collapse, and the implication of this to "Overlord" is obvious.

'General Eisenhower says that if the Germans had succeeded in perfecting these new weapons six months earlier than they did, our invasion of Europe could prove more difficult, and perhaps, impossible. He feels sure that if they succeed in using these weapons over a six-month period, and particularly if they make the Portsmouth-Southampton area one of their principle targets, "Overlord" might have to be written off.'

They were all silent until the C-in-C sat back in his chair to conclude:

'So we have a bog, but I hope we will soon be able to unstick things.'

As the others left, he requested Coningham to remain, and immediately produced a number of Photographic Reconnaissance Unit pictures of Amiens, and its prison in particular. At first neither commented. Coningham was then handed a report to read. Allowing him a few moments to absorb the document, Leigh Mallory admitted:

'Intelligence don't like it, the Air Ministry don't like it, and nor do I. Now it's your turn to think about it. All I can say is that bombing Amiens, Cambrai and Arras junctions would seal off Belgium during the invasion, so we need all the helping hands we can get from the Resistance. But,' he cautioned, 'even if this proposal is at all feasible, if the enemy is alert and vigorous, I think casualties would be far too high and could not, therefore, be justified.'

There was really no more to be said. Time was needed to consider every aspect. From then on, as far as the C-in-C was concerned, Amiens prison was largely Coningham's conundrum.

Coningham, with the most astute Intelligence assessment mind in the air force, was the fighting force leader Intelligence sections themselves respected most. In consequence, he was also one of the very few with direct and instant access at all times to 'C' – head of Britain's M16 secret service department.

*

Everybody loved 'Mary', as Coningham was popularly called. Born at Brisbane, Queensland, Australia, but educated in New Zealand, he preferred to be known as a New Zealander and was proud of the nickname 'Maori' which gradually became corrupted to 'Mary'. Two days after the outbreak of the Kaiser's war he enlisted in the infantry. Invalided out and sent home after two years, he regained health six months later. Although he had never even seen an aeroplane, he travelled to England at his own expense to join the Royal Flying Corps, serving with great distinction, and winning the DSO, MC, and DFC as a fighter pilot, shooting down 19 enemy planes in 14 days.

Original architect of Tactical Air Forces – President Roosevelt conferred on him the Legion of Merit (Chief Commander) in recognition of his establishing and commanding the North-squadrons – he also commanded Tactical Air Forces in the field in Sicily and Italy, working closely with generals Alexander and Montgomery. Recalled to Britain to prepare for the assault on Europe, he staffed his headquarters with American and RAF officers, and representatives of the United States 21st Army Group, because he passionately believed in land-air co-ordination. It was his greatest contribution to victory, and its value was quite incalculable. To him, more than anyone, went credit for the initiation and development of joint land-air techniques. 'Mary' Coningham was definitely no ordinary character – what genius is?

On returning to his base at Uxbridge, in Middlesex, Coningham remained in his office alone studying a large-scale map of the Amiens area. To put him in front of a map was to entice into the open a shrewd calculating brain. He had also taken the aerial photographs from Leigh Mallory. Coningham was never one to make a forecast, plan, decision, or any remark that wasn't sound and didn't prove right. To him, war was an art rather than a science. Insistent though he was on administrative and technical efficiency, he always put morale first and material second – quality before quantity. His weapon was the rapier rather than the bludgeon.

After hours alone tussling with the problem, he did what he usually liked to do at such times – go away with a packet of sandwiches and have a 'quiet think', after which he indulged in a favourite relaxation and watched a Marx Brothers movie in the Mess. On this occasion it was 'Animal Crackers'.

On digesting the Amiens Intelligence report he concluded that the operation would depend equally on the effectiveness of land and air teamwork. An air strike on the prison could only succeed with ground back-up. After mentally exploiting the possibilities of the situation, he sent for Basil Embry.

Was it then to be all-out for Amiens?

*

When in answer to an urgent summons from his Chief, Basil Embry strode into Coningham's simply furnished '2nd TAF' headquarters office at Uxbridge, Middlesex – so contrasted to the stately elegance of the C-in-C's Bentley Priory abode – he was handed, without a word, the same Intelligence summary 'Mary' had received only hours before from Leigh Mallory.

It stated that some hundred Resistance patriots were at that moment awaiting trial and death in Amiens prison. The next batch of mass executions were scheduled to be carried out around the middle of February.

Embry's eyes moved to a calendar on the wall. The deadline was all too close. The report stressed shattering reverses and losses suffered by underground forces in recent weeks throughout northern France. Even the Germans did not realise just how successful they'd been. They were unaware that they had captured, broken, or completely wiped out entire networks upon whom the Allies were dependent not only for up to date information on the build-up of rocket missile sites, but also for essential back-up when invasion started.

With the Allies' friends in France so demoralised, there was desperate need for a striking demonstration of the ability and readiness to assist them.

'They say that if we can bomb the walls of the gaol and release those inside, it would rekindle the flame of hope in a region that has long been a Resistance stronghold, but where morale is now at its lowest,' Coningham said as Embry closed the report file.

'They need help, and our prayers,' Embry said grimly.

'The way to get prayers answered is to pray for the strength to answer them yourself,' Coningham said softly.

Embry nodded thoughtfully, and glanced again at the report.

It assessed that there was no way in which the prison could be attacked from the ground without enormous casualties and little more than a slim chance of success, but proposed that those still at liberty would wait outside to assist fleeing prisoners if, and when, the RAF bombed a way out for them.

'Nobody fancies the idea' Coningham admitted, 'and understandably so, when we might destroy the whole place, and maybe kill hundreds, without finally achieving anything.'

Embry stayed silent.

'In fact we have already turned it down, and told them so – not because of the risk to us, but because of the enormous risk to them.

'But,' – and Coningham's 'buts' were famous – 'I've given it a lot of thought and think it could be done – by your *Mosquitos*.'

'Possibly,' Embry tentatively agreed, 'but only with the loss of some prisoners' lives. I would want to examine the full implications of such an operation before giving you a definite answer. I would also need to know *fast* every single aspect of the prison that could help us assess accurately exactly what we'd be up against.'

Coningham smiled.

'Friends over there have beaten you to that point. For the past few weeks – before this request for RAF help they've been sending us what appeared to be simply routine information about the jail and its lay-out: everything from where guards are housed and their eating habits, to the height and width of outer walls, without specifying any purpose. Best of all, they even obtained a copy of the *original* architect's plans of the place. So we already have a lot to go with, and I've some photographs we have taken too. It's a job now for your Planning Committee and the model shop.'

Coningham knew the model shop was Embry's special baby. In the face of Air ministry opposition, he had established his own modelling section and Planning Committee with a hand-picked team of innovators and red tape rebels whose sole aim was to get things done in the shortest possible time.

Having gone to such lengths to develop techniques and training for low-level ops, because he was convinced this bombing would pay the biggest dividends, and as it demanded exceptionally high planning standards, he had formed a committee to treat each low-level attack as a major air operation. Furthermore, to ensure the best navigational accuracy and dead-on approaches to targets, he had established a relief modelling section within his own head-quarters to provide the facility to model each target and the run up to it. This became an essential element of 2 Group's success. All that was needed was a simple plaster model, devoid of unnecessary detail, available for pilot study at briefings.

Refusing a request for a separate modelling section at 2 Group Headquarters, the Air Ministry insisted on modelling being carried out at the Central Photographic Interpretation Unit. Unwilling to accept the dangerous delays red tape could cause, particularly for a tactical outfit on constant call to hit quick-notice targets, Embry took the initiative.

'I don't like long answers to short questions,' he growled

impatiently. 'The only way to be efficient is not to lose time discovering mistakes.'

There were moments of crisis in any man's life when he is overwhelmingly compelled to piss against the wind, which is what Embry did in this instance by defying the Air Ministry veto and forming a small modelling section of his own to provide speedily anything required – something he maintained the Central Photographic Unit could never do for him.

He was sure the man seated across the desk to him at that moment would have acted the same in his shoes, for 'Mary' Coningham was his idea of the perfect fighting leader.

'Never do anything to the enemy unless you yourself have first discovered the antidote,' were Coningham's parting words on the day he handed him the Amiens assignment.

# 5 The melting pot

Inmates of the musty, overcrowded, sprawling old grey stone prison buildings on Amiens' Route d'Albert would have been very surprised at the interest being taken in their welfare and questions being asked about them by the occupants of the elegant mansion in England's Middlesex countryside.

As far as the prisoners were concerned, there were only two sides to every question – the inside and the outside. And, lying on the rusty iron-frame bed in Cell 16, re-reading Victor Hugo's *Les Misérables*, Dr. Antonin Mans didn't doubt that gaol was the perfect place to indulge in escapist literature.

Spies, burglars, saboteurs, pickpockets, Resistance couriers and con men, murderers and forgers, guerilla fighters and prostitutes, pimps and Black Marketeers, thugs, shoplifters, evasion line aiders and vagabonds – name them, and they had them in Amiens gaol. Civil criminals, supposedly separated in different wings from Gestapo detainees, were thrown together in the same sordid sadistic melting pot. Consequently, the dividing line between 'political' and criminal was impossible even for the authorities to define and record accurately.

Prostitutes were not imprisoned for prostitution but for being thieves as well, or for helping escaping shot down Allied aircrews or agents. Many vagabonds hadn't stolen anything, but nor were some genuine vagabonds. With the country under enemy occupation nobody was necessarily what they seemed. Hundreds of thousands of names on identity cards were as misleading as the forged documents upon which they appeared, and with Germans and French jointly administering and sharing gaols, the penal system was inside out and upside down.

For most criminals, the country could go to hell and Hitler, though others cared for France, liberty, equality, and fraternity – especially liberty. One thing united them with 'politicals' in gaol – all were in the same stinking boat.

Dr. Mans, chief medical officer of the entire Somme region, found himself there after his home was surrounded by two hundred soldiers with armoured cars and two Gestapo: an uncomfortably clear indication of the measure of importance attached to his detention as suspected head of the Organisation Civile et Militaire – the OCM – the largest Intelligence network in northern France. Inspector Serge Dumant of the Sûreté – the French equivalent of Britain's Scotland Yard – who had spent a lifetime hunting criminals, was now sharing a cell with several because he loved his country more than his job. Maurice Holville was inside with ponce and Black Marketeer Jules Dumay because he insisted on wearing a borrowed railway official's uniform when spying on fortifications and troop and arms movements, unaware that he fitted the description of a wanted railway-uniformed man.

Some were imprisoned under their genuine names, whilst others, 'diplomatically' arrested by sympathetic policemen, were hiding in gaol to dodge Gestapo or Abwehr army counter-Intelligence.

Roger Beaurin was listed in the gaol's criminal records as a common bicycle thief. He wasn't. His teenage brother Jean was officially shown as a simple ration card trafficker. That wasn't true either, but they were gaoled with people like Pierre Kowalezick, separated from his wife and seven children for five years for stealing 329 packets of tobacco and cigarettes, 14 kilogrammes of chocolate, and 50 boxes of groceries; and gentle Marc Caron who unexpectedly returning home ill from work, discovered his wife in bed with his best friend.

'They both laughed at me and went right on doing what they'd been doing before I interrupted,' said Caron, recalling the moment for his cell companions, 'so I beat him unconscious, then strangled my wife.' The death sentence was commuted to life, otherwise he would have been guillotined at Amiens. The guillotine, kept in Paris, was taken to Amiens when required, as it was a few months previously when an ex-Gendarme who killed a woman to rob her, was condemned and guillotined in the prison.

The striking difference between criminal and 'political' inmates was that the criminals openly talked about themselves, though all too frequently claiming they had been wrongly convicted.

The gaol had two main quarters: one requisitioned by the Germans directly facing the prison main entrance, and the French wing on the right comprising three floors, with general services, including the kitchen for the entire prison, in the basement. The small women's quarters were supposed to hold only women criminals, but like the rest of the place, took overflow 'politicals' from the central building. Women under total German control were in the same wing as men, but on the second floor. One of the women wardens was the German-speaking collaborationist Frenchwoman, Lucienne, who also acted as interpreter between French and German quarters. Only those not sentenced, or condemned to death and awaiting execution, usually remained in the German section, but many were simply shot, or disappeared without ever being brought to trial.

Officially, Amiens was a short-term establishment. Cases on remand, awaiting trial or verdicts, were held there. Murderers, armed bank robbers, and various violent criminals sentenced to twenty or thirty years, did the first two years of their sentences there, and then transferred to long-term gaols. It was also a short-term stop for 'political' detainees as it did not usually take the authorities long to decide whether to shoot them or ship them to concentration camps.

Long-sentence men and women were completely uninterested in dates, though many walls were etched with pencilled calendars and ticked off days, months, and years. Scorning this, long-sentence types stressed from experience:

'Who cares what day, week, or month it is – if you want time to go faster, don't look at a calendar.'

Time could only be measured by light, and prison routine – they were the only clocks available.

You could be sick with loneliness, but never alone.

To ease boredom, life stories – or whatever portion of them inmates chose to reveal – were exchanged, though you never really knew the truth about anyone, because everyone was a liar of some sort. The most discussed topics were crime, money, and sex, which was also Jules Damay's main business.

From a distance, Jules' round face, prominent nose, and black hair looked almost boyish – not the gigolo type at all, like so many pimps. Close up his eyes told another story. By the time he was twenty-eight, he had been inside several times for procuring. Now he was sharing a cell with Intelligence agent Maurice Holville.

This lively intelligent parasite with the slightly clipped manner of speaking also ran a wholesale purchasing agency buying all he could below fixed official rates, then reselling the stuff to the Germans who'd buy anything. The Germans started the Black Market in France, but the French soon surpassed their masters. Black Market fulfilled two purposes – it was profitable, and demoralising.

'I don't know why, but girls always swarmed round me like flies,' Jules modestly confided to cellmates. 'I used to recruit them for brothels, then moved up and owned a first class Paris house. It wasn't in my name, but I owned it one hundred per cent. I booked appointments for clients who wanted specialities – some men like women to be acrobats. You know, when a bachelor goes to a brothel, he's needy, but when a married man does, he's usually greedy. I suppose the easier women are to get, the easier they are to forget.

'I fixed police protection where possible; settled disputes with the Madame who ran the place for me; took care of taxi drivers and club doormen who steered clients to us; managed the girls – you know, women deteriorate worse than men once they pick up men's bad habits, like not knowing when they've had enough booze.'

'That sounds like a full-time job,' Holville said, keeping the conversation friendly.

'Not really,' Jules casually assured him. 'I spent most of my time either playing cards with friends, or enjoying myself somewhere. Of course I had to beat up a girl now and then at the house, just to show them who's boss, but you know how it is . . .'

'No, I don't,' said Holville.

'Most tarts want some man to cling to, no matter how rotten he is, and most go into the game because they're lazy. A respectable job would mean getting up mornings like the rest of us . . . myself excluded, of course,' he hastily added, smiling.

'Of course,' Holville responded, returning the smile.

Warming to the subject, almost as if excusing himself and trying to prove he didn't force girls into slavery, he insisted:

'They're self-opinionated, self-indulgent, and haven't the guts to face normal work. They're not on the game through hunger, like years ago. They just want luxuries the easy way.'

Holville was wondering what excuse there was for someone so full of excuses when Jules' self-confession was musically interrupted.

'No you'll never get Alsace Lorraine! – no you'll never get Alsace Lorraine!'

'God, he's singing his bloody patriotic songs again!' Holville cried, looking with despair at the cell's senior citizen. 'I'd better listen out for the footbridge – thank Christ it's made of metal so that we can hear the guards' bloody great big boots coming.'

Holville stooped down and put an ear to the food dispensing panel set in the door base, which was the best point for picking up external sounds.

Master baker Vincent Darras, whom Holville knew from his hometown, was a real problem, with his partiality for putting heart and soul and maximum lung power into bellowing out patriotic songs. Officially he was imprisoned for trading in Black Market flour. This way, friendly Gendarmes helped him get lost in a cell with a false identity just as the Gestapo were close to nailing him as a Resistance suspect. Vincent, who had served in the first world war, hid evaders and stored arms in his home.

'Well, at least Vincent's not as bad as the Abbé Carpentier of Abbeville,' Holville consoled himself and his companions. 'That holy terror cycles about the town singing popular songs in *English*! Language apart, they're a dead give-away because they're *current* American and British ditties he could only have picked up through listening to the BBC, which alone is enough to get him slung in here with us.

'He rides back and forth across that river bridge at Abbeville – crawling with soldiers – singing away to his heart's content. I saw, and heard him go across one morning singing "There'll be bluebirds over the White Cliffs of Dover," and coming back in the afternoon singing "When Johnny comes marching home again, hurrah! hurrah!" – he scares the shit out of me.'

Maurice Holville, Vincent and Jules took turns to play draughts with Boris – they couldn't pronounce his surname – the fourth member of their cell community. Practically all they had in common with Boris, who didn't speak a word of French, was playing draughts with little bits of different coloured paper they had managed to keep. An eighteen-year-old Russian prisoner of war, Boris had been conscripted as a slave labourer to build coastal fortifications, but kept escaping from work camps, so they stuck him in gaol. For a few days, a retired lawyer from Paris who spoke

Russian was a cell fifth and interpreted for Boris, but when he left they were back to draughts again.

They also made a pack of cards by cutting out bits of red and black from pro-German propaganda magazines they were allowed to read, and sticking them on smuggled-in plain cards to make a pack.

Toilet paper – small sheets torn from newspapers and magazines – was another diversion. They read every word before putting them to their intended use, and when they were fortunate enough to get whole pages of books, it was even more entertaining.

Waking morning moments were the worst, as consciousness returned them to reality and the customary first visitor of the day – the slopman, who came to empty Tinettes (outsize tin cans which were the sanitary arrangement). The stench that hit new arrivals quickly became an accepted part of the atmospheric background. Sometimes, giddy from the smell and lack of air, a man would sit on the bed, stick his head between his knees, then jerk his head up fast, which could make him faint and pass out for a half an hour or so. Many pulled this trick for kicks, just to 'leave' the cell and the world awhile.

As the gaol awoke, sleepy voices of men and women filtered through the thick walls, and at seven, black acorn 'coffee' arrived with a piece of what the French call 'complet' bread. Stodgy, smelly, it couldn't be saved for long as it quickly went rancid, though some hoarded a little to provide an in-between snack, or to swap for an authorised or smuggled cigarette.

Smuggling wasn't easy without collaboration of friendly, or corrupt, wardens, but Henri Moisan, imprisoned as a Resistance suspect, released, then re-arrested a few months later, had a well organised message service. The messages were brought in his wife's food parcels, concealed under a false glass jam jar bottom which he could simply tumble out of the jar.

Everyone habitually retained minute pieces of paper, a mere few centimetres long, which could easily be hidden and kept for future message passing between cells, and sometimes to relatives and friends outside.

Dirty linen collected by families in exchange for fresh often bore bloodstained evidence of torture. Relatives searched laundry for possible ingeniously secreted minute scraps of paper with pencilled or pin-pricked coded messages and writing was sometimes even scrawled in blood. Some dipping the point of a pin in their own blood.

Moisan's cell companions were all Black Marketeers, like the

Laurent family, all five of whom were serving two years apiece for breaking into an abbatoir, stealing cows, and taking them home. Marie Laurent, her aunt Antoinette, and sister Gisele were in the gaol's women's section, whilst Uncle Raymond, and Gisele's fiancé, René were in Moisan's section. Farmer Alphonse Serrian, on the other hand, didn't need to rob abbatoirs as he had his own, having been sentenced for running an illegal abbatoir and selling meat without ration books.

Two more meat traders in an adjoining cell were imprisoned for totally different reasons. Both worked for the Luftwaffe. David Bertin, making regular pork deliveries to Luftwaffe bases all over the Somme, was discovered also to be making regular runs with Allied agents and escaping airmen, whom he delivered to cross-Channel naval services ferrying evaders back to Britain.

Paul Bourse's meat run wasn't so high-minded – he was in it solely for the money, and owed his imprisonment to a cow which didn't want to be slaughtered. Officially, his job was driving Luftwaffe transports from Amiens-Glisy air base to the Abbeville-Drucat airfield. Unofficially, he used the same transport for stealing cows from farms and selling them on the Black Market, that is, until he took one particular cow home to kill and slice up. Not keen on the idea, the cow put up a tremendous fight in Paul's kitchen, smashing crockery, cupboards, everything, as Paul chased it around the kitchen table with a large chopper. The diabolical noise woke the neighbours, one of whom, thinking someone was murdering his wife or something, telephoned the Gendarmerie. In the early hours, as curfew was ending, Paul finally dragged the cow's carcass into his camionette van. Just as he shut the rear doors with relief the Gendarmes arrived.

'What's in the camionette?' they demanded.

'You mustn't touch it,' Paul protested, 'it's German military property.'

The Gendarmes nevertheless opened the back, looked inside, and Paul found himself inside – having to accustom himself to gaol life.

Prison was the one place you could get used to anything, except guard dogs barking whenever those sentenced to death were led to execution. For those awaiting death, the tramp of soldiers' or guards' boots along the galleries always prompted the question: 'Are they coming for me?'

Feeling the strain, Henri Moisan requested permission to report sick to the Medical Room, established in ground floor Cell No. 3 following the arrest and arrival of Dr. Mans.

Prisoners reporting sick were supposed to line up and not to talk, but when the guards weren't looking, they managed to whisper and repeatedly changed places with each other to vary conversation. Nobody minded the length of the wait as even being sick was a break from routine.

Although Mans and Moisan knew each other, they could only risk general doctor-patient conversation with an ever-listening guard present throughout the examination.

'I won't crack up, doctor,' Moisan said. 'I've got a spirit of steel, but I must admit that although I'm a Christian, the cruelty of man creates doubt in me about God. From what I've seen of His work, so much of it is bad, because the world's bad. If I had the opportunity to make the world, I'm sure I would have made a better job of it.'

Dr. Mans, deeply religious, unwaveringly believed.

'We've suffered too much in this world not to hope for another,' he said, fervently feeling that blessed are they who believe in something.

Antonin Mans was listening to the BBC six o'clock morning news on 12 November 1943, when a ring at the front door made him prudently switch over to Radio Paris before opening the door.

'Police!' announced a blond blue-eyed young man in civilian clothes. 'You are doctor Mans?'

'Yes'.

Mans saw the double ring of soldiers around the house, and two armoured vehicles parked outside with machine guns mounted and manned.

'You will come with us, doctor,' the blue-eyed Gestapo ordered without offering explanations.

Soldiers entered the house and began searching every room as Mans went to the first floor to wake his wife and twelve-year-old daughter Yvette. Madame Mans packed a case for him, saying nothing that could be overheard.

Ushering him into one of the armoured vehicles, they drove him away, convoyed by soldier-packed military transports. After travelling some one-and-a-half-kilometres, Mans said:

'You'll have to stop – I must pee.'

'Absolutely not!' refused blue eyes.

'In that case I'll do it in the car,' Mans replied.

Drawing up beside the road, soldiers encircled Dr. Mans while he peed on the grass verge.

Marched into Cell 28 on the second floor of Amiens gaol, he pointed out that the broken window required reglazing, and the workman who repaired it deliberately left a small piece of glass which he immediately hid.

As he descended a staircase on his way to the Gestapo office in the gaol, he thought he saw a familiar figure going down the opposite staircase. When both reached the ground floor, it proved to be André Tempez, adjutant of the region's civil defence services, and second in command of his OCM Intelligence network. It was only then that he was struck by the enormity of what appeared to be happening – they were scooping up Intelligence and action group leaders throughout the region to disorganise and demoralise all key invasion back-up forces. If this was so, 12 November 1943 would go down as one of the blackest days in Resistance history.

Dr. Mans also recognised the man waiting at the foot of the stairs – Braumann, chief of Amiens Gestapo.

'I don't want that one,' he rasped, pointing at Mans, 'I want that one,' he demanded, pointing at Tempez. Mans guessed why – Tempez spoke German, so Braumann could interrogate him alone, without using an interpreter. Mans was taken back to his cell.

For the Gestapo, the chief danger to guard against was suicide. As soon as a man entered one of their prisons, they removed his braces or belt, razor, and anything else which could be used as a lethal weapon. Retrieving the piece of window pane glass from under the bed, Mans stared at it, knowing the Gestapo wouldn't relent until they broke him somehow. Nor would they ignore using his wife and twelve-year-old daughter as hostages or levers to destroy resistance. His family could be their trump psychological card.

Once they completed piecing together their complex jigsaw puzzle of information, he, and hundreds – even thousands – of others, would be shot, or put to slower death. They would start double-checking all his staff, connections, all past visitors to his Prefecture Office. Someone would no doubt recall the stranger who had been with him only days ago, and visited just once previously, in the spring. If, in some way, the stranger was identified, the enemy would never stop until they broke him, his family, and everyone around him, because the stranger was Colonel Passy, General de Gaulle's head of Intelligence, who had flown from London specifically to discuss invasion preparations. Passy's London files referred to Mans only as 'Mistral', and Tempez as 'Shakespeare'.

He smiled, recalling the surprise on Passy's face as German ranks and officers saluted their Prefecture car wherever they went.

Now the Abwehr and Gestapo were wiping out in weeks, years of undercover work and the sacrifices of thousands. The only comforting thought was his conviction that there were no utterly hopeless situations, only people who have grown hopeless about them.

The enemy were masters at creating and exploiting an atmosphere of dread and terror of the unknown. Execution, deportation and torture were highly potent threats, but Dr. Mans was determined not to allow himself to be used to make such weapons still more successful. The simple solution, he told himself, would be to cut an artery with the piece of glass in his hand and prevent any possibility of him breaking, talking, and endangering the remnants of his own network. He wasn't afraid, because those who fear suffering are already suffering from what they fear. Courage was easier than fear. He was purely afraid for others.

He considered suicide for a long time and was lost in unfamiliar territory until he realised that he had begun praying – Not simply praying for God to remember him, but also that he should remember God. In prayer he found the strongest source of energy he could generate. Once he really saw himself – discovered his fears, false pride and faults, then prayed to be better than he was, he found new power and new strength in himself.

When they sent for him again two hours later, Braumann posed only one question:

'What do you know about Roland Farjon?'

'Nothing – I don't know him.'

The door of the adjoining room was opened, and in walked Roland Farjon, with whom he had secretly worked for so long in Intelligence. Farjon had been arrested less than three weeks ago, on October 23rd, and taken to Gestapo headquarters in Avenue Foch, in Paris. This was his first reappearance since then. He was clean shaven, and wearing a freshly pressed suit.

'Do you know this gentleman?' Braumann asked.

'No.'

'You can speak, doctor,' Farjon said, 'they have all the files.'

'What files?'

Turning to Braumann, Mans insisted:

'I really don't know this man.'

One of the Gestapo smashed a fist into his face knocking him to the floor, breaking his jaw, then they left and he was hustled back to his cell without being given treatment for the jaw.

At daily interrogations over the next three weeks, names were ceaselessly flung at him for identification, but he kept to his story, realising that even the Farjon scene could somehow have been stage-managed: either fear-induced, or even drug-induced. It was impossible to be sure – but Braumann had done him a favour in introducing Farjon into the interrogation technique. Seeing Farjon, apparently within their control, he knew they could learn much of what they were anxious to know. Before, when he had been unable to judge what they knew or didn't know, it was far worse. Now he was certain he could win the mental battle. Death itself didn't worry him – a doctor understands death.

Night after night, Gestapo men kept deliberately waking him, but as he was endlessly arranging thoughts and organising his mental defences, he found it difficult to sleep anyway.

Salvation came through Dr. Kauert, the chief German medical officer for the region, who initiated the establishment of a treatment centre in Cell No. 3. As overcrowding was overtaxing the gaol's own normal medical facilities, Kauert saw no reason not to employ Mans as the prisoners' doctor. There were other doctor inmates, but Mans was senior and the most experienced, especially in dealing with epidemics. When free, he had frequently engineered 'suspected epidemic outbreaks' in fortification zones where he would have been forbidden entry without Dr. Kauert's personal clearance.

Even in gaol, Kauert daily consulted him on regional health matters, and allowed twenty-two-year-old Francois Vignolle, and his twenty-year-old wife Raymonde, to see their departmental chief regularly in his medical centre cell and bring him Prefecture health division reports into which they, and he, inserted coded messages, including prison gossip which might be useful outside.

Through his work, Mans had a clearer vision than most of the extent to which the distinction between 'politicals' and ordinary law-breakers disappeared. Inside, they were as one, leaning towards each other, brothers and sisters in survival.

'If we want to survive, we've got to think like they think, and know what they're likely to do, otherwise we'll never beat them,' sixty-year-old safebreaker patient Bertie Bovin assessed during a treatment visit to the medical room. 'I shouldn't be in gaol at all – I was *practically* honest for years, and now look at me! It's hardly worth trying to keep your nose clean. I decided to do a final job and then retire, and ended up here. What a rotten finish to a long career. This is my sixth sentence. I wish I was outside helping the country get back on its feet – if you know what I mean.'

Dr. Mans, and his nurse, Elaine Guillemont, who was a prisoner in the women's section, did know what Bertie, and others like him, meant when they dropped hints like that. Their intentions were good, for criminals are not intrinsically less patriotic than other groups in society, although the worst elements could barter freedom from arrest by providing information and identifying suspects. It was the Nazis who bracketed them with resistance. Nevertheless, resistance heavily depended on the skill of professional criminals – especially forgers and smugglers – for providing cover and contact with allies. The Resistance accepted and 'legalised' many forms of criminality by using criminals to fight criminals.

As common criminals preferred to feel you were 'one of them', many Resistance men and women in gaol didn't oppose and played along with this line, claiming to be thieves or Black Marketeers. It was suitable camouflage and made the criminals feel more at home and among their own, although the top professionals contemptuously looked down their noses at 'ordinary semi-pros' or 'amateurs' as they classified part-time petty thieves.

'If you're risking going to prison, at least go for something,' the pros maintained, justifying themselves by insisting: 'Many people are only saved from being thieves by finding everything locked up.'

For most inside, crime was a habit, a way of life, a weakness, a desperate way out, greed, or an accidental lapse, and nobody knew better than Sûreté Inspector Serge Dumant that the greatest evil was the number of people trying to get something for nothing.

For using this influential and knowledgeable position to aid the Allies, Inspector Dumant found himself in Amiens with the kind of criminal intelligentsia he had been busy putting away for years. 'Colonel' Adrian Leopold, of military bearing and outsize military moustache, was very definitely criminal upper crust, contemptuous of, and apparently unaffected by gaol surroundings. This hefty, well-educated forty-year-old strutted about as a uniformed French Air Force Officer until war put paid to that caper, compelling him to concentrate on other methods of obtaining money by false pretences, as a 'paper hanger' – someone who passes or issues worthless cheques. He preferred conning people to working.

Everyone – wardens and prisoners – called him 'The Colonel'. He used to work the larger hotels, but at times returned to the 'simple life', as he so aptly described gaol. Without real schooling, he largely educated himself and picked up culture from prison libaries and 'intellectual' criminal characters with whom he came into contact inside.

'Crime isn't glamorous, like so many youngsters think – crooks are mainly stupid, treacherous and scared, and most need a bellyful of Dutch courage before they do a job. Then afterwards they usually head straight for some tart to spend their money on, or blow it on drink,' Serge Dumant said with contempt born of long experience.

'If France treats her criminals like this, she doesn't deserve to have any!' 'Colonel' Leopold declared, gesturing imperiously at the overcrowded hovel of a cell they were sharing. 'If they can't stop crime, why don't they just make it legal then tax it out of business?'

'Some men will do anything for money, except work for it,' said Inspector Dumant, smiling broadly.

'I worked as a hairdresser,' Leopold bristled, 'until I discovered you can cut anyone's hair loads of times, but can scalp most people only once, so I became a confidence man, which means I've got confidence in my own ability to live on other people's gullibility.'

'I suppose you never know who you can do until you try?' Dumant queried sarcastically.

'Right!' largely self-educated, good-looking Leopold enthused. 'I always pretend to take people for what they are, so that I can take them for what they have and I use any switch to win confidence. I'd even hire a pickpocket to steal someone's wallet; give chase; retrieve the wallet out of the victim's sight, then return it, apologising for the pickpocket having got away. I was usually offered a reward, which, of course, I refused. Then the person was well on the way to being hooked.'

'There's little anyone can do today to keep from being done,' philosophised Dumant.

'And when I'm card sharping for a change,' Leopold prattled on proudly, 'I make sure the victim suggests the game – I wait for him to come up with the idea, and am never over-eager. I sometimes deliberately admit I'm a professional gambler and advise them not to play, and they always resent the inference of not having a hope of beating a pro at his own game. When I finally let them persuade me, I take them for a packet. I make them *want* to give me their cash. I like to get what I need without violence. Give me a wife, respectability, and all the comforts of home – and a nice clean con now and again to top up the coffers. I simply con whenever I need a bit of extra, so that I'm never short.'

Dumant couldn't help laughing, knowing human nature, ego, and greed for apparent easy money, would forever provide con men like 'the Colonel' with people who practically begged to be ripped off.

Dumant found forger Georges Danielou even more interesting, because he was a pupil and former assistant to Professor Ivan Miassojedoff and Solomon Smolianoff – two of the most ingenious internationally sought forgers. Danielou, who needed suitcases full of money to pay for his gambling excesses, lost fortunes at roulette and cards. Being a skilled lithographer, he merely printed more himself.

'I made money to make money,' he explained simply. 'The problem wasn't how to make it, but how to spend it, although my gambling managed to take care of the greater part of it.'

Inspector Dumant appreciated that a forger could be an intelligent and resourceful character with a thorough understanding of his opponent – the law – and well equipped to take advantage of every loophole. Dumant had also heard from authoritative sources that although Danielou was chronically crooked, he rendered invaluable voluntary services to Resistance forces, supplying, when required, false identity cards and other official-looking forged documents without payment, which put him a cut above the average.

'Those who say forgery is bound to be discovered in some way are talking cock,' Danielou claimed. 'Some forged signatures are impossible to detect, even for experts. Fortunately, there are a lot of people who think a signature is genuine if they can read it. The trick is to avoid a forged stroke appearing drawn rather than written. Lines can show indications of a tremble and stoppages while a stroke is being formed, but I've repeatedly beaten experienced examiners.

'Paper's the big problem. With banknote forgery, which I was mainly into last – apart from a nice sideline in forged bread coupons – ultraviolet light tests can expose you, but luckily people don't walk about with battery-powered lamps under their arms.

'I was forging five and ten-pound British banknotes, and American dollars and selling them in Paris at half their face value,' Danielou admitted. 'I could sell any quantity, but couldn't get enough because of paper supply difficulties, until I found a source of ready-printed stuff coming directly from Berlin. I dug around and finally learned the Germans are printing millions of dollars and pounds in Sachsenhausen concentration camp and my old tutor, Solomon Smolianoff, is running the show for them there. There's no sign of Solomon's old partner, Miassojedoff.'

Dumant was understandably fascinated, and certain he wasn't being shot a line.

'The best stuff – near perfect with only minute flaws in the Britannia figure on the British banknotes – is being shipped from Berlin to neutral countries to buy war materials. They're using the second grade for paying Nazi agents abroad, and third grade for paying agents and purchasing materials in occupied countries. Even the fourth grade are passable, if not examined too closely. Someone in Berlin with access to the hoard is skimming off a slice of it and making himself a personal pile by releasing thousands on the Black Market in Paris, and I've been using some of it to top up my own personally printed supplies. I was working with Solomon in 1939 and 1940, just before he was arrested and gaoled for counterfeiting British banknotes.'

Russian-born, skinny, moon-faced little Solomon Smolianoff, with the big ears and sensitive hands, studied at Petrograd Academy of Art under gaunt Professor Ivan Miassojedoff. They pooled talents to forge American and British currency and passports. Both were constantly wanted by police of a half a dozen countries.

'It took the Germans a long time to discover British banknote paper was made from second-hand rags,' Danielou laughed. 'Now they've got agents in Rome, Madrid, Stockholm, Paris, Amsterdam, Tangier, and Copenhagen, selling their forged notes and changing them into gold, jewellery, Swedish kroner and Swiss francs. In each territory, there's a chief salesman who gets twenty-five per cent of the turnover and is responsible for his own sub-agents, which is how I first got my hands on some of it. Thousands of Frenchmen are breaking their necks to buy the stuff on the Black Market, and none of it feels new because they've manually aged it by having supervised concentration camp groups rub them between their hands. Nor are they consecutively numbered – they've thought of everything – or rather, Solomon obviously has – poor bastard!

'Personally, I age notes I make by spreading them on the floor of a room and walking over them for a few hours, which is guaranteed to make them look well used without appearing as if they've been deliberately rumpled.'

Danielou stared at a white cloud passing the cell window and envied its freedom. Returning his attention to Dumant, he said thoughtfully:

'I don't know if either of us will get out of here alive, but if you do, see if you can get word to the Americans and warn them. They're buying francs on the Lisbon Black Market to finance their agents in France, and the Germans are manipulating the trade by listing series and denominations and then invalidating whole series to help them detect enemy agents supplied with such notes. This way they can make them operationally destitute. Also Gestapo money raids on shops, businesses, and private homes can turn up their incriminating funds. It's a diabolical game.'

More happily, he suggested:

'If we ever manage to escape from this hell-hole, stick with me and I'll help you to a new start because I always believe in forging ahead and have an attache case full of those phoney Berlin notes stashed away not far from here. We'll need finance if we're running . . . The offer goes for you too, Inspector,' Danielou said smiling. 'It would be for the best reasons, and anyway, imitation is the sincerest form of flattery. Except I suppose, when it's forgery, Inspector.'

The sudden flood of fresh detainees, resulting from the devastation of so many undercover networks, overwhelmed Somme region Gestapo and Abwehr counter-Intelligence to such an extent that they were forced to summon reinforcements from other areas to help them cope. Interrogators and torturers, working overtime, were beating their brains out – and other people's – striving to find indications of Allied invasion intentions and preparations. Prisoners were already sleeping on almost every inch of cell floor space in Amiens gaol. The Gestapo's prison interrogation room was fully booked twenty-four hours a day, whilst prisoners were shuttled day and night to Gestapo headquarters at rue Jeanne d'Arc, and to an annexe elsewhere in the town, in cars and in 'Paniers à salade' - the appropriately nicknamed 'salad baskets', Black Maria prison vans, in which prisoners were locked in individual windowless compartments.

At midday, it took great effort to swallow the nauseating soup – mostly cabbage based. Attempting to identify the mysterious lumps that appeared in it, was a favourite sport. On occasions, baker Vincent Darras and pimp Jules Damay liked to separate solids from soup liquid so that they could slowly savour the liquid, then start on the solids, whatever they were, thereby adding an extra course. The appallingly meagre diet was insufficient to keep them alive without supplementation by food parcels from relatives or the Red Cross, and the diet was actually killing poor Xavier Cresset. Xavier, who told everyone he was 'in the typewriter business', was a 'walk-in' thief who relied on the innocence of people. He strolled into business offices and announced he had come to repair and service typewriters.

'I always found one or two that were "faulty" and needed workshop attention, and simply walked out with the machines,' said Xavier, laughing, but in Amiens prison, he didn't have much to laugh about anymore because he was a very big man with a very big appetite. Eating and the welfare of his stomach were his main preoccupation. He had no one to send him in food, and was emaciated and in misery.

Cells intended to house, at the most, a couple of inmates, were stuffed with four, five, six, even eight. They didn't know where to lock up hundreds being arrested week after week. Intelligence agent Maurice Holville's incarceration with the likes of Jules Damay was typical of the situation. According to the rule book, only Germans were permitted to guard 'politicals', and French wardens, criminals, but massive overcrowding compelled the housing of 'politicals' in criminal wings, and made nonsense of the rules.

Some of the vagabond inmates were only 'wintering' there. When cold months approached, they simply committed petty crimes, such as vandalism, to enable them to spend winter in gaol. If a judge gave what they considered to be too short a term of imprisonment to cover the bleakest weather, they would insult him in court to provoke a longer sentence.

When not pacing the cells to keep out wintry cold, most inmates stayed on their beds, or on the floor wrapped in blankets.

'You know what they say,' said one vagabond gaol regular: 'Seventy-five per cent of body heat is lost through exhalation, so keep well covered.'

Many inmates were totally isolated, without contact with anyone other than their guards and interrogators. Luckiest were light sentence prisoners, allowed to work in a factory separate from the main building at the back, producing marine cables, cable reels, and also winding, making ropes, straw for chairs, and coal sacks. Work was paid for at fixed rates, half of which went to the prisoners, and half to the State. The worker's share was split in three – one part spendable in gaol on extras; the second to aid legal expenses; and the third rationed for him until he was freed. Rigidly disciplined long-termers stayed in the cells, as they were considered to be more dangerous and likelier to look for escape opportunities.

Slim, red-haired Maurice Mercier – only in his early thirties, but with an old man's face – wasn't interested in the long-term big coup boys.

'Just give me a nice straightforward thieving job, and I'm satisfied,' he told Gendarme Achille Langlet, the policeman who arrested him for thieving and was now in the cells himself for aiding shot-down Allied aircrew. Maurice was a 'ladder man' who broke into houses whenever he had too much to drink, which was often. Quick-tempered, rash, with a weakness for girls, he paid dearly for them because he financed his fancies by housebreaking. He selected theft-worthy places to rob by gathering information from waiters in the best restaurants. Even in gaol he loved borrowing old magazines with illustrations and descriptions of interesting homes and poring over them, squatting on the stone floor, with knees drawn up under his chin.

'I like studying those sort of places and figuring out how I would break into them, if I had the chance,' he confided to Gendarme Langlet. 'A thief's got to keep his mind in shape, you know, just like any other profession,' adding almost apologetically: 'I only screwed when I needed a bit of extra, so that I was never short – or when I had a bit too much to drink.'

Overhearing Maurice Mercier's final comment, safebreaker Bertie Bovin mused:

'Maybe we ought to stay in here while the war's on, let both sides fight it out, then when somebody's won, we'll be able to go out and start thieving again.'

Maurice Holville and the inmates of his cell were in the small courtyard for their daily twenty-minute ration of fresh air and exercise when a flock of birds flew high over them. As if one man, everyone in the yard lifted his head upwards to follow the birds longingly.

'That's what we need,' said Holville softly. 'Wings to help us fly away from here.'


# 6  Best laid plans


'Personnel are instructed to drive their balls down the fairway,' the officers' Mess notice board announced for the Mongewell Park golf course tournament.

Mongewell Park was a beautiful old mock Jacobean house in its own grounds, with a small private golf course, and a heated swimming pool that nobody used. Close to Wallingford, amid refreshing Berkshire countryside, this was headquarters of 2nd Group Tactical Air Force and Basil Embry's 'home'.

The red brick mansion was a war effort contribution from American railroad millionaire Howard Gould, who owned and used it whenever he came to England. Much of the interior was superbly wood panelled and, to preserve it for after the war, Embry instructed that all panelling be covered with asbestos and other heavy sheeting.

A runway had been constructed, mainly for Embry and his staff's personal air transports, and there were also several outbuildings. Embry's office, the Ops Room, Administration, and, in a tiny room upstairs, the modelling section, were all in the main building.

Almost at the entrance of the mansion was the giant hall, used as the Mess, and left of the hall was Basil's spacious office with its large stylish desk, and even more stylish WAAF officer secretary, Meg Hurll. Beyond his room were staff offices leading to nerve-centre Operations Room, with large-scale maps and batteries of telephones, mounting, despatching, monitoring round-the-clock operations controlled by New Zealander Group Operations Officer, Wing Commander 'Digger' Magill.

The initial step taken was to have the goal photographed and modelled, so a reconnaissance plane was sent the same day.

'We've asked them to shoot every angle of the prison and a large portion of the district around it, though our files are already loaded with stacks of material on the town,' Magill notified Embry.

'The PRUs (Photo Reconnaissance Units) have also been told to take a series of shots from 35,000 feet at 11.45 a.m. By working out where the sun will be at 11.45 a.m., we can, according to the length of shadows thrown by the sun or the nearest church spire, assess the heights of buildings.'

Being a major railway centre and consequently incessantly bombed, Amiens was already well covered by general background Intelligence and photographic files.

As soon as current photographs were interpreted, the modelling section was asked to produce a scale replica of the prison to simulate what crews would see from a height of a thousand feet four miles away.

In the little modelling room nestling under the roof of the Mongewell Park mansion, former Civvy Street publicity artists, instrument repairers and carpenters beavered away under the guidance of Intelligence Staff Officer, ex-architect Squadron Leader Turner-Lord, creating a miniature wood, papier mâché and plaster-of-Paris replica of the prison. Former wedding cake decorators were particularly skilful at this type of work. No one was permitted to enter whilst a mock-up was under construction. The room was under constant guard as no risks could be taken of the objective being identified and gossiped about.

Turner-Lord's team laboured virtually non-stop from the instant they had the necessary photographs and information. As soon as complete, the model was taken under guard in a locked wooden box to the AOC's office, which was usually used for planning conferences, and placed at the head of the table before the Group Commander's chair.

Nine men were seated around the table in the office when Basil Embry arrived with his secretary Meg Hurll to open the meeting, but only four present knew in advance the contents of the box, having been involved in organising documents, photographs, and other relevant material.

Senior Air Staff Officer David Atcherley had frequently flown with Embry on raids, most recently with a badly fractured arm encased in plaster. Just before take-off, as Embry vainly struggled to manoeuvre him into a Mae West life jacket, Atcherley had finally told him to forget it, and climbed aboard without it. Pickard led, and Embry and 'Batchy', as Atcherley was affectionately called, flew rear-end Charlie in the formation. 'Batchy' was half of the notorious identical Atcherley twins. Both were group captains, wore the same decorations and shared a huge dog. Until David broke his arm and carried it about in a plaster cast, it was impossible to tell which of the identical twins was tearing you off a strip.

Another of the AOC's regular flying companions at the meeting was Squadron Leader Ted Sismore acknowledged to have the finest navigation brain in the RAF. He had acquired the nickname 'Daisy' because of his babyface, but preferred Ted. He had got into planning largely because of his intimate knowledge of *Mosquitos*, having served in the earliest Mossie bomber forces, as well as with the *Pathfinders*. Mossies required a whole new technique, so an experienced planning section was established, staffed by men who knew the aircraft inside out.

Group Intelligence Officer Pat Shallard, and his No. 2, Squadron Leader Edwin Houghton, had been advised of the target in advance of meeting. Also at the table were the man responsible for Signals arrangements, Wing Commander Geoff Eveleigh; indefatigable staff officer, Group Captain 'Bull' Cannon, who by lowering his head and charging at any administrative obstacle could always be guaranteed to get the best out of anyone; and Peter Clapham, credited with bomb accuracy improvements which reduced the average for visual medium altitude bombing from 1200 to less than 200 yards. Additionally, by the use of radar, in which Clapham specialised, the Group was able to reach unseen targets from medium altitudes with an accuracy of between three and four hundred yards. The technique of ground-level bombing had made it possible to hit even small targets in the heart of a large city with an accuracy almost measureable in inches. Embry fashioned a new post specially to utilise Clapham's talents, appointing him Radar

Operations Officer of his Operational Planning Staff.

Amiens planners finally included the emperor of Mongewell Park Ops Room, 'Digger' Magill; and the sole military member of the planning team who was always, directly or indirectly, involved in such matters, Major John Pullen, MC, of the Royal Artillery, the Group's Flak Liaison Officer. Pullen actually belonged to what were known as 'Gubby' Allan's boys – a military intelligence team who, through espionage, underground contacts, photo reconnaissance, from ground and air, plus all manner of other sources, managed to supply remarkably accurate details of enemy anti-aircraft gun defence. After careful study of the build-up of ack-ack defences in north-west Europe, Embry correctly assessed that the struggle for air supremacy was becoming a battle between the aeroplane and the gun, and would be even more so as the Luftwaffe's strength continued to be weakened by increasing onslaughts on air bases, aircraft factories, and fuel supplies.

There was ample evidence that with gun density alone, the enemy could achieve air supremacy over limited areas. The solution, therefore, was to locate high gun-density zones, and avoid them. To this end, Embry established an anti-flak section on his staff to secure information for accurate map siting of all known light and heavy anti-aircraft guns. Even aircrews were recruited into this intelligence exercise, being asked on returning from sorties to map-position any new gun emplacements which fired on them. John Pullen assessed these, and reports from outside sources, to up-date the enemy ground defence picture. Although nearly a million-and-a-half men were being used for German ground defences, there were still periodic ack-ack manning gaps. It would be up to John Pullen to advise on the ground battery strength likely to be waiting when, or if, it was decided to try and smash the prison walls.

Embry carefully extracted the stark functional model of the gaol and stood it on top of its box. Most of his audience were still unaware of the identity of the objective, until he declared:

'We have been asked to look into the feasibility of a special raid on Amiens – the prison.'

They had heard all kinds. This was new.

Embry went on to explain some – but not all – the background behind the request for the attack. This was to be the first of many Amiens discussions, for such a plan, with all its complex implications and problems, could not be wholly put together at 'formal' meetings. It had to evolve from a progressively cumulative effort. Only Embry and his senior officer, Atcherley, would know all. Others were told only what they needed to know. Information sources and Resistance planning partners weren't even mentioned initially. As 2 Group officers frequently flew sorties, the possibility of any of them being shot down and interrogated had to be considered, but due to the delicacy of the target, those involved were, on this rare instance, told more than usual.

'We know, and so do those who have asked us to try and do this, that no matter how precise the bombing, many prisoners are liable to be killed too,' Embry said quietly, 'but I'm assured that they accept this fact,' he stressed firmly, 'therefore so must we.

'It's the first time this Group's been asked to do anything to help some of those who have so often helped us when we've been shot down, and whose efforts as fighting men and women we so much admire, but it's at the definite risk of killing many of them in the process.'

Everyone in the room realised the twist which had put the lives of Amiens prisoners into Basil Embry's hands, because they knew that he owed his life to the Resistance when he was shot down over France and taken prisoner in May 1940. Aided by patriots, he had become the first British airman to return after escaping from the Germans.

'I know it's all very well for us to be told that a very considerable number of the inmates are about to die anyway at the hands of their captors,' he continued, 'but we are expected to arrange for our crews to drop bombs on the place in which they're being held, and although we have a high opinion of the crews who would have to do the job, the risks are there.'

He paused . . . 'It's quite an undertaking.'

He explained that he had instructed photographic reconnaissance to cover the prison extensively, ordered the mock-up, and called for advice from someone who could supply details of internal and external construction of the prison and its surrounding walls, plus the internal lay-out with all possible information about the cells, locks to the doors, and general prison routine.

Embry's conferences and briefing style were normally very forceful, with occasional touches of underlying wry humour, but today was otherwise. Friends and allies were inside the target. He hated the thought, but nonetheless had to concentrate on how to do it, if it was to be done at all. There were dozens of points where assumptions could go wrong. To make sense out of something, you had to put sense into it.

'It's obvious the prison walls would need to be broken in at least two places in order to effect escapes,' he went on, 'so both ends of the building would have to be hit.

'I want advice on the amount of explosive force needed to break the thick prison walls and force the locks on cells and prison doors at the same time. It is crucial to know precisely what effect specific bombs would have on the walls.

'It will be an easy target to find, just outside the town, parallel to the Route d'Albert, with the main road from Albert pointing straight at it like an arrow.'

Before giving way for the initial Intelligence report, he concluded:

'We have been told the Resistance intend encircling the place to assist all who get out, which means bombing has to be spot on, otherwise we could blow up outside Resistance units as well.'

As always, it would come down to care, cunning, patience, and guts.

Group Intelligence Officer Pat Shallard took over presenting to the planners a large selection of oblique and vertical photographs obtained during previous raids over the Amiens area. After they had studied them and turned their attention again to the prison model, Shallard happily declared:

'For an opening meeting we have an abundance of riches, in fact we've been practically swamped with information from the other side, including a set of the original architectural plans of the prison specifically stolen for us from Amiens municipal archives.' He laughed, gesturing at a mass of large photostated drawings on the table. 'So we have exact dimensions of all the buildings and know what the walls are made of. We have also been obligingly supplied with sketches of alterations and additions to the buildings since it was first constructed.'

Switching to the model he pointed out:

'We're advised that the gaol is three-storeyed and cross-shaped. The longer arm holds those we want out, and the extensions, which have been added at both ends of this arm, are German guardrooms and eating quarters. As the likeliest method of opening the place is by breaching the outer wall in two places to make an exit at either end, we must eliminate as many of the guards as possible by destroying their sections of the buildings.

'Most German guards usually lunch at noon, and the majority of prisoners assemble for their meal about the same time in a central hall, so it might be best to attack at midday in case our bomb vibrations fail to open cell door locks.

'The height of the surrounding prison wall is twenty-two feet. It's difficult to make an exact measurement as yet of the thickness of this wall. This doesn't appear to be unusually thick for its height and, as may be expected, is thicker at the base than at the top. We can say, however, that it does not exceed four feet in thickness and is probably less.

'We are still analysing all available information. Meanwhile we have already asked Medmenham to organise and give us a further double-check interpretation report on the buildings.'

The Central Photographic Interpretation Unit at Medmenham, which significantly contributed to the success of the airborne raid on Bruneval radiolocation post, had also been responsible for spotting what appeared to be a small aircraft-like object some twenty feet long with a similar length wing span, beside an airfield at Peenemunde. This proved to be the first sighting of Germany's secret rocket weapon.

Ted Sismore, who had been given time to consider Amiens navigational problems in advance, confirmed:

'Though it's certainly correct that identifying the target will be dead easy, not so easy is the fact that it is within sight of Galland's Abbeville base. This would unquestionably be the biggest threat to the attack.'

The Luftwaffe's Abbeville boys were the finest of the fighter squadrons commanded by 31-year-old Adolf Galland – Germany's youngest general, with 70 'kills' to his credit. His Abbeville-Lille-Calais sector, controlled from Le Touquet, was notoriously the hottest, toughest fighter-patrolled zone in Europe, and mixed gaggles of *Focke-Wulf*s and *Messerschmitt*s often came at Allied bombers in formations of fifty.

Galland calculated that, since half the Luftwaffe pilots would parachute safely to the ground, whilst shot down Allied crews were prisoners on German-controlled soil, the advantage was the enemy's, even given Allied superiority in men, materials and training potential.

'To outfox the Abbeville pilots we can route the Mossies in such a way as to make it difficult for them to guess where we're really headed until it's too late,' Ted Sismore prompted, routinely emphasising the obvious. 'With low-level attacks hard to trace, being below radar, we can make it a guessing game for Luftwaffe controllers and pilots as to what we're up to. We can route so that various turns should be enough to throw their fighters off our true directions.

'We'd have four main fighter bases in the area to contend with: Amiens-Glisy, Abbeville-Drucat, Poix de Picardie – only 32 kilometres away – and Mons en Chaussée, near Peronne. For good measure we ought to throw in Meharicourt – 52 kilometres from

Amiens – also a Luftwaffe chasse (fighter) base, and, 55 kilometres from Amiens, the fighter and bomber base at Montdidier.'

David Atcherley butted in:

'Is dive bombing worth considering because of the accuracy required to avoid hitting anything other than what actually needs to be hit? Maybe that's the way to minimise the risk of killing prisoners?'

'I've thought about it,' Sismore countered, 'but as the buildings present an upright obstacle against which bombs can be thrown, low-level would be more secure than dive bombing. The place is like a large house in open ground unobstructed by trees, so unquestionably low attack would be most effective. A big building like this, with such a good clear run-up, could be either completely destroyed or more accurately hit low, although approach would be the same as for a dive bomber at about 7,000 to 8,000 feet, out of light and medium flak range. When the prison's in sight, they can dive to ground level, straighten out for the last quarter or half mile staying high enough to just clear the top of the building, then about seventy yards away release bombs so that they crash through the side of the walls.'

For an attack of this nature, it is usual to go down in pairs, using a short delay on the bomb fuses so that each pair struck just after the last pair's bombs had exploded. If the target was heavily defended, four aircraft going down in two pairs were all that could reasonably get away with this type of action. Carried out quickly, and with bombs placed accurately, it was the safest attack method for small numbers.

'We'll need boxes of six planes at a time to go in,' Sismore suggested, 'staggered at brief intervals, across a spread of about a hundred yards, each plane carrying four bombs, all to be dropped at once at low level, aimed horizontally at specific sections of the prison. If one lot fails to get a target, the next lot has to go for it.'

'With Abbeville so close, it's simply got to be one single drop run for each plane – in and out fast,' Peter Clapham interjected. 'It'll all happen so quickly that no one will have time to get bored, as they sometimes complain they do in high-level stuff.

'At deck height we should be reasonably immune from flak, although an unlucky bastard might still cop a packet, but our altitude will help us dodge any *FW 190*s around.'

The *FW190*, the *Mosquitos*' arch enemy, could travel twenty to thirty miles an hour faster above 20,000 feet, but Mossies could usually pull away at near ground level.

'Flak shouldn't have time to open up at us,' Clapham calculated confidently, 'unless our aircraft present a visual target, which we don't intend to let them be for long. As John Pullen reminds us often enough, gun defences need an adequate early warning system to be efficient, especially against fast low-flying planes. Guns need to be pointing, and spotters looking, in the right direction before aircraft appear if they're to engage successfully.'

Pursuing that line of enquiry, ack-ack specialist John Pullen cautioned:

'It isn't safe to assume guns won't be alert on the approaches and in the target area. We mustn't allow squadrons routeing choice – not in such a heavily defended zone. I'll try to discover the number of guns that may be brought to bear on the run-up, as it's unlikely, considering the intended speed of attack, that there'll be time for our aircraft to neutralise gun positions as they go for the target.'

Experience had shown that when enemy anti-aircraft batteries, in excess of twelve guns, were at any time able to counter-attack, squadron losses were usually above average.

'There's certainly some uncomfortably close ack-ack at Rivery – just by the prison – protecting the Glisy air base.' Pullen warned.

'Johnny's always good for bad news,' Peter Clapham acknowledged with a grin.

The ten planners examined the model; pored over the old architectural plans and the translated technical details and explanations accompanying them; studied a large general situation map with the anticipated bomb line already clearly marked on it; and gave particular attention to the terrain around the target – nothing dared to be missed or underestimated.

'We have little time to do our homework, make the decision and, if we agree, attack,' Embry pointed out. 'The Gestapo have scheduled mass executions of a large number of the prisoners for some time in the middle of this month, so this has top priority over everything else. I want answers *fast*.'

After nodding thoughtfully, Peter Clapham couldn't resist commenting:

The trouble is that as soon as you think you've got the answers, somebody changes the questions.'

When Embry asked for action, he got it, mainly, he believed, because he worked with a small, tight, efficient administrative team. He gave responsibilty and allowed initiative, expecting both to be exercised at all times. If you couldn't look him straight in the eye – probably at less than six inches range – then you had no place in his outfit.

'Larger administration staffs increase complications and slow down the giving of decisions and action,' he admitted.

'These difficulties work in two different ways on two different sorts of people. The first are those who want to get things done. For them, too many rules and restrictions impose a great brake on efficiency and initiative. The second set have various reasons for not wanting to get things done. For them, over-complications provide an almost endless series of excuses into which they can disappear as a visitor into Hampton Court maze, to rotate endlessly about a problem without ever coming nearer to it, though often crossing their own tracks.'

For hours they argued and examined, tossing around pros and cons, seeking to agree on basics. Embry was never certain unless he knew.

'With the deadline we've got, and current rotten weather outlook, the whole thing – if it's on at all – is more likely to depend on Jock's weather than anything else,' remarked 'Digger' Magill, who, living and breathing forecasts day and night in his Ops Room and only too conscious of this overriding factor, felt the point should be made.

'Jock' Cummings, the Group's Met man, would of course be a key figure in the decision on whether it was finally 'Go' or not. It was impossible for the weather man to be sure about the weather, so they were never too sure about the weather man.

'Too true,' Embry agreed, 'but at least we're certainly not suffering from lack of information about the target, so let's just hope that if it's eventually feasible, we get fighter bomber weather. I should mention that I've asked for even more information regarding the extent of outside ground assistance escaping prisoners could hope to receive.'

As the planning meeting was about to break up, he summed up:

'One more thing. The operation has been code-named "Renovate" '.

Peter Clapham grinned. 'Someone has a nice sense of humour. If we do prang the place and give it a really good going over, it'll *need* renovating.'

*

God couldn't handle everything, so he made mothers like Mama Beaurin, who chose to get herself arrested to join her sons Roger and Jean in gaol, and warn them the prison was about to be attacked.

Word had come from London that should the RAF attempt to shatter the walls, it would be timed for mid-day, and Mama Beaurin was determined to tell Roger and Jean to ensure that they and their comrades inside would at least be ready to duck, then run for their lives.

Solemn-faced, twenty-nine-year-old Maurice Henri Holville – they called him the 'Curé of Montparnasse' – who was in the next cell to Jean Beaurin, though neither realised it for some while, had suggested mid-day as most suitable for attack because it was lunchtime for prisoners and guards. People outside would be safely off the streets, at home or in restaurants; and it also wasn't visiting time for inmates' relatives or friends, who would otherwise innocently be at risk.

Smuggling messages inside wasn't easy. Everyone and everything was checked, and as always, the Germans were thorough. Nevertheless, a note, sewn into the hem of a pair of trousers for Jean, had reached him a couple of weeks back. The minute scrap of paper in the hem advised that the building might be attacked to aid escape, but didn't indicate how.

Although neither a land nor air attack was definitely on, Dominique Ponchardier, anxious to sustain hope of some last-minute act cheating the execution squads, thought it best to attempt to get a warning through.

When Maurice Holville assisted in the preparation of Amiens prison raid plans, he wasn't yet one of the inmates. Mostly he went about his Intelligence gathering in a borrowed railway official's uniform, helpfully provided by his Amiens stationmaster friend Monsieur Bluet. Holville was called the 'the Curé' because people – especially girls – had the habit of confessing troubles to him, usually on trains. He'd inquire: 'Have you been greedy? – Have you eaten too much forbidden fruit?' and, as he confessed himself: 'My serious priestly face seemed to encourage most to talk to me intimately, though I used to counsel that honest confession is bad for the reputation, and only good for the soul in the sense that a tweed suit is good for dandruff.' The Montparnasse tag was tacked onto the 'Curé' title because his solemnity camouflaged a man in reality as fun-loving as the most outrageous inhabitants of Paris's no-pleasures-barred Montparnasse district.

Apart from Intelligence work, one of the 'Curé's' additional specialities was escape aid, for which he kept a constantly replenished stock of forged identity cards, as well as other official papers useful to evaders such as shot-down American and British airmen; parachuted espionage agents; and fellow countrymen on the run from the Gestapo.

As one of the shrewdest evasion experts in the area, he was

automatically approached for potential methods of freeing colleagues in Amiens gaol. He began by providing himself with a permit authorising him to deliver parcels to prison inmates, which he did three times a week – a convenient way of studying the place, enabling him to draw lay-outs of the buildings, Dominique Ponchardier augmented Maurice Holville's rough sketches and general information, with a set of ancient architectural blueprints stolen from official Amiens archives. Another escape researcher pleasantly double-checked gaol details in the course of apparently using the shadows of prison walls for love-making with a girlfriend. Old drawings were consequently revised and fresh lay-outs drawn which, for greater safety, were split in two – one part retained by Pepe, Commandant of Ponchardier's Sosie action group and chief of the Somme sector. The second portion was entrusted to Serge, one of Pepe's associates. All quarters, prison wings and German barracks were mapped and daily routines listed. No confirmation could be secured of dimensions of the old walls – a factor eventually to become crucial as not Holville, Pepe, nor Dominique Ponchardier was aware that the giant stones largely comprising the great perimeter walls hadn't been embedded with cement.

Despite the fact that the practice of shooting hostages and reprisal prisoners selected at random was frequently carried out following Resistance action, it was considered at first that an armed raid on the gaol would be the fastest and best course.

'We could try a massed land attack,' Pepe proposed to Dominique Ponchardier – 'break through the walls, kill the guards, and get our men out. We've got plenty of explosives and arms for the job stored in the false ceiling and under the floorboards of a house conveniently near the gaol.'

For Pepe, it was always better to act and not suppress a fundamental impulse. He knew all about prison buildings and prison walls – had studied several, attacked some, and appreciated the problems, but life has a way of happening to us while we're making other plans . . . Just when he thought he had the attack in the bag, the bag broke . . .

Serge was trapped at the Café Beaulot, behind Amiens railway station, as he was sipping coffee, waiting to rendezvous with Pepe, Maurice Holville, and other members of the group.

Catastrophe news moved fast – it needed to – and reached the 'Curé' virtually around the corner from the police-encircled bistro. Miraculously, at that moment the 'Curé' spotted Pepe with his wife Maria and their little boy Jean, heading for the café. Holville whispered, when he wanted to shout:

'Don't go there! – Serge has just been arrested!'

Pepe, who always carried grenades strapped to his body, ready to blow up anyone who tried to arrest him, as well as kill himself, unhurriedly strolled on with Maria and little Jean. Moving in the opposite direction, Holville, who never went armed, was suddenly battered to the ground by two men.

'Mers! Mers!' he yelled which was all he could think of then, and was where he wanted to get to – his home at Mers. He only got as far as Boulevard Alsace Lorraine and Amiens headquarters of the notorious St. Quentin brigade of the Milice, the French Gestapo, after which he was transferred to the house on rue Jeanne d'Arc to be confronted by German Gestapo chief Braumann, and the hosier from Place René Goblet – Lucien Pieri. Four hours of interrogation later, he was thrown into Cell 18.

'We know all about you from a young man we arrested in a cemetery the other day,' Pieri boasted.

Holville took the statement with a pinch of salt, recognising it was standard procedure to advise victims: 'Why be tortured when we know everything?'

But this time Lucien Pieri was telling some element of truth. An eighteen-year-old youth, apprehended and tortured in a cemetery, had confessed that arms were being organised by 'someone working at Amiens station who comes from Mers'. He didn't actually know Holville's name, but it was enough to start a Gestapo drive against all uniformed railway personnel from Mers. For once, Maurice Holville almost regretted borrowing his uniform.

Serge was shot in the groin and died from the bullet. On him they found his half of the prison layout plans. Their significance was obvious.

Anxious to confirm whether or not it was in fact Serge in the morgue, one of his friends was smuggled in by a nurse.

'They've got the plans – they *know*,' he said on seeing the body.

Eighty more soldiers were immediately assigned to reinforce prison guards, and a round-the-clock-manned machine-gun installed in the main courtyard. Pepe conceded that any direct land assault attempt on the gaol would now be almost suicidal – attackers would simply be mown down. Security had been further alerted through an abortive attempt to release prisoners from nearby St. Quentin gaol, where attackers had suffered severe losses, and not a single inmate had escaped.

Just as Pepe was making a copy from memory of Serge's half of the plans, Mama Beaurin and Maurice Holville's brother arrived at the Chapelles' little house at Pont-et-Marais.

'Somehow, something must be done to save them,' Mama Beaurin demanded determinedly. Pleading wasn't in her nature.

'We want to get them out, but need more than we've got to achieve it – we need help from abroad,' Pepe explained. 'We want to rescue them, not only because we owe it to them to try, and to show they are not forgotten when caught, but because we need their strength so badly. Even criminals in the gaol could usefully reinforce us. The only way to get them all out is to blow up the main perimeter walls, but the increased guards, machine-gun, and additional security precautions they've just introduced make ground attack success chances appallingly slim.'

When Mama Beaurin suggested: 'What about trying something from the air?', Maria plainly approved.

'As a matter of fact,' said Pepe, 'Maria and I have already discussed one or two planes possibly helping us in some way – maybe creating a simultaneous diversionary attack to switch attention from us at the right moment. It's worth putting it to London to see if they can come up with any useful ideas.'

René Chapelle escaped from a German prisoner of war camp in 1941. Since then, whether called Pedro, Gustave or whatever elsewhere, he remained René the bicycle repairer in his home village of Pont-et-Marais. He repaired the bikes of German soldiers, as well as those he and other members of his group stole to obtain spares for Resistance requirements.

'It's necessary to work for the Germans,' René explained to critics, 'to enable us to work for France at the same time. We need the umbrella.'

René's German clients almost ceaselessly complained about the sub-standard quality of bicycle chains that broke so often, and tyres with an abnormally high puncture rate. Whilst openly sympathising with unhappy customers, René sustained his private policy of never repairing anything too well.

Dark-haired, wiry, stern-faced René the bicycle man was vivid proof of backbone being the one thing more important in life than background. Though small, he was big in courage. He'd learned to lead, and kill ruthlessly and coldly, fighting with the International Brigade during the Spanish Civil War. Because of his International Brigade reputation, the entire Communist FTPF freedom-fighting organisation in the region devotedly followed him. Independently of the FTPF, alongside Dominique Ponchardier, he also commanded Sosie group resistance for the whole north zone, controlling action and intelligence. Although officially one authority rung below Ponchardier, Pepe, as he was known to associates, was the

on-the-spot decision man. Ponchardier stayed in the shadows –
never directly contacted, always reached through an intermediary.
It was better that way, because if anyone fell, it would stop there and
go no further. In line with this, Pepe's orders were for all sections to
stick to their own districts, so that if houses were searched, strangers wouldn't be found – only locals, thereby arousing less suspicion.

He was one of those rare leaders who always knew the size and
scope of his organisation and virtually what it was up to at any given
moment. If an action sounded right, he instantly exploited it. He
cleared mines from a number of strategic Channel coast beaches,
leaving the enemy comfortably believing the beaches were secure
against invaders although he, Washington, and London knew the
areas were now safe alternative landing points. Faced with situations he couldn't handle, such as rocket missile ramps or tank
concentrations, he passed them on for Allied bomber or Commando
attention through his Paris contact who, via Dominique Ponchardier, got them to Allen Dulles.

After Mama Beaurin and Maurice Holville's brother had left the
Chapelles feeling a little more hopeful, Pepe, trying a fresh thought
on Maria, suggested:

'What about a couple of planes precision bombing the walls and
making a hole in them for us to get through? *Mosquito*s could do it, if
we give them all the information they need and tell them what to hit,
and what to miss.'

Why not? He wouldn't be asking simply to free two or three men.
The Gestapo and Wehrmacht counter-Intelligence were having a
field day mauling the Resistance and filling prisons. Including the
Sosies, he counted seventy Resistants that he alone knew of in
Amiens gaol, some caught by French Gendarmes, some by German
police, some by counter-espionage. Most had been betrayed,
though he wasn't as yet certain of the source of the treachery. If they
weren't freed, they'd be executed, so why not chance an air attack?
If invasion didn't come in the next few months, he was certain
Resistance action and intelligence networks in France would be
virtually made ineffective – already comparatively few were left.

'I realise only too well, Maria, that an attack of this kind could be
dangerous for prisoners and people living in houses close by, but as
so many are to be shot anyhow, at least if some survive, they'll be
alive and able to rejoin and strengthen Resistance, which needs all
the help it can get right now,' said Pepe, arguing it out with himself.

Petite, black-haired, black-eyed Maria Benitas, who had met and
married René Chapelle during the Spanish Civil War, then fought

alongside him from the moment Germany occupied France, suddenly answered the questions in his mind.

'When the rest of the world is walking out on you, you need a true friend to walk in, so better risk being killed with honour by friends, than die hoplessly before your enemies' firing squads,' said Maria.

Duplicating the prison plans as well as all the additional details he had on the place, Pepe handed them to Maria to take to Admiral Edouard Rivière in Paris, to pass along the line from Dominque Ponchardier to Colonel 'Gilbert' in Geneva, and Allen Dulles in Berne.

'It's a good idea, now let's see what London thinks of it,' he said, as Maria dressed little Jean warmly for the wintry train journey to Paris. Jean was René's child by another woman, who had died.

Taking Amiens prison plans and other information regularly to Paris once or twice weekly, then returning with news and instructions for Pepe, was exclusively Maria's assignment. If asked, she'd reply that the train journeys were 'for family reasons'. Maria and Jean would frequently accompany Pepe to a rendezvous, then, instead of going home with him, immediately leave for Paris with Intelligence information he wanted transmitted to Dominique Ponchardier or Allen Dulles. Pepe would sometimes accompany Maria and Jean as far as the capital, then let her and the child go without him to see his contact – Admiral Edouard Rivière, employed by the Germans in the Oceanographic Service. If a man with the Admiral's qualifications didn't work for the Germans, he didn't work at all, and was instantly suspect. Making excellent use of his everyday official duties, the Admiral was influentially placed to carry on unofficial work effectively – directing Intelligence.

As the three trudged through the bleak, icy Pont-et-Marais village streets to the railway station, with notes on revised prison attack proposals hidden in little Jean's underclothing, Pepe talked of the other Jean – his protégé Jean Beaurin – and the Beaurin family. Since Papa Beaurin had been deported in 1943, Pepe had felt personally responsible for the family's safety and welfare, as Mama Beaurin had unstintingly done so much for him and his men.

The Beaurins lived resistance – feeding freedom fighters, hiding them in their restaurant and home, providing safe meeting rooms for action discussions.

With the help of her sons, Roger and Jean, Marthe Beaurin ran her popular cosy café restaurant in the Somme coastal town of Mers, to supplement the modest wages which her husband earned as a railway repair shop mechanic.

Long-haired, deceptively frail-looking Jean, with head buried in railway time-tables and books about railways of the world, when he wasn't helping to wait on tables, was in his early teens.

'He's just crazy about railways,' laughed Mama Beaurin, as everyone called her. 'I suppose he'll end up driving engines, or at least doing something connected with railways,' she added. As Pepe appreciatively knew, she was so right.

For teenage Jean, the future wasn't what it used to be, so he had developed into the deadliest railway saboteur of the war.

Pepe recruited him; gave him the contacts and directions. Neither Pepe nor Jean Beaurin personally saw Dominique Ponchardier, although the three worked as a team. After cutting his teeth stealing arms, Jean had persuaded Pepe to let him concentrate on what he knew best. His obsession with train schedules and technical data became the basis of derailments and the rescuing of people in transit to gaols, forced labour, or concentration camps. The Amiens-Arras section of the very busy Paris-Lille line – key troop transport and supply route to all fortifications of the region, including coastal and military centres – also happened to be the one most frequently used for sending troops to Normandy and Russia.

Five tough older men gladly took orders from schoolboyish Jean, because he was the most technically knowledgeable. Working through the night, usually starting from ten o'clock, they took rails apart, unscrewed bolts, always hiding whenever trains passed, which is why time-tables and train delays needed to be taken into account. It took a good week to prepare a derailment. They were of course grateful for Allied aerial bombing of marshalling yards and other rail centres and communications, but were better placed to achieve damage to specifically important trains. Their efforts seriously affected the enemy not only because they destroyed strategic shipments, but because wrecked rails brought long delays. 'Its hard work, Pepe,' admitted Jean, 'but the finished product – pure sabotage – is very satisfying, and I like the word pure related to sabotage.'

Altering signals could also be devastating, if accurately timed.

'According to the latest train schedule information we've received, there's an SS leave train heading for Germany, and a troop train going to Russia about the same time on the same line section,' Jean informed Pepe. 'If they're on schedule and we switch signals at the right moment, we could polish off two trainloads.'

Pepe nodded, satisfied.

'It's a big one, so be extra careful, Jean,' Pepe cautioned his protegé, though he usually emphasised that the biggest dangers often arose through taking too many precautions.

'Don't forget that if you try to cover ground too quickly, the ground is liable to cover you.'

Jean smiled, but took the point.

Noting green signals, the engineer driving the special SS leave train maintained speed until startlingly in his headlight, a train suddenly loomed ahead on the track. Braked wheels hurled leave train passengers from their seats, and as the second train, choked with troops and tanks for the Russian front, rumbled across a bridge, the leave train telescoped into its rear causing carriages from both trains to catapult into the river below. Over a hunded SS men, ninety officers, and the general of an SS division died, and the entire train load of tanks were destroyed.

Jean's boyhood hobby had become a deadly weapon.

He was also expert at securing two pieces of plastic to a track, fixing the detonator and time-fuse for possibly ten minutes' delay, then walking unhurriedly away. All it took was a two-pound plastic 'split' charge shaped to fit in the 'T' of a rail; smoothed so that it wouldn't be noticed, except on close examination. Once the fuse was crimped, he knew he only had a couple of minutes. Always, at this point, his legs longed to run, but his brain kept repeating: 'Never run, because if you stumble and fall, you won't be far enough away before it explodes.' So he walked.

Derailing a troop train on the Tréport-Abbeville line towards the close of 1943, he killed two hundred Germans and injured four hundred.

Congratulating Jean, Pepe said:

'We have no prisons to protect us from dangerous characters, so we simply have to kill them to stay alive ourselves.'

When Jean was finally arrested at the end of December 1943, it wasn't for all the death and destruction he had caused, but for possession of illegal ration cards. The two local Gendarmes instructed to make the arrest – friends of Mama Beaurin and long aware of Jean's activities – had no alternative but to carry out their orders or be suspect themselves.

'Don't ask why,' one said almost apologetically to Jean when they came for him at his mother's restaurant. 'We've just got to take you.'

He was transferred to Abbeville, then quickly on to the criminal section of Amiens prison, into which his brother Roger had already been consigned a month before. When not working in the café, Roger concentrated on seeking military information and 'safe houses' to shelter people in emergencies. Like Jean, he hadn't been detained for Resistance contributions – they'd gaoled him for stealing a bicycle.

'Don't worry,' his mother assured Jean, during a visit to the gaol, 'our friend will soon have you out of here.' The friend, a judge working with the Resistance, often managed to help those who happened to get arrested for minor crimes. He began to move wheels to free Roger and Jean, then two weeks later stopped when, significantly, Jean was moved to the German-controlled section of the gaol. 'Someone's talked,' Jean told his mother, 'and connected me with the train sabotage. Prison lists are regularly checked in case the name of someone wanted on another charge turns up. I've already had a Gestapo session at rue Jeanne d'Arc.'

Eleven of Jean's comrades had just been shot, so he had no illusions, when, charged as a saboteur, he appeared in court at the Palais de Justice in Amiens. After cross-examination, the Judge, without actually proclaiming sentence told Jean:

'Because of your age, you might be pardoned by the general.'

'Why would the general pardon me, if one of my comrades, who was only sixteen, was shot?' Jean questioned.

'Well, all right,' said the Judge, 'then maybe you have no hope.'

Returned to his cell, still unaware of the court's decision, Jean was later unofficially advised that he had been sentenced to death.

Mama Beaurin knew what had to be done as soon as aerial destruction of the prison walls became possible. A warning to Jean, Roger, and others to throw themselves flat or take cover the instant they heard attacking planes could help them escape and save their lives. They had to be told.

Realising that with her sons identified as Resistants, she was also liable to be hauled in for sheltering her children, she decided not to wait for the Gestapo to come for her. *She* would choose if and when to be gaoled to suit *her* convenience, thereby making certain of getting escape details to her boys.

Walking through the prison courtyard to the main gates, after visiting Roger, she began loudly cursing Germany and Hitler for taking her husband and sons from her, and humbling her country.

'Quiet, woman!' one of the military guards yelled at her, 'or you'll join your sons permanently inside!'

Mama Beaurin didn't stop shouting to heaven for retribution on the Führer, and as she stomped through the main exit into the street outside, a furious German sentry moved threateningly towards her. Mama Beaurin erupted – pushing and punching the sentry, screaming abuse. Overcome by guards, and with a rifle between her shoulder blades, she was prodded back into the gaol.

Learning, soon afterwards, that her second floor cell was in the same wing as Jean, she was satisfied.

*

To raid or not to raid was still the question when Bill Donovan flew into London direct from Moscow to discuss, among other things, Amiens prison with Justin O'Brien, ex-Professor of French at Columbia University. O'Brien was deeply involved with Northern France where he controlled OSS agents in the field, in close co-operation with MI6.

An uncharacteristically angry Donovan confessed to having come closest ever to breaking his no swearing rule through the exasperating off-hand tactics of the Russians who, impatient for the opening of a second front in Europe, ignored him for seven days over the 1943 Christmas period, giving him, and America's Ambassador to the Kremlin, Averill Harriman, the freeze.

'They know we're in bad trouble because of Gestapo successes, and that desperate action's needed to save invasion from further delay,' Donovan said, 'so they're giving us a hard time. Fill me in on the latest . . .'

O'Brien, after detailing all the developments gleaned from 2nd Tactical Air Force, including their serious concern as to whether they could be precise enough with bombs to avoid appalling casualties among the very people they had been asked to save, added:

'We've also some interesting news from Amiens. It seems there are now a couple of Americans inside the gaol. We don't know who they are as yet. There's also at least one unidentified Briton, almost certainly Intelligence. Two of the agents in there are said to have only recently dropped.'

Shrewdly analysing the information as always, Donovan, who, as American's General 'Hap' Arnold asserted, was: 'Incapable of a defeatist Intelligence answer,' suggested:

'Talk to Dansey – find out what the old fox has heard. I know a lot of people are trying to come up with fresh ideas on the subject and that a new broom sweeps clean, but the old one knows where the dirt is.'

'Uncle Claude', who took a direct interest in evasion plotting of any kind, had already alerted Airey Neave, who with Lieutenant-Colonel Jimmy Langley ran the MI9 escape organisation associated with MI6, that their services might be called on for a possible imminent large-scale escape operation in Northern France. America's MI9 counterpart, MISX, was also advised. MI6 controlled all MI9's clandestine work in France, Belgium, Holland, Spain and Portugal.

Dansey was partial to the Ivy Restaurant, Brown's or the Savoy Hotel for meals. He arranged to dine with Justin O'Brien at the Savoy Grill Room, and when Claude Dansey shouted 'Waiter!' the response was as swift as that of a guardsman responding to an order from the regimental sergeant-major.

'Two large dry martinis, and be sure it's pre-war gin, not that ersatz stuff you dish out to Americans.'

He didn't inquire whether O'Brien drank dry martinis, he simply ordered them.

Manetta, maître d'hotel of the famous Grill, hurried across to whisper in Dansey's ear.

'Excellent – you know how I like it.'

When O'Brien broached the subject of Amiens, Dansey, who preferred to eat in silence, snapped:

'I never discuss business in public. You never know who's listening. We'll talk in my office afterwards.'

On reaching Broadway Buildings, Westminster, Dansey said for openers: 'You know, I'm sure, that we prefer to keep ourselves very much to ourselves, so let's first get one thing clear – you must undertake not to give detailed reports of our discussion to anyone without my agreement – especially refugee governments.'

'Uncle Claude' had the lowest possible opinion of the security of various governments in exile, often refusing to exchange particularly sensitive information with some of them.

'You might as well hand it straight to the Gestapo,' he said sarcastically, believing in the necessity for security at home, as well as in the field.

Receiving the assurance required, he confirmed Justin O'Brien's news of American and British prisoners in Amiens gaol; informed him of evasion back-up preparations, and current assessments of success chances from 2nd TAF and agents in the area; and emphasised that no final decision authorising the attack had actually been made.

Before Bill Donovan returned to Washington, O'Brien again consulted Dansey to further up-date his chief on Amiens. Concluding his verbal report on the meeting, O'Brien told Donovan:

'Before we parted, I asked Dansey what he would advise if the decision whether to raid the gaol or not was his, and all he said was that Allen Dulles once remarked to him that an ounce of example is worth a pound of advice.'

Donovan smiled.

'That's what I call a real diplomatic answer. Dansey is a lot like Dulles – both are masters at the art of being crafty and the craft of being artful.'

*

André Manuel was standing warming his backside before the gas fire of his cramped little office, warding off the ice-cold morning and wondering whether winter always felt longer because it came in one year and went out the other, when the red 'Most Secret' phone on his desk rang.

Temporarily in command of General de Gaulle's BCRA – Intelligence and Action Bureau – during the absence in Algiers of his chief, Colonel Passy, former Paris lawyer, Manuel, known as 'Maxwell', welcomed the voice at the other end of the telephone.

'We have something interesting for you to see, and are sending it over immediately,' announced his good friend and MI6 opposite number, Kenneth Cohen. The 'something interesting' that arrived some fifteen minutes later at BCRA's 27-room suite of offices at 10 Duke Street, behind the giant Selfridge's Oxford Street department store, was Dominique Ponchardier – flown in by *Lysander* plane for forty-eight hours to discuss Amiens prison.

Facing for the first time the Jekyll and Hyde who, though still only in his twenties, led both action and Intelligence groups, Manuel instantly sensed why the Gestapo had put the man at the top of their 'Wanted' list. He oozed dynamic leadership.

Although unaligned to BCRA, Dominique had been security-cleared by Captain Beaumont of MI5 (British counter-Intelligence). Kenneth Cohen had asked for help, and Manuel knew the Ponchardier brothers were working with the Dulles-Groussard team in Switzerland, which automatically meant Donovan and his OSS were also backing the co-operation request.

'What can I do for you?' Manuel asked.

'I want to know everything BCRA knows about Amiens gaol,' Dominique demanded, 'inmates, administration routines, personnel – German and French – and the buildings themselves.'

Manuel didn't probe as to the purpose of knowledge required. It was clearly important enough for Dulles, Donovan and Dansey to send Ponchardier in person to him.

'Have you been in touch with Dunderdale since your arrival?' Manuel inquired.

'Not yet.'

'He could have some useful guidance and background for you too.'

'I know. I intend seeing him today or tomorrow – I'm only here for forty-eight hours.'

Efficient, tough former Navy Commander Wilfred Dunderdale, totally independent of Kenneth Cohen's MI6 sphere and de Gaulle's BCRA, working with non-Gaullist French and the Dulles-Groussard team, also looked after them when they were in London.

With his own offices in St. James's – comfortably distant from MI6's Westminster headquarters – Wilfred Dunderdale never missed a trick, even bugging his own waiting room with two hidden microphones to record visitors' off-guard comments.

Dunderdale's St. James's offices were also conveniently close to some of the hideouts Dansey used, such as 5 St. James's, for people MI6 wished to keep out of sight. Consulting Wilfred Dunderdale was high on Dominique's London schedule.

André Manuel started the ball rolling. Telephoning Ponchardier's requirements to BCRA's Director of Counter-Espionage, Francois Thierry Mieg, known as 'Colonel Vaudreuil', whose offices were just around the corner in Manchester Square, Manuel stressed:

'Find all you have, and I need it yesterday.'

He didn't explain why.

Thierry Mieg assigned two of his staff to check every souce, and an initial list of thirty-five names resulted: French and Belgian agents; Resistance; captured RAF pilots; and some civil criminals. But there were undoubtedly many more freedom fighters and Allied agents inside, whose identities were still unconfirmed. Researchers were even uncertain whether any on their list might already have been transferred elsewhere, although names were constantly updated. All information was filed in case it could be of value sometime.

The following morning, Manuel called Manchester Square again.

'Do you have your prisoner list and general information ready?'

Thierry Mieg confirmed he had.

'Well I'm sending Dominique Ponchardier to see you about it.'

On hearing who the material was for, Thierry Mieg was positive this was all in aid of preparations for a land attack on the gaol.

Captain Bienvenue, André Manuel's No. 2, escorted Dominique to Manchester Square to introduce him.

'Many of my own people are in there, as well as those taken from other groups,' Dominique explained as he scanned Thierry Mieg's list of names. Particularly gratified at being provided with the method of control for entry and exit from all sections of the prison, he exchanged information about the place for about fifteen minutes, still keeping close-mouthed as to the full purpose of his visit and enquiries. He said no more than he had to, or wanted to.

'This was definitely one of the occasions when a man had to force himself to tell half his secret in order to conceal the rest,' an intrigued André Manuel remarked to Thierry Mieg after Ponchardier departed.

# 7  Courvoisier the pimp

'Napoleon to Josephine . . . Napoleon to Josephine . . .'

The code signal from the Abbeville district, picked up by radio at Bletchley in Buckinghamshire, brought news that finally sent the Amiens prison balloon up.

Every coded message initially passed through the British monitoring station at Bletchley. When things went wrong, operatives in the field used the very fast LMT (Last Means of Transmission) emergency code.

The 'Napoleon to Josephine' signal, passed straight to 'C' and Claude Dansey, notified the arrest the previous day of thirty-five-year-old Raymond Vivant, Sous-Préfet of the town of Abbeville. Confirmation was radioed from a second source. The implications were enormous. Without Vivant's supervision and complex system which he alone controlled, remnants of the extensive OCM Intelligence network covering northern France would be leaderless, in useless disarray. No OCM chiefs were left in the Zone – all were now in gaol. But, as 'C' and Dansey realised, this was merely part of the Vivant catastrophe.

Vivant's working method for the area consisted of recruiting key people in six strategic centres, augmented by aides in every village, to amass every bit of information they could find on defences – especially coastal defences along this vital stretch of invasion-sensitive coast. Keys to the network were village mayors who collected news from individual informants, then brought it to Vivant. The set-up was ideal as it was normal for mayors to visit the Sous-Préfecture regularly on official business and see the Sous-Préfet. It was equally natural for Vivant to visit them, as well as other places, such as schools, on 'official matters'. He personally collated and considered all information, passing everything of possible value, no matter how apparently insignificant, to his exclusive contact and courier.

The Vivant Intelligence link had started in 1940 when he was Secretary-General to the Préfecture at Nièvre, between the Vichy France demarcation line and Paris. A 45-year-old ex-pimp named Courvoisier, appropriately code-named 'Napoleon' ('In honour,' as he proudly put it, 'of the cognac bearing my name which was Napoleon's favourite brandy,') initiated Raymond Vivant's first association with an organisation linked to the OCM. Courvoisier, who ran the organisation, always messaged London – 'Napoleon to Josephine'.

Explaining why he retired from pimping, he confessed:

'I used to run a team of prostitutes in Paris, but had to leave as I couldn't work there anymore – or rather, I couldn't work my girls anymore because I hated being anywhere where there were so many Nazis, and Paris was full of them.

'When I came to Nièvre, I was broke; without income, so had to look for a new line of business. Understandably, I wanted something to keep me in the style to which I'd been accustomed. At the same time, I wanted something that would allow me ample leisure and opportunities to fight the Nazis any way I could, using every crooked trick I knew – and I know most of them.

'Nazis are criminals, and I'm a criminal, so I understand them better than ordinary decent people.'

Courvoisier selected as his new career thieving and dealing in anything and everything that was in short supply. He was very particular whom he robbed, and specialised in raiding the homes and businesses of collaborators. He also made a deal with local Government and German authorities to find and keep abandoned cars – many of which belonged to people forced to run for their lives for one reason or another. He contrived authorisation to collect and sell all abandoned cars, giving half the proceeds to the authorities and keeping the balance as commission. So successfully and profitably did he run the scheme that France's notorious, traitorous ex-Prime Minister Pierre Laval even authorised him to extend the business to other areas.

Jack-of-all-trades – especially illegal ones – Courvoisier hated Nazis so much that, although not normally in favour of violence, he'd kill them with his bare hands whenever he had the chance.

There was a knock on the front door of the Vivant home one

evening. Jane Vivant opened it to find a somewhat dusty, slightly dishevelled Courvoisier.

'Good evening, Madame. Is your husband home?'

'Yes, Monsieur Courvoisier. He's in the salon. Please come in.'

On entering the hallway he immediately requested:

'I would like to wash my hands first, if you don't mind.'

As she showed him to the bathroom, he casually brushed dust and grime from his trousers. As they moved into the salon after he had thoroughly washed his hands, he calmly informed her:

'I just strangled a Nazi in the street outside your home, so I had to wash the smell of his neck off my hands before sitting down with you and your husband.'

He had done what he said. The dead German's body was almost beside their front door.

OCM and other Resistance members had qualms at times about working with Courvoisier, but his patriotism was indisputable. He was treasured by the British and Americans in London, both of whom he was ever-ready to serve as long as there were Nazis to kill and an enemy to defeat. He guided evaders from crashed planes; smuggled refugees across the demarcation line into Unoccupied France or on to Spain and Britain; and supervised reception arrangements for agents parachuted into France. One of the parachutes he presented to Madame Vivant.

'Make yourself a nightdress from it. It's excellent material and will look good on you,' he gallantly suggested.

Courvoiser and the Vivants parted company in April 1943 on Raymond Vivant's promotion to Sous-Préfet of Abbeville, but a few months later he called from a public call box.

'It's me, Napoleon. I'm in Abbeville and need to see you.'

Meeting at a little railway station near the town, in the privacy of Vivant's car, Courvoisier explained:

'I'm on the run. Things have become too hot for me in Nièvre. I need to protect myself from my enemies, and I don't mean only the Germans who've begun to suspect I'm not all I appear to be, though I'm sure they've no actual evidence against me. But, as you know, suspicions alone can be dangerous, and certainly restrict my Resistance activities, which is why I've come to you, my friend, for advice.'

They drove to the Préfecture, where Courvoisier stayed in the residence's official VIP guest room for eight days. Vivant cautioned him to keep in hiding awhile and not surface too much through travelling extensively.

'I think I'll risk going back to Nièvre to settle a few things, unobtrusively, of course,' he smiled, 'and then return to my old Paris haunts where I feel I can lose myself, especially as I've been out of the Paris criminal scene for so long. Fortunately, I've managed to put aside enough to afford a period of inactivity, so I won't need to start running girls again.'

Vivant and Courvoisier lost touch, but one day he reappeared and announced: 'I'm a Maquis Commandant now – self-appointed, of course.' It was true, but although this Napoleon's army was mainly concerned with the Nièvre and Lyon regions, he still had ears and eyes working for him in the north, which is why he learned so swiftly of Vivant's arrest.

On assuming his Abbeville post, Vivant went to pay his respects to the Somme's Préfet at Amiens, and was ushered into the Préfet's chamber by his amiable secretary, Mademoiselle Solange Caillé. She then introduced him to two senior Somme Préfecture officials – Public Health Officer and Defence Chief Dr. Antonin Mans, and a Captain André Tempez.

'Do you know someone named Jasmin?' Mans asked him when they were alone. The 'Jasmin' code signal identified Mans as his new OCM contact. Mans and Tempez were his superiors in the extensive network known as 'Centurie'.

The vast assortment of Resistance groups and circuits were largely self-formed by local leaders, but most were eventually reorganised, guided, and supplied by London and Washington. For security, they remained self-contained, unconnected, and, generally, unknown to each other. Their activities, motives and politics were diverse, but all were patriots with one common enemy and a single objective – freedom.

The Somme Préfet's gentle secretary, Mademoiselle Caillé, was in such a sensitive, well-informed job that she offered her secret services to two important Intelligence groups – the OCM and 'Centurie' networks, and one of her most significant coups was stealing a copy of the secret code used by the despicable Gestapo-associated French Milice organisation.

Sous-Préfet Raymond Vivant's first unofficial Abbeville assignment was receiving and assisting parachuted agents from London. One – an American – he housed in the Sous-Préfecture's guest room normally reserved for visiting Government Ministers.

A Préfet and Sous-Préfet's post and duties are, in many respects, similar to a Governor of a province or an American State, except that they are Government-appointed civil servants, not publicly elected administrators.

From the day reconnaissance photographs of the Peenemunde

Baltic research centre showed a tall object standing on a fan-shaped expanse of asphalt – a rocket resting on its fins – highest priority was given to secret weapon searches by American and British planes roaming the coast from Cherbourg to Belgium. Giant concrete structures spotted in the area were confirmed by Vivant and his colleagues to involve secret weapons, so the US 8th Air Force bombed them.

One man working on eight sites near Abbeville, on Vivant's doorstep, didn't understand what the contracting firm employing him was actually constructing. Each site was partly in woodlands, largely obscured at ground level by trees, but still visible from the air. None was served by rail spurs or even near a railway. At all the sites near Abbeville, the longer section of a rectangular concrete slab was aligned on London, with a square windowless concrete hut or shelter at one end of the rectangular slab exactly in line with it, with an open side also facing London. Vivant decided to look at the site himself.

In his capacity as Sous-Préfet, Vivant appointed Captain Tempez Director of Defense Passive, which covered Civil Defence, ambulance, rescue, fire and first aid services. Through Tempez' official sphere of duties he therefore facilitated for them both considerable freedom of movement throughout the area, enabling them to check personally stolen blueprints of launching ramps and blockhouses.

Returning to the Préfecture he confided to his wife:

'I have some terrible news, but am happy I have got it because at least we can warn the British . . . The Germans are building ramps from which they intend to launch rocket bombs against England.'

'I know,' his wife said.

'What do you mean, you know?' he asked incredulously.

'I also heard all about it today – from my hairdresser. She sleeps with a German officer who told her they have a new flying bomb weapon that is going to help them win the war.'

This was the confirmation he wanted.

But patient, painstaking collation of information lost novelty for impetuous young Roland Farjon – fourth key figure of the region's OCM network. Farjon tended to throw his weight around.

The Baignol and Farjon industrial dynasty, with its factories in Boulogne producing items used by every French school child – from pencils, pens, rubbers, to school stationery – made son of a Senator Roland Farjon a pre-war millionaire. Oustandingly courageous, but highly temperamental, he was related to General de Gaulle, and liked reminding associates of the fact.

Even Courvoisier, who originally knew Farjon from Paris, warned Raymond Vivant to be wary, and Vivant had good cause to respect Napoleon's instincts about people, as he was usually proved right. Repeatedly counselling caution in dealing with Farjon, Courvoisier assessed:

'In every way he's too much – too rich, too daring, too imperious, too dangerous, and paying too much attention to his reputation, which marks him as a weaker shallower character than he appears.'

Meeting with the Vivants, Dr. Mans and André Tempez in the ground floor salon of the Abbeville Préfecture, Farjon sought to pressurise them into ordering combatant action. Impatient for invasion landings, he demanded:

'We can't go on waiting like this for the Allies to invade – we must take drastic action ourselves. Our role is too dull. We must do something big, something important and *now*!'

Appalled, Mans protested.

Beginning with Roland Farjon's Gestapo detention during the last week of October, arrests had swept the area, with disaster after disaster striking individual unconnected groups – Dr. Mans, Captain Tempez, and their OCM network, the Ponchardiers' 'Sosies', 'Alliance', and others. All knew they were largely being wrecked through wholesale treachery, and that northern France was in imminent danger of being left virtually leaderless, helpless, and open.

Colonel Alexis von Roenne, the senior Intelligence chief whom Hitler expected to reach the right invasion answers for the High Command, concluded that the Allies were likely to come within three months – early in February 1944. This was why mass counter attacks began to exterminate possible military and civilian support in sensitive zones such as the Pas de Calais. The slightly hilly rural area protruding into the Straits of Dover was the historic region fought over by the Counts of Flanders, the Dukes of Burgundy, Bourbons, Frenchmen, Spaniards, Austrians, and was the terrible battleground of World War I.

Said Colonel von Roenne, in his report to Hitler:

They can dash across to Calais from Dover where the Channel is only twenty miles wide.

To which Hitler taunted:

The A-4 (the flying bomb) can decide the war, and what encouragement to the home front when we attack the English with it! This is the decisive weapon.

The Führer was also depending on the product coming from a lonely valley of the Harz Mountains. In a system of caves, V2 rocket production lines installed in enormous long underground workshops were staffed largely by concentration camp inmates to eliminate all contact with the outside world.

American Intelligence also knew that Germany had converted forty of their biggest sugar refineries to the production of bacteria yeast in preparation for germ warfare.

With the loss of Roland Farjon, Mans and Tempez, the burden of northern France Intelligence fell heavily on Raymond Vivant, as the last surviving Intelligence leader able to manipulate essential strings. A courier, to replace the transmission function previously supplied by Dr. Mans, was sent to handle everything Vivant could get on the massive build-up of missile sites and coastal defences. Vivant advised that the sites could be built from start to finish in six weeks, and that because of American bomber attacks, Lieutenant-General Erich Heinemann – artillery commander with overall responsibility for flying bomb and long-range rocket action – had decided to continue work on existing sites as a blind whilst preparing less vulnerable positions.

Concentrating on what was now classified in London and Washington as 'Invasion Intelligence', Vivant's team swiftly located the alternative launch pads. To help him interpret stolen fortification plans and other material, he created an official technical consultation excuse to send for his brilliant engineer and mathematician friend, Clerc, with whom he had worked in Nièvre. He almost regretted doing so when the irrepressible Clerc stepped off the train at Abbeville station.

'Ah, there is the friend of the Marx Brothers!' Clerc yelled as soon as he spotted Madame Vivant. Everyone knew the standing joke about the Luftwaffe fighter base at Abbeville. As it was generally agreed that nobody ever saw more than three planes coming from there, locals tagged them 'The Marx Brothers'. They were wrong about the base – it was one of the Luftwaffe's finest fighter units.

As the Vivants led the happy Clerc to their car, he suddenly burst into song:

'It's a long way to Tipperary, its a long way to go . . .'

He loved singing British songs.

Jane Vivant diplomatically slapped a hand over his mouth to shut him up.

Clerc's detailed technical assessments of rocket emplacements and new coastal fortifications were gratefully welcomed by the US 8th Air Force and 2nd Tactical Air Force. Clerc returned to his official and unofficial work in Nièvre . . . and to his death. The Gestapo caught him, then decided he should be brutally executed with a butcher's meat hook.

Seeking to be granted a final request, Clerc, a devout Catholic, asked:

'If I have to die this way, I would like a priest to kill me.'

A priest was brought.

'I realise it's a terrible thing to ask you to do,' he confessed to the priest, 'but if they insist on doing this to me, I would rather be crucified by a priest.'

The priest stuck the butcher's hook into his throat, and later personally conducted a special memorial service for him at the Church of the Invalides.

*

At the end of 1943, the OCM proudly notified London that they had an effective membership of 100,000 and the all-important 'A' region had 12,000, who were now in Vivant's hands. So much now depended on his maintaining the flow of current information on deployment of enemy forces, coastal fortifications, and missiles.

The Joint Chiefs of Staff in Washington discussed reports from Donovan and one from US. Air Force headquarters depicting the possibility that the enemy might achieve a stalemate in strategic air offensive by devastating Britain with bacterial weapons, poison gas, or revolutionary explosives of an unusually violent character.

It was reported to Washington in January 1944 that the Germans intended using their long-range projectiles for bacterial warfare, as the very small payload in such an expensive vehicle could not be explained in any other way

As General Eisenhower insisted to his Air Force Commanders:

'Until we can be certain that we have definitely gotten the upper hand of this particular menace, its top priority bombing must stand.'

Moreover, it was clear that unless and until underground armies and networks could be reorganised, re-officered, and reinforced, Raymond Vivant would have to be the key repository of invasion-support tactics. Unavoidably, he was now too essential and knew far too much for his own, or the Allies' good, so they couldn't afford to lose him too. André Dewavrin – 'Colonel Passy', Chief of de Gaulle's BCRA Intelligence services – confidently told Claude Dansey at a meeting they had on 8 February 1944 that he was certain reorganisation could speedily be carried out.

'I think there is still unexplored potential that could be harnessed in France, so that groups of under a thousand might grow to a strength of ten thousand, once presented with arms and opportunity,' Passy assured Dansey. For northern France, much of the success of this forecast now depended on Raymond Vivant.

At 10.00 a.m., on Tuesday, 14 February 1944, Vivant received a telephone call to say he was required at the Kommandatur division responsible for overseeing German civil affairs. He rang his friend Victor Samson, a former mayor, to say he might be late for lunch.

Whereas he was usually shown into the Kommandant's office, on this occasion he was taken before the young, paunchy, red-haired police chief who, after asking him to be seated, hastened to explain:

'I regret this very much, Monsieur le Sous-Préfet, but I am not responsible – it is the other services. Security officers are conducting a very important enquiry and would like your opinion on a certain matter.'

He said nothing more for twenty minutes, when Vivant, impatient, but still cautiously courteous, broke the silence.

'I would remind you that as Sous-Préfet, I have many urgent matters to attend to, and if these security officers don't show up in five minutes, I shall go,' he announced curtly.

'I'm certain they'll be here any minute,' the police chief reassured somewhat anxiously.

Five minutes later, two smartly-dressed young men in civilian clothes – one wearing a bottle-green hat – arrived. After talking in German to the policeman, the shorter one, turning to Vivant, demanded:

'You are the Sous-Préfet of Abbeville?'

'Yes.'

'You're Monsieur Raymond Vivant?'

'Yes.'

Vivant's temper was almost at breaking point when he suddenly felt something hard poked into his side.

'Arms up!' the second young man commanded.

Checking Vivant was unarmed, he motioned him to sit again.

'Monsieur le Sous-Préfet,' resumed the short one, 'we must arrest you.'

'Here we go with another German judiciary blunder,' Vivant answered sarcastically, 'and by no means the first.'

'We'll talk about that later, Monsieur, but for the moment, you must consider youself our prisoner.'

'What am I being arrested for?'

'I can't say.'

Vivant remembered what he'd said to his wife when Mans and Tempez were taken:

'You know there's always the possibility I also might be arrested. If I am, I'll escape, and if you're arrested, you must escape quickly.'

Leaving him temporarily in the custody of the red-haired police officer, the two black-raincoated Gestapo agents forced their way into the Abbeville Sous-Préfecture and the Vivants' private quarters. A manservant tried to stop them, but they merely knocked him aside. Bursting into the first floor main bedroom, they found Madame Vivant confined to bed with a severely sore throat.

'Get up and come with us!' they ordered. 'We want you with us as we search everywhere.'

Operating more on the instant than on instinct, intuition told her it wasn't the moment to ask reasons for the instrusion. Asking them to leave the room to enable her to put on a housecoat, she said stiffly:

'I don't understand why you've come, but I'll show you everything.'

She started with the Préfecture offices on the right of the small interior courtyard; switched to the elegantly furnished ground floor salon, dining room, first floor bedrooms, guest room and kitchen. They took both the Vivants' address books. On coming across the final chapter, entitled 'Inquest', of a detective book manuscript Madame Vivant had been writing as a pastime, one triumphantly exclaimed:

'Ah, – Resistance!'

They grabbed miscellaneous papers, but found no compromising documents. Still more fortunately, they missed the map of Saint-Valery coastal fortifications Raymond Vivant had hidden among a batch of boring administrative files.

Before going, they advised Madam Vivant, almost courteously, now to pack a valise for her husband, mentioning for the first time:

'He'll be in gaol for a couple of days.'

She packed what they suggested – blanket, towel, dressing gown, handkerchiefs, pyjamas, toothbrush, toothpaste, soap and comb and as they left with the bag, was glad she had never been afraid of fear.

Raymond Vivant somehow trusted in God, though he wasn't religious. His mother was Catholic; his father a Freemason. As a boy he had belonged to a Protestant Boy Scout troop, but he had gone to church only to keep his mother happy.

He knew he'd be taken first to Gestapo headquarters, and concentrated his thoughts on how to escape. As the Gestapo car stopped on occasions in the traffic; he calculated his chances of making a run for it. He'd been a chair-bound Civil Servant for many years but he was thirty-five, strong, a good athlete, regularly exercising and working out with two local physical training instructors with dumb-bells, bars, weights, the lot. Somewhere along the line, all that keeping fit could save his life.

Studying the Gestapo man on his right, and noticing the obvious revolver jacket bulge, he considered going for the revolver, but the armed Gestapo thug beside the chauffeur made the idea seem too risky. Unless he could reach a gun fast, it would be hopeless. Instead, he studied chances throughout the journey, considering every possibility in case another journey and another opportunity presented itself.

On reaching the notorious Gestapo H.Q. in Amiens' rue Jeanne d'Arc, he was taken into a small plainly furnished room where he was confronted by a young Gestapo officer seated behind a desk. The officer stared at Vivant, then glanced at his watch, and announced:

'I'm going to lunch – we'll talk afterwards.' Whereupon he left.

When hours later the officer returned, the questions he rapped out simply concerned civil details such as:

'Name . . . age . . . place of birth . . .' etc. A man at another desk wrote the replies on a sheet of paper, after which, with the same escort, the black Citroen Gestapo car drove him to Amiens prison, veering right at the main gate to the building staffed only by German military.

Two soldiers took him to an office where one senior officer and one junior officer were waiting. Another soldier seated at a desk had, as in the Gestapo office, a sheet of foolscap paper in front of him. The unexpected was a dark, petite, sharp-featured woman in a plain grey dress standing in a corner of the office. Other than Vivant, she was the only non-uniformed person present. She was the interpreter, spoke good French and fired all the questions which, at first, were a repetition of the Gestapo sequence – name, age, place of birth, etc. Suddenly, the routine broke as she asked rudely, almost simpering:

'What *is* a Sous-Préfet? – What does he *do*?'

Coldly, Vivant answered:

'I represent the State, and in Abbeville, am the representative of Marshal Pétain.'

When questions ended, one of the soldiers searched him, removing his two wallets, fountain pen, propelling pencil, papers, but allowed him to keep his tie, gold watch, braces, and even his grey suede gloves and black Anthony Eden-style homburg hat with his initials in metal inside.

When led to Cell 16, on the ground floor of the gaol, by the senior officer, junior officer and one soldier, with the woman interpreter hovering a few metres behind, he was quite a sight. Accepting it all without a hint of resignation, he looked the epitomy of what every well-dressed man should wear in gaol – from the stylish hat and suede gloves, double-breasted black jacket with neat white folded handkerchief in breast pocket, smart waistcoat and navy-blue overcoat, to the impeccably creased pin-striped trousers and highly polished shoes.

The junior officer opened the cell door, and Vivant entered to note a metal wash basin (cold water only, of course), a tie-up wooden table attached to a wall, and a metal bed which folded against the other wall. The bed base was simply metal strips covered with a hair mattress. Observing that the mattress didn't fit – it was half a metre short – Vivant protested:

'That's impossible! – I am one metre seventy-three centimetres tall, so why can't I have a mattress which fits the bed and permits me to sleep comfortably – or is this deliberate?'

He hadn't actually been charged with anything yet, was still Sous-Préfet, and determined to let them know it.

The senior officer promised to do something about the mattress. Nothing, in fact, was done.

There was no cup, no cushion, one blanket, and it was freezing, so he kept his hat, coat, and gloves on. Hours later, the cell door was unlocked to admit a German guard, followed by a prisoner with a large soup container. Vivant made signs to the guard, who only spoke German, that he had no bowl or plate for the soup. The two men disappeared, leaving Vivant without food or drink that day. The night was unremarkable, apart from his consciousness, from time to time, of the duty sentry staring through the cell door peep-hole. It was bitterly cold. He didn't sleep.

At 8 a.m. he was handed a cup of coffee, which inmates called something else. He was permitted to keep the tin cup, and given a tin plate and spoon. Shortly after 11 a.m., the Gestapo returned for him, and from then on the routine was repeated daily. There were plenty of people about the streets at that period of the morning, so he continued to be watchful, hoping his escort might get careless, or that an unexpected halting of the car might offer a chance to disappear into the crowds. The journey from the gaol to the Gestapo building took fifteen minutes. Philosophically, he was confident it would all work out in his favour, though he hadn't the slightest idea how.

At the Sicherheitspolizei (the Gestapo's official Security Police title) the same officer who had received him the previous day was waiting, but the questions were different:

'What were your clandestine activities, and to what group do you belong?' he barked. Vivant felt his interrogator knew too much about too many things, and was playing with him to test reactions. He tried to build a shelter with his silence until, as before, at one o'clock the interrogation stopped.

'I must eat, you understand,' he smiled at Vivant.

'Bon appetit!' said Vivant, as he was led to an adjoining room with a fixed bench as its only piece of furniture. At 3.30 p.m., interrogation resumed. When Vivant was driven back to his prison cell, he was overjoyed to receive a parcel his wife had been allowed to send in, accompanied by the valise of spare clothes and toilet necessities. The parcel contained food from his friends, the Tenaillons, wholesale grocers in Abbeville, with one white and one yellow and blue table napkin. There was also two bottles.

'Alcohol, nix!' the German guard announced, smiling broadly, and then departing.

The food was a gift from the gods to Vivant by then, especially the sugar. He put five lumps in each of his pockets, thinking they could be of some comfort during the next long interrogation, if he managed to suck them without being spotted. His wife's parcel also contained an already opened bottle labelled 'Vitamin pills'. Possibly, he thought, she had sent them to counter prison undernourishment. He decided to take one a day (long afterwards, he was to learn his wife had sent him pastilles for his sore throat, and that they bore no resemblance to the bottle of pills the Germans had delivered to him).

Around 6 p.m., the single bare light bulb high in the ceiling, was switched on and 'Dinner was served'. The nightly menu was cabbage soup with a small lump of bread in it. This watery liquid, sometimes brown, sometimes green, always tasted the same, but on a good day it did include a few minute bits of meat. Served from an outside urn when the door was opened by a guard, it was ladled into the metal plate by a convict from the gaol's criminal section.

Untying the wooden table attached to the wall, Vivant regularly 'laid table' for his meal, spreading the white napkin as his tablecloth, and using the other as his serviette. He set out the tin cup, plate and spoon, and slowly savouring the soup and some of the things his wife had sent, dined as though in his favourite restaurant, ignoring the sound of the cell door peep-hole repeatedly opening as guards kept staring in at the spectacle. But that wasn't all.

After the meal, he took a 'constitutional', promenading up,

down, and around the cell. Guards outside queued to observe the gloved, overcoated, immaculately attired Sous-Préfet, 'walking off his food', wearing his hat and still Sous-Préfet, from head to toe. The German guards were impressed by the display because it smacked of something of the order they were conditioned to admire. Vivant knew he had them worried. Even in a cell, he was managing to assert an air of authority. He always remembered his father advising his mother:

'In front of a German officer, you do two things – protest violently or praise the German army as being human and just. Always remind him that he must not let the honour of the army down, despite the fact that others may be willing to act in an inhuman and uncivilised manner.'

He also recalled the occasion when a Wehrmacht Colonel and another officer having coffee with him at the Préfecture asked:

'What do you think of the war?'

'Do you speak to the Sous-Préfet, or Raymond Vivant,' he countered.

'We would like the opinion of Raymond Vivant,' they answered.

'Then I regret for your sake that Germany will be knocked out – will lose.'

The two regular officers – not Nazis – were shocked, but respected the frankness.

When he wasn't with the Gestapo, or busying himself with his cell meals routine, Vivant occupied long hours considering escape ideas, and philosophising about his predicament, without over-dramatising the obvious dangers, nor minimising them. This had always been his way – his parents' way. It was professionally ingrained in him. Oscar Wilde, he thought, had a point when he declared that philosophy teaches us to bear with equanimity the misfortunes of others. Right now, in the kind of situation he was in, philosophy was just about all he, Vivant the philosopher, had.

However, at rue Jeanne d'Arc the fencing was over.

'We know General de Gaulle has chosen you to be Préfet of Amiens after the "liberation", and we know *all* your friends,' the interrogator claimed, describing alleged members of the Resistance who had visited his office.

'You know very well that it is perfectly normal for a mayor, or other officials, to see me at the Préfecture,' replied Vivant. 'And you must also know that the nature of my duties also requires me to travel extensively, inspecting places, and seeing people,' he calmly replied.

He never mentally prepared himself for the Gestapo sessions, as he was accustomed to questioning and diplomacy. As far as he was concerned, parrying the Gestapo was the perfect justification for diplomacy as the patriotic art of lying for your country.

The interrogator became uncomfortably specific about the subjects Vivant had discussed with some of his Préfecture visitors. Smirking, the interrogator said:

'We know everything, because Roland Farjon told us all about the OCM and you.'

Doubting the finger pointed at Farjon, especially with the accusation coming from the Gestapo, although even the most courageous of men and women could be broken, he continued to reassure himself that they had no documentary proof. He had taken too many precautions against this risk. His only way was to compel respect for his position from the Germans, even though he was their prisoner. He was positive that the psychology was right, and would raise doubts as to whether they might have blundered in arresting him on someone's treacherous word, or someone's suspicions. As part of his fight-them-with-psychology policy, whenever he passed a German officer at Gestapo headquarters, or in the gaol, he raised his Homburg hat, keeping an absolutely straight face. The gesture shook them every time.

Prison gossip spread the word that the new man in Cell 16, ground floor, was the Sous-Préfet of Abbeville, but many inmates disbelieved the news which was tapped from cell to cell on the plumbing pipes. Using the plumbing 'telephone', Dr. Antonin Mans called his new cell neighbour and learned it was Raymond Vivant.

On the Wednesday morning – third day of Vivant's incarceration – as the convict with the morning 'coffee' handed him his filled cup, he whispered:

'You are Vivant?'

'Yes.'

Furious at the no-talking rule being broken, the German guard shouted 'Raus! Raus!', grabbed the convict, and cursing in German, pushed him on as he slammed the door of Vivant's cell.

Within hours, one of Courvoisier's criminal fraternity friends in the gaol passed confirmation of the arrest via a French prison guard to an outside contact who, in turn, notified Courvoisier. Instantly appreciating the possibly enormous consequences, he desperately sent a 'Napoleon to Josephine' radio signal to London.

*

'C' passed the brief Bletchley radio station message to Claude Dansey.

The news reached André Manuel at the BCRA Duke Street office; General Koenig appointed by General de Gaulle to be responsible for all Resistance movements designated to supply invasion support; Bill Donovan in Washington; General Eisenhower; and Winston Churchill.

Commented Manuel:

'With Vivant they have a master key to the entire Somme Intelligence and Resistance – and more, much more. Although they probably don't realise it yet.'

Said General Koenig:

'Without Intelligence and other invasion back-up, landings would have to be postponed until we rebuilt the networks and our forces.'

Bill Donovan was equally forthright:

'At this point in time, minus Vivant we're like the three wise monkeys – virtually blind, deaf, and dumb – just when we need to be seeing, hearing and told everything possible, particularly in northern France. Vivant must be freed, or silenced. If he's made to talk, and no man's mind is safe from the Gestapo, they could wipe out an enormous slice of our operations over there just when we need them ready, and even stronger.'

Deeply perturbed about effects of Intelligence disruption on the anti-missile campaign, as well as D-day preparations, Eisenhower insisted:

'Everything possible must be done to secure the safety of Britain as a base for operations, and we're depending on an uninterrupted flow of Intelligence to help us.'

'C' similarly echoed:

'Invasion delay would give Hitler time to increase missile attacks which, as Ike rightly says, make themselves felt on morale, and not on civilians alone. Given time, Hitler might also be able to perfect some mass destructive weapon we fail to discover fast enough, or can't stop or master, so time is one thing we cannot afford to lose.'

Dansey summarised:

'All the networks have suffered severe losses, and although previous reservations regarding bombing Amiens prison were understandable because of the unavoidably large casualty risks, there can be no reservations now. It's clear what has to be done.'

As 'C' was about to leave for 10, Downing Street to report to Churchill, Dansey, concurring with Bill Donovan, concluded: 'We have to eliminate the Vivant danger – one way, or another.'

*

At all levels, and in all departments, nobody favoured the proposal. It was far too dangerous – for the prisoners. Even Embry, who had never shirked anything in his life, called it a 'hateful responsibility', but the ten planners were together again in his room after innumerable ad hoc mini-meetings, often between just two or three of them, to discuss and consider specific aspects coming within their special operational scope or expertise. There was fresh information from Amiens. Medmenham had completed their photographic sortie and interpreted results.

Squadron Leader Edwin Houghton – No. 2 of Group Intelligence – opened the morning conference with the Medmenham assessment that had reached Mongewell Park in the early hours.

Producing photographs taken of prison buildings marked A, B, and C, he began to recite details of the report on them:

The dimensions of the area enclosed by the prison wall are as follows:
Building 'A' – North side – 425 feet; South side, adjoining the main road – 410 feet; East side – 325 feet; West side – 315 feet.

The height of the main building to the eaves is approximately 49 feet, and to the ridge 62 feet. There are therefore four or five storeys, but the exact number cannot be ascertained from photographs.

No machine gun posts are visible in the immediate neighbourhood of the building, but these could of course be concealed.

Building 'B' appears to be a small housing estate consisting of a number of semi-detached two-storey dwellings with gabled roofs. The layout is regular, each house having a small garden. There is no photographic evidence to suggest the buildings are used otherwise than as private houses.

Buildings 'C' are buildings marked on the town plan as 'Hospice St. Victor' and their layout and design would correspond to that of an institute for the poor and aged. The grounds are surrounded by an 11-foot wall but there is no photographic evidence of military occupation. Outside the grounds, about eighty yards to the north, there is a trench near the road junction.

About the Hospice, Medmenham were wrong – it was being used mainly as a German military hospital. Houghton and the interpretation report confirmed:

Most of the German guards are definitely in their own quarters at midday, and these are separate from the main buildings positioned at each end of the long arm of the cruciform prison building, as shown on the sketch plan provided for us by those on the spot. Although there are guard houses at both ends, the guards' Mess room is at one end only. The attack therefore has to be sufficiently discriminating to ensure decisive force being used against the German Mess portion of the building as well as their guardroom at the other end to eliminate interference from them. And, as stated at a previous discussion, many prisoners assemble for lunch at virtually the same time as the guards, but in the central hall. Noon, on all counts, appears to be the perfect timing for us. Because we know precisely where most of the guards, and where the prisoners will be at midday, we can direct our bombs accordingly to keep casualties down.

His last two points were:

The courtyard appears fenced internally to segregate prisoners whilst at exercise.

Executions are definitely imminent within the next few days, so if an attack is to take place, it must do so quickly.

Embry hadn't as yet given a 'Yes' or 'No' but everyone felt he knew the answer. Now they sensed they were about to get it.

'If we place a number of bombs at the base of the prison, their explosion should throw doors out of alignment, making the locks ineffective and at the same time damaging prison building walls enough to allow prisoners to escape into the yard,' Embry emphasised, adding with extra significance:

'I have warned members of the Resistance with whom we're dealing, that we would be bound to cause casualties amongst the prisoners because even if all went according to plan and our calculations were absolutely correct, falling debris and the proximity to explosions would be certain to take their toll.'

In other words, revenge could be sweet, but not for all of the victims.

Knowing the feelings and attitude of each of his staff towards the proposed attack must, above all, be influenced – as he was – by consideration of the lives of the inmates, he slowly and deliberately stressed:

'In reply, I have again been assured they would rather be killed by us than by the Germans.'

The effect of the last sentence was written on every face. All felt it was 'Go', even though the word was still unspoken.

Ted Sismore cut through the atmosphere:

'Eighteen aircraft should do the job perfectly. The outer wall needs SAPs (semi-armour piercing hard-nosed bombs), but we'll have to be careful where they use those SAPs because they have been known to go through a wall and out the other side. Also, if they hit anything hard, they sometimes bounce – even higher than the plane that dropped them – and could even bounce right into one of the follow-up planes. I've known them to do this sometimes when hitting railway lines.

'We'll use medium-case bombs that explode on impact for the inner walls. We have to have exactly the right amount of explosive to achieve what we want – not too little, and definitely not too much.'

'Digger' Magill put his piece in:

'I'll fix a strong escort from "Jamie" Jamieson's II Group. He can give us *Typhoon*s from Westhampnett to rendezvous with our Mossies over Littlehampton, see them across and help take care, if necessary, of any problems from their fighters. We've done a little advance clobbering in that direction a few days ago – on the 8th, Mossies plastered the Amiens-Glisy base. Dummy aircraft were seen alight, and also two of the airfields, so we've hurt them a bit ahead of time.'

Both Sismore and Magill were already speaking as if the raid's approval was a foregone conclusion.

No one said anything more. All eyes were on Embry. It was his moment, his decision.

The raid itself was no problem, he thought. Actual operational implications were not all that involved and not nearly so intricate as in so many other ops they had carried out successfully, but as far as he was concerned, there were too many ifs, and only one but.

If they could do it in time to save the condemned prosoners. If weather permitted. If there were enough outside help for escaping inmates, and if ground assistance were able to shoot down any security forces hunting escapers. If the pilots could place the bombs in the right positions in the right wall, and if their explosions would do what was expected of them after delaying sufficiently to allow the second Flights to get *their* bombs into the guardrooms – if the aircraft managed to do it all at the prison's midday lunch period.

The biggest 'if' of all was those walls. If Intelligence information on their construction and depth was wrong in the slightest degree, all calculations on how the walls would behave when exploded would be wrong too, and hundreds of innocent people could die.

On balance, he should confirm the Air Ministry's original rejection of the proposal. There was so much against it. The solitary 'but' was that it could prove to be an appalling error. On the other hand, fear of being wrong was no justification for not attempting something – that kind of thinking was contrary to everything he had ever stood for. According to his book, one could fail by stupidity, fail by ignorance, by laziness or by error, but one should never fail through lacking the courage to make errors. Consequently he always insisted to men he commanded:

'Let us learn by our mistakes and if we do fail, at least we will not have failed through doing nothing.'

The single 'but' answered the question on his mind. He ended the silence of the room.

'I shall notify HQ today and ask them to send a message to our Amiens friends warning them to be ready to support any escapers outside the prison at midday any day from a date I'll finally determine after getting the Met outlook.

'Three Squadrons from Pickard's 140 Wing will do the job, but I shall lead, with Ted as my navigator. Percy Pickard will be deputy leader and I'll leave it to him to select crews.'

So it was on. All realised it could turn out to be a tragic blunder, but everyone agreed that it was better to try than stand back and let prison firing squads execute so many anyway.

The decision was passed along every link of the chain – from Embry to Coningham, who notified Leigh Mallory, who advised the Air Ministry, which reported to the Intelligence branches concerned, who despatched a courier to Allen Dulles in Berne, who told Colonel Groussard in Geneva, who sent for Dominique Ponchardier, who had initiated the whole thing and took the RAF plan to his Paris link, Admiral Rivière, then finally informed those anxiously waiting in Amiens and the rest of northern France.

Winding up the meeting, Embry sat back and said:

'I am making a slight change in arrangements. As so much depends on those walls tumbling down, I think, from now, the operations's code name should appropriately be – "Jericho".'

# 8 'New boy'

The Pissers of Mongewell Park were Jacks-of-all-jobs.

Rugged little *Piper Cubs* – Pissers to everyone in the air force, because they were forever pissing about doing almost everything, from ambulance duties, reconnaissance, flight instruction, to transport – could keep putt-putting about the sky in all weathers. At the start of the war, four out of five pilots learnt to fly in a Cub, which could take on all kinds of flyers. It was a very forgiving, obliging little aircraft, and one of them, cocking a snook at the bleak February sky, putt-putted Embry to Hunsdon air base, a few miles north of London, to brief Group Captain Percy Charles Pickard on the Amiens prison raid.

140 Wing had moved to Hunsdon on 31 December – many using Pissers to get there – from the peaceful Sculthorpe village, in Norfolk. Assigned 'No Ball' targets – the Buzz Bomb V1 rocket launching sites as their major task – they attacked V1 launching platforms the same day they checked in at Hunsdon for duty. The Wing had started rocket base attacks from Sculthorpe only nine days previously, when they were personally led by the Group's Commander, Embry, and their own Commander, Pickard, as his No. 2. Next day, they gave the secret weapon sites another pasting, this time with Pick up front, and from then on kept returning to them. Now they were to carry on the good work from Hunsdon, but on an increased scale.

Pick really felt very much at home at Hunsdon because, by coincidence, it was in fact a family residence – being the former country home of Helena and Cedric Hardwicks. The old country house, seated squat and comfortably amid iron-railed meadows, was a red-brick three-storey affair with eight bedrooms, several bathrooms, large grounds with fruit and vegetable gardens, a hard tennis court and a side driveway. The house fronted a quiet lane close to Hunsdon village. It also had servants' quarters, large kitchens, and ten acres of grounds with a river Thames tributary running beside it. Requisitioned by the RAF, the aerodrome attached to it, with brick crewrooms, small blister hangars, well dispersed aircraft parking pens, and concrete perimeter track and runways was close to the sector station at North Weald. The entire sector guarded London from anything coming across the east coast and Essex marshes, or up the Thames Estuary.

The bulk of the Wing's baggage was due to follow personnel on by road from Sculthorpe to Hunsdon. Anticipating the usual gremlin delays, Pick and several colleagues stuffed large bags containing dress uniforms, shaving kits and other personal belongings into their little Pissers because it was 31 December, and that meant by fair means or foul, a not-to-be-missed-no-holds-barred New Year's eve celebration party. The year 1944 – or any other year for that matter – couldn't possibly be permitted to be born without a suitable welcome.

Before departing Sculthorpe, he announced to a dozen of his friends in the Mess – 'I should like to propose, and second, that we have a party tonight.'

Inexplicably uncertain of the likeliness of his being at Hunsdon long, he thought it prudent to place Ming into the temporary care of his second-in-command at Sculthorpe, who was remaining behind.

'Don't worry about her,' he reassuringly counselled. 'Just stuff her full of off-ration rabbit and she'll eat out of your hand, and not it. Her bark is worse than her bite, though everyone prefers her bark. And remember that every dog isn't a growler, and every growler – as you should know – isn't a dog.'

Pick was a great party personality, so those invited to the New Year's eve do wondered what he would pull this time. Would it be as memorable as when he walked on the Mess ceiling at Dishforth after the famous Bruneval raid?

King George and Queen Elizabeth had visited the unit soon after to meet some of the men who had taken part in the raid, and lunching in the specially spruced up spick and span Mess, the King turned to Pick to inquire:

'Is there any significance in your ceiling decoration?'

'No, Sir,' a somewhat shaken Pick responded, suddenly realising that cleaning of black footprints running from the door and up the wall to the centre of the ceiling, had been overlooked.

'I'm afraid it's the result of the Mess party to celebrate our return from Bruneval,' Pick explained, his bearing recovered. 'At the height of the proceedings my shoes were removed, my feet blackened with boot polish, chairs stacked on each other, and I was perched at the top making the footprints you can see. I'm sorry, Sir.'

'But what are those two especially large blobs at the centre of the ceiling?' the King asked.

'I regret to say, Sir, that those are the marks of my bottom,' came the dutiful reply, and both the king and Queen were very definitely amused.

Pick's 1943 New Year's party was equally unforgettable because baby Nick Pickard arrived precisely on New Year's Day, and with bad weather grounding planes, it was a wonderful chance to celebrate the arrival of a son for the CO of 161 Squadron.

An oak beam, just below ceiling height, ran the full length of the Mess bar, and the Pickard first-born's head-wetting party was well away when the most daring were challenged to cross the length of the beam, hanging by their toes. Naturally, the host had to have a go, but half way across, booze took its toll, and Pick fell. The following day he visited his wife and son in the maternity ward with a broken thumb in a plaster cast.

Worried, Dorothy asked whether he had been in a flying accident.

'I fell down the steps of an air raid shelter,' was his excuse.

'That,' said Dorothy, 'is a lie. You've never been in an air raid shelter in your life!'

His great friend and No. 2 Group comrade, Colonel Livry-Level of the Free French Squadron, which had also flown the 'No Ball' site attack that day, was one of the guests at the 1944 New Year's eve party at the Waldorf Hotel, off London's Strand, as were other French aircrew with their distinctive Cross of Lorraine uniform insignia.

As midnight grew close, the Frenchmen at one of Pick's tables in the ballroom of the Waldorf became, as many revellers noticed, strangely silent.

As the first midnight strokes of Big Ben's chimes were relayed into the ballroom, everything fell silent, the orchestra rose to its feet, and the dancers remained still. At the final stroke of twelve, instead of singing en masse the traditional Auld Lang Syne, almost with one voice those who wanted to acknowledge the fighting Frenchmen torn from their homes and families slowly and almost reverently began to sing the Marseillaise, softly accompanied by the orchestra. The French rose to their feet as one to join in, but were so overwhelmed by the gesture that they were unable to sing a word.

'Happy New Year!' Pick shouted to his party, 'and may there soon be peace on earth, which isn't so impossible as we only have to keep wars from breaking out.'

Only days before, the BBC had broadcast a message, recorded by Colonel Livry-Level, to the people of France, Prophetically for one who was to fly as a navigator and sole representative of France in the attack on Amiens prison, he had said in his broadcast home:

'My dear friends – friends I know and do not know – it is one of your own people speaking to you. The walls of your prisons are not so high nor so thick that they can prevent you from hearing me . . .'

A couple of weeks later, a 'new boy', who had never dropped a bomb on enemy territory, reported to Pick at Hunsdon to take command of 'B' flight of the 464 Squadron. Firm friend of Basil Embry, he was soon to be closely involved with Pickard's life too, and to make a crucial technical contribution to bombing effectiveness and prisoners' safety in the Amiens raid.

Former aero club instructor Squadron Leader Ian McRitchie, DFC, was utterly new to bombing when he reached Hunsdon on 18 January, but an old hand as a fighter pilot. Leaving Australia to join the RAF as a pilot, he downed four enemy night bombers, and after 105 sorties, was transferred at Embry's direct instigation to the RAF's Farnborough Research Establishment as a test pilot. Flying 25 different types of British, American and German aircraft, he fast developed into a brilliant technical 'boffin' and started coming up with all manner of innovations and ingenious answers to tactical problems.

Too long on ops, McRitchie was rested, but was restless. Someone suggested phoning Embry, then commanding defence of southern England. Immediately Embry tried pushing McRitchie into a night fighter development unit, but he ended with the Armament and Instrument Development Flight and the Aerodynamic Flight at Farnborough as a test pilot and researcher. Anxious to get back into flying action, he subsequently badgered Embry for a 'No Ball' unit posting, which is how he got to Hunsdon one month before the raid that was to cost him, and Pickard, so much.

Pickard knew there was a special on when he was advised from Mongewell Park that Embry was on the way to him.

'No reflection intended, but this is one I feel I ought to lead – it's a very touchy op,' Embry said, putting Pick in the picture. Hearing the details, Pickard understood and placidly accepted the necessity for Embry being No. 1 and he No. 2, acknowledging that the raid called for exceptional delicacy of judgement.

Embry warned:

'Apart from advance briefing of the three Wing Commanders and their navigators, which we shall do together, no one else is to be briefed until the day of the operation, particularly in view of present Met uncertainty as to when we can actually go. Complete secrecy must be observed.

'Your fighter escorts should give plenty of protection from the 109s – especially the Abbeville boys, who are closest to the target.

'I'm arranging for a film unit to accompany you,' Embry reported. 'This is one of which we need a complete film and photographic record,' he paused significantly – 'for a lot of reasons.'

As he left, he announced:

'I'll let you know as soon as "Jock" Cummings advises me on the best day for it, and if the weather dies on us and we have to scrub it that day, we'll do it the next morning, or the morning after that – we've got to smash those walls – and soon.'

The following day, when inspecting a Wing, Leigh Mallory asked:

'What about "Jericho"?'

Embry explained in some detail, but not fully – the C-in-C didn't need, or want, to know everything. Details were for others.

'We'll plaster those walls as soon as the weather lets us,' he promised.

116

'It is terrible to feel that we can't stop what's going on, simply because of bad weather,' Leigh Mallory complained impatiently. 'With flying conditions restricting operations so much, everything today is perfectly bloody, and from my point of view there's nothing good.'

And then he inquired:

'Basil, who is leading it?'

'I am, Sir,'

The C-in-C made no comment. Embry sensed something wrong. That evening, Coningham phoned:

'In no circumstances are you to fly on this operation.'

'But I've already briefed Pickard and everything is set to go as soon as conditions permit,' Embry's voice rose with anger and bafflement. 'I decided to go solely because I'm the best we have for the job. Of the seven daylight sorties Pickard has done with 2 Group, I have flown on five to help break him in. He's essentially a night man, but as experienced as he is at night ops, he's still comparatively green at low-level day bombing, and there's too much at stake!'

As far as he was concerned, Pick was only just learning day bombing traffic laws, and he didn't want him to learn them by accident. It would be impossible to measure his value to the RAF and to the Allies as a courageous leader.

'There would also be "Overlord" at stake if you were shot down and captured and they discovered who "Wing Commander Smith" really is,' Coningham firmly reminded him.

Embry was reluctantly forced to agree, and added no further protest.

Leigh Mallory had told Coningham:

'The man determined to throw away his life for the cause for which he is fighting can always do so. We can't afford Basil to risk doing so right now.'

Sympathetically, Coningham insisted to Embry:

'I am sorry, Basil, those are Leigh Mallory's orders, and he's most emphatic about it, so I'm afraid you've got to accept it.'

So Charles Pickard was to lead instead of him. Embry was apprehensive at the thought of having to throw all the responsibility of leading the attack onto Pick, now that he was forbidden to go himself. Nor was it any use thinking that if at first you don't succeed, try someone else. It was now or never for those in the gaol.

He returned to Hunsdon, with disturbing misgivings, to tell Pick the change of plan. He felt concerned for him, and in some strange way, for himself as well. His heart had reasons which reason couldn't understand.

The Wing Commanders of 487, 464 and 21st Squadrons, and their navigators, were summoned that evening to a heavily guarded briefing room. As they entered, the six immediately noticed a bulky covered object on the map table, and were surprised to see the AOC also there. Now they *knew* it was important. The prison model was uncovered and Embry began the story.

When he finished the background, Pick outlined the attack. Then, whilst the three navigators went over the route maps in detail, the AOC, Pick, and Wing leaders Bob Iredale, 'Black' Smith and 'Daddy' Dale, discussed their roles.

The navigators calculated the travelling time to the target area at just under one hour fifteen minutes. This meant that the first squadron would be due off at 10.45, with the others taking off at five minute intervals. The strike *had* to start at midday when the guards would be lunching and least prepared for trouble. The bombing interval between Squadrons was set at three minutes, to allow for the eleven-second delay bombs and time for debris to settle.

Assessed Canadian John McCaul, Wing Commander Bob Iredale's navigator:

'We should start our Channel crossing between Brighton and Beachy Head to landfall between Cayeux and Berk, then north of Abbeville to Doullens. From that point south east to the Arras-Amiens road at Albert, which would start the bombing run just east of Amiens, as the prison is located on this road. The distance from Albert to the target is approximately five miles, which we should cover in one minute.'

'It seems like a fairly straightforward raid, but it'll call for accurate navigation and timing if we're to maintain target secrecy to the last.'

Briefing of the rest of the crews was set for early next morning, until 'Jock' Cummings' evening weather report came in. There wasn't a hope in heaven of take-off yet.

'We nearly always seem to get the roughest ops on Sundays – probably because so many of us don't go to Church regularly,' said 'Daddy' Dale, 'so I bet it will be Sunday.'

There were no takers.

It turned out to be a Friday.

Basil Embry returned to Mongewell Park, and with him went the model – for security.

'Be sure not to include anyone with the twitch,' Pick cautioned his Wing COs, 'this one's too dangerous for any pilots or navigators with break-up signs.'

To his Wing leaders, as they parted company for the night, he added: 'We can't take too many chances with those prisoners' lives.' Then, with uncharacteristic bitterness:

'One of the worst things about war is that it seldom kills off the right people.'

'Well, you know what they say – only the good die young.' 'Daddy' Dale, the 38-year-old 'grand old man' of Hunsdon cheerfully reminded them, trying to change the mood, unaware of the weight suddenly thrown on Pick's broad shoulders by Embry being barred from the flight.

'The good die young,' Pick countered, 'because only the young die good.'

Dense cloud with intermittent sleet and snow showers had deteriorated flying conditions so much that ops had been completely wiped out. Grabbing the opportunity, Ian McRitchie had taken a twenty-four hour pass to see his wife and nine-month-old baby daughter in Surrey. Arriving back at base early next morning and encountering his friend and fellow Australian Bob Iredale, he was informed:

'Basil was here and was sorry to have missed you.'

'And,' Iredale confided,' "Black" Smith, "Daddy" Dale and I were briefed by Basil and Pick for an important raid due any day.'

Iredale said no more than that about the briefing, but McRitchie knew that when Basil Embry personally stepped in on a briefing, it *had* to be something special.

\*

Twenty-year-old Anne Marie Chedeville was standing on a chair balanced on her oval-shaped eighteen-inches-wide galvanised iron toilet Tinette, getting a grandstand view through her cell window of the schoolboy football match on a pitch adjoining the gaol, and giving cellmates a running commentary on the match.

The laughter and excited shouting of children was precious contact with the world outside, because the sound of children was the sound of the future. Everyone inside gave a lot of thought to the future, wondering if they had any future to think of.

Anne Marie was one of a group of two women and eight men detained the same day for aiding the Abbeville escape organisation of Abbé Carpentier – the priest who had scared the hell out of Maurice Holville because he would sing pop songs in English whilst cycling around his parish. The second woman arrested with Anne Marie was the Abbé's mother.

The Abbé had a well organised identity card and forged paper service, even producing false documents on his own printing press.

Fearing for his sixty-year-old mother's safety, the Abbé had pleaded with her not to get involved with his escape work, but she still did her part in forging identity cards, and caring for American and British aircrew and agents seeking temporary shelter before being passed along the evasion line.

The women's quarters were also appallingly overcrowded with up to five in a cell with one bed and four straw-filled palliasses on the floor shared with the mice. The bed was given to the Abbe's mother.

Prisoners were only physically searched – *everywhere* – on arrival. Cell searches, spasmodically carried out thereafter, never discovered the smuggled pieces of mirror used for checking outside activity. By prising open a cell door spyhole's external cap with a mirror piece, then pushing the mirror through, the corridor or gallery outside could be watched.

Tinettes were emptied once daily. To relieve themselves with some measure of privacy, most women erected a bed blanket screen. Two or three Tinettes were stored in a cell cupboard. When due for emptying and washing with disinfectant, they had to be pushed through a hole in a wall secured by a locked door on the other side. Tinettes were removed through this door, and at the end of each section there was a special place into which Tinettes were emptied.

Fortunately for the Abbé's arrested ten, he was being held and questioned in Lille gaol. Through frequent visits, his curate learned what he had told the Gestapo, and, passing this on to the Amiens ten, was able to help them synchronise their stories.

None discussed dangers within the hearing of strangers, for even the most seemingly trustworthy could be Gestapo infiltrators. Apart from the Abbe's mother, Anne Marie knew another of her companions, but for some inexplicable reason the fourth woman made her instinctively nervous, although Madame Berthe was undoubtedly born and raised in Abbeville.

'They've put me in here for listening to the BBC,' she told them. Everything about her appeared to add up correctly yet even the Abbé's mother squeezed Anne Marie's hand extra hard – as a warning – when at one time she started to lower her guard a little. A message smuggled to the Abbé's mother finally revealed that Madame Berthe had, in fact, almost told the truth – her imprisonment was indeed connected with listening to forbidden BBC transmissions.

By denouncing her husband for tuning in to the BBC,

forty-year-old Madame Berthe had had him imprisoned so that she could more freely enjoy her affair with an Abwehr officer. When her sixteen-year-old son turned on her for her treachery, she had accused him too of listening to the BBC and the boy was deported to Germany and died there. Everything was comfortable for her until the officer lover was posted elsewhere. Fearing retribution from relatives or neighbours, she had arranged her own arrest on a civil charge, in the interest of her own safety. The facts of the case were smuggled to fellow prisoners, with a warning that Madame Berthe was now undoubtedly spying for the Gestapo within the gaol.

'Is that what sex makes you do?' asked Anne Marie.

Madame Berthe was, in many respects even more despicable than prostitute Alice Durand, in an adjoining cell, who wouldn't let any pimp live on her earnings, and chose her lovers from top thieves. Whenever she wanted to unload a lover, she would tip off the police to some thievery he was about to pull. He would get caught, and another thief would replace him in Alice's affections. She believed the best way of ending one love affair was to start another. Unfortunately, the last bank robber lover she put away, got away, escaping during transfer from one gaol to another. Heading straight back to Alice to kill her, he ended in the morgue himself. As he was beating her up, she snatched a handy pair of shears to defend herself, and stabbed him to death.

Alice's cell companion, Helen Brunel, was, on the other hand, the golden-hearted type of tart. Awaiting execution for stealing military documents from an SS officer client who shouldn't have had them on him in the first place when out whoring, this wasn't the first time she had done her bit for her country.

Helen had almost child-like features, yet even in prison her sensuality suggested a warm bed. She also had the deviousness of a child, and could cover the art of deceit with incredible simplicity. Slender, fluffy haired, blonde, with the most innocent eyes anyone had ever looked into, she claimed she had been forced into becoming a prostitute, but the words somehow didn't match the body and even more suggestive talk. It was true she had once been, as she put it, 'Charity goods' – a promiscuous girl who didn't practice prostitution – but the basic fact was that Helen was a nymphomaniac who took on all comers so as not to wear out her own man.

'I need men – lots of them – and was never able to stay away from bad ones, which is how I started on the streets when I was eighteen,' she told two of her cell companions, Else Burton, mistress of an Allied agent – a clerk working for the police – and Florence Dupont, a secretary, arrested for passing secret fortification papers to an Intelligence network.

'I first learned about whores from the Bible, but when I asked my mother what the word meant, she scolded me and said it wasn't a word nice girls should use, so I asked why it was in the Bible, but she wouldn't reply. I soon found out all about it from the other girls at school.

'We get a lot of business because too many women are aggressive, and a man always wants to be a man and dominate. I'm expensive and very business-like about it all.'

'I'll vouch for that,' Alice Durand butted in. 'She even used to put a sign on her apartment door saying. "Gone to dinner – go fuck yourself".'

Helen, who looked anything but what she was, enjoyed the crack with the rest of them.

'I must say she rings up a lot of change on her cash register,' Alice said with respect.

'Cash register?' Florence Dupont queried.

'Her vagina – you innocent!' Alice laughed.

'One good vice will get you more attention than a dozen virtues, and my ambition was to run a high-price stable of call girls in Nice or Cannes, and I'll do just that if I ever get out of here alive,' Helen said dreamily. Life to her had been a dreamworld, but she had to wake up sometime.

She stopped, blew her nose, was clearly on the verge of tears at the thought of the death sentence hanging over her. Then, recovering, she cockily asserted:

'I'll be in business as long as man's instincts are like a bull, and he believes it's his role in life to shoot his sperm into where it will do the most good, then get the hell out of there as fast as possible.'

The sudden shock of a baby's cry almost over-balanced Anne Marie Chedville from the Tinette perch beside her cell window.

'I hope to God that's not another baby in here!' she said anxiously, turning to her companions. 'The last one's only just gone.'

Although the authorities tried to keep prisoners' children outside with a foster family or some social service, a baby sometimes remained with its mother in gaol until eighteen months old. A special cell in the women's section, called the nursing room, was provided, particularly if a baby was breast fed. One woman who gave birth in the gaol kept her daughter in prison for a year.

Beneath Anne Marie's cell was the constantly used women's solitary confinement cell. One inmate occupied it as punishment for shortening the skirt of her prison uniform. She said she wanted to 'make it more fashionable.'

Women civil criminals wore brown dresses with a long white chemise, and a cape. Like the men, they could either use their own shoes, or be supplied with clogs. Some had slippers or sandals, and if they wore stockings at all, they were their own, for none were issued.

Women 'politicals' also endured daily Gestapo interrogator sessions, but fortunately there has never been a man who could judge what a woman is truly thinking by listening to what she's saying. As the interrogator's attitude was always: 'If you weren't guilty, you would talk,' most of the women were schooled to talk freely about everything, except what the questioners really wanted to know.

As even young Anne Marie observed:

'I never tell the truth to people who are not worth it.'

Guided by the misguided assumption that if a woman shares a man's bed, she must also share most of his secrets, the Gestapo often indulged in husband and wife arrests. Consequently several married and betrothed couples were in the gaol, but although on different floors of the same building, they rarely glimpsed each other. They were forbidden official contact or any communication whatsoever, and could only reach one another through smuggled notes or messages sent via the plumbing 'telephone'.

The heating pipe 'telephone', running through all cells, was an invaluable system. 'Ringing' amounted to knocking on the pipe, then, when the receiver replied, 'conversation' could commence between unseen 'voices' of relatives and friends. It was possible to 'talk' to prisoners several cells apart. It took ages to tap out words, but time didn't matter. The code was 1, 2, 3, according to the alphabet position of the letter you wished to send. In preference to tapping long drawn out messages to adjoining cells, some managed to speak directly into the hole in the cell corner through which plumbing passed.

The gaol also had a unique 'talking newspaper'. Information defiantly picked up from BBC transmissions by friends outside was smuggled to two men in the 'political' building, and the two took turns at shouting war progress reports through their cell windows. With the men's quarters so close to the women's section, voices carried sufficiently.

'The Shouters', as they were called, also identified new arrivals, names having been collected by the prison barber on his rounds. Every morning before lunch, the Shouters announced internal news, keeping everyone informed about what was going on, including who was to be shot. Both Shouters disguised and alternated their voices to make location and identification difficult. One talked at auctioneer speed, thereby ensuring that any French-speaking German would need to be totally fluent to understand. Craftily, they never shouted if there was a German in corridors or in the prison courtyard, into which once daily in the afternoon twenty or more women were led single file to walk in silence for approximately twenty minutes. Those who wished were permitted to take turn exercising with a guard-provided skipping rope. Those receiving solitary confinement punishment exercised alone, some with long chains manacling their hands and feet.

Claire Archibald had seen it all – many times – because she had been inside many times, but she was normally accustomed to staying in the best, or at least second best, class hotels. Although Claire was a thief, she paid hotel bills meticulously.

'Even if you're a thief, not to pay a bill is the sign of an amateur. Why attract attention?'

When younger, the once beautiful Claire, familiar in both England and northern France, had frequented the hotels the elderly favoured. But she had stayed only long enough to discover who possessed valuables, and then start a fire. As guests hurried out, Claire hurried into their rooms to clear them of jewellery and cash.

Put away several times for this, she had switched to advertising herself as a 'nurse' specialising in care for elderly invalids. If a place appeared to have possibilities when she visited a potential client for an interview, she offered to stay – 'for an hour or so to get to know you better,' as she so kindly explained.

Offering to make some hot milk or tea, or read to the lonely invalid, she suggested: 'Have a little rest and we'll talk more later,' helpfully offering what she described as a 'gentle sleeping mixture' – not a drug – 'just a vegetable extract'.

Drugging the victim, she helped herself to whatever she wanted, and in one instance telephoned for a removal van to remove all the best furniture and carpets, leaving an invalid woman on the floor.

Claire, who of course spoke excellent English, was sharing a cell with Muriel Leroy, who also happened to speak almost perfect English. Muriel would have been attractive if she hadn't been so muscular and so masculine. Even her voice was like a man's. With the war severely curtailing her criminal acitivities, she had decided to reform and use her multi-lingual expertise to become an Intelligence courier operating between France, Belgium and

124

Switzerland. Unlike Claire, who had been imprisoned again for roguery, Muriel was experiencing her very first sample of gaol because of good deeds.

'War ruined things for me because you can't get about so easily and my business was international,' she informed Claire. 'I couldn't trade anymore with London, Brussels and Amsterdam.'

'I used to go to Hatton Garden diamond centre in London to visit a diamond dealer – after the banks were shut. I'd ask to see diamonds of a particular weight and quality, select what I wanted, then immediately have them made into a packet for collection the following day when I could draw payment from the bank.

'Diamonds were packed in special blue-tinted paper, and already knowing the approximate weight and size I intended to choose, I carried with me an identical size packet in the same paper, but filled with gravel. I always managed to distract the dealer for a few seconds to switch packets. The fake packet would be placed in the safe for me to collect the next day, but I flew straight back to Paris and enjoyed a good night's sleep with a very handsome haul.'

Now her sleep was less comfortable, and neither was she anticipating a restful night the following night as she was due to appear in the morning before a Tribunal at the Amiens Palais de Justice.

As they say in France, 'If you sleep, you eat,' meaning sleep is food for the body. Many, in perpetual pain from hunger, slept as much as they could because sleep was the best thing to do when you had nothing to do and not enough to eat. Food of any kind was also the main substitute for sex. Stomachs hungered for food, and bodies for affection and recognition as individuals.

'We not only have the right to be individual, we're obliged to be one,' insisted Florence Dupont, expecting to face a firing squad for her offence against the enemy.

'It takes guts to be an individual, and it can also be lonely, but it's better than being a nobody.'

Every night the prison babel hushed as the sound of a lonely girl's lovely voice shared her emotions in old songs. Afterwards, everyone lost themselves in thoughts, memories, prayers, and sleep – if mercifully it came – and night was disturbed only by the creaking beds of restless prisoners, and Tinettes scraping the floors.

*

Every day was bad, but Sundays were the worst because the place was too quiet – quiet enough to make you want to scream, which many did. Sunday was also the day for suicides, and for Mass.

Single file, they marched to the towering central circular hall known as the Rotonde, to be parked in rows of tiny cramped boxes ringing the Rotonde's three floors. Each tight cubicle held one prisoner, with the first two floors reserved for men, and the top for women. The boxes were just sufficiently open on one side for prisoners to face and see the central raised platform upon which the altar had been erected for Mass. Sixty male and female prisoners could worship together, but as there was only a single Mass a week, those wishing to attend were placed on a rotating list which allowed them to join the service once every few weeks.

On Sunday, 13 February 1944, Father Wyplier, who visited the gaol during the week as well as conducting Sunday Mass, climbed the spiral iron staircase to the little bridge leading to the altar platform. Guards remained at key exit points on all floors. Devoutly religious Helen Brunel was among the worshippers that morning.

There was no music, but reflecting the flickering altar candles, the glittering crucifix became a living symbol.

'In nomine Patris, et Filii, et Spiritus Sancti, Amen . . .

'In the name of the Father, the Son, and the Holy Spirit . . .'

Crossing himself, Father Wyplier commenced the Mass, moving towards the altar incanting:

'Introibo ad altare Dei – ad Deum qui laefificat juventutem meam . . .

'I will go to the altar of God – to the God of my joy and gladness . . .'

The human beings locked in the boxes all around him, whispered the traditional words with him almost as one, and the opening psalm phrase which followed, translated with deeper significance.

'Give sentence with me, oh God, and defend my cause against the ungodly people . . .'

Gently addressing the congregation, Father Wyplier managed, as always, to inject double depth into his words:

'My sons and daughters . . . praying is as natural to me as breathing, and whenever I am in trouble, guidance never fails to come – usually in the form of some self-decision,' he confessed.

'Too many of us pray in the morning and sin the rest of the day. Lack of faith and understanding has brought our world to the edge of destruction. The one thing that terrifies the godless is the thought that some day, all those who believe in God will finally begin acting their beliefs.

'How do you get faith? – You don't. You *have* it, for nobody can be an unbeliever – we either need to believe in God, or in no God. It is pointless blindly to oppose what we don't understand.

'I ask you all, who have so much on your minds and in your hearts, to dwell on a prayer written by St. Francis of Assisi:

'Lord, where there is hatred, let me sow love; where there is doubt, faith; where there is despair, hope; where there is darkness, light; and where there is sadness, joy.

'O Divine Master, grant that I do not so much seek to be consoled as to console, to be understood as to understand, to be loved as to love; for it is in the giving that we receive, it is in pardoning that we are pardoned, and it is in dying that we are born to everlasting life.'

Father Wyplier liked the prayer because it placed total responsibility for its answer upon the person who said it.

Back in her cell after Mass, Helen Brunel cried bitterly:

'My belief in God will die if these bastards have to wait until they get to Hell before paying for what they've done to millions of innocent people. I want them to pay in this world too.'

Madame Joly's irrepressible good humour was as inspiring, in its own way, as Father Wyplier's sermons. Her habit of looking at the bright side of anything was worth a great deal to most of her gaol companions.

As Madame put it:

'We owe Hitler something – if it wasn't for him we wouldn't know how happy we're not. Let's face it, when the worst comes to worst, it needn't be so bad.'

It was because some Germans couldn't take a joke that she was imprisoned.

Secretary to an insurance agent, she was forever giving people something to laugh about in not-so-funny times. Her practical jokes were notorious.

'Laughing's the best way of forgetting,' she said, and mailed to dozens of relatives and friends black bordered In Memoriam cards stating:

WE DEEPLY REGRET TO ANNOUNCE THE SUDDEN
DEATH OF OUR BELOVED REICHSFÜHRER
ADOLF HITLER

The card bore the names of all Hitler's General Staff.

The joke was too successful and almost inevitably, one of the cards reached the Gestapo. Tracing its source, they raided Madame Joly's home, discovered more cards, found the printer, and arrested him too. The Nazis couldn't take a joke – they put you in gaol for making fun of them. Madame Joly was sentenced to eighteen months in Amiens prison, but nothing could squash her spirit nor her seemingly endless fund of stories, like the one about the hefty brown-shirted Nazi stormtrooper studying a public noticeboard above which was a slogan declaring:

'The Jews Are Our Misfortune'

A small, very short-sighted Jew wearing thick glasses, stood behind the Nazi straining to read the noticeboard.

'Excuse me, Sir, but what does it say?' he nervously inquired.

Looking contemptuously down at him, the stormtrooper sneered:

'It says the Jews are our misfortune.'

The little man turned away muttering:

'Let's hope so! – Let's hope so!'

Madame Joly, who kept right on laughing in gaol, and making others laugh with her, was a born optimist whose interpretation of the difference between an optimist and a pessimist was that the German optimist was saying:

'We are definitely going to lose this war.'

And the pessimist:

'Of course, but when? – When?'

Madame Joly, advising gaolmates that if they didn't laugh at their troubles now, they wouldn't have anything to laugh about when they were older, boasted:

'I've inside information that we're winning the war.'

'What kind of information?'

'Straight from a high-ranking Luftwaffe officer who told me a story going the rounds which proves the rot is setting in, because when they start telling them like this, we've got good grounds to be optimistic.'

'Well, come on – what's the story?'

Suddenly, Madame Joly was uncharacteristically serious.

'This isn't one of my usual jokes. This really *is* openly being repeated around Luftwaffe Somme bases, so I think it's a genuinely important indication.

The anecdote went:

Hitler, who was going crazy trying to decide the best way to invade England, was told that an old rabbi imprisoned in a concentration camp, was said to know the secret of how the Hebrews crossed the Red Sea without even getting their feet wet.

'If we learn that secret, my armies can cross the English Channel and conquer Britain – I must know it! – I must know it!' Hitler cried. 'Bring that rabbi to me personally.'

The old rabbi was taken from the concentration camp, driven to Berchtesgaden and taken before Hitler, who promised to free thousands of Jews if told the secret.

'Moses simply used a miracle-making wooden staff to part the sea, that's all,' the rabbi said, 'and that staff, with inscriptions proving its origin, was found, and is preserved to this day.'

'I must have it immediately at all costs!' the Führer screamed, almost biting the carpet with excitement. 'Where is it?'

'In the British Museum,' said the rabbi.

It was a swine of a day. 17 February was as bad as the 16th – foul weather cancelled all air ops. Deep snow blanketed the ground. Dense clouds and blinding blizzards didn't help either. Central Meteorological Forecasting Establishment's report deepened Embry's mood. There was no sign of weather let-up. The phone rang. It was Coningham.

'If we're going to do this raid at all, Basil, it *has* to be in the next twenty-four hours. We've just heard the Gestapo intend executing a hundred inside the gaol within a couple of days. And even more crucial is something I can't go into at the moment.'

'More crucial than a hundred executions?' Embry probed.

'Yes.'

Coningham didn't explain further.

'It's all the more galling because it is really a relatively shallow penetration job and the approaches are fairly easy,' Coningham continued. 'All we need is good weather, and a bit of luck.'

'That all!'

The solitary hope was improvement of conditions over northern France, because no weather was ever bad enough to assume there could be no attack. As always, the ruling factor was the state of weather over enemy territory. Final decisions were normally based on later afternoon information. When updated forecasts arrived, Embry was unhappy with the icing index, but at least there were indications the situation might be somewhat better over France itself by the morrow.

Nineteen aircrews – eighteen attackers and one photographic unit – had been isolated in readiness at Hunsdon for two days, with the entire station confined to camp the whole of the 16th and 17th. The three selected squadrons were a mixture of British, Aussies, New Zealanders, one Canadian, and one Frenchman – 45-year-old Colonel Philippe Livry-Level, or Squadron Leader Livry, as he was known in the RAF. Livry, now a 21 Squadron navigator, had previously teamed with Pick on many clandestine operations.

Security men were specially drafted to the airfield and its surrounding neighbourhood, to cover all local pubs and cafés as a precaution against leakages. Phones were tapped, mail censored. Not even a gossiping letter home about 'something interesting in the wind' was allowed to slip by.

One aircrew navigator phoned a girlfriend, explaining he wouldn't be seeing her for a few days because of 'special circumstances'. Security picked up the call and a furious Pickard summoned all the stand-by crews to a meeting to announce:

'One bloody unthinking fool put all our lives and a whole op in danger because he didn't think. "Careless Talk Costs Lives" isn't a load of propaganda crap but an essential warning,' he declared angrily, adding:

'If enemy agents over here get a sniff of what we're up to, they'll be on to it. If they find out too much, we'll have had it.

'I won't name the offender in front of you, but will deal with him personally. Remember, everything you say or do is being listened to and observed.'

Security-conscious Pick stuck on a crew room wall a poster showing a French peasant, in baggy pants, queuing outside a brothel, with a caption saying:

'Avant partir en operations prenez garde que les poches sont vides!'

Shortly before 5 a.m. in the darkness of 18 February, Embry's black Humber staff car drew up in front of the Mongewell Park main building. First to emerge from the HQ was Squadron Leader Ted Sismore, hugging an outsize wooden box housing the Amiens prison model which he gladly unloaded on the rear floor of the car, after which he and Embry stepped in and made themselves comfortable, feet propped on the model box.

The drive through darkness to Hunsdon along snow-carpeted roads took well over two hours. Weather was atrocious, but briefing was fixed for 8 a.m. Roused at 6 a.m., the 19 crews put their noses outside momentarily, then pessimistically withdrew them inside again. As blinding gusts of snow almost entirely obscured the runway, it was agreed by all that unless this was a very exceptional attack, it would almost certainly be scrubbed and postponed to another day. But the buzzing CO's bell, summoning Flight Commanders, instantly confirmed this wasn't a routine job. Moments later, the base throbbed with the roar of *Mosquito* engines under test; petrol bowsers topped up fuel tanks; armourers armed guns and prepared bombs; maintenance and servicing teams – riggers, fitters, electrical mechanics, radar and signals personnel checked and re-checked equipment in hangars and on workbenches.

Chatter was sparse among breakfasting crews in the mess. They remained abnormally silent until someone admitted almost not making it back to base, the night before they had all been restricted to camp.

'The car got bogged down in the snow, and the more the wheels churned it up, the deeper we sank until we were well and truly stuck. We had to wade back on foot through all that bloody snow, otherwise we'd have been forced to spend the night in the car . . . with the girls.'

A chorused moan rose from every throat in the mess, and the previously tense atmosphere eased an instant until loudspeakers in the barracks, messes and hangars blared:

'Pilots and navigators of 21,487, and 464 Squadrons report immediately to briefing room!'

Reaching the Operations Block, they found strict security enforced, RAF Military Police checking each man's identity card, ticking names off a list.

As they filed into the Briefing Room, crews noted all windows were closed, and blinds drawn. Everyone stared at the large sheet-covered bulky object resting on the table positioned at the front of the briefing platform. The five-feet-square, six-inches-deep box obviously contained a model of the target. It couldn't be anything else.

'What is it, Tony?' The question was aimed at Flight Lieutenant Tony Wickham, the photographic unit pilot, because photo crew generally gleaned advance information of a target to enable them to fit suitable cameras to their aircraft. 'Pick didn't fill me in on all the details last night, only told me where, the route, and that the raid would be very photogenic, so you'll have to be patient a little longer.

'When I asked whether it was a big factory of some kind, he said it was something like that and I'd understand the need for absolute secrecy when I heard about it at the briefing. Sorry, but that's all the gen I've got.'

Wickham had already fitted two fixed cine cameras into his *Mosquito* and stowed away two hand-held cameras in the nose, ready for use.

Some of the crews clustered around the briefing room stove warming numbed hands whilst waiting for things to start; others stamped cold feet, but speculation and stamping died as Pick entered, followed by Embry and Sismore. The door was immediately locked behind them by Security Police.

Everyone stood to attention as the trio strode to the dais, and Embry opened the proceedings.

'Right, gentlemen. Sit down.'

Pickard swept aside the curtains over the giant target maps affixed to the back wall of the room, and all eyes studied maps showing the entire approach, red markings on the attack and return areas indicating German airfield and anti-aircraft defence positions.

'Gentlemen,' Embry began, 'your target today – weather permitting – is Amiens, but not the marshalling yards this time – the prison.'

The gasp was unanimous. 'Prison!' echoed around the room.

Embry knew precisely how to gauge an audience, how to reach them, and get the best from them.

With an almost melodramatic flourish, Pick, also revelling in shock moments such as this, removed the sheet to expose the papier-mâché model of the prison on the table.

Examining it at eye level enabled the crews to obtain the same oblique view in miniature, as if flying over the original at anything from 50 to 500 feet. By selecting a combination of easily recognisable landmarks such as church spires and factory chimneys which could be adopted as navigation markers, a target approach route could be clearly defined. At the start of the approach the landmarks might be as far as two miles apart, but the distance between markers would be gradually narrowed until eventually it was like flying down a visual approach beam. Known positions of all light flak guns were marked and taken into account when deciding approach. The model helped crews recognise the objective and determine aiming points, especially if the attack was to be made by more than one sub-formation of six aircraft.

'This is a most unusual mission,' Embry continued, 'dedicated not to the destruction of lives, but to saving them. In your hands are at least a hundred valuable men we need freed to play their part in the invasion of Europe, when it comes.

'There has been much debate as to whether this attack is feasible at all. It can only be carried out by low-level *Mosquitos*. Inside the prison are more than a hundred who have been condemned to death and due to be shot at any moment for assisting the Allies, and there are hundreds more – men and women – expecting similar verdicts, some sentenced for helping airmen like us shot down in France.

'The prison is strongly guarded and there's no conceivable ground operation which could help these prisoners. Only by breaking the walls with our bombs can we give our friends any reasonable hope of escape, and that's what we are going to have a crack at today. We're going to burst that prison wide open.

'If we make a good job of it and give those inside a chance to get away, the French underground will be outside to take over from there.

'I've asked the Met man if God is doing his best for us this morning and he has reported "Moderate visibility for northern

France." I ask each of you to remember that should weather conditions prevent the operation from taking place today, it must continue to be regarded as top secret.'

Having said all he had come to say, Embry stopped, and let Pickard take over. As he moved to the back of the room, Pick stepped forward to the table and the model. The importance of careful briefing couldn't be overestimated.

'We've *got* to make a success of this,' he began emphatically.

'Eighteen of you are detailed for the trip. In addition, the Film Unit aircraft is coming to see what job you make of it. The first six of you are to breach the walls. The walls have to be broken, so this will need real low-level flying. You've got to be right down on the deck, and as the walls are only about twenty-five feet high, if we're not damned careful our bombs are going to bounce right over them, land inside the prison and blow everyone to smithereens. We've got to cut that risk down to minimum. You've got to be below the height of the wall when you let go – down to ten feet, if possible. There are no obstructions in the way on your run up, so you should be able to make it. Timing's essential if we're to avoid blowing each other up with our own bombs.'

Warming up and indicating the model on the table, Pick outlined:

'When you study this in detail shortly, you'll find the prison itself is in the form of a cross. At its east and west ends are small buildings, which, according to our information, are quarters of the Nazi prison guards. The second six aircraft are to prang those quarters. I don't suppose all the Nazis will be inside at once, but we're sure to get some and it'll add up to general confusion, giving prisoners a better break.

'The Photographic Unit aircraft will follow this second formation and orbit the target, filming results of the raid.'

He looked at Tony Wickham.

'We're dropping eleven-second delay bombs, Tony, so you'll have to lose a minute or so near the target to give them a chance to go off before you run over the prison. Then you can make as many runs as the cameraman wants and as you consider expedient.'

Tony nodded.

Pointer in hand, Pick motioned to the large-scale maps behind him.

'You see that the prison lies north-east of Amiens, outside the town and in open country on the road to Albert, which we'll initially make for. The prison is actually on Route Nationale 29, the Route d'Albert, a long straight road linking Amiens with Albert, some 29 kilometres away.

'The three-storey prison building is roughly cruciform, the longer arms of the cross run parallel to the road. One end houses civil prisoners – criminals – the other women prisoners. Extensions have been added to each end to house German guards. The short arm of the cross runs north-south, at right angles to the Route d'Albert, with the longer part of the arm holding so-called "political" prisoners – the ones we're trying to help. At the intersection of the cross, a watch tower has been built into the gabled roof, some sixty feet up, giving guards a virtually uninterrupted view of the prison and its rectangular compound, which contains various other buildings, including workshops and stores.'

He halted briefly to let details sink in. There was much to cover, and he knew the briefing held one devastating below-the-belt body blow, but that would have to be the final punch. He needed clear concentration now.

Then he dived into the attack plan:

'The first six aircraft have to breach the outer prison wall in two places. The Squadron will split into two sections of three. The first will run straight in along the Route d'Albert and attack the east wall here.' He pointed to the wall at the base of the model cross. 'The second section of three aircraft, ten miles from the target, will break away to the right at sufficient height to allow them to watch the leading three, then attack the northern wall on a north-south run, immediately following the explosion of the bombs of the leading section. That should give us our two breaches.

'It's vital to break two sides of the wall. Breaches on one side only could give guards a chance to seal off that side of the prison, but if two walls are smashed, that should be impossible.

'Timing for the attack – Zero hours.

'The second six, again split into two sections of three, are to lay bombs against the walls of the main prison building – the most delicate task of all. The leading three aircraft of the second Squadron will attack the south-eastern end of the main building, and second section of three the north-western end, similar to the first Squadron's attacks.

'Timing – Zero plus three minutes.'

Pointing to the two annexes at the base and the apex of the model cross, he explained:

'These two low extension buildings, the quarters of the German guards, are built right in the shadow of the prison, using the main prison wall as support. These annexes are to be bombed, using a section of three aircraft for each annexe. This should severely damage the main prison wall, shake every cell door off it hinges and every lock out of its hasp. Remember – watch your timing so you don't fly into the blast of each other's bomb's.

'The third Squadron is a reserve force. It will approach the target as in the previous two attacks – one section from the east and one from the north – but only bomb if it is seen that one of the previous attacks has failed, and employ the methods of the initial waves. Targets will be decided by me and attack timing will be Zero plus thirteen minutes.

'This is crucial because, according to Intelligence information on prison routine, most of the German guards lunch at noon, and it's also lunch hour outside the prison, which means there'll be more people around in the streets for escapers to mingle with. In addition, many prisoners will be in the mess hall for the midday meal, which should make it easier for them to break out into the prison courtyard during the confusion the bombing will cause.'

Route procedure details were Group HQ navigation officer Squadron Leader Sismore's job.

Completing the first part of his briefing contribution, Pick turned to Ted Sismore:

'Nav – it's yours from here.'

Sismore took over.

'Your course is west around London, just short of Reading, to Littlehampton, across the Channel to one mile south of Doullens, and south-east from there to the Arras-Amiens road at Albert, which is the start of your bombing run to the prison. It's a beautiful approach because the prison is actually on this road, and it's dead straight. You'll hit the road about four to five miles from the prison – just follow the road and you can't miss it.

'Once over the coast, you're virtually there, and should cover the distance from Albert to the gaol in little over a minute – an essential timing factor, as successive waves attacking at right angles require fine judgement to avoid mid-air collisions. With eleven-second delayed action bombs, timing errors could be appalling for following aircraft, so stick to the time-table. I'll tell you precisely when and where your bombs should land, and if you can't drop them in the right place at the right time, don't drop them at all.

'Your route is intended to mislead the enemy to maintain target secrecy until the last – they won't be expecting us to go for the prison. But this type of attack is in fact very close to what you have been carrying out these past weeks on "No Ball" sites, with pin-point targets demanding individual aim by each pilot. Remember, going in waves of six at ground level, echeloned to port or starboard, depending upon the direction of turn away from the target, is a hundred per cent accurate method of attack. As long as you fly in good formation it's possible to get six aircraft over the pin-point before bombs from the first aircraft explode. Remaining waves, of course, have more difficulty in seeing the target because of smoke and debris, but, if necessary, the leader will have to rocket to five hundred feet from time to time in order to locate his exact position.'

Sismore stopped an instant to give them time to swallow it all, then was off again:

'The IO [Intelligence Officer] will be filling you in on enemy defences, observation posts, flak batteries, and other possible interferences, but the AOC now accepts the policy of carrying out a reasonably long run to the target, flying straight and level, instead of taking violent action to avoid flak, as was the practice heretofore. Flak evasion for this attack will therefore consist mainly of turns of ten to fifteen degrees, combined with changes of height, with the proviso that flak on the bombing run must be accepted. A steady bombing run, in good formation, over-rides all other considerations. Unless we can put the bombs where we want them on the prison, we might as well stay home. We've found that if a target is to be destroyed, it's more economical to visit it once, complete the job and accept the casualties, rather than have to return to it two or three times. The cumulative casualties are usually higher than they would be if we accepted the casualties which occur from taking a proper and steady bombing run.

'A half-hearted attack is far more likely to be dangerous than a really vigorous one.

'The IO will also be detailing several blind spots between ack-ack batteries, which you can use on this trip for going in and out of France. There's one choice spot with forests of tall trees. The guns are all on the west side of the trees, so you can nip in low on the eastern side – up over the cliffs, below the trees, where the guns can't fire at you.'

'Each formation of six *Mosquito*s will have one Squadron of *Typhoon*s as close escort, and fighters will rendezvous with you as follows:

'First attack force – one mile east of Littlehampton at Zero minus forty-five minutes. Second attack force – one mile west of Littlehampton at Zero minus forty-two minutes. Third attack force – at Littlehampton at Zero minus thirty-two minutes.'

Navigators normally relied on the various flight plan headings provided on the operation day to steer the course, but maintenance of headings depended on wind. With virtually unpredictable conditions to contend with, Sismore was only too conscious the Amiens navigators would have to work wonders to keep the course and time-table, as well as take avoiding action.

'You'll be so low – below the radar – that they'll have to guess where you're headed,' he assured them confidently. 'They'll imagine you're going one way, then you'll turn and throw them. Although their Controller will try and assess your route, without radar he'll be mainly dependent on Luftwaffe fighters feeding him info as to your course, or artillery batteries saying: 'We can see six of them over us,' but by the time that's been relayed back, you'll have turned again. You'll be making several slight jinks [changes of course] to keep the Luftwaffe guessing and throw their fighters off. If you had no one else to worry about you could turn how you liked, but in a formation with five people behind you, it must be a slower longer turn. You must really watch it. If you're flying only thirty feet up you can't tip the wings, otherwise you'll hit the bloody ground. Whatever turns or avoiding action you have to take, don't forget the target isn't far inland, so you've very little time, and you won't be coming straight home out of France either, to throw their fighters off you.

'Following each attack on the target, sections of three aircraft of each formation are to endeavour to regain close company as soon as possible. For the homeward journey, turn right from the target for St. Saveur, Senarpont, Tocqueville, Hastings, and base, and even in this foul weather, acquaint yourselves with the position of the sun in the sky relative to the course home, in case your compass gets knocked out and you become separated.

'For emergency homing, head for Friston. Your special VHF codeword is "Renovate".'

From the back of the room Basil Embry's piercing eyes took in everything and everyone, knowing that the only thing that could be achieved without unstinting effort was failure. They were all fully conversant with his low-level bombing policies, and there were twenty-four DFCs and thirteen DSOs among them. This was one occasion when briefing couldn't afford to be sloppy or miss a single point, for an oversight could have fatal results. Emphasis of all possible factors was always vital, and never more so than today with the gamble greater than any in the room realised.

Pick positioned himself again behind the table.

'Before I ask you to gather round for a closer look at the model, and also invite questions you want to toss at me, or anyone else, I must touch again on the final phase of this op.'

'As I said earlier, when the last six Mossies arrive ten minutes after the second attack, their work will entirely depend on the success or failure of the first two sections. If the job's been well done, the third Squadron will pass north of Amiens and set course for home, bringing their bombs back with them.'

Wing Commander 'Daddy' Dale, C.O. of the RAF 21st Squadron, stood up.

'Who will decide whether the attack is a success or not, sir?'

'I shall be flying as number six of the second wave,' Pick replied, 'and when I've dropped my bombs, I'll peel off and circle – probably just north of the prison. From there I can assess the damage and radio instructions to the last wave leader. If I signal "red, red, red," he'll know he's being warned off and go home without bombing. If I say "green, green, green" they go in and bomb. The film aircraft will have just as good a view as myself of the whole show – perhaps even better – so as an additional precaution, it can act as cover. Therefore if you don't hear me give the signal and hear the answering acknowledgement, Tony can give the "red" or "green" himself before the third wave comes in.'

He halted. Although never the nervous type, he had qualms about what he was now to say.

'If I see prisoners escaping, I shall radio the third Squadron to return home.'

He faltered. It was unlike him, and everyone sensed it. Then, voice slightly lowered, added:

'If none are getting out, I will radio the Squadron to bomb the jail.'

The silence that followed said everything.

A shade less steadily, Pick went on:

'We have been informed that the prisoners would rather be killed by our bombs than by German bullets.'

The crews stared aghast at him. So the prisoners' choice was escape, or die . . . by German firing squads, or Allied bombs . . . *their* bombs.

Embry had warned all concerned with the planning of the raid, including underground in France, that it was bound to cause casualties among the prisoners, but had been assured repeatedly that even if the raid saved only a few, the sacrifice would be worth while. There was also the new element just added.

The idea of killing friends weighed heavily on his mind as he studied the drawn faces of the *Mosquito* crews who had just been instructed to do the killing. It was a terrible burden to have to issue such an order – one, Embry felt he had to carry alone.

'Those who haven't borne such responsibility can never fully appreciate the mental torment of the commander who says, "Yes, we will do it, and this is how it will be done",' he had confided to Ted Sismore as they drove to the briefing. 'And the burden will be made no easier by having to sit on the ground and watch others put my plan into execution.'

Pickard sliced through everyone's thoughts with –

'Any questions?'

The obvious was echoed in unison by almost the whole assembly:

'Who's in first, and who last?'

What they were really asking was, who might have to do the dirty job?

He had in fact decided the night before to send the New Zealanders in first because of a recent incident totally unconnected with the Amiens raid. Contrary to regulations, one of the Wing's New Zealand pilots had indulged in aerobatics over the camp. While trying one trick too many, he had stalled his *Mosquito* and crashed into the middle of the camp, killing himself, his navigator, and four WAAF parachute packers. Pickard couldn't afford to let this appalling indiscipline, nor the deaths it caused, pass without summoning all Squadrons and reading the riot act. The New Zealanders took it hard, and, to restore their self respect, he intended to let them spearhead the Amiens operation; but now, because of the effect of his final briefing bombshell, he wasn't too sure about the fairness of such an arbitrary choice.

Pulling a coin from his pocket, he gazed around with an embarrassed smile and declared:

'We'll toss for it. Loser stays in reserve.'

The three Wing Commanders stepped forward to call – 'Black' Smith of the New Zealand 487 Squadron; 'Daddy' Dale of the British 21st, and Bob Iredale of the Australian 464 Squadron.

The tension was electric.

He tossed.

Smith and Iredale called 'heads'. Dale, 'Tails'.

The British had drawn the 'dirty job' and showed their unhappiness.

'God, you're lucky bastards!' exploded Dale.

'Too right we are!' Aussie Iredale replied typically with a broad grin of relief.

So it was after all to be 487 Squadron in first, and 464 next, with the 21st in reserve.

At this point Pickard announced:

'I want you all to come and have a look at the model of the prison and get every detail fixed in your minds.'

Surging forward, they clustered around the table, crews staying together, concentrating on the sections that concerned them. For an hour they studied the model, checked and rechecked maps, routes, timings, call signs. From the Signals Officer they were informed that the first attack's call-sign would be 'Dypeg'; and their ground control call-sign 'Ailsome.' Their fighter escort's call-sign was 'Garlic'.

The second attackers' call-sign would be 'Canon'; their ground control call-sign 'Bellfield', and fighter escort call-sign 'Cajole'. The final bomber Squadron's call-sign was to be 'Buckshot'; ground control's call-sign 'Greenship', and their fighters' call-sign 'Dunlop'.

All bomber leaders would be permitted to call their escorts direct in emergency.

Ian McRitchie had a query that he felt it would be wrong to raise for all to hear until he was sure of the answer. He took Pick aside.

'Have HQ considered that there has to be a speed limitation on putting bombs into a brick or bluestone wall?' McRitchie asked.

Having a very healthy respect for McRitchie's perceptive knowhow mind, particularly remembering his experience in the Armament and Instrument Development Flight at Farnborough, Pick was attentive.

'What's the point?' he asked.

'Faster than about 240 m.p.h. the bomb casing is likely to fracture and render the bomb useless,' McRitchie unhesitatingly answered.

The words floored Pick. If bombs fractured, not only would the whole raid be abortive, but there wouldn't be a second chance as the ineffective attack would have told the Germans, as clear as if we had written them a letter of our intentions. Mass executions would be carried out before we could even try again, that is if we were insane enough to do so.

McRitchie had thrown a timely spanner right into the planners' whole minutely worked out concept. If right . . .

There was no Embry to consult – he had already gone with Ted Sismore and was somewhere on the roads in a staff car and impossible to reach before scheduled take-off time. To postpone, with every minute counting, could also be disastrous. It was his baby now.

'Hold it, everybody!'

Pick silenced the chatter.

'I've an extra point to make – It is *absolutely essential* for pilots to keep bombing drop speed *under* 240 m.p.h.' He paused before emphasising: '*This is a must!*'

Within minutes, McRitchie followed up with another invaluable caution:

'On the run-in for the bomb drop, don't fly in formation, as we usually do for bombing. Follow the line astern. This should enable us to get the bombs straight into the guardhouse.'

Pick passed this advice on to all the others, and reflected that McRitchie's posting to Hunsdon only four weeks ago could prove an extraordinary touch of destiny – if he was right about the bombs. If he was, then God *must* be keeping an eye on those poor bastards in the gaol.

At ten o'clock hot tea was served, as crews continued to familiarise themselves with the prison model until they knew it almost as well as their own homes.

'I've just called Group HQ,' Pick outshouted the hubbub and chit-chat, which immediately stopped again.

'It's still snowing over south-eastern England, visibility's bad, but we can get off the deck and "Jock" Cummings and his Met gang say it may improve across the Channel, so Group have given the OK but have left the final decision to us. Well, as far as I'm concerned, this is one raid where further cancellation is unthinkable. If the slightest hint gets out of what we're up to, those Amiens prisoners will have had it and be shot instantly, so we'd better get going and make a good job of it.

'*And, absolute radio silence all the way.* If any bugger opens his mouth up there, he'll be off my station tonight. What's more, if anyone brings a bomb back to this aerodrome without a damned good reason, I'll deal with him. Everyone got that? It's *got* to be a bloody good show, so off we go!'

When someone somewhat nervously raised a last-minute navigational query about the route, Pick, jutting his face towards the questioner, snorted impatiently:

'Bugger the course! – Just follow me – you'll be all right.'

If he had been born out of this century, he would have been a Cavalier or Roundhead. He wasn't the greatest station administrator, but he knew how to lead and how to fight.

'No more ifs,' he insisted. 'It's now, or it's too late – we can't wait for better weather anymore.'

Tomorrow could be two days too late for yesterday's job.

With that slow boyish smile of his, Pick added softly.

'Let's just hope the Met boys are bloody right about it being clearer over France, otherwise we're liable to have to get out and walk.'

Recovering vocal volume, he bellowed:

'Synchronise watches, please!'

# 9 Opportunity knocks at noon

'There's a lot of flu about so take care.'

An unusual number of phone callers in and around Amiens seemed to have the same solicitous thought on Friday, 18 February. The epidemic warning was simply cautioning those scheduled for the now daily mid-day stand-by duty close to the prison, that there were a lot of Germans about. The dangers were over-confidence, excessive daring, and waiting at rendezvous points.

Some hundred locals outside, and sixteen prisoners inside – including Dr. Mans, Maurice Holville, Jean Beaurin, his mother, and twelve other Sosie group members in the cells – were in on the secret of the raid being possible any day now.

A week ago, Pepe had told his assistants only one fact:

'If aerial bombing take place, it'll be at mid-day, so from today on, make it your business every day to be in the vicinity around that time.

He added:

'Opportunities, like eggs, come one at a time, so it's up to us to take full advantage of every one of them.'

At least knowing there was a fixed hour meant they needn't risk hanging around the gaol too much, arousing suspicion through constantly being seen in the area. It was obvious the authorities were expecting trouble – heavily increased guards and extra-frequent motorised patrols were proof that the portion of prison plans found on their shot comrade, Serge, hadn't been forgotten. As all one needs to be a pessimist is to look at things as they are, many waiting to help escapes were pessimistic about the chances. Others calmly accepted that the only thing to do was to make the best of the worst of it.

All were aware that the main entrance was heavily guarded by machine-guns covering every approach, and that a direct telephone line connected the prison guard room with the SS barracks within the walls. Frontal attack would be hopeless unless the planes caused enough chaos. A dozen look-outs were positioned in the very few houses close to the gaol. Several, who spoke fluent German, were wearing borrowed SS uniforms with special Resistance recognition markings. There were no houses opposite the prison, which had fields back and front.

Pepe, who had launched the boat, wasn't at the oars on the day – he was in Normandy, in Caen, checking possibilities of attacks on gaols at Caen and Rouen to free others.

He left on Wednesday afternoon and, to cover during his absence, Admiral Rivière and Dominique Ponchardier found professional excuses to come to Amiens early Thursday morning. Their dual presence was highly dangerous, because if both were arrested or killed, the Sosies would be severed from their life-line link with Allen Dulles in Switzerland.

Before leaving, Pepe established controls for the Admiral and Dominique to enable them to direct without breaking cover. The ready-made arrangements they took over envisaged an incredible range of requirements.

Stand-by transports were especially difficult, as it was unsafe for any vehicle to hover too long in the prison vicinity. The midday schedule eased the problem by limiting the parking period. Each day, about noon, ten large trucks – a butcher and a baker's delivery vans, plus several private cars – made a point of being in the area. All were gazogene vehicles. Only Germans and their associates had privileged petrol cars, while ordinary Frenchmen chugged about in contraptions with a small rear furnace, which supplied wood gas to a balloon-like container on the roof. Top speed of the gazogenes was around 30 miles per hour – if you were very lucky.

Everyone with a car or truck with acceptable reasons for being on the roads, and ready to assist, was recruited. Apart from briefly parked vehicles, some arranged journeys to pass the prison at the right time.

Finally, Pepe, the bicycle repairer, naturally also provided a supply of bicycles stored at nearby houses and shops, as well as a few Velo-taxis – the heavy two-wheeled bicycles towing a wickerwork seat for two.

Redoubtable Madame Vignon, 'Wardrobe mistress of Amiens', had been requested to provide a consignment of clothing of all types, shapes, and sizes – male and female. A lot of shot-down American and British airmen had said 'Thank you' for their lives to petite, plump, grandmotherly Madame Vignon, whose contribution to their freedom was collecting old clothes from wherever she could and keeping them for force-landed Allied aircrews on the run. Her big house in rue Jules Barni, next to the largest Amiens military barracks, resembled an over-stocked secondhand clothes warehouse. A devoted fan of American and British airmen, whom she looked up to as gods, she sometimes hid a dozen aircrew at a time in her home, and even had a two metres deep hole dug in her courtyard and covered by a metal sheet to shelter evaders from bombing while they were staying with her. She notified two of her emergency wardrobe suppliers – Gendarme Edouard Robine, and building contractor Michel Dubois – that her courtyard shelter, at present unoccupied by aircrews, was available for gaolbreakers. Robine, Dubois and Lieutenant Marceau Laverdure of Amiens Gendarmerie jointly ran an Allied Intelligence service and escape chain which had its own mobile radio transmitter, in direct contact with London, operating within Amiens itself. It was garage proprietor Raoul Debeauvois' responsibility to keep transmissions constantly on the move to avoid detection. A network of Gendarmes passed Allied aircrews, including wounded, from one Gendarme to the other, to Madame Vignon's house, after which rescue operation details were exchanged by radio with London, and escape routes organised. Now the network was to be summoned into action to aid another kind of evader. With the courageous Madame Vignon, they constituted a formidable back-up team for assisting the escape of prisoners whom some of the Gendarmes had themselves put in the gaol.

Main 'annexe' for Madame Vignon's storage facilities was at her friend Madame Barré's house in rue Delpech. Madame Vignon had been advised that because of prevailing freezing weather conditions, an adequate supply of overcoats was of primary importance for the urgent special order. Within a few days, Madame Vignon and Madame Barré signalled they were ready with the goods.

Part of the Vignon order was collected each morning then loaded into the butcher's and baker's vans before they made their noon way towards the prison. The vans had been designated as 'changing rooms' for escapers in need of different clothes, although many, expected to emerge in civilian clothes, would mainly need overcoats.

The several groups on alert for the raid included armed teams with sten guns, grenades and pistols, prepared, as outer prison walls were breached, to go in to locate and help escapers. Extra arms had been parachuted to them, sufficient to arm instantly many of the escapers.

As Pepe reminded action teams:

'When you go in, remember the Resistance saying that the duration of each contributes to the duration of all. The rule is keep your head at all times, otherwise you will very likely lose it.'

'Safe houses' in, and far beyond Amiens, were notified to expect an outsize intake. All Resistants in the cells were aware of emergency hideouts in Amiens, Abbeville and Arras, to which they could fly like homing pigeons.

An interpreter working for the Germans got his hands on a treasure of blank identity cards, passes and official stamps, and Pepe's helpers, prepared for any eventuality, amassed a fantastic collection of professional cards, demobilisation notices, military papers, official seals, and even family records, in readiness for prison escapers.

'It's always been like this in France – you need papers for everything, and have to show papers to get more papers,' said Pepe. 'All we were short of were the Germans, who are madder about papers than we are. Count them – from birth certificates to identity card, draft card, labour card, ration cards for meat, butter, wine, bread, textiles, tobacco, and if you've had your cock circumcised, you need a baptismal certificate to prove you're not Jewish.'

All papers bore authentic stamps and signatures – some copies, some stolen. Genuine seals, of towns destroyed with all their records, were used, but false paper services, who could make moulds for virtually undetectable forgeries, worked day and night until Pepe felt he had enough documents to create new identities for the escapers. Forgery carelessness could cost lives, so forgers had to familiarise themselves with the writing and printing idiosyncracies of individual offices, such as the small 'i' of the French Government Printing Office which had an almost invisible cross stroke through the middle.

The incredible seventy-five-year-old Monsieur Deloison, retired Director of Customs for the whole of northern France including all its famous ports, was the region's master identity card forger, and, assisted by a Monsieur Buffet, a teacher, and Monsieur Gros, a secretary at Amiens town hall, he operated his forgery 'factory' inside the Somme préfecture itself!

Deloison was a character. Dapper, grey-haired, apparently shy, immaculately dressed and never out without a jaunty small-brimmed Anthony Eden-style hat perched on his head, his pince-nez glasses, tape-attached to a jacket button, were forever falling off his nose. With his neat moustache and little Napoleon-the-third-type pointed beard, he looked the complete traditional conception of the cavalier Frenchman.

Punctually each weekday morning he arrived as the Préfecture doors opened for business. Strutting straight to his office 'Bon jouring' everyone in sight, he set to work forging his daily output of identity cards and 'official' papers in an 'office' that didn't even have a door – it was merely a section of corridor furnished with table, chair, table lamp, and little cupboard to which he alone had the keys. In it were genuine official stamps he had acquired, supplies of blank identity cards and the rest of his forgery paraphernalia.

No one at the Préfecture – other than Dr. Mans and two of his closest associates – knew the precise scope of Monsieur Deloison's 'work' and none realised he was one 'employee' whose name didn't figure on the Préfecture payroll for the simple reason that he wasn't being paid.

Monsieur Deloison, a widower with one daughter, putting to good use his years of experience in dealing with devious smugglers, assured Dr. Mans:

'The way of the transgressor is hard, if the police find out, but it takes two to make a criminal – one individual and one society.'

One of his false paper colleagues had only just been caught. Ex-carpenter Raymond Bompas, a war invalid with severely maimed legs and back, unfit to continue his old trade, became a Concierge. He then linked up with the 'Noah's Ark' Alliance network, to whom he passed information, but it was largely his work in the provision of false identity papers which landed him in an Amiens cell.

Even Belgian espionage agents and Resisters in Amiens gaol were catered for, with a supply of blank frontier passes of the type Belgian workers daily used for crossing into France. A Feldgendarmerie stamp for Lille region was copied so that the passes could be impressively stamped.

Accomplices in official positions – Préfectures, mayors' offices, police stations, hospitals, German departments, rationing offices – borrowed specimens from which copies could be turned out. Town hall employees also managed to produce a substantial quantity of completely authentic documents by locating names of people who had left parishes years before. For each name, which would be genuine with proper legal status, some fifteen identity cards could be produced, as it was unlikely that two of the same name would be presented at a single check-point in the same day.

The identity card suppliers were without another of their

colleagues who had been imprisoned since mid-November last – Préfecture bureau chief Gruel, in charge of General Administration, which covered the division issuing and controlling identity papers as well as the seemingly endless variety of official papers governing everyone's lives.

Striving to break him, and the identity card traffic, the Gestapo beat Gruel regularly. When his twenty-two-year-old son Pierre visited the goal on 31 December, his father's face was swollen so badly that he could barely speak, and both his eyes were blacked.

'Why is your face in such a state?' Pierre asked.

'Oh, I fell down a staircase,' was the excuse.

'Please ask your grandmother to bring my prayer book and rosary next time she comes,' were his parting words to Pierre, who was never to see him again. Hating his son seeing him beaten and battered, he insisted thereafter that only his seventy-five-year-old mother and fifteen-year-old daughter visit with food-parcels. His wife died in 1938.

Everyone connected officially and unofficially with Monsieur Gruel liked and respected the moustached forty-seven-year-old Préfecture bureau chief, who was always ready to do favours. Favours put him in gaol.

When his mother and daughter arrived at 11 a.m. on Friday the 19th, they brought food and a change of clothes. The previous week he had requested civilian clothes, as he was still dressed in the Préfecture uniform, with distinctive light beige riding breeches, in which he had been arrested.

'They moved me into a different cell two days ago, he told them. 'It's the same cell Dr. Mans occupied when they sent him here.'

Clutching the prayer book and rosary which his mother had brought, he suggested quietly:

'Maybe God sends us trouble because that's often the only time many people think of Him.'

'Let us hope He answers prayers,' his mother replied.

Managing a smile, Gruel said:

'And I suppose if they're not answered, the answer's no.'

He didn't explain why he no longer wanted to wear his distinguished uniform. He couldn't. He knew an attack was coming, with the opportunity of escape, and the uniform would be too easy to spot if he got out of the prison gates.

Prison doors and gates particularly concerned Pepe, Dominique Ponchardier and Admiral Riviére. Apart from breaching the walls, they wanted the main gates open to enable getaway transport to drive freely through to collect escapers. Only the gatekeeper possessed keys for the main entrance leading to the Route d'Albert. Wardens had one key each to open all doors. When going for a meal, they required to hang their key in a little cabinet in the warden's office, and the cabinet was kept locked. On general duty, they carried the key in a pocket, but took no chances in the criminal section and usually kept a hand on the key to prevent a pickpocket lifting it, as in fact happened to careless wardens. Pepe further ascertained that most locks were not self-locking and required the manual turning of the key in the lock.

What if bomb blasts didn't blow open cell and communicating doors? The whole thing would be totally futile unless they could be certain of opening the right doors at the right moment. Every second would count for achieving fast getaway. The doors question plagued Pepe. The insurance had to be someone they could use in the gaol. Not all the wardens were pro-German. It had been noted that a number of them habitually favoured a little café near the prison for an end of duty drink. This was clearly the best contact-making point, but before reaching this stage, the background of wardens who patronised the café needed checking – their personalities, politics, reputations, everything. The first approach *had* to be right.

Pepe chose well, and found one warden willing to co-operate, who further promised to sound out colleagues whom he thought might also be willing to assist. Recognising that inside aid could be restricted by whether or not helpful wardens were actually on duty at the time of attack, or if they happened to be in the crucial wings of the buildings, he assessed still more insurance was necessary – ideally, a set of prison keys. Pepe had the locksmith to copy them once he could lay hands on either wax impressions or drawings of the keys. Different keys were required to open specific doors.

The answer came from Victor Pasteau, a professional burglar and lock specialist, in the cell adjoining Roger Beaurin. Victor was the kind who'd steal anything movable. In his early thieving days, he used even to steal toilet pedestals and sell them to a plumber.

'Burglars are only those who feel they're not as rich as they ought to be, which is why I always tried to live within another man's means.' Victor explained philosophically to his cellmates.

Resourceful, small, balding Victor, with a single tuft of hair dangling over his forehead, never appeared to be thrown off course by anything. Whatever you asked for, he managed somehow to supply. Although his cell companions could not think for the life of them what he had to sing about, he almost constantly hummed to himself. When things were going well, he always rubbed his hands together and switched from humming to whistling softly.

Observing Chief Warden Magiras in conversation with one of his staff, Victor photographed the key with his eyes, mentally recording a deep 'Y' cut, four notches down one fork, and five down the inner fork. After also noting the grooves on the outer flanges, the cut of the key was imprinted on his mind. He drew it, and the sketch was smuggled to Pepe. When ready, the key had to be tested. It would be stupid to chance using it for the first time when it was really needed, only to discover it hadn't been cut accurately and required adjustments. It had to work from 'Go!'

'I daren't check it!' the go-between warden told Pepe. 'If I'm spotted trying a key I shouldn't possess, it'll be the end.'

Again Victor Pasteau had the answer:

'Leave it to me,' he confidently boasted to the co-operative warden.

Adept at striking a light by using a steel button, a piece of thread, a small flint and a piece of tinder, Victor sparked a flame then carefully blackened the key with smoke. The following morning he contrived to stand with his back to the door which the helpful warden had said was the one the copy key should fit. Sliding the key into the lock, Victor turned it as far as it would go without actually attempting to unlock the door. It only moved slightly anyway, so checking was justified. The impression of the inside of the lock was clearly imprinted on the smoked key. Snatching prison workshop opportunities to file and smooth the key, he gave it another test, and it worked. Victor then concentrated on further key duplications.

'If there's hope of us getting out of here sooner than we're supposed to, I think we'd better have some reserve keys just for ourselves,' he informed his cellmates, then proceeded to follow through by fashioning skeleton keys from the lattice-work iron strips of his bed. When asleep, he kept the keys in his boots. Victor thought of everything, except, unfortunately, that apart from being a chronic thief he had a major failing – he was absent-minded. Now no man knows what absent-mindedness really is until he finds himself dialling his own telephone number, and when free, Victor was forever phoning himself. Forgetfulness about phones put him away the time before last. Robbing a bistro, he imprisoned the proprietor in the café's telephone booth by jamming the door handle with a heavy chair, then started looting the place. He even helped himself to a couple of croissants and coffee. The police were waiting outside – Victor having forgotten that the bistro owner in the booth could ring for Gendarmes.

Absent-mindedness was largely the reason why he was more

inside gaols than out. His current Amiens sentence resulted from an early morning robbery – he preferred 'working' early and having the rest of the day to himself. He waited for milk supplies to be delivered at a café where the proprietors lived on the premises, then, masking his face, holding a milk bottle in one hand – he felt that was a nice touch – and a gun in the other, he knocked on the front door. The revolver was only for show – he hated violence. Thinking it was the milk delivery man, the owner opened to find a gun pointing at him. After binding the husband and wife, he ransacked the place, forcing cabinets, emptying drawers on the floor, slitting mattresses, even ripping clothing apart in the hunt for hidden valuables or cash. Carefully selecting the most saleable items, he packed them into a large suitcase he found, and departed.

Within minutes, he was stopped in the street and arrested. Victor couldn't understand why, nor why the Gendarme had a perpetual grin on his face as he took him to the police station. Only there did another Gendarme, almost helpless with laughter, say to him:

'You can take your mask off now.'

Poor absent-minded Victor had forgotten all about the mask. It was understandable that so many of the criminal fraternity nick-named him 'Lucky Pierre', because when absent-minded, he was anything *but* lucky. Nevertheless, when on form, he was a very good thief. With him, bad luck never lasted – it usually continued awhile, and then got worse.

Pepe had a final task for Victor Pasteau's professional abilities. Asking for help in a smuggled note, he explained:

'I sympathise that, as soon as you can, you'll want to get far from the place as fast as possible, but before you do, help yourself and others inside. Use your duplicate keys to get into the administration office in the main block; break open filing cabinets and burn all the prison records you find. This will make it harder for details of escaped prisoners to be circulated. They don't always keep prisoners' photos with their files, but all physical and other details are there, including judgements and individual notes on each of you.'

Copy records of prisoners involved with the Gestapo were also kept at the house in rue Jeanne d'Arc, but that was another problem.

Contemplating the note, thinking there's nothing worse than a born scoundrel handicapped by his conscience, Victor shrugged his shoulders and accepted that he owed it to those who were offering him early freedom to fulfil this extra request. Without going into what was now expected of him, he announced to the other two cellmates:

'It looks like I've got a job to do before we get out of here. All I hope is that I don't have to do it on a Saturday – that's always been my unlucky day. It went wrong for me three times on a Saturday, so that day's out as a working day for me. Sunday would be fine – a lucky working day for thieves. Mind you, if I'm about to do a Sunday job, I always attend Mass first – I don't believe in pushing my luck too far.'

Having said that, he popped Pepe's note into his mouth, chewed it, then swallowed it.

*

Although Admiral Rivière and Dominque Ponchartdier didn't know it at the time, estimates of the number of 'political' prisoners in Amiens gaol were wrong. Officially, 'politicals' were supposedly all housed in the German section where, according to current information, there were said to be some hundred inmates – men and women. The remainder, in the criminal sections were listed as civil criminals – murderers, thieves, pimps, black marketeers, mostly scum who deserved to be there. This was misleading, and the numbers inaccurate because excessive overcrowding compelled the Germans to put 'politicals' with civil criminals, and many, like Jean Beaurin and Maurice Holville, had been apprehended for offences apparently unconnected with Resistance activities.

A further factor affecting the estimates of numbers imprisoned was that Gestapo and French militia constantly detained victims in cells for weeks without reporting them to judicial authorities.

According to the chief warden's tally, on Friday 18 February the total was 832, including 180 in the German quarters. The following day, 26 men and 3 women, housed in the French quarters with common criminals, were scheduled to be shot by firing squad, along with others from the German section. Most had been sentenced to death by an Amiens Tribunal.

Overcrowding was so appalling, that in innumerable instances up to eight prisoners took it in turn at night to snatch sleep as there was insufficient room for them all to lie down at the same time.

Rivière and Dominique were unaware that the stakes were far higher. If the raid succeeded, it could save not a hundred, as they believed, but hundreds of freedom fighters – Sosies as well as countless other réseau members; Maquis; American, British, and Belgian espionage agents; captured Allied airmen; and Raymond Vivant – the man Washington and London wanted freed, or killed.

Five espionage agents were kept in solitary confinement, strictly away from all other prisoners. Three were British spies, one American, and one Belgian. There were three more Americans who, although captured in civilian clothes and claiming to be shot down airmen, were nevertheless classified as suspect spies, which of course, they could well have been.

The eight were almost daily visitors to rue Jeanne d'Arc for regular treatments – personally supervised by Gestapo chief Braumann, frequently with the treacherous Lucien Pieri present – of head-under-water and hands crushed with heavy weights. Beatings, brutality and traps could often force involuntary admissions. The Gestapo called it 'Physical Culture'.

Elaine Guillemont, 'action terrorist' prisoner and 24-year-old nursing assistant of Dr. Antonin Mans in his Cell No. 3 'medical centre', was ordered to attend a sick man held in one of the special case special discipline cells in the basement bowels of the gaol. Passing through an outsize gate to reach the solitary confinement cell, she was shocked to find her patient manacled and chained like a dog to an iron grille that looked as if it weighed a couple of tons. Chaining was standard procedure for anyone confined to this classification cell. Even if someone knocked down the walls, escape would be impossible, for nobody could carry that grille on his back.

As she took his pulse and checked the fever, her brief diagnosis and probing queries – questions needed to be brief with the watchful German guard in attendance – were answered in alternate flawless French and English, which the prisoner was delighted to find she understood. She'd been engaged just before the outbreak of war, to an Englishman living in France who managed to get back to Britain in 1941 to join the RAF.

The cell patient's eyes, fixed on hers, said far more than his words. Heroes, she thought, are often made in moments of defeat.

'I'll be okay,' he said, just about managing a reassuring smile. 'I'm a patriot, which means I claim the right to go to hell my own way.'

'I still worry about you . . . and about France,' she said wearily.

Gripping her hand, counselling her almost as if she, instead of him, was the patient, he said:

'Don't worry so much about France. How can anyone permanently conquer a country that has two hundred and forty six kinds of cheese?'

She was almost ashamed of suddenly hearing her own laughter in the musty cell.

As she was about to leave he said firmly:

'I'm positive I'm not going to die – at least, not in here.'

He was an English spy, condemned to death, but the Gestapo

were anxious for him to receive medical care to get him fit enough to stand before a firing squad.

In a day or so, she knew there'd be commotion in the corridors, as the place echoed with the clink of keys, slamming doors, and clanking chains, when the next batch of manacled death-sentenced prisoners were prodded outside to be shot. Possibly the Englishman would be one of them, unless the Gestapo hadn't finished with him, and so would her fiancé, Pierre Bracquart.

A second British agent, alone in an adjoining cell, was left unchained for the simple reason that he had only one leg.

In his early thirties, 'Johnny' – the sole name he ever gave the Germans – still somehow retained a distinguished air, despite the squalor of the windowless cell. He also spoke French like a native.

The first time he was parachuted into the region, he had returned safely to Britain, but during his second mission he was gravely wounded. After a German surgeon amputated one of his legs in the military-reserved Hospice St. Victor, around the corner from the gaol, he was imprisoned as soon as he could move and put through the interrogation mill by Braumann.

On hearing from inside-Germany sources of the one-legged spy in Amiens gaol, and the importance placed on his capture by Berlin, Allen Dulles requested an identification cross-check on top agents active in the region. Admittedly, the name was a fragile connecting thread, but he wondered if Amiens 'Johnny' could possibly be thought by German High Command to be a shadowy character named 'John' who had been second in command of 53 spies, plus innumerable sub-agents operating mostly inside Germany itself. 'John', also known as Augustus de Fremery and Captain Jan Hendricks, worked closely with Dutch Military Intelligence. At one period he had been based at 57 Nieuwe Parklaan, a quiet residential street on one of the canals at the Hague. If it was 'John' from the Hague, then his extensive knowledge of highest-level espionage and his Gestapo detention and questioning could be of tremendous significance for the enemy and the Allies. Dulles was unable to identify the 'Johnny' in the gaol positively.

Elaine Guillemont swiftly learned that if you obey and smile at the enemy, he may let you live.

Nursing in a hospital at Péronne, she first worked with an escape route, getting people to Britain through Spain. Subsequently linking with a Somme espionage group directed by a British agent, she extended her scope by also joining a sabotage unit headed by telephone engineer Pierre Bracquart. André Priestley, with an English father and French mother, was also a member. Pierre equipped the Renault building in Amiens, occupied by the Germans, with two phone systems: one for them, and one for him and his colleagues to eavesdrop on calls day and night. Changing jobs in 1942, after taking a course, he progressed to Income Tax Collector in Péronne, and worked undercover with two organisations – one run by Colonel André Loisy-Jarniere, known as 'Captain David', and the second acting for General Giraud in Algiers, and Allen Dulles in Switzerland. Elaine Guillemont, who had become Pierre's fiancée, was one of the eleven-strong Giraud-Dulles unit.

Overlooking the street from his office, Pierre, spotted ten Gendarmes heading for his building. Sensing that they were coming for him, he dashed into the toilet to flush incriminating papers down the pan. When he emerged, Gendarmes were waiting outside the lavatory cubicle with revolvers drawn.

Nine of the eleven, including Elaine, were arrested that day. Only Pierre knew of the surviving two.

Guarded by six soldiers, the nine were transported by military truck to Amiens gaol, and separately questioned the same evening by the Gestapo. As there wasn't room anywhere else, the men were housed in the French criminal section, whilst Elaine was put on the second floor in the women's section of the German wing. Because of her nursing qualifications she was assigned to Dr. Mans to help with sick inmates, and spent most of her time assisting the doctor in the 'open' or 'surgery' cell on the ground floor.

For a time, Pierre was also in the German section, but on 8 February 1944, after months in the gaol without trial, he was informed the Section Spéciale had considered his case and sentenced him to 20 years forced labour and 20 years exile from France. He hadn't even been allowed to defend himself before the tribunal. Later that day, without any explanation being offered, he was told the verdict had been altered to execution, which would be carried out within eight days.

The 'Arabic telephone', as the gaol's heating pipes were called, conveyed the news to Elaine. Consoling her, Dr. Mans said:

'You never know, they may change their minds again, so let's hope for the best, and if we get it, let's hope for something better.'

16 February arrived, but soldiers didn't come for Pierre.

As dusk fell and window light disappeared, Elaine and Pierre lay on the lumpy palliasses of their separate cells. In tomb-like silence interrupted only by guards' footsteps, they prayed the reprieve would continue.

*

Sipping ersatz coffee, waiting together at a little café within easy walking distance of the gaol, Admiral Rivière and Dominique Ponchardier checked their wristwatches almost simultaneously. It was drawing towards noon. Would it be today?

The risk in appearing openly together was enormous, but both realised there are occasions when playing for safety can be the most dangerous thing in the world. Urgency had been heightened since the institution on 20 January of a new courts procedure, aimed at making anti-invasion measures bite even harder. Legalised murder by courts-martial was authorised. Tribunals comprising three anonymous judges had commenced sitting in secret inside gaols, and their no-appeal sentences were carried out on the spot without delay. There was neither prosecutor nor defence counsel, and white wood coffins were always waiting outside.

'It *must* be today, or more lives will be lost,' said Dominique, for only that morning they'd been told many inside were due to be shot tomorrow. Originally set for 16 February, the execution date had been moved to the 19th, and a large mass grave had already been dug for the bodies.

Jean Beaurin, Maurice Holville and Pierre Bracquart heard that their grave was ready.

*

Following 'old Pick', the 'Pied Piper of Hunsdon', they all trooped out of the briefing room, their departure noisy, but the tenseness even louder.

'I've a feeling they're really telling us sweet FA about this trip,' a Flight Lieutenant ventured.

'Why don't you clam up,' another countered. 'You're always airing your knowledge, which is why you're so full of wind.'

Banter couldn't really camouflage strain. The thought of what 'Daddy' Dale's RAF Squadron might be asked to do in the event of initial attack failure was still clearly uppermost, but, for the moment, it was Egg Time – time for the pre-raid ritual of ordering and consuming eggs in the Mess with a cuppa, and perhaps a sandwich. Civilians and Service men and women, in general, had to accept the very limited wartime egg ration, but for pilots and aircrew it was almost always eggs immediately before and after a raid or sortie. It had become a kind of status symbol habit, as well as a superstition. Someone had introduced it sometime, and flying personnel were great ones for superstitions and 'lucky charms'. The selection of weird and wonderful Hunsdon 140th Wing superstitions included a bird's wing, a hunting horn, a steel shaving mirror, girls' or wives' stockings, a red white and blue scarf, and rabbits' feet. Many wouldn't think of taking off without their own bits of witchery, and 'lucky' items of clothing had to stay unwashed for months in case their owner had unexpectedly to fly without it.

Superstition knockers cautioned that if you depended too much on luck, you could soon have nothing else to depend on. But some had good luck, some bad luck, and others had no luck at all.

Hanging around for take-off after briefing was always nerve-racking. No one knew what to do with himself, and no one was talking much. Some stood around in small circles, sipping soft drinks, tea, or not drinking. There were no snifters before take-off to provide Dutch courage. Perhaps a single glass of beer with a meal, but anything more or stronger was absolutely out before flying. Even the wildest knew the risk and wouldn't touch the stuff, not only for their own sakes, but also in case alcohol-influenced misjudgement cost the lives of comrades. It was necessary not only to stay sober, but also to avoid the calls of nature at inconvenient moments. When you were fighting for your life you didn't want to worry about taking a leak.

Flasks of hot coffee would stay unscrewed until well on the way back, at a lower altitude and within easy distance of home. The pre-op drink at Hunsdon – on CO's 'recommendation' – was milk. Pick loved his glass of bitter beer, but drank gallons of milk, downing huge glasses of it like many beer drinkers swallow pints. Hunsdon's crews were 'advised' to drink milk before going on a job.

'It gives you extra stamina before a raid,' insisted Pick. 'If you have to come down and float about in the sea for hours, you'll be glad you drank milk before leaving base.'

Pre Amiens take-off, some played billiards; others lazed, listening to the Glenn Miller Orchestra on the radio; one concentrated on reading a copy of *Lady Chatterley's Lover*; but most just sat in chairs picking up papers and magazines, throwing them down, staring into space, waiting for the clock on the wall to show the time when they would have to go for their flying kits.

Pick strode into the Mess, gazed around, and asked with the shadow of a smile:

'Any complaints?'

To which somebody suggested:

'Couldn't they improve the desserts?'

'What do you mean?' Pick demanded. 'You've got a bloody good aircraft to fly – what more do you want?'

Hunsdon's roomy Mess had a well-stocked bar; pretty batwomen of all shapes and sizes; central-heated quarters with constant hot and cold water; and female corporals to wake crews up in the morning, make their beds, and keep the place tidy – and, thankfully to further loosen strain in the Mess that morning the crews' favourite batwoman – a girl with a great pair of boobs – arrived on duty.

'What a lovely pair of twin engines you've got!'

'Cocky', an extrovert overgrown schoolboy yelled at her – 'I wonder how fast you take off?'

In the air, 'Cocky' was totally different – serious, fanatically intent.

Time dragged for the waiting aircrews, but the three Wing Commanders and their CO were up to their eyes in it, going over everything with the navigation and signals 'kings'; consulting yet again with the Met man, or seaweed basher, as they preferred to label him.

From signals section a stack of bumph had to be collected, including the 'Q' code, full lists of frequencies and callsigns, beacon identification, and secret list of colours and code letters of the day, printed on rice paper, to be eaten in the event of 'unscheduled descent among hostile natives' – forced landing on enemy territory.

Phones rang ceaselessly.

'There's always a bloody something!' Pick exploded.

Despite all the preparatory activity, the rest of the camp was totally oblivious that it was a very special action day. As far as they were concerned Squadrons could be about to depart on yet another training flight.

Pick, the solid pre-war RAF type, had been commissioned two years before the war started, but there were those who fought alongside him who stubbornly insisted that he'd been in the Service so long that when he joined up the Dead Sea hadn't even reported sick.

Although he made a really strong stab at being a Station Commander disciplinarian type, it wasn't easy for someone with a reputation for saying what he thought in front of anyone.

Returning from an evening off during his first Hunsdon week, he drove past the duty guard without stopping, braked suddenly, wound down the car window and yelled at the guard in his sternest Station Commander voice:

'What kind of security do you call that? It's about time you knew that you're supposed to shoot anybody going through the gate without stopping!'

He glared at the guard, who stared right back and asked:

'Would you like to reverse and try it again, sir?'

Pounding the 'No Ball' targets – the V1 and V2 launching pads and rocket storage caverns – were the Hunsdon Squadrons' main assignments during January and February, weather permitting. But newly transferred *Mosquito* pilots unfamiliar with Hunsdon's runway middle dip kept buckling and bending the precious aircraft far too often on landing or taxi-ing, so Pick ordered a giant notice posted in the crew room stating:

'The next person to prang a *Mosquito* through finger trouble will be posted to the bloodiest job in the Air Force.'

Pilots didn't doubt he meant every word.

The day after the notice appeared, a *Mosquito* returned to its hangar with a bent tail wheel – piloted by Pickard.

Though not by nature an office wallah, considering being chair-borne a fate worse than death, from the instant the Amiens briefing ended he had toiled non-stop tying up final details, feet up on desk, puffing at the pipe that was virtually a permanent extension of his mouth:

'Cigarettes and bombs are the quickest way to smoke yourselves to death,' he commented with disdain to chain-smoking staff.

Lifting the phone, he rang the head engineer.

'Is my aircraft okay?'

'Good, I knew it would be. That's fine.'

Ringing off, he raised the phone again to call Group head-quarters.

'I'm sure we'll have a maximum effort today,' he reported. As long as his aircraft was okay, he was confident of a maximum effort. But Embry was worried. He had chosen Pick as deputy leader for the Amiens task because he intended leading the raid himself. Now forbidden to do so, he just couldn't put another leader in Pick's place.

Disappointed, he confided to Ted Sismore:

'A slight like that could all too easily destroy a man whose courage, devotion to duty, fighting spirit, and powers of real leadership stand him out as one of the great airmen of the war.'

Despite the severe wintry weather, twenty-two ops had taken place during the first fifteen days of February; but Pick had only been on six daytime low-level attacks, and needed more time to adjust his vast night flying experience to daylight low-level rules.

Basic general rule for *Mosquito*s was in fast, and get the hell out fast, always avoiding going round again for a second try, the motto being – those who fight and run away, live. Luftwaffe fighters presented little problem to a *Mosquito* flown tree-top height on full throttle. Only flak, a church spire or tall tree could be a danger.

Embry had taken the precaution of accompanying Pick several times, including that very first rocket site attack when forty-eight

*Mosquitos* – twenty-four led by Pickard, the second section by Embry – pounded Hitler's secret new weapon. Having gone along to break in his new Station Commander on day attack ropes, he had thereafter barred him from flying actions without his personal permission until he had completed a minimum number of 2 Group-style low-level ops. As a leader Pick was supreme, but he tended to take lots of chances – not with others, with himself.

Almost to the last, Embry strove to convince his superiors to let him lead the Amiens raid, using Pickard to head the 21st Squadron. He appealed once more to Coningham, stressing misgivings.

'I agree with you to an extent Basil,' Coningham admitted, 'but the C-in-C has a point too, and he is adamant so it will do no good to raise it with him.' Making absolutely certain Embry didn't disobey the veto, Leigh-Mallory ordered him to report to Fighter Command HQ immediately after the briefing.

Disconsolate, he returned to Mongewell Park to give the sad news to Ted Sismore, who was to have flown as his navigator.

After he had repeated Coningham's conversation, Sismore contentedly drew attention to the indisputable fact that:

'Neither Coningham nor Leigh Mallory have barred me, so who do you suggest I navigate for? – I'm going anyway.'

'No you won't!' Embry whipped back. 'If I don't go, you don't go!'

Bomb dump wallahs beavered away preparing the 500-pound eleven-second delayed-action bombs. Once trollied, they were tractored down to the dispersals and left for the armourers to load. Meanwhile, the armourers prepared gun ammunition, checking, positioning in the belt machine, and lapping the ammunition belts into the narrow boxes. Immediately air tests were completed, they would carry out pre-flight checks in readiness for the actual op. Four Browning machine guns in the nose and four Hispano cannons could be fired together with the impact of a three-ton truck hitting a brick wall at over 50 m.p.h. Empty cartridge outlets were well back under the fuselage.

Despite relatively narrow bomb bays, Mossies could carry an extensive range of explosive stores.

When engineers and electricians finished, bomb doors were opened, armourers moved in with their laden trollies, hooks were lowered and hoists operated. Finally everything was locked and checked, with safety fusing wires and safety pins staying in position until aircrews arrived.

On being doled out extra chocolate, sweet rations and chewing gum, the latter supposedly to keep mouths moist, several crews drifted from the Mess to their quarters to write letters to wives, girl-friends and parents – in case. Some, with married quarters in houses in the surrounding districts, didn't need to write, although the security clamp down on the base had prevented them going home for the past few days.

Air Marshal Sir Arthur Harris, of Bomber Command, had actually issued an order forbidding any wife to live within forty miles of her husband on a bomber base. Exceptions were made for those already living out, but there were few of these. Fighting and living at home was rough on any man – and wife.

'You're one of the lucky ones – you can usually go home and enjoy your wife's cooking,' remarked one of the less fortunate.

'Don't be too sure about that . . . you've never tasted my wife's cooking. I bet I'm the only one on this base who packs a lunch to take home.'

Crews also headed for the aircraft-recognition-chart-papered crew room with its illustrated dinghy-drill procedures and security warnings blessedly relieved by a selection of busty pin-ups of Betty Grable, Alice Faye and Rita Hayworth. A gramophone was soon blaring out a record of the Forces national 'anthem' – Vera Lynn's 'We'll Meet Again' – and within minutes the tobacco-laden fug could be cut with a knife.

'It isn't good for you to concentrate so much on those pin-ups just before a flight, "Bull",' someone shouted through the smoke. 'The bags under your eyes are bad enough already . . . What were you doing – playing with yourself all night?'

'Bull', real name Ferdinand, was a complete contradiction of his identity, and definitely no bull with the girls.

It was absolutely freezing outside, and a bunch of airmen stayed in the dispersal huts to keep warm. Cold could be one of the worst dangers to be faced. Unless you were warm enough in the air, it could make you physically and mentally inefficient, and so drowsy that your only desire was to sleep.

Snow showers still pelted down. Cloud base was now estimated at a thousand to twelve hundred feet, and everyone was convinced the Amiens op was due to be the kind that was a great laxative – better than a bottle of castor oil.

As the Mossies' engines were run up and vapour trails sprayed from the propeller tips, crews took to drifting about dispersal pens and Flight Offices.

A mass of radar aerials astride one of the huts identified the Special Signals Officer's abode – a favourite navigators' hangout before and after a raid, when they usually turned up to blame their own failings on the AI sets supplied by Special Signals.

Crewmen, enveloped in their customary haze of cigarette smoke, were also sprawled around the nearby Intelligence hut, presided over by the Squadron Intelligence officer – a wizened, dry old Scot, formerly in the fish business, who constantly seemed to be trying to retrieve scattered documents from the floor, answer the phone and withstand ragging, all at the same time. He was also forever covering the phone mouthpiece, turning to others, and shouting: 'Wull you fellows no be quiet a minute?' Flying Officer 'Robbie' Robertson was a Hunsdon character, as was Senior Flying Control Officer Squadron Leader Bradshaw-Jones, who, in all weathers, was out on the balcony of Castle Keepfit – the name, acquired from its radio call-sign, of the square, camouflage-painted Control Tower of Flying Control, which with its radio direction finders, tele-printers and landlines monitored all comings and goings.

Tall, gaunt, 'Brad', standing sentinel on the balcony of his kingdom, was the finest welcome home sight any Hunsdon airman could wish for. No matter how exhausting or nerve-tearing an op they'd endured, returning crews loved to see 'Brad' wearing the revolver and thigh-length waders he inexplicably favoured. He had such a nautical, piratical air, that airmen were ever expecting him to whip out a cutlass. Calm, confident, friendly, no matter how bad things were, he was respected not only for being thoroughly efficient and thinking of everything to provide maximum take-off and landing safety, but also for riding a motor-cycle around the mess billiards table with four passengers aboard.

But now Senior Flying Control Officer Bradshaw-Jones was calculatingly considering all the problems of the imminent triple-S-quadron departure in blizzard conditions. Take-off depended not only on the kind and state of the runway, but also on bombload and weather conditions. Bombed up aircraft normally took off singly, one after another, with sufficient distance between them to ensure one aircraft didn't start moving off until the aircraft in front of it was just leaving the ground. With the exception of bombed up aircraft, and when weather conditions allowed, take-off was done in sections of two. In the case of fully loaded aircraft, or even with two 250 pounders and a drop tank, special care was a must to ensure that take-offs were three-point without excessive bouncing that could endanger plane and pilot.

As the empty bomb trolleys parked, phones stopped ringing, and a sudden strange peace descended, except among gossiping crews tugging flying kits from lockers and manoeuvring into them . . .

'Do you remember when 88 and 107 were billeted in a convent

school and found a notice in each room advising: "Ring if you require a mistress", and everyone did? . . .'

'They shot away his rudder bar, but that shouldn't have worried him because, according to that old lineshooter, he never needs it anyway' . . .

It all sounded carefree, high-spirited, but it camouflaged emotions and pre-flight tummy flutter – the common complaint for which the only remedy was getting into the air.

Squadrons were at the dispersal area, a quiet corner of the base, just before ten thirty. Navigators impatiently swung aircraft compasses. Then the CO's pick-up was spotted motoring along the peritrack and everyone nervously wondered if the appalling weather might yet have caused a change of plan, or even postponement. Low-flying Mossies could cope with minimal cloud bases, but had to able to see where they were going and precisely where to attack the prison – this was vital. As Pickard's pick-up drew up beside them, he didn't even get out to announce:

'Met reports moderate visibility for northern France, so we're going to have a stab at it, and now it's – "Time, gentlemen, please!" ' The phrase raised comforting smiles, at the thought of the celebration pub drinks they hoped to enjoy on their return.

For New Zealander Pilot Officer Sparkes, one of the three captains due to attack first, Pick then put into words what he was certain they were all beginning to feel when he said:

'Well, boys, this is a death-or-glory show. If it succeeds it will be one of the most worth-while ops of the war. If you never do anything else, you can still count this as the finest job you could ever have done.'

Shuffling out in their flying boots, they all headed for the flight trucks, lugging their parachutes, ear-phoned leather flying helmets, Mae Wests, maps, briefing bags and other flying paraphernalia. They tossed some of the gear into the transports, climbed in after them, and the pick-ups then moved round the perimeter to the aircraft on the hardstandings. All tried to keep to their own individual favourite aircraft.

Out at the dispersal area, cockpit and engine covers had been removed, and wings and tailplanes were being swept as clear as possible of snow. Crews tried to allow a half-an-hour at dispersal before take-off to complete detailed inspection of their aircraft and to get comfortably settled in the cockpit. *Mosquito*s stood ready, in clusters of three and four, slender as wasps.

Helping Pickard, with ever-present pipe in mouth, struggle into his Mae West was his quiet much-decorated friend, 22-year-old navigator Alan Broadley. He complained:

'I could never figure out why they make us wear these bloody uncomfortable things in the winter when they warn us that we couldn't stay alive very long anyway if we come down in the freezing Channel or North Sea.'

'It's obvious,' said Pick. 'It makes the body easier to find.'

No military aeroplane proved more versatile than the wooden *Mosquito*, from the moment its originator, Geoffrey de Havilland, spun around the sky in it. Two Rolls-Royce engines, thousands of horsepower, super-plywood construction – everything revolutionary, except for ordinary windscreen wipers, just like any car.

The first thing that struck you about it was the line-beauty of the fuselage, tailplane, fin, engine cowlings, cockpit and undercarriage. Justly called 'the Wooden Wonder', it could withstand a severe hammering and still fly on one engine, because the wood not only stayed well glued, but proved outstandingly able to remain in one piece even after rough battle damage. There were countless cases of Mossies flying through intense heat of exploding aircraft with no worse effect than superficial charring, blistering and stripped fabric on control surfaces.

It really never occurred to any of the crews that they were flying in a wooden box with all the associated frailities of plywood; and at least it could be out in all weathers without rusting. Deservedly, they acquired such a reputation that the day some new type Mossies arrived at a base, the American Signals Officer commented:

'Gee, they *must* be fast ships – they've nearly beaten the rumour!'

A great love affair developed between airmen and the *Mosquito*, although there were problems.

The crew consisted of a pilot and an observer, who also acted as bomb-aimer, radio operator, and navigator. For two average-sized characters the cockpit was reasonably comfortable, enabling the navigator easily to grab the control column if necessary. But with bulky beings, it was another story, and the difficulty of baling out in the somewhat confined space could be a snag, to put it mildly.

After climbing the steep telescoping ladder leading to the nose hatch on the starboard side, Pickard had to squeeze himself through the hole, less than three feet square, in order to enter the somewhat cramped cockpit.

'I'm always amazed how a big bastard like you manages to get into this plane,' commented Broadley with his navigation board tucked under his arm.

'I don't get into it – I put it on,' Pick laughed.

The ground sergeant rigger helping them get started raised his thumb, collapsed the ladder immediately they were aboard, handed it up, then slammed the hatch cover and locked it. Pick checked the catch. Broadley strapped the ladder into place as Pick started groping for the various cocks and switches – the drill was automatic.

Cockpit drill was the most important thing of all. You needed to know the position of every tap so that you could fly without even looking down for controls. Movements had to be as automatic as car driving. A second's distraction could cost your life.

'Check petrol-cocks.'

'Petrol-cocks SET.'

'Check booster-pumps.'

'Booster-pumps ON.'

One by one, Broadley answered, completing the list, checking the battery of superb equipment, although some pilots never left ground without a supply of rubber bands and chewing gum for emergency cockpit repairs.

Inside, the pilot sat with his seat pack and dinghy facing the maze of instruments, whilst the navigator's seat was no more than a shelf on the main spar of the starboard side wing of the cockpit, set back slightly so that once in, he could relax his left shoulder just behind the pilot's seat. His parachute was elsewhere stuffed for lack of headroom. Both checked their watches – everything, from now, had to go by the watch – every second crucial.

They didn't need to worry about reloading guns as they were in fact sitting on top of the four cannon and their boxes of ammunition, separated from them only by the cockpit floor. Muzzles were set in the underside of the aircraft's nose, and the bomb sight was also in the nose, necessitating the navigator to move into this position before bombing, using the clear view panel provided for aiming.

In addition to all the radar equipment, the navigator had to keep his eyes on oxygen supply and petrol taps, as these were more accessible to him than to the pilot. Control of these was governed by strict routine ingrained into pilot and navigator to safeguard against trouble.

They had a good view above the horizontal to the sides, front and above, and could see moderately well to the rear. However, their view downwards and backwards into the area they had to search was bad, partly due to a blind spot and partly to the fact that both faced forwards, making it difficult to search thoroughly as they could only look over their shoulders. Broadley sometimes knelt on his seat facing backwards, having discovered this made an improvement. They were only too aware that an enemy fighter could often approach from the rear and below without their even being conscious of its attack. Fortunately, mirrors installed in the blisters fitted to the sides of the cockpit did help them to keep a look-out to the rear and slightly below.

Pilot protection comprised 7mm thick armour plate extending from the level of the seat to the top of the head, whilst a 9mm thickness of armour plate protected the navigator at the rear. The circular section of bullet proof glass behind his head provided an unhindered rearward view, and the upper part of the armour plate was hinged to enable operation of the radio at the back of it. The engines were not armour-protected.

*Mosquito*s were already only too familiar to the Amienois – had been, in fact, through the past year, since they had opened 1943 campaign operations with attacks on rail installations at Amiens, Mons and Tergnier, delivering bomb loads from shallow dives or runs as low as 50 to 100 feet, or 1,000 to 1,200 feet with bomb fuses set at 11 or .025 seconds. Low level meant low level, because 100 feet was considered high, and many often found themselves flying *through* power cables. Accurate marking was essential for accurate bombing of specific targets, and accurate marking could only be reliably done at low level.

During the first ten days of February 1944 alone, fourteen sorties had been flown over Amiens, Compiègne, Cherbourg, Dieppe, and the rivers in the Douai area. These had mostly been for the purpose of obtaining photographic reconnaissance for future invasion use by the Allied armies.

Pick pressed the starter and booster coil buttons while ground crew primed the engine as rapidly and as vigorously as possible. Turning periods couldn't exceed twenty seconds, with at least thirty seconds interval between them.

An ignition cracked, engines spluttered, roared and raced, straining against chocks, like racehorses waiting for the 'Off', until the field was alive with sound, exhaust flames, whirling propellers, shuddering aircraft. With freezing outside temperatures, it was necessary for ground crew to continue priming after the engine fired until it picked up on the carburettor. Happily, it wasn't cold inside the aircraft as the Mossie's cockpit heating was exceptionally good, and even at altitude in such severe winter, no bulky flying clothing was needed. This was a blessing for which outsize Pick was more than thankful, because those cockpits were tight for small characters, and murder on big bastards like him. He knew they'd soon be sweating, which was why old *Mosquito* hands always cautioned against wearing full flying kit.

One advantage in winter flying was not having to put up with windscreens smudged with a mass of squashed summer flies. Insects and birds could be a pain. Birds could shatter Perspex with the velocity of a shell, stove in a wing edge, or choke engines.

Testing the engines and equipment after warming up, Pick and Broadley checked the operation of each engine-driven hydraulic pump by lowering flaps with one engine opened up to 2,000 r.p.m. and raising them with the other engine 2,000 r.p.m. They opened up to weak mixture cruising boost to check operation of the airscrew; tested each magneto in turn at rich mixture cruising boost to ensure the drop didn't exceed 150 r.p.m. They opened throttle to climb position to check boost, then opened fully to check boost, oil pressure and static r.p.m.

The liquid-cooled Rolls-Royce Merlin engines and the radiators were set into the centre section of the leading edges of the wings, with only the thin wooden shell of the fuselage separating them from the cabin. The ear-splitting stub exhausts of the Merlins rose to a snarl, as thirty-eight engines burst into life in quick succession creating deafening pandemonium.

Pick signalled ground crew:

'Chocks away.'

One of the ground crew ran from the plane tugging a wheelchock at the end of a long rope.

Aircraft became more and more sophisticated, but chocks, plain ordinary simple chocks to stop a plane moving forward when engines are running, were the same as they had always been from the birth of flying.

There was a hiss of air as brakes were released, and the plane with the distinctive 'F for Freddie' marking – Pick's Mossie – moved off around the perimeter track allowing others, including slow starters, ample warm-up time. As Pick taxied, he checked brake pressure was at least 200 pounds, and kept flaps fully up. The close-cowled Merlins had a tendency to overheat during prolonged taxiing, so he made sure everyone moved to their allotted positions with minimum delay.

Converging to the airfield rendezvous point, the aircraft stirred up such thick clouds of snow that several disappeared from time to time. Finally assembled in a long line on the downwind side of the field, pilots double-checked trimming tabs were all at neutral; fuel mixture, high; airscrew speed controls fully forward. Fuel cocks and contents of the ten self-sealing tanks, with their total capacity of 543 gallons, were also checked, as were flaps, superchargers, and radiator cooling switches. Cockpit drill was over. They were ready.

The first six, of 487 Squadron, swung off the approach track onto the runway. Astern, the other Squadrons queued in line to follow, all in correct order for take-off at eleven. Pilots switched off their now satisfactorily warmed up and checked aircraft; nose entrance doors opened; extending ladders lowered, and pilots and navigators descended for a final leg stretch or smoke. The combination of cold and excitement weakened bladders, so crews congregated at the rear of their planes to christen the tail wheels.

'Daddy' Dale seemed an interminable time standing legs astride behind his tail wheel, until someone cried:

'You're not taking a leak, "Daddy", you're making a lake!'

'A man daren't even drink a cup of tea before an op in this weather,' Pick joked.

Others stamped around to keep circulation going, and gossip and banter went on to the last . . .

'There's no doubt about it – the aeroplane has brought a lot of places closer together, including this world and the next . . .'

'Do you know on our last trip, bullets that ripped into the cockpit just missed my best assets. And I thought it was meant to be a "No Ball" attack . . .'

'It's all in the lap of the gods, but with a bit of luck we should pull off this one in time to save those poor bastards in the gaol.'

'Yes, and if we succeed it'll be luck – just ask anyone who's failed and that's what they'll tell you.'

All were cheerful, raring to go, but chatter was slightly more tense now.

As time approached, crews climbed back into their cockpits and counted minutes.

New Zealander Sparkes sat at his controls thinking that if this had been an ordinary operation it would almost certianly have been scrubbed out or postponed to another day, but it wasn't an ordinary job. Every day, perhaps every hour, might be the last of those men and women in Amiens prison, so although it was no kind of weather to go flying in, he knew they must.

Leading the first section of six from the New Zealand Squadron was Wing Commander I. S. 'Black' Smith, DFC and bar. The second section was from the Royal Australian Air Force, led by Wing Commander R. W. 'Bob' Iredale, DFC, and the British Squadron's section commanded by 'Daddy' Dale.

The Aussie and Anzac Squadron badges were Hunsdon favourites. The 464 Squadron's badge appropriately depicted a piping shrike, the piping shrike being a bird indigenous to the Australian mainland. The Squadron's motto was 'Aequo animo' – 'Equanimity'.

The New Zealand 487 Squadron was even more colourful – a tekoteko holding a bomb. The grotesque Maori figure shown holding a bomb was not only an indication of the Squadron's activities, but also true Maori legend. Whare-whakairo, or meeting house of the tribe, was usually ornamented by grotesque but beautifully executed carvings, the tekoteko usually appearing at the apex of the gable above the entrance in an attitude of defiance, generally brandishing a weapon as a challenge to all comers.

The 487's motto was 'Ki te mutunga' – 'Through to the end'.

'Set?' Pick queried.

'All set,' Alan Broadley replied.

Both throttles were slowly opened to take-off position, right rudder maintained to check the plane's tendency to swing to port; tail raised by light forward pressure on the control column. Broadley made certain undercarriage locks were up, and now they could hear the familiar howl of *Mosquito* Merlins tearing along the runway ahead of them. The cacophony rose to a crescendo as throttles pushed forward and, one after another, aircraft roared into the sky.

They took off east to west at intervals of a hundred yards between pairs until all three Squadrons were airborne. Nobody climbed until the safety speed of 170 m.p.h. had been reached. Tails lifted and swayed; the runway rushed at them as they rose. Pilots reached across for the undercarriage lever, wheels thumped into position, and in next to no time wheels and flaps were up.

Barely off the ground, they plunged deep into snow and ice, left hand on the trim-wheel, feet on pedals, glancing frequently at the altimeter. Then they levelled off, to circle the airfield and immediately form into groups of three before vanishing from view, heading south towards Littlehampton to meet their *Typhoon* fighter escorts.

Tony Wickham just had time to check again the cameras of his Photographic Unit plane, before taxiing for take-off, and, a moment or two after the second six had gone, he too belted down the runway in a shower of fine snow. Aircraft ahead were already invisible, and the ground could be seen only vaguely through the swirling blinding snow. His cameraman was Flight Sergeant Lee Howard.

It was just past 11 a.m. on 18 February.

Miles away at Sculthorpe air base, at the precise moment of the Hunsdon Amiens departure, Ming padded out into the icy cold and blinding snow from the warm quarters of Pick's former second in command, and despite repeated pleadings, cajoling, and even offers of tempting rabbit, steadfastly remained outside in the bitter cold, scanning the sky.

# 10 The madame and the maid

As the *Mosquito*s headed for Amiens, action was also imminent in the town at 41, Port d'Aval.

Louise, the chambermaid, tidied the seven oblong tables set before the padded benches in the bistro-like Salle du Choix (Selection Salon), then swept the barely used postage-stamp size dance floor, although there was little time for dancing downstairs as the girls were usually too busy upstairs. It was almost rise and shine time for the eighteen sleepy girls, aged between twenty and twenty-six, sharing thirteen bedrooms.

Madame Jacqueline, owner of the house, had left with her husband the previous day for Paris to attend to financial and other affairs and wasn't due back until Saturday. She had arranged for her sous-mistress to take care of the cash desk, and Louise to look after everything else. Drink supplies also needed restocking from Paris. Wine was rationed, but beer was the drink most Germans demanded. Madame Jacqueline charged 2 francs 50 centimes for a beer, and 10 francs or more for a girl.

Answering the front door bell, Louise unlatched the barrel spy panel and opened it to a familiar face.

'Bonjour, Louise!' Dr. Gerault, accompanied by the regulation two French police officials, greeted her. He had come to do his routine blood and urine test checks on the girls, who always fussed round the witty, handsome young doctor from Cherbourg. He was the one man who could mean trouble for them. Madame Jacqueline wasn't allowed to be present in the examining room. Whenever things weren't satisfactory, he would send the girl into hospital. He always joked and gossiped, relishing endless anecdotes about brothels in which he had worked, such as the one near the Hôtel de Ville, in Paris – 'A vitesse – a very quick house.' he laughed. 'The girls there handled up to a hundred customers each a day – really rapid! Pace wasn't quite so frantic at the luxurious establishment at Port St. Martin, or that incredible place called "The Sphinx" which catered for Government Ministers and the like.'

Enjoying the tittle-tattle, which eased the tension of the visit, the girls swapped comments on their clientèle.

'You've had French, German, English – which do you prefer?' Dr. Gerault asked a group of the girls as he was about to depart.

'We like the English because when they finish, so many of them announce – "Very good, thank you" – said Antoinette. 'They're always so correct, although we don't think it's genuinely polite.'

'And the Germans?' Gerault pressed.

'With them it's something else,' Lucille laughed. 'When *they* finish, they bring out photographs of their wives and children to show us!'

As the front door closed behind the doctor, the girls immediately returned to their rooms to make up and change into the tutus – very brief ballerina-type skirts – they usually wore, with little else, for working hours.

What was the connection between *Mosquitos* flying to bomb the prison, and 41, Port d'Aval?

If it hadn't been for plump plain Louise, the brothel's chambermaid, there would have been far fewer serving sentences for thieving and Black Market offences in the criminal section of Amiens gaol, and far more awaiting execution for 'political crimes' in the German wing.

Louise put a lot of men and women in the cells because a cell was one of the best places to hide if the enemy were on to you. If you got wind that they were, the trick was to get charged with a comparatively minor misdemeanour, then, with the additional aid of false identity papers, conveniently to disappear for a few months inside a cell until official inquiries into your activities and whereabouts reached a dead end. Aware of this, Louise, listening to tongues wagging too freely at 41, Port d'Aval – the best bordel in the town – had arranged for many of her countrymen to be gaoled for their own good and to save their lives. In fact, they weren't actually her countrymen, for Louise wasn't the simple uncomplicated soul she appeared to be. She spoke French like a native, but equally English, German, Italian, Dutch, Spanish, Greek. Only her Russian wasn't of such high standard. Louise happened to be the wife of a Canadian soldier.

Lieutenant Laverdure and Gendarme Robine of the central Amiens Gendarmerie were two co-operative officers who often put people threatened with undesirable attention safely out of circulation awhile by gaoling them for petty offences. Gendarme chief Lamont, at the little village of St Sofleur, near Amiens, did the same, although sometimes, when Gestapo were too close, he would hide suspects in his own local Gendarmerie cell until able to transfer them to Amiens gaol. He didn't like retaining them long locally, in case nosey German officials turned up, as he kept a large store of explosives for sabotage purposes in his Gendarmerie too.

Louise's 'Maison de Tolérance' – pleasure house – also labelled a 'Maison Fermé' because from outside it appeared totally closed, with all street-facing windows permanently shuttered, opened its front door for business from 1.30 p.m. to 11 p.m. every day except Mondays, which proprietress Madame Jacqueline decreed should be 'A rest day as the girls get so tired'. Chaperoned by Louise, all eighteen girls trooped out on Mondays dressed in their best, and promenaded to the nearby Brasserie where they could gossip and enjoy an aperitif. Mothering them, shopping with them, taking care of their comforts, cleaning their rooms and ever changing bed linen, Louise laughingly told them: 'You're the only girls who wear out more bed sheets than shoes.' She did all the donkey work, while her mistress was always on hand to take the money.

The bordel's entrance, somewhat resembling a café, wasn't open to all comers. Reserved for Germans only – supposedly solely military personnel – it welcomed the Luftwaffe, Wehrmacht, SS Feldgendarmerie (military police) and the Gestapo, although civilians were forbidden, but Gestapo didn't consider restrictive regulations applied to them. The first occasion a Gestapo bunch turned up, all of Madame Jacqueline's 6 feet and 128 kilogrammes arose from her small reception table strategically positioned in the well-lit hallway. Barring their way, she firmly declared:

'I'm sorry, you're not allowed in here.'

People were always surprised by Madame Jacqueline's inappropriately frail voice and almost doll-like face, so strikingly small for a woman of her formidable size.

Recovering from the shock of being refused anything, one of the civilian-suited Gestapo crowd reacted sharply:

'We *are* allowed in, and we're coming in!'

'No you're not!' unwavering Jacqueline retaliated, towering above the Gestapo man like a boat prow defying the storm.

Hearing visitors raging at her mistress, Louise ran down the main staircase.

'They're not French, you know, although the man speaks good French,' she advised.

'Even if they're not French, they're civilians, so they shouldn't be here,' Jacqueline insisted.

Prattling away in German, Louise explained the military restrictions and answering in German, their leader replied:

'My name is Braumann, I am head of the Gestapo in Amiens, and these,' he said, gesturing towards the others, 'are some of my staff. They are soldiers of the Third Reich too, and are entitled to enjoy the same relaxation facilities provided for other fighting personnel. I take full authority for ordering you to allow us entry today, and every day you are open.'

Louise translated to Jacqueline who, experienced at the art of handling threatening animals by saying 'Nice dog' until able to lay her hands on something heavy to hit them with, conceded the issue.

'I accept your assurance, but would appreciate written authority to cover future visits,' she told Braumann.

Louise was even more delighted than the Gestapo at the concession. The Feldgendarmerie, in on so many anti-Resistance raids, were often valuably talkative in the brothel, boasting to girls about what they had done, and areas and places upon which they were concentrating. Gossiping Gestapo could prove of still greater use for, as Louise well knew, it wasn't only pants that men let down in brothels – inhibitions and caution also dropped.

Madame Jacqueline wasn't afraid of the Gestapo or anyone.

'I can shout louder than they can – I've a louder voice – and I'm bigger than most', she boasted. It wasn't an idle boast.

If they were courteous, she was nice to them, but if any caused trouble, she'd grab them bodily and shout:

'Shut up! – or I'll throw you out myself!'

Clients called her, and her husband Louis, 'Mama and Papa Pouf' because when German soldiers said they were going to 'have it off' with a girl, they announced: 'I'm having a Pouf today.'

Gestapo clients of four neighbouring bordels, some fifty yards away at 5, 9, 27, and 34 Boulevard du Port, also carelessly provided Louise with valuable information via chattering chambermaids, although none of the other maids was aware of her unofficial activities. Nor was Madame Jacqueline, for more than a year. The only person who knew, from the day she arrived from Paris, the true reason why she had taken the brothel job was someone Jacqueline christened 'Monsieur Bahnhof' because he looked French, wore German uniform, and worked at the station. Bahnhof is the German word for station.

Aged about forty, of medium height, with glasses and a little black moustache, 'Monsieur Bahnhof', who despite his credentials and attire, wasn't German, was still around when the Allies reconquered the town, except that he wore a different uniform. 'Monsieur Bahnhof' brought Louise instructions, and collected messages. As far as Madame Jacqueline was concerned, the less she knew about all this the better. The brothel was all she lived for, from the day she took over in 1941, at the age of twenty-nine, inheriting it from her wrought iron worker husband's aunt. Until then, she had been a waitress in a brothel at the naval, commercial, and fishing port of Lorient.

A great disciplinarian, she fitted perfectly into the skin of a bordel Madame.

'You would have made an excellent hospital matron, or a very good director of my clinic,' Dr. Gerault, the brothel's official doctor, complimented her. In charge of venereal disease treatment for the area, Dr. Gerault, – a friend of Dr. Antonin Mans, Chief Medical Officer of the Region, inspected all five Amiens brothels twice weekly at fixed times, plus making a third always unannounced surprise visit. He treated mainly French women as German personnel had a German specialist. There was also a house of prostitution catering for Luftwaffe fighter pilots at Poix, sixteen miles south-west of Amiens. This house wasn't classified as a full-scale brothel, but those in Amiens were officially licensed and controlled. Dr. Gerault, began as a junior at St. Lazare Hospital for Women in Paris, to which prostitutes from the streets and bordels were brought by the vanload. He was promoted to looking after brothels around Beauvais, Chantilly, and Saint Lys, then transferred to Amiens in 1940. Headquartered at the Hospital St. Charles, he was made medically responsible for all the local brothels by Dr. Mans.

Few other bordel clients walked the dimly-lit Port d'Aval-Boulevard du Port quarter at night, because there were always too uncomfortably many German military and Gestapo around. The largest establishment – Madame Jacqueline's – averaged a daily minimum of 250 customers, but often satisfied 800 in a day. There were twelve to fifteen girls per house.

Allied Intelligence and Resistance networks considered brothels among the safest of 'safe houses' for hiding spies or men and women on the run. Some bordels kept one or two rooms permanently free for threatened Resistants, escaping shot down aircrews, or agents in transit or awaiting transport back to London, so Pepe accordingly reserved bordel emergency accommodation as temporary shelters for some of the anticipated gaolbreakers. Houses were seldom searched because all invading Gestapo or police were likely to find in them were Germans.

Amiens brothel streets were rarely without crises of some kind, but as Dr. Gerault remarked to Jacqueline one morning:

'You have to have drains in a town otherwise we would be treading on shit all the time.'

One evening, Dr. Gerault received a panic call from one of the Maison de Tolérance Madames:

'Please come quickly, doctor – my husband has just hanged himself!'

He was dead, and when the police came, one of the girls pleaded with the officer in charge:

'Please give us the rope he hanged himself with, because a noose brings luck.'

The policeman gave them the rope, which they cut into small lengths to keep among their belongings as lucky charms.

Another night, Dr. Gerault was summoned again – Jacqueline's husband had acute appendicitis. Dr. Gerault despatched him to the local clinic staffed by nuns and run by Dr. Gerard Perdu. Every morning after the operation, four or five of the girls arrived at the clinic with bouquets of flowers, until you practically couldn't squeeze into the private bedroom for flowers.

'Sister, take the flowers to your chapel,' Jacqueline suggested to Mother Superior, Sister Marie.

'That is very gracious of you,' said the Mother Superior who, several days later, asked Dr. Perdu:

'Who is this lady who comes every day with all those nice young ladies to bring all those flowers for our chapel?'

Dr. Perdu replied:

'She's the Mother Mary of Port d'Aval.'

One of the Boulevard du Port houses was run by two Madames who looked so alike that they could be taken for twin sisters. Yet the boss' wife was fifty years old, and his mistress, thirty. Dr. Gerault congratulated him on acquiring two women, with a twenty-year difference, who looked virtually the same as each other.

'It won't be women that'll be the death of me, doctor,' forecast the Patron, 'it'll be Pastis.' He was right. All that the husbands of the Madames ever did was play cards and drink Pastis. They had nothing to do with the running of the brothels. As ever, the pimps did nothing. The Madame, chambermaids, tarts did all the work, whilst the pimps just spent money, wore beautiful rings, and died of cirrhosis of the liver from drinking so much Pastis.

Although there weren't separate bordels for officers and other ranks, officers never entered Madame Jacqueline's high-ceilinged large communal main Salle du Choix, with its blaring record player, garish neon lights, and completely mirrored walls. Jacqueline would emerge from her office, or momentarily cease poring over account books on her reception desk to signal to Louise to usher officers straight upstairs to prearranged girls. Regulations restricted officers from patronising brothels, but they went, and usually got drunker than lesser ranks. Only the night before she left on her current Paris trip, she had been compelled to call for a car to remove a high-ranking Luftwaffe officer. The officer's batman arrived;

stiffly saluted his stark naked superior, who could hardly stand and was vomiting all over the place, and addressing him as if nothing untoward was happening, carried him alone to the official staff car outside.

Dr. Kauert, Chief of German Medical Services in the area, which included responsibility for medical care provided for prisoners of the Amiens gaol 'political' wing, unwittingly presented Louise with opportunities of access to genuine official German Army stamps and documents.

Jacqueline lived in the house beside No. 41. The two buildings had connecting passages. The ground floor of Jacqueline's home was locked and empty, except for one part used as a store room. Dr. Kauert inquired:

'Is the house next door yours, Madame Jacqueline?'

'Yes.'

'Then we'll requisition it.'

'You can't do that!' Jacqueline protested. 'I live on the first floor.'

Although Kauert spoke a little French, and was always co-operative and reasonable, Jacqueline, anxious that his understanding of French might be insufficient for her explanations to get through to him, sent for Louise to translate.

'He wants to use the main ground floor room as a German health centre for all the brothels,' explained Louise.

'That's different,' said a relieved Jacqueline. 'It's only a junk room, so you can have it as a medical centre.'

She offered to paper and paint it, and install a basin and hot water supply in the room. Thereafter, it was manned by two male nurses on less busy days, and four or five nurses at busier periods. A big Red Cross was painted on the door, and all personnel were ordered to attend there before and after patronising a brothel. The Feldgendarmerie issued little brothel forms which were required to be presented at Jacqueline's medical centre for a 'before' physical examination, during which the form was stamped. Only if the paper was officially stamped would Jacqueline sell a contraceptive and at the same time accept payment for the girl. Contraceptives were compulsory. On the way out, clients had to return to the health room to be re-examined, when their paper was re-stamped, and the name of every visitor logged in a register.

War makes strange bedfellows, and so does prostitution, but Jacqueline and Louise handled the almost daily crop of troubles with calm discipline – nothing seemed to throw them, not even almost regular American and British bomber pounding of nearby rail marshalling yards. Whenever bombers knocked out the town's electricity supply, it was still business as usual, with Louise giving candles to each customer to light his way into the bedrooms. Just once she lost grip on herself and let her mask drop, when long after the house had shut for the night, she unlocked the front door spyhole in answer to persistent knocking.

'Madame, it's a Luftwaffe officer,' she informed Jacqueline.

'Tell him we're closed.'

She did, but he rudely demanded the door be opened, and that he and his comrade be provided with girls.

Angrily shouting at him in German, Louise slammed the spyhole. The banging continued until Madame Jacqueline, not understanding what Louise had finally said in German, flung open the door to give a mouthful in French. As she did so, the officer charged in waving a revolver screaming:

'Where is she? – Where's the bitch who insulted me like that?'

Keeping well out of the way, Louise let her mistress tackle the situation.

'Come back tomorrow and you can have our best, but not now, otherwise if a Feldgendarmerie patrol spots you here after hours, you'll be court-martialled,' she warned.

The words hit target, and they went.

'My God! – What did you say in German to make him blow his top like that?' Jacqueline asked.

'I called him son of a dog,' Louise replied sheepishly, bitterly regretting the words.

'No wonder he exploded – even I know that's one of the worst things you can throw at them. If I'd known what you said, I would never have opened up to tell him off myself.'

It was a never-forgotten lesson for Louise who realised her momentary lapse of control could have brought disaster to her and others, and to the camouflaged existence she had maintained since soon after the outbreak of war.

The only time she disclosed a hint of her true identity, was when close to death.

She cut her hand; the cut became infected, and poison swiftly spread beneath her arm causing high fever and excruciating pain. Jacqueline asked Dr. Gerault to examine Louise when he came on one of his VD check visits. A couple of days later he diagnosed:

'Gangrene.'

He came twice daily, Jacqueline and the girls took turns nursing her, but she deteriorated fast and was near dying.

In the middle of the night, Louise's eyes opened and, seeing

Jacqueline keeping watch beside the bed, clutched her hands and pulling her forward, whispered:

'Madame. There's a small package I've hidden in the attic. Destroy it. If the Germans ever find it, you'll be shot.'

She slid again into unconsciousness. Suddenly stripped of her customary self-discipline, Jacqueline went straight to the attic to find the parcel that could destroy her. It was there. Superstitiously, she decided not to open it as long as Louise was alive, but felt she needed someone to confide in – Dr. Gerault. She knew he had been fighting the enemy in his own fashion by issuing medical certificates declaring people to be sick when they were not, to prevent their deportation to Germany as slave labour. He also dished out certificates to stop men being sent to Glisy, the Luftwaffe fighter base outside Amiens. Labour forces were constantly recruited to fill in bomb craters at the aerodrome and repair runways – a dangerous job, as workers were open to repeated attacks by Allied bombers aiming to put Glisy out of action as often as possible. Jacqueline was also aware that the sympathetic German medical services chief, Dr. Kauert, advising Dr. Gerault that excessive granting of medical certificates could be classified as sabotage, had warned:

'The German services have got their eyes on you because you are giving too many certificates which help people avoid compulsory labour.'

Louise was in a coma when Dr. Gerault came in the morning.

'I've done as much as I can medically,' he told Madame Jacqueline. 'It's up to her now. She's strong, only twenty-nine, so if she has enough motive to live, she could still come through. Some prayers wouldn't hurt, either.'

'If she dies, doctor, there'll be a complication for which I'll need your help,' Jacqueline said.

'What do you mean?'

He saw the mental struggle on her face, and waited.

She told him about the package in the attic. Brothel Madames are usually expert at assessing men's characters. She was sure she wasn't wrong about him.

'What's her background? – Where did she come from?' he probed.

She's a Swiss who married a Canadian before the war. They were in France when fighting broke out. He returned to Canada to join the army and was posted to an armoured division, but Louise, for reasons she's never frankly explained, remained in Paris. At first, she was unemployed, so God knows how she lived. Then a friend sent her to me. She is, as you know, an incredible linguist, and I wondered at first why anyone with her language abilities needed to be a bordel chambermaid. But she knows what makes people tick, and I was glad to get her – she's a great asset.'

'She's also, without doubt, an Allied Intelligence agent,' concluded Dr. Gerault. 'Her background, talents, what she confided last night, and the package, add up to nothing else.'

'She admitted she was a spy,' said Jacqueline, 'but didn't say who she was working for.' Inexplicably, Jacqueline found herself not telling about Louise's friend – the mysterious 'Monsieur Bahnhof'.

'You're right about not opening the package yet. If she miraculously recovers, we may never have to, so we'll postpone facing that problem.'

The miracle happened. Louise didn't die. She continued arranging for Gestapo-hunted people to be hidden in Amiens prison cells, and providentially was in charge of 41, Port d'Aval the day the *Mosquito*s came to smash the gaol walls.

# 11 Visibility zero

'Hitler's just like any other man who gets too big for his breeches – he'll be exposed in the end,' Robert Beaumont soothingly assured his wife Liliane. She said she was feeling depressed about what the future held for their eight-year-old son and nine-year-old daughter, and needed a shoulder to cry on.

'It's no good being despondent,' he stressed. 'We must take depression for granted, knowing that as long as we don't get obsessed with it, it will pass.'

It was typical of him. Nothing seemed to dampen his spirit for long but there was another side of him nobody saw. For years this had made him terribly alone even among family, friends, and neighbours in the picturesque village of Warloy-Baillon, some twenty-three kilometres from Amiens.

Everyone around, including his wife, thought they knew him. He was the local doctor. He was also a British spy.

Robert, who believed in luck, had long enjoyed the kind that couldn't be boasted about – the luck of not yet being found out. At 3 a.m. on 15 February 1944, his good luck ran out.

Like so many doctors, he was ideal for espionage, able to travel justifiably and extensively, averaging a hundred kilometres a day covering his widespread clientèle. Using 'emergency calls' as an excuse, he was also entitled to the priceless privilege of being permitted to venture safely out at night.

Documents for London were sometimes picked up at night by *Lysander* planes, which made a quick rendezvous in the fields around the Pérronne area.

He received a small petrol ration from the German authorities, who regularly checked his mileage which he regularly altered. Extra mileage for clandestine activities he achieved with home-distilled alcohol supplied through farmer friends. By fitting a secret second tank, he was able to fill one with petrol and one with alcohol, and switched easily between them.

His widespread practice provided access to places where other agents would have been unable to operate without arousing suspicion. Professional calls meticulously logged in his day book gave him perfect alibis, and pharmacy records and signed prescriptions, subsequently confirmed his visits. Everything he did as a doctor was dove-tailed into his medical behaviour pattern to keep cover intact at all times.

The only occasion he put his wife's security at risk too, was when the Canadians abortively raided Dieppe and thousands were captured and manacled in reprisal. Three French Canadians – Conrad Lafleur, Guy Joly, and Robert Vannier – who escaped from what the locals termed 'the false invasion', reached the Somme and crawled through fields, eventually finding refuge in a private house. Vannier had an injured spine, and all needed medical attention. Robert Beaumont treated them, provided money, clothes, and false papers, and arranged chaperoned transport to Paris, Spain and England.

A year later, Conrad Lafleur returned to see Robert. Lafleur, now a spy, was working out of a house in Belgium.

'His coming here can threaten us all,' Liliane pleaded. 'Strangers suddenly turning up in any village create suspicion.'

Robert made no comment and offered no explanation for Lafleur's reappearance. The silence wasn't golden – it was guilt at having even remotely to involve his wife and children. When conversing with Lafleur, they spoke English to ensure Liliane, who didn't understand the language, heard nothing she could unwittingly give away.

Robert aided another Canadian from Montreal, who had been parachuted in to build and lead a sabotage unit specialising in blowing up railway lines, shunting sheds, and signal boxes. But the primary objective nominated as No. 1 sabotage target by Allied Chiefs of Staff, was the canal system. Besides its importance as an industrial and rail centre, St. Quentin lies at the heart of the north east France waterway systems. Military and industrial materials for the enemy war machine were transported along the canals passing through St. Quentin, which is why the lock gates were a constant air offensive and land sabotage target. German and French teams were forever repairing them. Limpet charges and time bombs – dropped from London – were attached to the locks by Robert Beaumont's associates, who lay flat in drifting, apparently empty little boats on the canal. Under the eyes of German soldiers guarding the canals, another little boat would 'drift' – aided by some hand paddling – alongside dozens of just-laden craft, and more than forty barges were blown up.

Apart from sabotage assistance, Robert, who had direct contact with London, co-ordinated escape for dozens of American and British airmen, and his evasion route connections were put to unexpected use when Lafleur, in trouble in Belgium and on the run, turned to the Beaumonts for help. For a month they hid him in their home until Robert arranged for someone to get Lafleur back to Britain. Two weeks after his departure, police searched the Beaumont house for three hours, and found an American revolver.

At 6 p.m. they led him handcuffed from his home, and drove him to the Gestapo house at rue Jeanne d'Arc, where Braumann and Lucien Pieri were waiting. Grilled until 3 a.m., he was taken to gaol, then interrogated again later that morning. The interrogation continued next day. Then the early morning Gestapo session, scheduled for Friday, was suddenly postponed until the afternoon. Robert was particularly relieved because he had been officially advised that his wife was being permitted to bring him a parcel at 12.30 p.m. The prison grapevine unofficially informed him there were two other doctors inside – Dr. Mans, whom he knew, and a Dr. Guy Guillot.

Liliane Beaumont was on her way to the gaol to see Robert for the first time since his arrest. It was nearing 11.20 a.m.

\*

Visibility was zero.

By the time the planes had risen a mere hundred feet or so, the men couldn't see a thing except the soupy driving mist of swirling snow beating against their perspex windows. There was fat chance of getting into formation, let alone staying in it. All they could do was hope and head for the Channel.

Leading the Australians, Bob Iredale levelled off at a thousand feet and his Canadian navigator, John McCaul, somehow managed to guide an accurate course to their scheduled first turning point, east of the town of Reading. Turning on time, still in blinding snow, they pointed themselves at the south coast. McCaul got some cold comfort from noting on his map that they were at least on a good route for avoiding high ground in such a low cloud base.

In and out of clouds at 270 m.p.h. several of them, including Pick, completely lost themselves as well as losing contact with the main body.

'It's a bloody good thing that although Mossies are such sturdy, pugnacious little brutes, they're so friendly to their pilots,' 'Daddy' Dale shouted through the intercom to his navigator. He had frequently been thankful for this. There was the time his aircraft went through a set of high-tension cables, yet returned to base only slightly bent; and also the sortie when, despite severe damage, with full bomb load still aboard, it saw them home safely on one engine. A *Mosquito* had the happy knack of being able to land on its belly with little damage. It had even stubbornly ploughed home with elevator controls severed, solely controlled fore and aft by flaps and throttles. Blessed be He who had given them the *Mosquito*, 'Daddy' thought, and its creator, Geoffrey de Havilland, too – to fly them out of trouble so many times, and, if prayers were answered, out of blizzards battering them now.

It was an aptly named aircraft as it stung vital and unexpected places. It would do its damndest even today, he was sure – despite the bastard weather – to retain its reputation.

It was freezing outside, yet sweat poured from his brow beneath his flying helmet, trickled down his back, and soaked his shirt.

As soon as they entered the clouds, ice built up on the aircraft, particularly on the windscreens.

*Typhoon* escorts, taking off from the Westhampnett and Manston bases, were having troubles too. Due to converge on Littlehampton to rendezvous with the *Mosquito*s, they ran straight into ten-tenths low cloud with the same opaque snowstorms, and soon became split up.

Three of the six support *Typhoon*s of 198 Squadron scheduled to accompany the first wave were forced back to base by snowstorms, but the eight *Typhoon*s of 174 Squadron, keeping tabs on the second *Mosquito* wave, and the eight from 245 Squadron, managed their rendezvous with the third wave.

Fifteen of the Hunsdon *Mosquito*s, including Tony Wickham's film unit plane, were pressing on to get to the Littlehampton area to meet the fighters; but four Mossies – two from the RAF 21

Squadron, 'Daddy' Dale's RAF 21 Squadron, and two from Bob Iredale's 464 Squadron – were helplessly lost, their crews straining to peer through snow-bespattered windshields as their wipers fought to clear a vision arc for them. It was futile. It would be an aerial work of art just to get back to Hunsdon, let alone struggle on to the target, even with the radar equipment tucked under the roof behind the pilot's seat, which enabled them to use the ground radar beacons dotted around the country to make them independent of ground control for fixings and homings.

'Bloody useless!' – one of the disgusted 21 Squadron navigators yelled, switching on the intercom to his pilot. 'If we can't get there on time, and we can't now, then we might as well not bother to go!'

There was no alternative. If being bang on schedule was the make or break factor of the whole exercise, this was already impossible. Time had run out for stragglers. The best they could do in the circumstances was to try and get their aircraft, and themselves, back home in one piece on blind flying instruments alone.

Pick and Broadley almost became the fifth duo not to make it at all to Amiens, and not simply due to losing their course in the blizzard.

464 Squadron's Dick Sugden had never before undergone such a terrible flying weather beating, and keeping even a reasonably tight formation was a task few of the raid pilots had ever had to do in such conditions.

As Sugden's Mossie burst from a cloud, he found himself heading straight for another *Mosquito* weaving right in front of him.

As he opened up the throttles, almost cartwheeling his *Mosquito* to avoid seemingly inevitable collision, the whole airframe shuddered, engines howling wildly. Everything depended on the shaking airframe and screaming engines staying in one piece.

Almost in the same seconds he yelled furiously over his RT:

'Get the hell out of it, you bastard!'

The other plane lifted with a violent surge, wheeling away, and as it did, the identification letter 'F' on the *Mosquito*'s side hit Dick Sugden between the eyes.

'My God, it's Pick!' a shocked Sugden exclaimed to his equally shaken navigator, who had missed the ident letter but thought they would never miss hitting the other plane.

'My God!' Sugden repeated softly to himself this time, at the thought of having told his CO to go to hell, calling him a bastard, and breaking his rigidly enforced radio silence. What had been Pick's last words at the briefing? – 'If any bugger opens his mouth up there . . . he'll be off my station tonight!' Well, he'd certainly

182

opened his, to Pick in person, and didn't fancy the roasting he was bound to get despite what he considered excusable events.

Sugden's timely appearance put Pick and Broadley back on the road again.

'Closer escort *Mosquito*s to Pas de Calais. Formation divided in snow storm and three aircraft returned to base.'

The signal from Westhampnett base came through to 'Digger' Magill's Operations Room at Mongewell Park via the Filter-Room at Fighter Command headquarters at Stanmore.

There was more bad news by the time Basil Embry arrived back at his own HQ from Fighter Command, to which he had promised to report in person after the Hunsdon briefing – a thinly camouflaged Leigh Mallory tactic aimed at scotching any last-minute attempt by Embry to participate in the flight itself. A second signal from Westhampnett notified that a fourth fighter had been compelled to abort, and the escort force was consequently reduced by a third.

Returning *Mosquito*s, forced to give it up as a bad job, started to report in. 'Digger' signalled each of the four planes in turn to transmit for a fix, after which he speedily counted from one to ten, then switched off. As he did so, three radio-fixer stations took bearings which were plotted on the table, then each of the lost pilots, flying blind on instruments, were advised where he was and what course to steer for home.

So the attack tally was now only twelve Mossies for the initial two waves; the stand-by 21 Squadron had four left to do what it had to do, if necessary, and there were just eight fighter escorts to nurse them through.

They could still do it, and they were at the Channel.

Another fighter signal came in:

'Made r/v at Littlehampton with 4 *Mosquito*s, 3 more joined while crossing the Channel at zero feet.'

*

It was the kind of bitterly cold February day that pilots hate, when cloud and sea merge into a grey blanket.

The sea looked cold and rough, and anyone unlucky enough to come down in it would be a goner in an hour unless rescued.

Pick had given crews time to settle down after the murderous take-off and frustrating, exasperating nightmare of a journey to the coast. As pre-arranged, they moved into cloud at intervals of a few seconds to minimise collision danger. Then, at last, they broke out from cloud and snow into reasonably clear sky.

The surviving fighter escorts followed watchfully above as the

Mossies skimmed across the sea at nought feet to duck below enemy radar. Propellers were only fifteen to eighteen feet above water, and, fortunately, there were no waves that day.

Tony Wickham's filming aircraft was about three minutes late for his *Typhoon* escort rendezvous. It was the first time he had been offered the luxury of a fighter escort, as normally *Mosquito*s operated alone. But with the target so close to so many enemy fighter airfields to ensure him getting a fairly free hand to do a good photographic job of work, two of the *Typhoon*s had been assigned to cover him and chase off nosey aggressive Luftwaffe fighters. Being late for the meet-up with the 'Tiffies', he was concerned that he might have missed them. As he tore over the coast, hurrying to catch the second six Mossies, with 'F' for Freddie among them, he almost jumped from his cockpit at the surprise of suddenly finding two *Typhoon*s flying alongside, one on each of his wing tips, and they stuck to him almost as fast as the glue that held the wooden Mossies together.

'I'm sure if we go down a railway tunnel they'll come right along with us!' he said laughingly to his navigator.

The Channel looked a yard wide, and would take ten minutes to cross.

*Typhoon*s were accustomed to crossing the Channel at low level to dive bomb the notorious Abbeville base, and try and knock out *Focke-Wolf*s and *Messerschmitt*s flushed out by the attacks.

The further across the channel they skimmed, the better the weather became. Two miles from the French coast even the sun appeared, and suddenly, thankfully, it was beautifully clear.

The omen seemed good.

According to the 'Y' service, a powerful listening device in England which was tuned to German fighter VHF and W/T frequencies, the enemy had tracked the Mossies over the Channel in spite of their low-flying tactics. The defensive guns on the French coast had developed the habit of dropping shots into the sea just ahead of low-level aircraft, making huge spouts of water which sometimes downed and drowned a low-level plane. All it needed was for the engine to suck too much water into the air intake, and that was your lot. It was a neat trick.

Rapidly climbing slightly on approaching the coast to clear cliffs, trees or other high obstacles, the Mossies immediately dived back to deck height to slide under enemy radar again. Going flat out, skimming houses and tree tops, the lower the better, it would be hard for Luftwaffe fighters to clobber them.

'Whoops!' Ian McRitchie's navigator, Flight Lieutenant

'Sammy' Sampson, yelled over his intercom, 'That was nearly too low.'

'Those villagers down there also thought so,' McRitchie laughed. 'Did you see the way they all threw themselves flat?'

'Were we that low?'

'Darn right, we bloodywell were!'

Beneath their wings, the web-like pattern of ice-fringed estuaries and salt marshes of the snow-blanketed Somme coastlands were like a vast map. On crossing the Dieppe-le Tréport road, they swooped low again, tracking the contours of the Somme valley, the plains of Picardy stretching below them with the now almost unbroken white surface only occasionally relieved by dark contrasting hedgerows and isolated farmhouses. They headed for Amiens over the battle-fields of that almost forgotten war, against the same enemy.

\*

A ringing alarm bell signalled overture time in the Luftwaffe's 'Battle Opera House'.

The bell was followed by a message from the Channel warning:

'British bomber units crossing French coast.'

The Officer Commanding, seated next to his Intelligence Officer, lifted one of the battery of phones before him to speak to the OC of a unit.

'Where are they headed?'

'Uncertain – they're undoubtedly on a deceptive course to mis-lead us.'

The constantly alert Wurzburg sets, with their powerful radar ears listening fanwise to the English coast, had detected the incoming aircraft. At once, 'Opera Houses' warned Luftwaffe fighter groups.

The 'Battle Opera Houses', as the central combat stations of the Luftwaffe's fighter divisions were ironically called by their staffs, were newly-created in 1943. Before 1944 the air Intelligence services of the Reich had even worked without radar equipment. Until then, the normally super-efficient Germans had depended largely on eye-and-ear observations. Incredibly the most sophisticated technical equipment had been pairs of binoculars. Intelligence battalion reservists, pensioned policemen, retired civil servants, men unfit for military service and hordes of women and girls manned observation posts, telephoning and telegraphing reports to centres which, in turn, notified air observation commanders responsible for notifying anti-aircraft batteries, air raid warning sections, and strategic rail and industrial centres. Finally, these activities were unified with army-run front-line air intelligence in operational areas and the fighter radar division, into an organization co-ordinating everything to provide complete air situation pictures for fighter and all other air defences.

The five giant 'Opera House' bunkers at Arnheim-Deelen, Döberitz, Stade, Mertz, and Schleissheim, orchestrated counter-attacks.

As the *Mosquito*s flew on, 'Battle Opera Houses' alerted Luftwaffe Sector Stations to direct fighter units towards them, but the Squadrons were flying faster than the Luftwaffe estimated, so intercepts were late. Black splotches from the Somme infested the sky like a spreading rash as gunners on 88mm. batteries hurled ironmongery at the Mossie pilots and navigators, tightly packed in their wooden boxes.

The guns couldn't have made the message clearer – German air defence were tracking every twist and turn, trying to guess where they were going, anxious to alert ack-ack batteries and fighters in the vicinity.

'Opera House' girls were methodically doing their job too. Behind the great frosted glass map panel in the centre of the room, female signals auxiliaries, wearing headphones and laryngophones, drew in *Mosquito* positions with thick sticks of charcoal. Behind the plate glass, their shadows could be seen ceaselessly marking with strokes and arrows on the huge map, the ever-altering battle scene. Light spots, projected onto the panel, illuminated the written positions, altitude, strength and course of the enemy, as well as of defending Luftwaffe formations. The map represented the air situation in a fighter division sector with only about a minute's delay. Each dot and every change shown were motivated by reports from radar and listening posts, aircraft observers, reconnaissance and other contact planes. Radio and phone messages were all pooled, sorted, analysed.

Attending the debut of the 'Battle Opera House', General of the Fighter Arm Adolf Galland, who had long pressured for super combat control, had commented:

'It's like a huge lit up aquarium with a multitude of water fleas scuttling madly behind the glass walls.'

But on 18 February 1944, the 'Opera House' didn't as yet know what show the attacking *Mosquito*s were staging for them.

On rising steps like an amphitheatre, seated several rows deep before the glass map scenery, fighter-director officers issued directions to units, based on the dispositions of the battle in progress. The artificial light on the faces of the directors and their 'stage-hands' – the innumerable telephone operators – created an eerie theatrical effect.

The network of telephone links connected command and other outside posts directly to the balcony of the theatre, from where productions were conducted.

'Notify fighters units in the Abbeville-Lille-Calais sector!' the Kommandeur ordered.

'If they are attacking in such bad weather conditions, and they must have ploughed through worse over England, they obviously have a very urgent target,' surmised the mystified 'Opera House' Kommandeur. 'What's so important for them to stick their noses out in this weather?'

He knew all northern France airfields were being swept by strong gales and snow flurries. Ground staff were working round-the-clock clearing snow-covered runways. It had snowed so heavily during the night that by morning only the tail and airscrew blades of aircraft were visible. Snow was still falling, and a hundred feet ahead was as far as you could see. Normally, they would have welcomed a brief bad-weather breather, but this was a different situation – they couldn't afford to remain grounded now.

At this point, none could estimate the bombers' objective – they were sure to try and throw them off scent with turns, diversions, or decoy attacks. It was still too fluid a picture to commit to a definite forecast. Fighter bases in potential attack areas had already been signalled to load hurriedly with fuel and ammunition for moments-notice take-off, and even now ground crews on auxiliary fields were trundling out petrol bowsers and ammo trucks ready for refuelling and reloading fighters which might force-land away from home bases.

Fighter pilots and ground batteries depended on the 'Opera House' for the minute-to-minute course changes of the attackers, for details of the size and altitude of the force, and every other bit of useful information they could provide.

A stuttering teleprinter broke the train of thought.

'What's the latest Met report from the area?' he demanded.

'Driving snow still sweeping across our airfields, although Met is sticking to its improved weather forecast.

'I hope they're right.'

'They could be going for one of their short penetration targets,' the IO suggested. 'Either Rouen, Meaulte, Amiens, or Richthofen II.'

Two 'Richthofen' gruppen were at Abbeville-Drucat, with deta-chments at Le Touquet-Etaples and at St. Pol-Brias. The spate of

Allied airfield attacks had been causing a shortage of operational aircraft in the 'Richthofen' Geschwader, and everyone recognised these attacks as a run-up to invasion. Apart from in-and-out low-level attacks by *Mosquitos*, *Flying Forts* of USAAF were also going in for surprise attacks on the very dangerous Abbeville-Drucat base.

The 'II' was to distinguish the new Richthofen Fighter Group, born in 1935, from the original World War I group. Adolf Galland had been posted to it from the start. Specialising in aerobatics, he crashed, and after months in hospital with multiple skull fractures and mutilated face, he emerged half blind – his left eye badly damaged – to become the Luftwaffe's Richthofen of World War II.

In the stale cigarette-smoke-filled air, ventilators hummed and teleprinters clacked ceaselessly away, accompanied by the disciplined murmur of the 'Opera House' chorus of voices – visible and invisible battle-disposition personnel, striving with their Kommandeur to unravel the *Mosquito* attack puzzle.

*

They were close. Bob Iredale peered down through his window blister, then checked his watch. Timing was so essential on this one – especially keeping that midday lunch appointment with the prison guards.

Shells were spouting up, reaching for them. As soon as they spotted initial bursts from an ack-ack battery, they altered course slightly, trying to outsmart them. Knowing shells took twenty seconds to get at them, they had to move course a few degrees after fifteen seconds, and from then on take pot luck as to which way the cats were going to jump. The sky was already speckled with flack.

'Blimey! – that was close!' 'Black' Smith's navigator breathed heavily down the intercom to his squadron leader partner. 'I thought we'd had it.'

'You and me both,' Smith breathed back.

There's an old saying among those who shoot game birds that 'They must be hit in the beak.' Birds don't mind their tail feathers being shot away. But with aircraft, the tail is vital, which was why German gunners were aiming at their tails.

Radio silence was strictly maintained – except for emergencies and irrepressible Aussies, and there were a few of those on this trip, who had some choice things to say as bloody great lumps of flak pelted them.

It was one of those pieces of flak that started 'Tich' Hanafin's troubles in 'Q' for Queenie of 487 Squadron.

Fight Lieutenant Hanafin, son of a Scots colonel from

Inverness-shire, was leading the second section of three *Mosquitos* in 'Black' Smith's first section of six. Heading towards Albert – the target run-up point – he felt the aircraft shudder. Black smoke plumed from the port engine.

'I'm going to feather it!' he shouted to his navigator.

Pressing the feathering button, then letting go, he instantly closed the throttle.

'Shut the petrol cock!' he yelled.

'Fuel off!' his navigator replied, carrying out his part of the emergency procedure for feathering.

Increasing starboard engine power, Hanafin re-set the aircraft's trim, pushed the extinguisher tit, praying that if the engine was ablaze, flames would now die. Pushing ahead on one engine, he miraculously managed to maintain position in the flight. All he could do was hope the freezing atmosphere would sufficiently quickly cool the malfunctioning Rolls Royce Merlin to enable him to re-start and restore stability in time for the target run-in. He was going to need maximum power when the bombs had gone. Maybe he should permit himself a faster getaway by using the laughing gas cylinders?

At the start of the year, backroom boffins had come up with the idea of achieving increased engine speed by mixing nitrous oxide – the laughing gas dentists used to use – with petrol. Gas cylinders and piping were installed in aircraft, but gas use was limited to only a few minutes at a time. The idea was to provide extra power and speed boost if it was desperately needed.

It was time to try unfeathering the engine.

'Airscrew control set fully back!' he notified the navigator, who immediately switched on the fuel.

Pressing the feathering button until revolutions per minute had reached six hundred to eight hundred, he released the button, letting the engine windmill until warm. He knew if the r.p.m. rose higher, revolutions could be reduced by pressing the feathering button momentarily then pulling it out again. When the engine was warm, he'd press the button and hold it in, making the airscrew feather then instantly unfeather, and after releasing the button when r.p.m. had risen enough, the airscrew should return to normal constant-speed operation. But things didn't always go according to the book. Although it restarted, the engine was malfunctioning and getting dangerously hot.

Almost there – but ten miles away – 'Q' for Queenie's port engine started misbehaving again, uncomfortably over-vibrating. As the Mossie's nose dropped, followed by one wing, 'Tich' held the control column back, regaining control by increasing his speed, but found he was still losing the other two of his section of three of Wing Commander 'Black' Smith's first section of six. To continue, arrive late, and throw out the so-essential timing schedule of those ahead and behind, could endanger everything. He had to drop out.

As 'Black' Smith ordered the remaining two to continue without 'Tich', Hanafin banked unhappily and turned for home. Escort *Typhoon*s couldn't help – they had to take care of the others. 'Tich' had no alternative but to attempt it make it alone on one engine – an easy unprotected duck for any ack-ack crews spitting metal at him. As if that wasn't enough, he still had his bombs and might have to crash-land. Coming in on one engine was never a piece of cake. Ground defence batteries would have spotted he was in trouble. The mere fact of parting company from escort cover and the others would have told them as clearly as a special delivery letter that he had a full bomb load aboard – a tempting morsel for them to aim at.

'Bomb doors open,' he ordered.

The doors opened, and the navigator gripped the bomb release.

Checking position, he saw they were over open farmland without a building or person in sight.

It was nice virgin territory, but in the state they were in, any target must have looked like a whore at that moment.

'Jettison them!' 'Tich' commanded.

'Bombs going – bombs gone,' came the reply with a note of relief. 'Tich' and his navigator watched the bombs fall in the fashion of all bombs, apparently drifting lazily below the aircraft for a few seconds, then nearing the ground, accelerating across the country-side. They didn't even kill a cow.

'Close bomb doors,' ordered 'Tich'. Then, as they closed, he added:

'Now let's get weaving!' and they weaved over the countryside like cross country runners streaking for home – to fly straight into a fierce flak barrage. First came a burst directly below them, then a second burst closer than the first. An anti-aircraft battery was obviously predicting their course on radar. Ground gunners had them taped and opened up. Metallic shell fragments accurately and noisily rained on the fuselage without piercing vital points. 'Tich' dodged, but with only one good engine, fierce avoiding-action tactics such as corkscrews were out. The best bet was virtually to point themselves straight back to Hunsdon, and then a dirty great lump of flak smashed through the perspex, and 'Tich' had copped it. Shrapnel tore into his neck, blood poured from him, and he felt his right side becoming paralysed.

Eternity seemed to pass for the navigator until 'Tich' spoke.

'Give me a shot of morphine' he asked, not releasing controls, still somehow keeping the Mossie on course.

Morphine helped pain, but not the paralysis.

As shells continued hammering 'Tich', assisted by his navigator, held on, and went on, knowing that as long as there was enough height, and speed wasn't less than 135 knots, with flaps lowered less than 15 degrees, it *could* be done. 'Tich' headed for home on one engine, one leg and one arm.

\*

Friday 18 February began memorably for Amiens prison warden Gaston Brasseur – he was arrested in his own gaol.

Warden Brasseur, mainly concerned with administration duties, wondered which criminal with a grudge had given him away. Heaven help those who help others to help themselves, he thought. He'd probably been shopped by someone who believed that the only people you should try to get even with are those who have helped you.

At 9.30 a.m., Braumann came to his office with his mistress – Nazi-loving Warden Lucienne Den, who, as usual, interpreted for him.

'Would you like to come with me a moment, Monsieur Brasseur?' Braumann asked with unaccustomed politeness.

'Yes, of course,' he replied, regarding the man whom he knew wielded the power of life and death.

As the less a man knows about you, the politer he normally is, Brasseur knew he was in trouble now that inquisitor Braumann – a sadistic headhunter type – was about to try and learn more about him.

He was led to the German quarters office where, after having him searched, by a guard, Braumann's whiplash voice snapped:

'Give me your pass keys and the keys to your office!'

As Brasseur placed them on the desk, Braumann, who rarely talked much, or used long sentences, said:

'Now we're going to your place.'

With that, the hated, red-haired ox of a man left, with the almost inevitable Lucienne following dutifully behind. Brasseur felt a chill on his skin at the thought of the corrupt pair in his home with his wife and fourteen-year-old daughter Yvette. He waited taut, mentally crossing his fingers.

Remaining under guard in the German Adjutant's office, he nerved himself to keep control and struggled to think clearly, knowing control of an interrogation solely relied on the temperament of the officer in charge – an undertaking for which these officers received no specific training, which is why methods varied so much. The bloody fool who attempted playing it clever was just the sort they loved meeting. It was wiser to play dumb, but say just enough. Steadfastly holding out was, he knew, the biggest blunder because it made you more obvious and vulnerable. Whatever it was they were after, it was smarter to give them something on account, to let them feel they were getting somewhere, or had all there was to get. Unflinching refusal wasn't courage – it was madness.

He wondered if they had discovered the message-smuggling traffic he operated through prisoners serving food and handling Tinettes. One German soldier and two prisoners came daily to the communicating door between German and French quarters to collect giant metal food containers and Tinettes. Letters were hidden beneath Tinettes, then secreted by prisoners under a little ramp alongside his office. There were sometimes two or three letters there, which he hid until the evening postman called and he was able to slip them into a stack of already checked and censored letters. Among thirty or so letters, two or three were never noticed and he had only done such favours because, after all, he was French.

But it wasn't the letters. His other habit, of distributing American and British propaganda leaflets dropped by bombers, started the inquiry, and a little notebook he kept at home finished him.

When Allied planes dropped leaflets in French with the latest news and developments, such as 'The Germans are retreating in Russia', and inciting people to sabotage the enemy's war effort with non-cooperation or sloppy work, he often got hold of leaflets and put them around the gaol to cheer prisoners. As leaflets moved from cell to cell, inmates indulged in excited tapping discussions about them on the prison plumbing. Someone – almost certainly one of the criminals – must have wanted to put him well and truly in the dung heap, and talked.

Ransacking his house, Gestapo found a notebook he had kept from Warrant Officer days, in which he'd written the names of all men serving under him, even noting their gun registration numbers. The book also contained the name and address of his brother-in-law – Sidney Canfield, a British military police regular army Lieutenant-Colonel whom his sister met during the first World War, and married in 1919.

'So you have an English officer brother-in-law,' Braumann stated almost tonelessly, jabbing under his nose a photograph of Sidney Canfield in uniform. Then flipping pages of the notebook taken from the house, he inquired:

'And what does this list of numbers mean?'

Behind the cold eye every detail was shuffled, indexed, and filed for the future.

Involuntarily, Brasseur clasped his hands tightly, trying to keep a grip on himself. The man probably thinks those gun registration numbers are a code! What with Sidney and the suspicious numbers, he knew it was enough to put him in one of his own cells.

'We're arresting you, and will commence a fuller inquiry later,' Braumann concluded emotionlessly, whilst his mistress and interpreter, moon-faced Lucienne – justifiably nicknamed 'La Chienne' (the bitch) – stood in a corner of the office savouring every second. 'The guilt's written all over your face!' Braumann jumped to his feet, shouting and shaking his fist.

Brasseur didn't have a chance to counteract the frenzy of accusations.

When Adjutant Eugene Schwartzenholzer started entering his name in the German quarters' register, Warden Brasseur knew he was about to join two other imprisoned officers of the law – Sûreté Inspector Serge Dumant, and Gendarme Achille Langlet – in the 'political' wing of the gaol in which he had guarded others for so many years.

*

'Achtung! Achtung! – All flights!

'Achtung! Achtung! – All flights! –

'Stand by for immediate take-off!'

The BBC dance music blaring from the loudspeakers in the Abbeville-Drucat air base Mess suddenly faded for orders.

Mechanics poured from hangars running, slipping, sliding on ice and snow to prepare aircraft, dumping camouflage screens into the snow, and opening canopy flaps in readiness for the pilots.

'They *would* turn up just in time for lunch,' one of the pilots in the Mess complained. Nobody had expected action in such weather conditions, particularly as they were aware of how bad it was over England. The Kommandeur had been entertaining staff, squadron pilots, and Commanding Officers of neighbouring units. Instead of oil flying suits, they were in smart white or dark-blue uniforms, white shirts and, in accordance with squadron custom, loose-fitting white socks. Mess conduct was expected to be correct. The Squadron Welfare Officer always wore 'English cut' uniforms, and 'Papi', as he was known was old enough to be almost any pilot's father.

Everything about Galland's famous Abbeville Officers' Mess in the attractive red-brick farmhouse, was gallant. Waiters in white coats served real English tea and sandwiches, Galland usually smoked English tobacco – it could have been an RAF Mess, but for the uniforms, and for the fact that one of the popular pastimes was showing camera-gun films of Allied ships being bombed and sunk.

The tables of the Mess – the furniture had been requisitioned from local houses – were loaded with warm drinks, food and a good supply of French Cognac. Everyone agreed:

'You've got to hand it to the French – they know alcohol.'

But the pilots' attention was now held again by the base loud-speakers:

'Achtung! Achtung! – Enemy aircraft – *Mosquito*s heading for Amiens!'

'Why bother with the railway yard in this weather?' – was the general question. There'd be other, better flying days.

The Kommandeur rose.

'Kameraden! – The Abbeville boys (they liked their RAF nickname) always do their duty and go! To the health of all true knights!'

After downing a quick toast to each other while their *FW190*s were being ground-crew inspected from head to tail, pilots, quickly donning flying kits, hurried to the aircraft bays in their heavy fur-lined boots.

The Kommandeur was nattily dressed in a plain linen flying suit, and bright yellow life jacket hung loosely across his shoulder and chest. A black, white, and red ribbon showed from under his collar.

Hanging around their planes, shivering, cursing, stamping their feet, impatient for mechanics to finish, like fighting airmen every-where, pilots joked and gossiped as they waited to go, knowing whoever fired first had the best chance of survival.

'I love the smell of aircraft "halitosis" ', someone cracked, referring to his plane breathing its mixture of petrol, rubber, oil and hot metal at him.

'Even in this lousy weather we're expected to die for the Führer and the Fatherland.'

'Maybe you will, but I won't. If I die, it will be for the People and the Fatherland.'

'But the Führer is the Fatherland.'

'Not to me he isn't and many more like me nowadays. I don't want to have to express my thoughts and feelings for the rest of my life behind locked doors.'

'Sometimes when I look at enemy pilots' faces, I see our own. What a tragedy! – We're killing *ourselves*!'

Even the Abbeville boys – the best of the Luftwaffe – had begun to question the war, and why and how long they would have to endure 'Freund Hein' – (Death) – waiting around for one of them to slip and fall into his lap. And today, they were about to face *Mosquitos* which, living up to their names, were stinging the Luftwaffe to death.

Mechanics sat on wings as pilots fastened their harnesses, and inertia starters began to wail.

'Hals und Beinbruch! some of the pilots laughingly shouted to each other, which literally meant 'break your neck and bones' but was the Luftwaffe fighter pilots' substitute for 'Good luck!', which was considered a bad luck greeting before take-off.

'Contact!'

Ground crews closed canopies and slid off the wings.

Ignitions on, engines thundered, the clouds of glistening snow whirled into the air. They would need full throttles to plough through the snow. Sixty engines all around the broad airfield started up. The four squadrons' dispersal points lay in the form of a square, so that their take-off paths crossed each other. This crossing over was very dangerous as, at the centre of the field, with one's nose slightly up, it was impossible to see across the other side, and take-off collisions were usually fatal.

As a continuous stream of instructions poured from ground radio, throttle levers gently pressed forward and aircraft roared off with only metres separating them from each other. *Fockes* trembled with power as acceleration force pushed pilots back into their seats.

At 105 m.p.h., they were airborne. A drop in height indicated wheels were safely up, and buttons pressed to close flaps at the trailing edge of the wings, gave additional lift to the aircraft on take-off. After a left-hand turn for a final parting look at the airfield, they climbed high, in radio silence, into woolly masses of cloud which could be guardian angels when you wanted to hide from an enemy out to kill you.

You got used to everything in war – especially killing.

As the *FW190*s headed for Amiens, still unaware that the prison, not the railway centre was the *Mosquitos*' target, the Abbeville boys were only too conscious of also being 'Galland's boys'. Abbeville and Galland had been synonymous since the Battle of Britain, when both the man and the place had earned the reputations they were to sustain throughout the war.

Quiet, pleasant Adolf Galland was good-looking dark-haired, with a little moustache, and burn marks around the eyes. His tunic full of medals included the Oak Leaves to the Knight's Cross – highest military award apart from the Grand Cross, which was reserved for Reichmarschall Goering. Galland, whose favourite activity, when not flying his fighter, was playing with model trains, was healthily respected by the Allies as their most dangerous Luftwaffe opponent. Never a Goering 'Yes' man, Galland got himself into lots of trouble because of his stand on many issues.

Asked by Goering what he would think of an order directing him to shoot down pilots who were baling out, he replied, 'I should regard it as murder, and would do everything in my power to disobey such an order.'

Cigar chain-smoking Galland, who hated the idea of joining the General staff as he had no intention of losing contact with his men, made the JG26 'Schlageter' Geschwader at Abbeville, the most feared and famous among all Allied airmen. He gave himself permission to smoke on operations, and flew the only German fighter equipped with an electric cigar lighter for his twenty-a-day.

Hitler complained that cigar chain-smoking was a bad example, but Galland wouldn't stop – not even for the Führer. A frustrated Hitler had to settle for vetoing photographs of Galland with a cigar in his mouth.

In the summer of 1941 when legless Wing Commander Douglas Bader was shot down in a Pas de Calais dog fight and taken to St. Omer hospital, it was Galland who agreed to Bader's request for a spare pair of tin legs to be flown to him by the RAF.

They cherished the legendary story in the Abbeville Mess of Galland being awarded Diamonds to the Knight's Cross. Goering studied the decoration and grimaced:

'These aren't diamonds at all. Just ordinary stones. The Führer knows a lot about guns, battleships, and tanks, but hasn't a clue about diamonds.'

Goering promised to replace the decoration with a real diamond version.

Told about the stones, Hitler sent for Galland, who was by now wearing Goering's set, took it and gave Galland a replacement, also with real diamonds

'Now you can see the difference,' said Hitler.

Goering was right – where diamonds were concerned. Hitler didn't have a clue.

Neither did he really have a clue as to the full seriousness of the air war, particularly in northern France, which was Galland's special responsibility.

'The Allies are coming, I feel it, know it,' Galland insisted, 'and we're short of fuel, ammunition, pilots – everything. Nobody tells the Führer this because he doesn't want to hear it, so we go on – not facing facts.'

Although the Channel Front had provided the backdrop for the greatest triumphs of the *FW190*s and Galland's boys, at the very time *Mosquito* squadrons were en route to Amiens gaol, he was reporting to Berlin loss in daylight fighting of hundreds of his flying personnel within the first couple of months of 1944.

'Among them were many of our finest Squadron leaders, wing commanders, and group commanders,' he said angrily. 'We have trouble closing these gaps, not with numbers, but with experienced pilots. The problem is that the Americans have created air superiority, so we must build our fighter arm. We cannot replace losses in existing conditions.'

Top Allied priority from the start of the year had been destruction of the Luftwaffe, especially Galland's fighters in the west which had been strengthened to some 1500 aircraft by January 1944.

'Destroy the enemy air force wherever you find them, in the air, on the ground and in the factories,' had been the New Year directive of all Commands from the USAAF Chief of Staff, General Arnold, and Galland's men were priority number one on Arnold's destruction list.

Allied fighter sweeps aimed mainly at provoking German fighters into having a go, but Galland shrewdly preferred saving forces for intercepting American day bomber raids. It was his Abbeville Squadrons in particular which were acknowledged to be the biggest risk factor at Amiens prison. Defiant Galland, had once been asked by Goering at a conference what the requirements were to improve his squadrons. He answered:

'I should like an outfit of *Spitfire*s for my group.'

It was one of the rare occasions when Goering was left speechless.

But as *FW190*s took to the sky that grey February morning to meet *Mosquito*s and *Typhoon*s, the line-up appeared to be Embry and his planners, Pickard and Co., and a whole invisible army, including remnants of the Resistance in northern France, versus Adolf Galland's Abbeville crews. But not one of them knew what was truly at stake.

It wasn't, as the attackers believed, the lives of so many already condemned prisoners. It was, above all, one man's life or death – and with it the success, failure, or postponement of the Allied invasion and liberation of Europe in the summer to come.

\*

They were late, three minutes late, but lucky to have made it at all, if you could fairly call it luck, because more courage, more effort, and more work – all that luck is most of the time – is what really got them there. That, and navigators' innate sense of direction guiding them truer than compasses.

Snow-disguised landmarks could have fooled them, yet they found their way to turning point after turning point, finally bringing the aircraft to the main Albert-Amiens road.

'There it is, skipper – straight ahead,' 'Black' Smith's navigator cried, starting his stop watch.

The snow-crusted Route d'Albert pointed long and straight, like a white finger, directly at the mass of dark prison buildings rising in the distance above surrounding walls.

'Three minutes to go, skipper.'

Smith, leading the three, streaked along, hugging ground as low as possible. Parallel with the road, barely missing black telegraph poles, with the propellers' slipstream kicking up a snowy wake, he throttled back, slowing to the lowest possible speed to ensure greater bombing accuracy.

The road was lined with tall poplars, and Pilot Officer Sparkes, one of the two captains accompanying their Wing Commander in the first wave, found they were flying so low that he had to keep his aircraft tilted at an angle to avoid hitting the tops of the trees with his wing. It was then, as he flew with one eye on those poplars and the other watching the road ahead, that he was reminded they had a fighter escort.

'Jeeesus!' was the only suitable comment as he nearly jumped from this cockpit seat as a *Typhoon* came belting across, seemingly from nowhere, right in front of the three *Mosquitos*.

'Two minutes to go.'

The two surviving Mossies of the second section – minus 'Tich' Hanafin – were swinging northwards in a wide arc, turning just in time to watch the first of the action. For safety they had all been flying in somewhat loose formation until nearing the run-in, but now everyone tightened up, wing-tip to wing-tip, to concentrate the bombing. They passed the first little row of houses on the far side of the road, the beginning of Amiens' suburbs.

'One minute to go.'

'We've *got* to blow the walls down to let the prisoners out; *got* to blow the ends off the buildings to kill the guards who should be eating by now, and we've only *seconds* to do it in' – were the uppermost thoughts in 'Black' Smith's mind as his navigator started the final countdown for him, the first *Mosquito* to go in.

'Open bomb doors.'

'Bomb doors open.'

Final check: course – exact; speed – exact; height – exact; thumbs on bomb release, aiming for the base corner of the east walls. Navigation was perfect – they'd never done it better. It was like a Hendon or Paris air display demonstration.

'Forty seconds . . . Thirty seconds . . . Twenty seconds . . .'

The poplars suddenly petered out and there, seconds ahead, was the prison.

'It looks *just* like the briefing model,' Sparkes shouted as they were almost on top of it.

A German patrol suddenly appeared, marching outside the wall, and a short burst of *Mosquito* machine-gun fire scattered them.

Aussies of 464 Squadron, arriving at Albert, could see the New Zealanders diving in.

At rooftop height, Smith's navigator didn't need to look into a bombsight to judge when to release their 500-pounders.

'Steady – hold it – bombs gone!'

*

It was soup time, but the young prisoner in priest's clothes, sharing a cell with false identity paper specialist Raymond Bonpas, was momentarily more interested in the sound of the unusually low-flying aircraft. He looked to the sky.

'Ask and it shall be given to you – that's what they say father,' said Bonpas. 'Well, a lot of us in here have asked hundreds of times but we're still here.'

Father Janin, still only in his twenties, gave a slow beatific smile and replied: 'We can't simply demand God's help when we need it. Prayer can't easily unlock prison gates, or bring relief from suffering, but it can help sustain us.'

Bonpas wasn't too sure whether his clerical companion was genuine, or a 'Mouton' – mutton dressed as lamb. The Gestapo were partial to slipping fake prisoners into cells in the hope of picking up unguarded comments. 'Moutons', stool pigeons, informers, traitors, collaborators – however they were branded – recruited from enemy and Allied ranks, were as a rule, embittered characters who went in for this line through greed, love, selfishness, fear, ambition, racial or religious prejudices, or plain stupidity. The most despicable were the double crossers who tried working for both sides.

English-speaking Germans sometimes appeared as 'prisoners' in USAAF olive drab, or RAF dark blue, possibly with a bandaged arm or hand and not too well shaven. They passed information through German guards, or when taken to the Gestapo for 'interrogation'.

Raymond Bonpas couldn't confirm whether Father Janin was a genuine priest or not, but had to admit the saintly soul knew how to spout the right words.

Prisoners from the factory at the rear of the main building had been marched back to their cells for the mid-day break, and German NCO Otto, with two young Belgian 'political' prisoners, was beginning the rounds with the heavy cauldron of soup.

At five minutes to twelve, Jean Beaurin studied the sky through the window of his cell. For three noons he had done this, wondering if Pepe and Dominique Ponchardier would truly deliver the RAF. No matter how great the daily disappointment he never gave up hope. The sun was bright on the snow-covered fields beyond the gaol. He watched the guard change on the tower opposite him. As the bell of the church some distance away rang noon, he counted the twelve strokes and accepted planes weren't coming today either.

The final toll of the bell had hardly died when air raid sirens wailed in the town and Jean, hearing screaming aircraft engines, scanned the small square of sky visible through the window and saw a bomber with RAF markings.

'Look out! – They're here!' he yelled to his three cellmates.

*

The ringing telephone sounded shrill and shocking in the room, and prison Warden Gaston Brasseur felt hairs on the back of his neck prickle and an alarm bell ring in his head as Braumann stared at him. He was taking a call, and it obviously concerned his case. God only knows if there's a God in heaven, Brasseur told himself, praying someone or something was watching over him. Then he heard the plane.

Adjutant Schwartzenholzer crossed to the barred big bay window of his office and seeing the first bomb falling, flung himself to the floor.

As Braumann dived under the table, Brasseur saw the beautiful *Mosquito* coming in even lower than the buildings, then soaring up over the building as it vanished. Two more bombs hurtled down heading straight for the German barracks.

Brasseur thought of trying to grab the Adjutant's revolver from the holster hanging on a hook on the wall. If he got it, he thought he could shoot the others in the room, which for him would have been the best solution. There wasn't time.

As he went for the gun, more bombs fell – one next to them. Another hit the prison kitchen.

As he twisted his body awkwardly to snatch the revolver, bomb blast racked him with pain; bricks rained down; bomb fragments ripped his clothes, and his glasses splintered.

Picking himself up from the floor, Adjutant Schwarzenholzer made for the door. Almost as he opened it and stood at the top of the

Maria and René Chapelle, with little Jean

The Ponchardier brothers who co-led the extensive 'Sosies' Intelligence and action network. This photograph was taken after the war when Pierre, on the left, had become a Vice-Admiral, and Dominique, on the right, was acknowledged as a Lieutenant-Colonel

The face of a traditionally publicly faceless leader of MI6 – Britain's Secret Service. Sir Claude Dansey – 'Uncle Claude' – always avoided being photographed but, like everyone else, had to have one on his passport. This was it

Allen W. Dulles, with his inevitable pipe, on a visit to London

'Pick' and Ming

Teenage railway saboteur Jean Beaurin, reunited with his
fiancée Ginette, after escaping from his cell

*left* Raymond Vivant, back in uniform after the Liberation

*right* The prison mo[...] used for crew briefir[...]

*left* The wartime identity card photograph of Dr. Antonin Mans

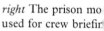

*right* The Luftwaffe' top ace – Adolf Galla[...] (left) – with some of 'boys'. Galland's pil[...] were the most dangerous threat to [...] gaol strike

One of the *Mosquito*s making its low-level attack

*top right* Flight Lieutenant Broadley making a final adjustment to Pick's Mae West just before the Amiens prison attack take-off

*below right* All that remained of Pickard's *Mosquito* after it had crashed at St. Gratien

A ground photograph of the damage at the junction of the north and west wings, looking from the main breach in the west outer wall

Admiral Edouard Rivière, Maria Chapelle's Paris espionage contact, presents her with one of the many decorations she received after the war

brief staircase immediately outside, a bomb landed and he simply disappeared in a terrible flash.

Braumann didn't reappear from under the table, so Brasseur assumed he had been knocked unconscious by the explosions.

Minus glasses, blinded by bomb dust, and suffering internal injuries, Brasseur, though unable to walk properly, reached where the stairs should have been, but they weren't there anymore. Stumbling into the remnants of the main prison interior out into surrounding gardens, then through a bomb-torn breach in the perimeter wall at the back, he headed for the small housing estate on the left. A couple of homes ahead and one adjoining the gaol requisitioned by Braumann for his personal use, had been demolished.

As he staggered on, body bent from bomb blast, covered with debris dust, his wife ran past without recognising him, until he breathlessly managed to shout after her:

'Hey! – Where are you going?'

She stopped, turned, then realising who the grime-covered apparition was, cried with tears streaming down her face:

'You're not dead!'

'Obviously not,' he replied.

*

'Black' Smith dropped his bombs from a height of ten feet – less than half the height of their target – pulling hard on the stick. The three Mossies pulled up to hurtle across the gaol buildings, throttles wide open, their deafening roar shattering the midday calm.

When the bombs went, the planes bobbed up violently, lightened by load loss, and after their leap-frogging over the prison, banking in tight blood-draining turns that made their aircraft structure shake, they flattened out almost to street level making passers-by either throw themselves flat, or rush into doorways.

'Bloody hell!' exploded Ian McRitchie, from afar, 'From here it looked like the buggers were going to land!'

For a split second he was certain 'Black' Smith's plane was going to smash itself against the wall until, gracefully, its nose went up as its underbelly virtually scraped the top of the towering wall.

'Christ!' – Smith cried out – 'Our bombs went right through that first wall, across the yard and into the wall at the other end!'

Even if they had wanted to, this was no time to stop and look – the minute-by-minute schedule made this impossible.

After a small ninety-degrees sweep to the north to allow for the delay fuses of the three leading aircraft, two *Mosquitos* flown by Pilot Officer 'Merv' Darrell and Pilot Officer Bob Fowler blew holes in the northern wall.

As Iredale's 464 came down the run from Doullens towards Albert and spotted the New Zealanders attacking, his navigator, John McCaul, instantly realised the timing had gone wrong.

'We've got problems, Bob,' McCaul warned Iredale through his intercom. 'Even though we're bang on time, the first lot weren't, and if we follow them over the target at low level at less than a two-minute interval, it won't be healthy.'

'What do you suggest?'

'Make a left-hand circuit to waste a minute-and-a-half or two minutes,' McCaul advised.

They had flown together so much, relied on each other so closely, that Iredale didn't question. They had been a team from 1941 days, together in the Officers' Training Unit. Twenty-eight-year-old brawny six-feet-one thirteen stone McCaul – a paper company employee from Toronto and Montreal – was attached to the RAF whilst serving with the RCAF, and on completing a tour in Blenheim bombers with Bob, both were awarded DFCs. They knew each other backwards. Swinging immediately to port, Iredale indicated to the rest of his crews to follow – including Pick, who was flying with them.

The deviation brought them within range of ground defence batteries, and the Amiens-Glisy Luftwaffe air base. As they passed over it, they saw ground crew and pilots tearing towards their aircraft to get them airborne.

Flak from ground defences came at them at first in spasmodic flashes as booming ack-ack poked around trying to improve accuracy, then suddenly defences erupted. Mushrooms of dense flak were everywhere, and smoky black puffs all around them were doing their damnedest to bang them out of the sky.

'God, that was close!' one of the navigators shouted.

'I could smell the cordite!'

Although violent evasive action near the target could be necessary, they knew the run had to be steady, regardless of opposition, until 'bombs gone'.

On completing their holding circuit, they were again on the Albert approach road. Coming up to the prison they could just distinguish, through obscuring smoke and billowing debris dust what 487 Squadron had achieved.

'There are holes and breaches in two walls, and a large part of the end of the main building has been hit!' Iredale shouted to McCaul.

Now it was their turn. Diminished by the two forced back to base by the weather over England, they had reformed to attack in sections of two.

Iredale knew they had to do the job right. There's no margin for error, he told himself, as they came in, so I won't even entertain the thought of missing.

No big breach had been made in the eastern wall.

'Let's go for the eastern wall and try overshooting with a bomb to take care of that guards' quarters at the base of the building's cross section,' he shouted to McCaul, and the first Aussie section of two swept in, going for the eastern wall at fifty feet altitude. As they slightly overshot, it was precisely 12.05 p.m. when their bombs dropped.

'We've scored a direct hit on the guards' quarters!' John McCaul yelled.

'We *just* cleared that wall, and no more, after the bombs went,' 'Black' Smith shouted to his navigator, who had been holding his breath.

487 Squadron's reduced second section, already swooping in to breach the north wall, also had a perfect view of the first wave's results and were staggered to see bombs go straight through or over the eastern wall careering erratically across the prison courtyard between buildings before embedding themselves into the far side western wall where, eleven seconds later, they exploded. But one bomb hit the main building, and another the northern side of the eastern building.

The two aircraft attacking the northern wall breached it, in two places, and the junction of the northern and western wall also collapsed.

Again a solitary bomb struck the main building. Stray bombs crashed into the northern horizontal arm of the cross-shaped prison – the wing housing 'political' prisoners. But oncoming crews witnessed another fantastic sight – bombs, and no one could judge exactly whose through the pall of debris dust already spewing up from the prison – tobogganing across snow at 300 m.p.h. knocking down fences and houses without appearing to lose velocity, then slithering to a halt on open ground hundred of yards beyond the prison, and exploding.

Two factors the planners hadn't anticipated had taken a hand. The first was undiscovered until years after the attack – *the stones of the outer prison walls hadn't been securely concreted when originally constructed*, and were therefore far weaker than the planners, or anyone had anticipated. Consequently, some of the bombs simply sliced through them like cheese, flying on to buildings they were never intended to hit.

The second unforecastable factor was unpredictable ground ice. Nothing could safeguard accuracy as bombs, tail-fused and pitched horizontally, struck and skidded along the ice-covered ground, helplessly out of control.

'Whoever says it's a piece of cake is a bloody liar,' said 'Black' Smith as they set their return course. 'Now it's done, I'm completely shagged – spent.'

It was Ian McRitchie's task in the third wave, which included Pick, to place bombs into the barracks situated at the top end of the prison buildings' cruciform. After the initial explosions, everything was smoke, flames, and confusion, and McRitchie could see stray bombs jumping and sliding through the snow like frightened rabbits.

Nearing the gaol, he turned to starboard, climbing for a clearer view of the scene to judge points those before him might have missed, and where, other than his specific barracks target, further bombs could be effectively placed.

Moving in with his navigator, Flight Lieutenant 'Sammy' Sampson, with Pick close by, Ian McRitchie's eyes were held by the scene of destruction. He decided in the final seconds that he would rather break his neck in the attempt than overshoot the target and thus be indirectly responsible for a holocaust that would undoubtedly follow. Every single man in the force, he was certain, must feel similarly, and everyone in the first two Squadrons, he was equally sure, would be relieved not to be burdened by the overwhelming thought plaguing 'Daddy' Dale's 21st Squadron: would they be made the executioners of all the prison inmates?

Plainly seeing Bob Iredale put a bomb into the wall at the Albert end of the gaol, McRitchie cautioned Sampson:

'We've got to wait until Bob's bombs go off – We can't risk running in and having his bombs shooting debris at us and fouling our visibility.'

McRitchie's second section, with Pick as 'Tail-ass Charlie', swung wide to the right to attack the farther end of the prison, 90 degrees away from Iredale's approach. Going in they bombed the wall and the guardhouse, then climbed hard, barely missing a gargoyle figure on the building. Continuing their climbing turn almost over the Albert road, they happily saw their bombs go off in the guardhouse, and as they rounded the back of the prison, the holes in the wall made by the two belly bombs and one wing bomb were satisfyingly visible.

'Good on you, Mac!' 'Sammy' Sampson congratulated McRitchie, thumping him on the back.

The entire prison and courtyard were practically invisible under a blanket of bombing dust and smoke. McRitchie knew somewhere behind him, Pick was circling around waiting for the pall to lift sufficiently for him to check and decide what he had to do as last man in, and whether or not 21 Squadron needed to carry out their appalling stand-by assignment. In the terrible smoke-obscured visibility conditions, he knew it would have been suicide for Pick to make his run at under twenty feet for accurate placing of his bombs, as the slightest miscalculation of height could cause the bombs to jump the wall and hit the main building housing the prisoners. McRitchie prayed, as he had never prayed before, that Pick would see prisoners running through holes already blasted through the walls and not have to give that order to 21.

Too occupied with putting bombs in the right places, navigators had little chance to check results. Turning from his own bombing run, John McCaul witnessed McRitchie and Pick dive in, saw Pick peel off and climb to assess results, then blessedly, men in dungaree-type outfits running through the gaping breaches in the outer wall and stumbling across adjacent fields.

Tony Wickham's RAF Film Unit also spotted and focused on escapers. As his cameraman, Lee Howard, filmed, they both saw 'F' for Freddie orbiting and reconnoitring almost alongside them, whilst escort *Typhoons* practically figure-skated over the target ground.

Crouching in the nose, enthusiastically getting pictures, Howard kept demanding, whenever Wickham suggested it would be healthier to about-turn and make for England:

'Oh, no! – do it again – just once more.'

Putting it all on film, they were equally conscious of the terrible final decision Pick was, at that moment, having to consider for 'Daddy' Dale's crews.

As they completed the third circuit, Howard challenged:

'You know how you can tell the Nazis from the prisoners?'

Wickham didn't.

'On our every run, the Germans throw themselves flat on their faces, but the prisoners keep right on running like hell – *they* know whose side we're on!'

Circling the prison, evaluating damage from five hundred feet up, Pick and Broadley could see the west wall had got the worst of it, with a large section completely gone at the junction corner with the north wall which had several smaller breaches. Though hit in places, the east wall hadn't been sufficiently breached, but there was a beautiful gap in the south wall close to the prison main gates. Few of the outbuildings within the courtyard were unscathed, and the German guards' quarters had been well and truly taken care of. The extent of damage to the main building was still partially overcast by the stubbornly hovering pall of smoke. Best of all for Pick was the magnificent sight of gaping holes disgorging fleeing inmates, their tiny black ant-like figures starkly contrasting against the dazzling whiteness of the snowy landscape.

Moments later, Bob Iredale and John McCaul heard him calling 'Daddy' Dale and his 21st Squadron –

'RED DADDY – RED DADDY'

'Well, fan me with a plate of soup,' said 'Daddy' Dale, relieved to receive the 'Go home' message from 'F' for Freddie.

The signal for their return to base without further attack meant they were off the hook – the bombing had been satisfactory. It was the last any of them ever heard, or saw of Pick.


# 12  Nobody got soup


Only two of the seven Denis children were at home when *Mosquitos* started aiming their delayed-action bombs at the gaol, and home was a little too close for comfort.

Five of the smaller Denis children had gone with their mother to stay with an aunt in Normandy because of incessant Allied pounding of Amiens, leaving their eighteen-year-old brother Michel and twenty-year-old sister Marie Louise behind with their father.

Their neighbour, nine-year-old Marcel Bellanger, off sick from school, was sitting up in bed listening to the roar of the *Mosquitos* attacking the prison when a bomb completely stripped off the roof above him. Michel and Marie Louise, home for lunch, saw the same bomb miss them miraculously; strike a twelve-centimetres thick iron reinforcing bar in their backyard wall; bend and bounce off the bar; skid across a snow-covered field and go straight through the rear prison wall without exploding.

When the bomb blew up seconds later, blasting an enormous hole in the wall, a German soldier climbed through the opening, rifle slung on his shoulder, but without an arm. He stood motionless a moment, as if on guard, then collapsed on a pile of rubble.

Fifty-year-old Sosthène Denis was cycling home fifty metres from the gaol when he spotted the bombs coming. Diving off the bicycle, he hurled himself into a ditch and stayed there until the explosions stopped. He grabbed his bicycle, and pedalled perilously and anxiously along the icy road to his children, grateful that his wife and the younger ones were away.

Inside the gaol, nobody got soup. The two young Belgians carrying the soup urn were flung right across from one balcony to the other, like a pair of cats, and with cat's luck, were unhurt. Otto the Rhinelander – the hated NCO accompanying them on the soup round was pulverised to pieces.

Préfecture bureau chief Gruel was exchanging his conspicuously resplendent uniform of office for the ordinary civilian garments his mother and daughter had just brought him, when the bomb killed him. He was found in the cell – formerly occupied by Dr. Antonin Mans – wearing only a vest and pants.

Dr. Mans's ground floor cell door was ripped from its hinges. Stunned, but apparently unhurt, he moved in a daze into the courtyard until he heard someone calling:

'Doctor! – doctor! – let us out!'

André Tempez, shut in a first floor cell, had seen him.

Hurrying back into the building, he felt a key in his hand but couldn't remember where he'd picked it up. Maybe he had unconsciously grabbed it from a table in what was left of the Gestapo offices? The staircase to the first floor had gone, but its iron supports were still hanging down. He somehow scaled them to reach Tempez and found that the key he had unconsciously acquired, unlocked cells. From all directions men and women shouted to be freed. Passing the master key to someone to open the rest of the doors, he slid down the staircase supports to the ground, followed by Tempez.

Lying amidst the debris on the floor of Tempez's cell was a book his friend Raymond Dewas has brought him – *The Decadence of Rome*.

As Tempez and Mans headed from the smashed main gate, they saw a woman on the ground, legs severed at the thigh, with a man on his knees, cradling her head in his arms. It was her husband. She had been due for release that afternoon, and now, even in her agony, was trying to help her heartbroken husband, telling him:

'Don't cry, you'll make another life for yourself.'

'I can't leave her, or any of the injured, André,' Mans said. 'I'm staying to do what I can.'

'So will I,' said Tempez.

A voice added:

'I'm with you, too, Doctor.'

Despite injuries, Gendarme Achille Langlet, due to be executed for aiding American and British parachuted agents, joined them.

'Let me bandage your head, Langlet,' Dr. Mans offered.

'There's others worse than me who need you more,' he declined, and started digging with bare hands into a pile of rubble from which the cries of a trapped woman could be faintly heard.

Desperately tearing at the entombing mound of bricks and stone, relinquishing his own chance of freedom and life, he inexplicably found himself recalling the Chinese proverb he had pasted in a scrapbook on the morning of his arrest . . .

'Better to light one candle than curse the darkness.'

In Cell 15, with Amiens municipal council member Louis Cellier and four others, including a Belgian espionage agent who had only arrived the previous day, Gendarme Langlet just had time enough to glimpse the bomber's undercarriage before explosions smashed their window to pieces; black cloud enveloped the cell, and a violent blow on the right knee tore his trousers and soaked them with blood. Twice more planes came, and twice more shrapnel tore into his face. His knee was on fire, so using a soup spoon, he extracted the walnut-size piece of shrapnel from it, with the moans of the trapped and dying torturing his ears.

Smashing at the door with a stool, he shoved his arm through a hole he had made and opened it from the outside, but their exit was still barred by mounds of rubble which had fallen from the upper floors. The main roof had gone, as had most of the even number cells. All that he saw in Cell 17 next door, was a shoe he thought had belonged to Raymond Vivant.

One of the first bombs hit the guardhouse, where soldiers, anticipating lunch, died seated around the table. In what remained of the place, Gendarme Langlet found his belt – taken from him by a soldier – hanging from a hat peg.

The Route d'Albert entrance to the gaol had collapsed, but instead of attempting to escape, Langlet searched the battered buildings.

'Are you looking for your wife?' Warden Lefevre asked.

'Yes.'

Uppermost was the fear that his wife, who had just delivered clean laundry for him, had been caught in the bombing.

'Your wife, and other women visitors left just in time,' Lefevre assured him, but Langlet still didn't try to run for it. Returning to the wrecked gaol, at the largest collapsed section, he found Dr. Mans and Captain Tempez tending wounded.

Also sacrificing escape, others stayed to assist.

'Check if the operating table in the medical room is in one piece,' Dr. Mans ordered. 'There are syringes, drugs, and some general supplies there too – we need the lot.'

The table and equipment were brought intact into the courtyard. Laying the desperately injured woman on it, Mans gave an injection, but couldn't save her. With his assistants he attended everyone – fellow inmates, and wardens, and injured guards.

'Back into the cells, scum!' a German soldier, blood streaming from a gash in his head, screamed at the doctor and his team. Sole survivor of a patrol gunned by a *Mosquito* as they were marching outside the perimeter wall, the berserk NCO staggered around threatening everyone with a sub-machine gun. One of his wounded comrades, shouting in German, halted him long enough to give Mans an opportunity to calm him, and bandage his head so completely that he couldn't see well enough to harm anyone.

Cell 18, which housed 'The Curé of Montparnasse', wasn't damaged, and Maurice Holville, pimp Jules Dumay, Boris the young Russian, and baker Vincent Darras were unhurt.

Sûréte Inspector Serge Dumant was dead, but con man Adrian Leopold and forger Georges Danielou were gone.

Assessing that the weakest part of the door would be adjoining the bottom panel through which soup plates were usually pushed, Maurice Holville attacked it with a stool. Still in the railway official's uniform he had been wearing when arrested, Maurice rushed into the courtyard and collided straight into Jean Beaurin.

'I've been looking everywhere for my mother and Roger,' Jean said, 'but there's no sign of them.'

'Maybe they've already left, so don't look anymore, or you'll never get away,' Maurice warned.

Twenty-two-year-old Marius Couq, one of Dr. Mans's imprisoned liaison agents, trapped in the mass round-up, also decided to remain with the doctor.

To stay meant certain recapture and the firing squad, so almost blessing the third bomb that blew open their cell, Jean Beaurin and his three cellmates, scrambling over the rubble, located the gaping hole in the outer wall, and ran into the fields.

Jean's mother, wounded in the head, had been taken to hospital. His brother Roger was killed by falling masonry.

Masonry only narrowly missed doing the same to Henri Moisan, who wondered how many times you could die when he couldn't breathe under a ceiling which had collapsed on him. Fortunately, the ceiling, still in one piece, precariously propped up by a lump of stone, just stopped short of crushing him completely. Shouting for help seemed to suck air into his suffocating lungs, so he kept shouting until pulled out.

When bombing began, he thought D-Day had come. An agricultural broker and spare-time collector of information on fortifications and troop movements, which he passed to André Tempez, Moisan was put in an ambulance by rescuers, and delivered to his brother-in-law Dr. Filachet's house, instead of the hospital. Using lumbar injections, Dr. Filachet made Henri appear sicker than he was, in case anyone came.

Lying in his bed, reflecting on the events which had put him there, Henri Moisan thought the story of the prison attack almost worthy of the previous occupant of his house – Jules Verne – who had written so many of his extraordinary novels in it. But Moisan hadn't the remotest notion of the true length and depth of the gaol bombing story, nor that it was, in fact, more incredible than any fiction conceived by even Jules Verne's fantastic imagination.

*

Some people are born good, some make good, and some are caught with the goods, but Victor Pasteau the thief had no intention of letting himself or others get caught again through criminal identification dossiers in the prison Governor's office. This time he wasn't absent-minded about his promise to burgle the office and destroy the records.

Once Pepe fixed into Victor's mind the idea of duty, it couldn't get out. Admittedly, he was a crook, but he was also a patriot and ready to give his last drop of blood for his country, though he was in no hurry to provide the first drop.

Accepting that the best way to get rid of duties was to discharge them, he scurried from cell to cell happily opening doors with copy master keys fashioned from metal strips extracted from his iron bed, then switched attention towards the Governor's bureau in the Administration block at the front of the main building. Slipping a skeleton key into the door separating the prison's central Rotonde from administration offices, Victor was professionally proud to discover how efficiently it worked. The Governor's room was empty, and the uncomfortable aftermath silence of the whole building was only broken from time to time by moans from the wounded. Victor concentrated on metal filing cabinets.

The art of picking locks is something speedily acquired by prisoners. Two bits of stiff wire, each bent in the shape of an L, is all that is needed. With one you lift the spring of the lock, and with the others you feel for the notch in the bolt and slide it along. Victor generally favoured sardine tin openers. The only trouble was that the process could be slow, and someone might walk in at any second. He couldn't help worrying, but worrying wouldn't help either.

A cabinet lock clicked, and the first was open. He opened folders and scanned and thumbed pages. Hastily glancing at documents, he saw some had prisoner's photographs attached and some hadn't, as Pepe forecast. Victor stacked them on the Governor's desk and started on the second steel cabinet, which opened faster. He pulled out a drawer, and it held hundreds of cards with photographs – full face, and profile, with general descriptions, plus 'political' or criminal records. As he bent over the fresh batch of files he had piled on the desk, he felt he was being watched. Whirling around he found himself confronted by a lean man of about thirty, with grey eyes and civilian suit to match. Was he Gestapo or a prisoner from the 'political' wing? Victor was branded a criminal prisoner by his double-breasted regulation brown jacket and trousers and beret – shaped like German first world war berets – perched on his head. When the coarse uniform material forced Victor to scratch himself, his sole consoling thought was that Franciscan monks used the same material for their clothes.

Casually leaning against the door frame with a hint of a smile the man asked:

'What are you in for?'

'Thieving.'

'And what do you intend doing with those files?'

Victor, who had always watched his step even when he wasn't going anywhere, who had lived most of his life on the basis that honesty wasn't the best policy, decided that on this occasion, it could be the safest.

I'm going to burn all the shitlists,' he replied.

'I'll help you,' the man said, and removing a box of matches from a trouser pocket, struck one and set fire to a stack of documents.

Borrowing the matchbox, Victor announced:

'The next lot's mine,' and put a burning match to them. They watched the flames char the papers and the Governor's desk.

'What do you want to do next?' the man inquired.

'A crap,' said Victor.

'Well, what are you waiting for – to mess up this nice clean floor? – Go on – get it over with!' the man grinned.

Shaking off his fear, Victor disappeared into the Governor's toilet, and on his return, the man said quietly:

'You know we ought to finish the job properly.'

'What do you mean?' Victor asked, somewhat nervously, as for the first time, his acutely sensitive ears caught a slight accent in the man's fluent French.

'There are a lot more files – mostly, it's true, affecting people such as me – in the Gestapo house at rue Jeanne d'Arc. We should burn those too.'

Victor suddenly felt tired.

'The Gestapo! – You want to burgle *their* place?'

'Yes, and I could do with your expert help – we could save a lot of lives.'

'I'm scared,' Victor said, almost inaudibly.

'Well, we'd make a good pair then, because the idea also scares me, so maybe if we stick together we'll be good for each other!' Seeing the look on Victor's face, he added encouragingly:

'Nobody's expecting you to become a hero overnight – a step at a time will do. Don't worry – fear's nothing to be afraid of. We all need it; can't do without it. It's a natural part of our make-up and the motivation of so much we do.'

Victor regarded him with nervous curiosity.

'Anyway, first we have to steal some ordinary clothes for you from somewhere,' the stranger concluded.

Victor let out his breath slowly.

'I'd steal anything,' he said, perking up again, relieved to be back on familiar ground. 'If I can lift it, I'll pinch it, but at least this time I'll be doing it in a good cause.' Despite the apparent firmness of his resolution, the mere thought of the house on rue Jeanne d'Arc scared the hell out of him, but some tasks, although seemingly impossible, are so important that they have got to be tackled. Even Victor the burglar knew that.

He needed the answer to one more question.

'You're not French, are you?'

'No, American – Call me Freddie – it's as good a name as any.'

*

As hundreds fled blindly from the devastation, streaming through gaping holes bombers had ripped out of the front and back prison perimeter walls, Dominique Ponchardier and an armed unit ran into the gaol.

Others, accidentally in the area, also ran into the devastation to help, but the pall obscuring everything made it virtually impossible to distinguish friend from enemy. With Resistants, criminals, French wardens, and German guards mixed up and looking alike through the dust covering their clothes, there was incredible confusion.

Unlocking unopened doors looking for imprisoned comrades, guns ready for opposition, Dominique and his men realised there was little breathing space to scour thoroughly the rubble and ruins for anyone trapped before German reinforcements and police swamped and surrounded the place. If they couldn't find their friends in the cells, they would have to leave without them.

Fifteen were located, but not Jean Beaurin nor Maurice Holville.

Solitary confinement dungeon cells in the prison basement were either smashed or open and empty, with manacles and chains still attached to remnants of stone walls, but the occupants had gone, including the one-legged spy.

Christiane Lecaillet, secretary at the chair factory, fifty metres from the gaol, saw one of the dungeon maximum security cell inmates leave.

They usually didn't stop work at the factory until 12.30 p.m., but today was different. Bombs were falling.

Christiane was watching diving, cannon-firing RAF *Mosquitos* attacking when the exodus of dust-bespattered prisoners through the snow began – some running for freedom, others trying to get away from the bombs. A black leather-suited German officer, stalking from the ruins with whip in hand, commenced pacing up and down muttering to himself, apparently completely oblivious of the hordes escaping past him, including two brown-uniformed prisoners from the criminal section carrying between them a small man in civilian clothes. He wasn't injured – simply couldn't walk in the deep snow with his feet chained together and heavy metal balls attached to each foot. In gaol, every human instinct and all the traits of the lower animal within man, surfaced – suspicion, greed, ego, selfishness, viciousness, intrigue. The single element mitigating the negative, to some extent, was the quality of giving comfort and encouragement to each other. In aiding their chained comrade, the escapers in criminals' uniform were striking their blow for freedom and victory. The three disappeared into the street where Pepe's mobile 'changing room' transports were standing by.

'Check houses around here in case some of our men were hurt and have taken temporary refuge,' Dominique Ponchardier ordered.

'We can only hope Beaurin and Holville have already got away,' he reported to Admiral Rivière awaiting news outside.

It was total disorder, with prisoners and guards frantically running in all directions.

'We'll help whoever we can, including criminals,' said Dominique. 'We are not justice. Their punishment for being criminals didn't include being bombed, and we brought about the bombing. They've been punished enough so we'll get them out of prison uniforms into fresh clothes, then let them go their own way.'

A hundred men and women changed clothes in the butcher's and baker's delivery vehicles parked in nearby streets, after which those anxious to go it alone were advised to walk away from the area. Most of the rest were piled into the small fleet of gazogene trucks and private cars standing by to vanish as fast as possible before the inevitable flood of security forces descended.

Trucks and cars distributed them all over the Somme before the town could be sewn up. Thereafter, they were quickly moved singly, and in twos and threes from 'safe houses' to Paris, central France, Spain and even to Britain. Two Allied agents brought out by Ponchardier, went it alone.

'They have their own contacts,' Dominique told Admiral Rivière. 'They don't know ours, and we don't know theirs – it's better like that.'

The first twenty-four hours offered the best hope of freedom before the Wehrmacht, Gestapo and Gendarmerie search parties could become efficiently operative.

'After that,' added Dominique, 'anyone still in the area won't be able to move for a minimum of several days until the Germans possibly let up a little.'

One of Gendarme Achille Langlet's cell comrades ran across the Route d'Albert into a barber's shop. The barber took him into the back room, gave him fresh clothes, a shave, and a haircut. Reappearing completely transformed, he strolled away perfumed and impeccable.

Seeing a bomb-shattered house on the right of the prison with a wardrobe of clothing strewn about, an escaping man and woman, both in prison brown, dived at the clothes, snatched overcoats, then bundling up a suit, dress, boots and shoes, ran with the bundles under their arms behind another house. Stripping to their prison underwear, they dressed again and calmly walked away arm in arm, whilst another escaper, in civilian clothes, 'borrowing' an empty handcart standing in the street, methodically loaded it up from the same bombed house with some general junk and clothing he felt might come in handy for on-the-run colleagues he expected to meet elsewhere. Pushing the load past the noses of German guards, he headed down the Route d'Albert for town as Lieutenant Marceau Laverdure tore up it on his motorcycle towards the hundred-metre-high cloud of debris dust engulfing the gaol.

Minutes before, he had been looking after the 'cabbages and goats,' as he called his office routine at central Amiens Gendarmerie, until explosions started, a phone jangled, and a secretary rushed in shouting:

'They're bombing the prison!'

She said nothing of British planes, so he automatically assumed someone had either planted bombs or was attacking to get colleagues out, but looking through his window he saw planes circling. Alerting his Resistance Group co-leaders, building contractor Michel Dubois and Gendarme Edouard Robine, by telephone, he headed for the gaol. Why were the RAF bombing the hell out of the place? What was the purpose? There were so many questions, and even more bodies strewn everywhere. He had to return to duty at the Gendarmerie to liaise the salvaging and rescue of those still alive in the ruins, and to organise help for the wounded. Assistance for escapers he would have to leave to Michel Dubois and Edouard Robine, who was fortunately off duty.

Dubois and Robine were there within minutes. It was ghastly. Bombs hadn't completely annihilated the gaol, but when you're just a few metres away from explosions, you're shaken, no matter how tough you are. Pounded by bombs, men and women imprisoned for terrorist acts, hardened professional criminals, and Black Marketeers were all crazily running for their lives. Making no distinctions – 'They're all human beings' as Michel Dubois said – forty of them were collected and guided to the back of some houses almost opposite the prison.

'We'll take you somewhere you can hide,' Robine calmed them.

Using his own building firm's transports, he took them to the caves of St. Pierre – deep natural tunnels once used for mushroom growing – in the St. Pierre district of Amiens, practically under the shadow of the gaol. A hill camouflaged the solitary utilised access to the vast caves, which were cool in summer and fortunately, with ice and snow so thick everywhere, warm in winter.

'You'll be warmer still when we bring you extra clothes – and food and drink,' Michel Dubois promised, then departed to fill transports with clothing from the secret storehouses of Madame Vignon and Madame Barré, after which he joined Robine to look for more escapers.

*

When the *Mosquitos* had gone, Michel and Marie Louise Denis ran to inspect the rear yard wall beside their father's stonemason's work-shop. The massive iron wall support the bouncing bomb had struck

215

had been flung into the middle of the neighbouring field.

Satisfied the planes wouldn't attack again, and that his son and daughter were safe, Sosthène assured Michel:

'I don't understand why they did this, but I'm positive they're not coming back today, so I must go to the prison to help – Julian is certain to be there soon.'

Charles Julian commanded the technical advice division of the Defense Passive, and Sosthène was his deputy. Slipping on his official armband, Sosthène was about to hurry towards the devastation when they saw prisoners pouring from the gaps in the rear prison wall, slithering, sliding and colliding on the ice and snow as they fled to freedom. Some couldn't run; some limped; some were carried by fellow prisoners, some supported walking wounded. The bizarre bloody scene set on a snow white background looked something like Napoleon's retreat from Moscow.

The Denis house, so close to the gaol, was one of the first invaded for help, and the trickle fast became a flood. Fourteen arrived in one batch – some civilian clothed, others prison uniformed. All the inmates were covered in muck and exhausted. Two were even carrying a prison guard whose leg had been blown off.

Whilst firewatching at a local hospital accidentally hit by bombs, Michel had experienced a similar disaster. With his father he began organising aid for the gaol victims, while Marie Louise gave cups of water to the dust-choked men.

The kitchen became the blood-spattered treatment room. The right arm of one man was only attached to him by his jacket sleeve, and he was holding it by the wrist against himself with his other arm. Using tea cloths for tourniquets, they tightly bound his torn arm.

The Denis trio could hardly cope with the ever-increasing numbers as dozens more came through the front and back doors. Many paused only long enough for second breath and a drink to relieve dust-parched throats before departing, realising that killing time could end in their own corpses being mourned, as it could give the enemy time to destroy them.

Seven prisoners left en masse on seven of the Denis family's bicycles.

'We're only borrowing them!' one of them yelled over his shoulder as they pedalled away like a cycling club on a day's outing. 'You'll get them back!'

Reassuring Michel, his father said:

'Don't worry – many people are as good as their word.'

'But maybe their word's no good,' said Marie Louise.

Some prisoners left the Denis home to hide among the gravestones of the little St. Pierre cemetery, just beyond the field adjoining the house, but only remained there whilst deciding best directions to take. Deep snow would obviously be one of their greatest enemies, because it would retain footprints.

All but eight left the Denis house, and the gravely wounded eight urgently required hospital attention.

'I either take you to hospital, or you bleed to death here,' Michel told them.

The old seldom-used Citroen van with racks strong enough for bearing memorial stones, and therefore able to support makeshift stretchers, was the best vehicle they possessed for ambulance duty. The small fuel ration allowed for business purposes opened the door to augmentation with Black Market petrol, as they could always claim to be running on authorised supplies, so Michel had enough to get the engine going and warm it while they loaded up with injured. Depressed at having to return so many to their gaolers, he headed for the hospital through streets already swarming with curiosity-spurred people making for the gaol.

Some time later, the telephone rang in the Denis home, and a voice without a name instructed them to go to a specific rendezvous.

'Your bicycles will be waiting there for you, as promised,' the caller explained. The line went silent, but Michel didn't hang up, sensing the man was still at the other end.

'Thank you,' the voice suddenly added, 'thank you for so much.'

*

The consequences and results of the attack were enormously underestimated, largely because security barriers separating combat and Intelligence networks made accurate information impossible on the numbers and individuals held in the gaol.

In respect of one aspect of the raid, Pepe's forecasts were accurate and rewardingly effective.

Apart from trucks, cars, identity papers, and civilian clothing, he prepared a reserve item – stolen German Army uniforms.

Briefing members of his units before departing for Caen and Rouen, he explained:

'Depending on whether German guards are sufficiently knocked out for us by the bombs, some of you may need to wear their uniforms to provide freer movement – but don't start picking each other off by mistake. Stick to shooting the enemy.'

Pepe outlined the rest of the idea, but when the moment arrived for it to be put into action, more fake German soldiers came out than went in.

'There's plenty more German uniforms here!' one of the escaping prisoners shouted, gesturing at dead soldiers lying in the rubble as Pepe's men escorted him out. Bodies were stripped of uniforms, greatcoats, and rifles, and several prisoners, after speedily transforming themselves into 'Germans,' developed Pepe's proposal much more effectively than even he had planned. 'Politicals' still in civilian clothes, with others in prison brown, were herded into groups and marched from the gaol across the Route d'Albert with rifles pointing at their backs.

Little crowds gathered around the gaol, watched in silence until someone cried:

'God help them!'

'It's all very well asking for God's help, but too often we expect Him to do the whole job Himself,' said another onlooker bitterly. All knew it was pointless trying openly to assist the oppressed unless they were prepared to take on the oppressor and risk mass public reprisals against their families, so they just watched helplessly.

Security Police screening squads had absolute discretion as to which hostage members of the public, or prisoners in gaols, should be taken away and executed. Sheltering under the responsibility-avoidance umbrella of 'Orders are Orders!', SS and other security forces did anything with a shrug, no matter how evil. Obedience was their excuse for listening to the voice of evil, rather than the voice of conscience. Obeying authority without question was the main reason intelligent men and women committed such appalling crimes.

'They're probably transferring recaptured prisoners to a more secure place now that the gaol's wide open,' somebody guessed, without realising how accurate this was, for the rifles threatening the inmates were in the hands of Pepe's 'soldiers,' reinforced by recently 'German-converted' prisoners. Those 'soldiers' were doing a great disservice that day for the Fatherland.

*

'We've got company.' John McCaul warned Bob Iredale.

Adolf Galland's fighters were streaking towards them, but largely through having been deceived by a couple of *Mosquitos*' diversionary feint on that old target friend, Amiens' railway marshalling yards, they were late. The raid on the gaol was almost over.

Luftwaffe arrived on the scene from both Abbeville-Drucat and Amiens-Glisy bases, but *Typhoons*, encircling their charges in a defensive ring, brushed off the initial flock of angry *FW190*s.

Some Canadian fighter pilots had craftily painted their engine cowls yellow – like Abbeville aircraft – to create confusion.

Galland's boys were nicknamed 'Yellow noses'.

A brace of *190*s manoeuvred as though poising to launch their notoriously effective head-on tactics. Swinging around in a wide U-turn, a dozen came in from twelve o'clock in pairs and fours, spitting ammunition at the *Typhoon*s rushing to meet them. As soon as the *190*s stopped pressing the attack, *Typhoon*s resumed position around the *Mosquito*s some on the starboard flank, others above, on the port flank.

Someone yelled over their R/T:

'*190*s at twelve o'clock, diving now!'

*Focke*s swooped onto targets from 12,000 feet until they screamed down at 400 m.p.h. with airframes vibrating violently from the demands being made upon them. Several half-rolled ahead of bombers, firing from inverted positions, then pulling sticks back into their stomachs to escape with vertical dives.

Keeping out of line of fire, a Mossie slithered under a *190*'s belly. The Luftwaffe pilot, realising he couldn't out-turn the bomber, dropped into the cover of some cloud below.

The sky was filled with the howling of German BMW engines chased by the snarling Merlin machines of argumentative *Typhoon*s. Some Canadian pilots were close enough to opponents to be able to reach out and touch the Luftwaffe black crosses.

Spotting a *190* obviously eyeing his aircraft, a Mossie navigator readied the gun-sight mounted several feet above his guns and awaited the pounce he was certain was coming. *Focke*s had to be hit dead right – fast – because they were the kind of customers who were never in a hurry to buy anything.

The *190* was sitting around beyond range on the *Mosquito*'s left, and staying there for the moment, obviously reporting to rein-forcement Luftwaffe squadrons headed towards them.

Easing back his control column, the Luftwaffe pilot took his machine up in a gentle climb, training forward guns on the bomber, anticipating that it would dive steeply to port as soon as he attacked. Only just beneath it, he opened up, but the Mossie's cannon replied with interest. The *190*'s machine-gun muzzles raked the bomber's fuselage fore and aft, ripping though its body.

Badly hurt, the aircraft twisted and pushed itself upwards at full power into the sky. Flying suit soaked with perspiration, hands wet on the sticks, sweat pouring into his eyes near blinding him, the Mossie pilot turned to counter attack.

As the aircraft soared, the pull-out force almost made him black out. Bending his head between his knees to bring the blood back to it, he prayed nothing would ram him while he was striving to regain total consciousness. As his head cleared, the *190* became larger every second until it filled his vision and his navigator's sights. Guns firing, they almost crashed before the *Mosquito* plunged away vertically.

There was a flash from the *190*, and it lurched. Swooping back over it, trying for a coup de grace, the Mossie fired again. The *Focke*'s complete cockpit cover split away and the *Mosquito* pilot and navigator dodged pieces of fuselage as the shattered aircraft disappeared beneath them.

'God, those bullets missed your foot by an inch!' the shaken navigator shouted.

'Yes, it's lucky I've got short legs!'

Even now they joked with strained bravado, but their plane was wounded too, and would be one of three *Mosquito*s seriously mauled, with barely strength enough to make it back to England.

*Typhoon*s darted everywhere, shooing away *190*s and *Messerschmitt*s from their Mossies like mother hens; others sat on *190*s' tails. One *Focke* engine fell to earth; another's wings disintegrated as cannons tore them apart.

Flying low at Poulainville, four miles north of Amiens, Canadian *Typhoon* pilot Rennie felt his aircraft almost stop in its tracks as a shower of flak seared into it. Yanking the stick and pulling back hard on the controls did nothing. Suddenly nothing worked, so the only thing left to do was to attempt to get the machine and himself down in one piece. In case of trouble, it was standard procedure to go as low and as fast as possible. To achieve this the r.p.m. control had to be pushed into the fully forward position, with throttles fully opened, and the 'panic valve' also pulled. The valve was a lever which when pulled, gave full supercharger pressure on the engines, and the three operations could be done almost simultaneously.

Notifying his leader that he was forced-landing, Rennie crashed, was captured, and hospitalised with a wounded knee.

Once clear of the target area, all the crews started talking, releasing tensions . . .

'Leave tomorrow . . . I'm going to sleep for two days . . . I'm going fishing . . . I'm going to fix myself a date and do some shows in London . . . God! what a sweat that lot was back there . . . Yes, God's always waiting around for us to prove ourselves . . .'

*Mosquito*s had become a real plague to the German High Command, with their deadly 'Oboe' bombsights and so effective ability to undertake day and night raids at comparatively little loss to themselves. Even when located early enough to be passed on from radar station to radar station, they were a pest, as, made of wood, they only came up as very faint blip signals on radar sets.

Maddened by *Mosquitos*' hit-and-run raids and habit of chasing people out of bed at night, Goering formed two special fighter wings armed with all kinds of 'souped-up' tricks, as an anti-*Mosquito* 'lotion', but neither unit ever shot a *Mosquito* down, so German people continued to grumble:

'The Fat One can't even cope with a few silly *Mosquitos*.'

All the way back to the Channel, Amiens crews and their escorts had *190*s and heavy ack-ack to contend with – there wasn't an instant's let-up. As they headed home, all that most of them thought about between flak bursts and keeping an eye on the Luftwaffe, was whether Pick and Broadley were safe. Pick had probably lingered to check results, they told themselves.

Practically at the coast, approaching Dieppe, white puffs began exploding around Ian McRitchie's plane as a battery got him within range. Despite ducking and weaving to avoid the trap, the boom-boom-boom-boom of the flak continued pounding at him. They were tracking him accurately now and not letting go.

Suddenly the plane lifted like a toy and his flesh burnt as flak tore through his right side from head to foot. Out of control, the aircraft plunged into a dive. The windshield was spattered with blood, and blood streamed down his face. Reaching forward for the stick, he found he couldn't make it – his right side was completely paralysed and right eye blinded.

'Sammy!' he called for his navigator to take over, but there was no answer.

Paralysis wasn't thank God affecting his left side, and his left arm and foot still responded.

Tugging at the stick with his left hand, he somehow brought the plane out of the dive and wiped some blood from his face hoping to clear the vision of his right eye. It didn't, but his left eye could see the ground coming fast at him. As he saw approaching fields and scattered trees, he found himself repeating aloud emergency landing instructions which he had so often recited to pupils at the private aero club back in Melbourne, and then repeating the *Mosquito*'s own mislanding instructions . . .

'Open throttles fully and climb at about 140 m.p.h. . . . Flaps should come up quickly and not be raised until a safe height has been reached . . . They should be raised in stages and the aircraft trimmed tail heavy before raising them the last twenty degrees. . . .' He thought of his wife, Joyce, his baby daughter, and her godfather – Basil Embry.

The Mossie was doing 300 m.p.h. at 50 feet. Then there was a slide, a heave, a terrific jolt, and they were down – amazingly in one piece – a few feet from a giant oak tree in a snow-covered field. McRitchie struggled to prise open the windshield, then for the first time was able to look back at 'Sammy' Sampson. He was dead. Manoeuvring his half-paralysed body from the cockpit, McRitchie dropped to the ground, and despite his shocked gravely wounded state, attempted to set fire to his wood plane to keep it from enemy hands. It didn't work. He couldn't stand, so he dragged himself away from the *Mosquito* and dropped just in time to avoid being riddled by a burst of bullets.

When he awoke, he was in a Dieppe hospital. He was taken back to where he had just come from, to Amiens, and the Hospice St. Victor, about a mile from the prison he had bombed – the same Hospice that the Mongewell Park planners had been advised was probably a 'home for the aged and poor.' It was a military hospital.

'One of your bombs – or comrades' bombs – even hit this place during the raid on the prison,' a Hospice St. Victor orderly bitterly informed McRitchie. 'We were hit soon after midday and fifty soldiers were killed in a ward.'

# 13 A burglar's lot

Clothes can easily proclaim a man to be what he's not, and when Victor Pasteau reappeared from the back of a baker's van parked in a street off the Route d'Albert, you could have taken him for a member of the Gestapo – he looked the part.

Victor's clothes problem on his departure from gaol was soon remedied by a visit to one of Pepe's mobile 'changing rooms'. He stepped into the baker's van in convict's uniform brown, and stepped out in black jacket with matching overcoat and hat. He was already wearing black shoes when he escaped. Some prisoners who didn't want to wear out their own boots or shoes wore officially issued clogs in the gaol, but clogs were noisy, and noise, for someone who had spent so many years silently burgling people's homes, was a stench in the ear. As Freddie was issued with a grey overcoat from the van. Victor, with a tinge of disappointment said:

'Now we don't need to steal any clothes.'

The pair walked – running was unwise in the circumstances –

away from the gaol, towards the town centre as ambulances, police cars, military trucks, and people on foot, hurried towards the prison disaster area. Victor was carrying the narrow, long newspaper-wrapped package with which he had left the gaol. On enquiring about it, Freddie was informed:

'It's a crowbar and a screwdriver.'

'A crowbar! Freddie said wryly, 'where the hell did you get that?'

'Made it myself. I persuaded one of the warders to loan me a screwdriver and a pair of pliers, and worked on the bolts and nails of my bed. I loosened the iron bed base slats, then temporarily set them back in their original positions. I mean, a professional never knows when he's likely to need tools – you've got to be ready for anything.' Freddie nodded and grinned. You could read most of the chapters of Victor's life in his face – they were all there, but Freddie was a closed book. The stroll gave Victor almost his first opportunity to study him. The deceptively lean frame obviously camouflaged a muscular, fit character, looking like a Humphrey Bogart type in a Bogart private eye role.

'I used to be an afternoon burglar, so that I could have some home life.' Victor said, making conversation. 'Mind you, in my younger days I used to work all shifts.'

'You don't look like a burglar,' said Freddie, immediately regretting the remark. 'That was a stupid thing to say – you'd think burglars were all comic-strip characters with five-o'clock shadow, wearing masks and carrying a torch and a piece of lead-filled rubber hose to knock people unconscious.'

Victor smiled broadly. 'We criminals are creatures of habit,' he explained. 'We usually stick to our own specialities and styles. You never hear of forgers going safe-breaking, or con men doing a bit of blackmail for a change.'

Freddie didn't offer in return any deeper insight into his own background, nor the circumstances which put him in an Amiens cell. Knowing he was American, fluent French-speaking, clearly familiar with Amiens streets, and in civilian clothes, told Victor enough, and as much as he expected to learn. Reaching the tall old brick-built house at the corner of rue Jeanne d'Arc and rue Dhavernas, they walked straight past it.

'I know the place a little – been inside a few times to keep Braumann company,' Freddie said, indicating for the first time that he had been through the Gestapo mincing machine. Answering Victor's unspoken question he said coldly:

'They run the whole range of techniques – from leaving you in total solitude in the hope you'll be overcome by despair, doubts, depression, conditioned to sign a confession, to handcuffing you to a hook on the end of a long double chain hung from a pulley on the ceiling. When the chain's pulled, your feet can't touch the ground and your arms are practically torn from their sockets. When they pulled the ropes up hard, it was excruciatingly painful as they tried to make my shoulder blades and elbows touch – the bastards know it all. My policy was to give them little bits of truth among a pack of lies and let them sort it out. The most important part of lying is knowing when to tell the truth. You stick to your cover story for as long as you can, and they keep torturing to get at the truth until finally they either shoot you or deport you to a slave camp. The most important safety element for someone like me is luck, and if your luck runs out . . .' He paused emphatically, then added emphatically:

'Only an inexperienced man doesn't believe in luck.'

Trying to forget the hours spent in the house merely made him remember them more. It would be easier to forget after he'd got even. He glanced at Victor, about whom he still knew comparatively little. Most of us live on islands of separateness, but feelings and thoughts can't forever bear being unexpressed. Freddie wondered why we hid so much from each other, then heard himself saying:

'I'll hold my job only as long as I hold my tongue,' which was the closest he came to revealing anything significant about himself to Victor, whose puckered brow indicated he hadn't missed the hint.

Then Freddie added:

'We're all thoroughly trained on how to behave if we fall into enemy hands, but when they've got you, you can't refer to those official behaviour recipe books. When interrogation ingredients aren't exactly cooking according to the book, you've got to use your own mental salt and pepper.

'A lot of Abwehr counter-Intelligence interrogators, and even Gestapo, cunningly cash in on our automatic expectation of torture, maltreatment and degradation by deliberately ignoring such techniques for a time in order to throw detainees off balance. Calculated consideration and softly-softly methods often achieve more rewarding results. Some interrogators claim to get all they want from ninety per cent of prisoners by using an unexpectedly gentle initial approach. Of course, they never mention that leaving heat off in cells in freezing winter months, and forgetting to serve meals, also helps!'

Momentarily, Freddie paused, thoughtful again. Then, suddenly disciplining his thinking to the task ahead, he said:

'The bathroom which they use for tricks other than washing their dirty hands, is along a narrow corridor leading to the administration room where the files are probably kept, and that's our target!'

Crossing the street, they strolled back down the other side as if looking for an address. There were none of the customary notorious Gestapo Citroen cars with their 'PQL' (Polizei) number plates outside the house.

'The prison emergency could have flushed them all out,' observed Freddie hopefully. 'We might be in luck.'

'The only certainty about luck is that it'll change,' said Victor cautiously. 'Anyway, we can't make a frontal entrance, in case there are a few of them left inside. We'll have to get in from the back through another house.' Victor had already noted drawn blinds in an adjoining place, possibly indicating the owner or tenants were out. Marching straight to the front door, he rang the bell.

'If they answer I'll ask if Madame Pasteau is at home, then apologise for having got the wrong address,' said Victor.

Getting no reply to the first ring, he tried several times more, to be sure, then using a knife borrowed from the gaol, slid it into the crack of the door, manoeuvring until the catch edged back.

Entering and checking the house was in fact unoccupied, they studied the rear of the Gestapo building. They got a good look at the back and sides and assured themselves there were no patrolling guards.

'There's a handy strong-looking drain pipe we could possibly shin up,' Freddie suggested.

'Too old-fashioned, too visible, so too dangerous,' Victor criticised with professional authority. 'Ground floor windows are the things to go for. Ordinary screw locks attached to window catches are usually useless.'

Satisfying himself that no one was in the room they were aiming for, he was about to break a window pane and put a hand in to unscrew the catch, when he realised the window was unlatched.

'They assume nobody's mad enough to want to force their way in,' he laughed. Gently raising the window, they climbed into a sparsely-furnished room with a desk and a couple of chairs. The blinds were drawn, and after the intense daylight the room seemed dark, until they adjusted vision to light seeping through the slats, and even amidst shadows saw the stained plaster-crazed walls. Victor crept to the large desk, examined two telephones, then looked under the desk for any alarm connections. There were none. Unlocking the desk drawers in turn, he skimmed through their contents.

Gently opening the door confirmed that it led to the hallway. There wasn't a sound anywhere. Incredibly, the place seemed completely deserted and they were wondering whether all hands had been summoned to the gaol when footsteps creaking down the stairs told them the assumption was wrong. Slipping back into the room, leaving the door slightly ajar, they waited, marshalling their thoughts. A beefy man, whom Victor sensed Freddie instantly recognised, appeared, and stood with his back to them facing the street front door, as if on guard.

Victor dipped his hand into an overcoat pocket, extracted the knife he had used to force entry into the adjoining house, and offered it to Freddie. There was no disguising the hint of agreement around Freddie's mouth. Taking the knife, he opened the door, crept into the hall, and stabbed the guard between the shoulder blades, puncturing life out of him like a balloon.

'He's the one who operated the ceiling pulley-chain contraption, nearly pulling my body apart,' Freddie said icily, 'and he so obviously enjoyed his work.

'There are always men and women who, given the opportunity and lack of restraint, will behave like beasts towards others.'

Victor stared down at the dead face. Its open eyes stared back at him, and the mouth still had its final tortured grimace. He felt sick, but safer.

'I don't relish murder,' said Freddie, 'even though we've good cause to hate. I've simply learned to kill without developing the drugged killer type mentality.'

Every time Victor met an apparently impossible situation, he experienced the tortures of the damned, but once through it, he felt freer than before, gaining strength and confidence from facing up to fear.

Silently exploring the rooms, it was plain that the whole Braumann crew had rushed to the bombed gaol, leaving only the solitary guard. Victor was drawn like a magnet to the old fashioned square safe standing in the corner of one office.

'I can resist everything except temptation,' he said happily. 'This safe brings back memories. Let's look at its arse – help me shift it away from the wall.'

Pushing and pulling together, they slowly inched it round until the back was visible and reachable.

'You soon get the knack of spotting the safe that looks safe but can be got at from the back,' Victor explained authoritatively. 'If a safe's really good, and small, we usually haul it away intact and deal with it in comfort elsewhere.'

Scraping paint at the back with his screwdriver, he located the joint. Using the screwdriver he forced the metal from the rivet.

'These old safes only have a thin sheet of steel covering riveted at the back,' he explained.

Using his cell-made crowbar, he worked it down above the rivet, gave a tug, and burst the rivet. Working from rivet to rivet, he popped them open one by one, and within minutes, the back of the safe was on the floor. Removing the fireproof asbestos backing exposed a second metal back, so he simply repeated the first procedure and they were in.

It contained all kinds of documents and files – and cash.

'Now that's nice! – very obliging of Braumann to finance our getaway,' Freddie said, grabbing the thick wad of franc notes and stuffing them into his inside coat pocket without bothering to count them.

'We'll split them later,' he assured Victor who was looking at him somewhat questioningly.

'There's no point in examining files – the best thing is to destroy everything.'

Victor agreed. Hanging about unnecessarily could push good luck too far. Unlocked administration office filing cabinets helped.

Making a bonfire of all 'political' files and records in the middle of Braumann's office, they watched them burn to ashes, then left through the ground floor back window. The prison Governor's records were gone, and so were the Gestapo's. Now nobody would be circulating these descriptions, photographs, nor other details of escapers.

\*

Right now, they all felt a long way from home, wished they'd never have to go again, but knew they would, and would want to.

The remnants of the Amiens bomber force were almost at the Channel and the last leg to Hunsdon, but knew they weren't out of the Luftwaffe woods yet, and wouldn't be until they were actually over England. It wasn't much further, but far enough with flak still belting up at them and *190*s and *Messerchmitts* vulturing overhead, sticking around to peck to pieces any who straggled, strayed, or became separated from their *Typhoon* escorts. And those Luftwaffe boys weren't the only enemy they were facing – mid channel, the foul weather that hit them almost made them want to scoot to the clearer skies of France, except for those viciously hungry clusters of fragmentation ack-ack shells back there aching to do their utmost to tear jagged holes into them, *and* the *Messerchmitts* and *FW*s.

Most of the Mossies found themselves strewn about by weather and winds, and many totally deprived of escort cover. Several tried ducking under cloud base, only to see nothing through the Perspex roof other than thick smothering vapour.

Oh, those Met forecasts! – they could be such a load of bull at times.

Cloud had lowered to a hundred feet over the Channel and they constantly hit giant snow clouds. In a particularly dense one a Mossie saw the menacing shape of an aircraft ahead, and its navigator was about to grab the firing button when a waggling of wings signalled 'Friends'. As soon as they emerged from the cloud, Mossie and *Typhoon* closed in almost wing tip to wing tip – nearly holding hands, and continued to keep each other company, feeling safer together in such weather. Pilot Officer Sparkes was literally wide open for trouble, with a two-feet by two-feet-six-inches hole blown in his wing making the aircraft a handful to handle. He kept it on full rudder trim, but it was still murder to hold level as he struggled to remain close to the others.

His ship, 'T' for Tommy, was a flying wreck, thoroughly ripped, riddled, and reeling, with their engine also hit by flak.

'If she doesn't hold out, we might have to come down in the drink,' he warned his navigator, thinking that at least a forced landing on water was preferable to a parachute descent into the sea. After touching down on water, a plane usually stayed afloat between forty to sixty seconds – long enough for the pilot to unstrap and scramble out, hoping to be one of the fortunate fished out by the superb Air Sea Rescue Service.

Everyone moaned about the Mae West, rubber dinghy, flare bag, Very pistol, and innumerable other emergency accessories weighing them down, but they could be life savers, although looking down at the grey uninviting icy Channel, he wondered how long they'd be able to hold out in that lot before a rescue launch managed to locate and grab them. Not a comfortable thought.

The air over southern England that afternoon hummed with 'Mayday' signals from stricken aircraft warning they couldn't remain airborne much longer, and this was no weather for Channel swimming. Radio homing channels were filled with requests for assistance from exhausted crews as they vied with each other to get down.

From control towers, signals flashed back to them advising those in greatest trouble to divert to alternative airfields where grim-faced controllers fought the clock to sort out landing priorities to get battered machines down fast.

Blood-soaked, half-paralysed morphine-sedated Flight Lieutenant 'Tich' Hanafin and his banged up *Mosquito*, compelled to abort his mission and turn back only ten miles from target when the flak got him, had with his navigator, taken terrible flak pounding all the way back to the French coast. Luckily, Luftwaffe fighters were too engaged at Amiens to bother about his winged and wounded *Mosquito*. They left him to anti-aircraft batteries. With the help of his navigator, 'Tich' chanced his remaining movable arm and belted straight through the massive gun barrages, and prayed that the wooden Mossie wouldn't be their wooden coffin. The only thing that existed in the whole world right then was the *Mosquito* fighting for its life, his navigator, and himself.

In blinding blizzard and nil visibility both he and his navigator glued their eyes on their artificial horizon, air-speed indicator, and variometer. The machine had to lie exactly on the 'horizon' and the speed must not drop too low. Undercarriage lowered, landing flap down, fuel reduced. Steady back with the stick – steady – a slight side-slip – steady – the undercarriage struck the ground and he stamped on the brakes, blood singing in his ears and head feeling as if it was about to burst.

God must have been with them all the way. Something or somebody certainly was, because they were the first to make it back, landing at the nearest south coast base they could reach where a station 'blood wagon' was ready and waiting to rush 'Tich' to hospital for emergency care.

Leigh Mallory was in 'The Hole' at Fighter Command HQ, Stanmore, seeing what was 'on the board' – Fighter Command term for aircraft plotted by radar. The deep-down 'Hole' – centre of things – was reached by descending the many-flighted staircase to its steamy, stale atmosphere.

At Mongewell Park, Basil Embry and almost all the other original Amiens raid planners were with 'Digger' Magill and his Ops Room team, keeping their eyes on the thirty-feet-wide wall blackboard and its 'Time Landed' space, listening to incoming Mossies, with faces mirroring anxiety every time the girl mounted the ladder to fill in spaces, chalking results in red.

A phone shrilled – the Observer Corps reporting another *Mosquito* crossing the coast. It was Pilot Officer Sparkes with the hole in his wing. Everything else might be in one piece, but that hole was bound to cause landing trouble. He was 'Taken in charge' – ground radar classification for taking over pilots as they moved about, with one ground station after another taking over in turn. But he couldn't get as far as his base control tower and had to be seen in at another airfield as soon as he reached the coast.

Reducing speed to 150 m.p.h. Sparkes set the radiator switches to OPEN, then carried out the Drill of Vital Action.

'Undercarriage!'

'Down!' his navigator replied, checking by indicator that the undercarriage and tail wheels were down.

'Mixture!'

'HIGH!' – the fuel tanks hadn't been hit, thank heaven. Sparkes scanned Pitch to ensure the airscrew was fully forward.

'Superchargers!'

'MOD!'

'Flaps!'

'Fully down!'

They were almost there now. With flaps up and engine assisted at 135 m.p.h. and sweat trickling down his back, he watchfully checked the reduction of elevator control when lowering flaps to see if tail heaviness was very marked, as it should be. It was.

As they headed in fast on the approach he concentrated on the runway, wanting, but not daring, to look at the shattered wing that was a stone-cold certainty to knock his stability for six. It didn't disappoint – with a juddering wallop they met the ground, an undercarriage leg collapsed and they pancaked, slewing all over the place but finally, thankfully, stopping – reasonably in one piece. Sparkes measured that gaping wing hole to check his estimated size of it. The guess had been right almost to the inch.

Within sight of the English coast, some of the Luftwaffe hunters made a last ditch stab at wounding or downing more Mossies, dropping on the tails of a bunch of them in long diagonal dives before opening fire. They knew they had little time left to score as it usually took them approximately a half an hour from their Pas de Calais and peninsula bases to reach the English coast at the Channel's narrowest point. Most of them therefore only had a tactical flying time of some eighty minutes, so time was definitely now scant for them to notch up a *Mosquito*.

From virtual ramming distance, one of the *190*s shot up a Mossie tearing lumps of wood from the plane. At mid-air collision point he pulled up his nose and soared over her, firing cannon and machine-guns at a counter-attacking Canadian-piloted *Typhoon*. Canadian pilots had a reputation for toughness and he soon had the *190* scurrying away, but not before it had managed to shoot up the *Mosquito*'s fuel tank and radiator, which were both leaking heavily. Seeking to outclimb each other to gain height advantage, dogfights between German and *Typhoon* fighters soared to ever-increasing heights whilst the bombers pressed on home.

Twice within minutes, Luftwaffe pilots attacked, bursting through formations like whip cracks in a final life-and-death struggle. Most of the bombers retaliated, but mainly left their defence to the *Typhoons*, two of which, badly shot up in the final dogfights, had to seek emergency landings at south coast bases other than their own.

But one of the *Typhoon* pilots was a weather casualty. He was last seen climbing into a thick snow cloud twenty miles south of Beachy Head, along the English coast, and never reappeared.

Suddenly it was over. The Luftwaffe force turned, pointing themselves at France. Then, as they headed back, one of the English coastal listening posts tuned to the battle was astounded to pick up the sound of one of the German pilots singing in English. As he streaked away they heard him sing over his R/T:

'Oh give me a bright silver *Focke*
'Put the joystick in my hand . . .'

at which point in the song he lapsed back into German, either through not knowing any more English or maybe from simply having had enough of the English for the moment.

On crossing the coastline, blurred in cloud and haze, one after another of the bombers radioed ETA (Estimated time of arrival), and put their noses down for Hunsdon. Calling control three minutes from base, they were advised the height to fly. Their next call in was over base for height of circuit required. Aircraft were staggered at 500-feet heights and brought down in stages until ordered to land. Pilots called in again to control when in the funnels and clear of the runway after landing.

'Cut the nattering!' ordered 'Brad' – Flying Control Officer Bradshaw-Jones – sharply to some of the crews chattering away on their radio transmitters to each other, as they queued to come in. 'The sooner you cut it out, the sooner you'll get down,' 'Brad' reminded them, always a stickler for rigid R/T procedure.

Bob Iredale and John McCaul were among the first in, landing at 1.00 p.m. In ones and twos the remainder struggled through snowstorms and dense cloud, several not reaching Hunsdon until dark, after diversion to different airfields by the weather. It was rough enough battling the Luftwaffe and German ground defences without English weather joining the enemy as an ally.

Gratefully gulping enormous enamel mugs of hot tea laced with rum, each said his piece to the Interrogation Officer, then headed for Mess bacon and eggs, and waiting around for the rest of the homing pigeons. They talked of the bombing, of the prison walls, of the fleeing inmates, of the Abbeville boys . . .

'Wasn't it terrible?' said one.

'Yes, it snowed like blazes,' said another . . . and they talked, of course, of the weather. It was a long wait. All felt a strange mixture of elation at the success of the operation, and depression at not knowing what had happened to Pick, McRitchie, and their navigators.

Some believed they had seen McRitchie hit by flak, but none knew what happened to Pick after they left him orbiting around five hundred feet over the gaol.

'Pick not back – it's unbelievable!' said Dick Sugden, echoing everyone's thoughts aloud. Pick *couldn't* have bought it – not Pick! They were all positive he would stride in at any moment calling for a pint. Mongewell Park also couldn't accept the loss, and were equally certain he would turn up somehow. 'Digger' Magill felt especially deeply and personally the disappearance of 'Sammy' Sampson, whose friendship went back years to days in Cambridge, New Zealand, when 'Sammy' was a boyfriend of his sister. The wait was probably hardest on Basil Embry. Had what he feared, happened? – had Pick's comparative daylight inexperience told? Had the ban on him personally leading the raid cost them Pick?

Questions without answers tortured.

\*

A car drew up near the shattered front gates of the gaol. The driver, the twenty-year-old son of a friend of Dr. Antonin Mans, sat in the car awhile, shaken by the devastation before him, then got out and walked into the prison courtyard which resembled a battleground with dead and wounded everywhere.

Some inmates and German guards were simply wandering aimlessly about, dazed and in shock; some were burrowing into mounds of rubble; others were bending over casualties.

The newly-arrived visitor found Dr. Mans examining an injured woman.

'I have a car outside, doctor – come quickly!' he urged.

'No, I'm staying.'

'But doctor – please come!'

Dr. Mans shook his head.

'I can't, it would also be too dangerous for you, but you can do one thing for me – let my wife know I'm alive.'

Answering the telephone, Madame Mans heard an unidentified caller say:

'Your husband is well.'

'I don't understand,' she replied cautiously, ever wary of possible

Gestapo manoeuvres, 'my husband is in prison.'

'Yes, Madame, but the prison has just been bombed and many have been killed. I have just seen your husband, and he wanted you to know that he hasn't been hurt.'

'The prison has been bombed!' exclaimed Madame Mans, 'but . . . Hello?'

The caller had hung up.

Madame Mans immediately phoned the Perdu Clinic to seek more news of the bombing and, hopefully, of her husband, but all three Perdus had gone to the prison. Dr. Gerard Perdu and his brother Jean François were surgeons, and their uncle, Dr. Christian, was deputy Mayor of Amiens.

The three Perdus witnessed the RAF attack from a terrace of their clinic, situated on a hill overlooking the town, then left with emergency medical equipment and a nurse for the scene.

On seeing Dr. Mans, they pressed him to leave and get away from the region.

'We have transport for you, so grab freedom while you can,' all three Perdus insisted.

'I am needed here,' Mans said determinedly. Although, as the Perdus could see, still severely in shock, his working mind was clear. He steadfastly refused to go.

'But we're here now, and soon there will be many more doctors and nursing assistance, so save yourself while you can!' Gerard argued.

'Like you, I have medical obligations to perform,' Mans said, 'but thank you anyway.' As he turned to treat a casualty, the Perdus, seeing it was pointless attempting further persuasion, started to tend the injured.

Gerard Perdu wondered what had happened to two of his friends. Jean Bellemere was a solicitor who had deliberately broken seals of some top-level official German documents in order to copy them for Allied Intelligence. Bellemere had been lodged in the gaol only days ago, as had Dr. Robert Beaumont, who was one of Gerard Perdu's closest friends. The day before his arrest, Robert Beaumont had laughingly reproved Gerard for solely confining his English conversation practice to when they were alone together in a car, away from anyone else's ears. Gerard Perdu was anxious to polish up English in anticipation of the expected invasion.

Shortly after the Perdus arrived, a body was dragged from a cell whose walls had entirely collapsed. The inmate's head had been crushed by masonry, but Gerard Perdu recognised the victim. It was Robert Beaumont.

Gerard Perdu didn't know it, but Robert's wife and father had come to Amiens that day to visit him for the first time since he had been taken. Also, with a truck in a street near the gaol, was Robert's sister, Madeleine Gandon, praying she might be fortunate enough to see him and help him escape. She stood by with the truck throughout the night, waiting.

The incredible mass breakout of prisoners had taken everyone by surprise. Hundreds had gone, although not all ran. Some, serving minor sentences, decided to stay because they were due for release anyway, while others, lost and uncertain where to go, chose to rescue the trapped and help the wounded. How each reacted largely depended on what they had been facing in gaol. Dr. Mans, Captain Tempez, commander of Amiens civil defence services, and Gendarme Langlet remained from a sense of duty, fully aware that gratitude has the shortest memory. They shared their courage, but kept fears to themselves.

The significance of the raid and size of the breakout took a while to really hit the German authorities, who were convinced the main target had been the station and railway marshalling yards. On realising the prison had been the true objective, German command headquarters in the hotel adjoining Amiens Préfecture ordered the Commissariat Central, housed in the basement of the Hotel de Ville, to locate whatever copy records it had of prisoners. There were some, but they were totally inadequate to aid effective identification of escapees. Freddie and Victor Pasteau had done a worthwhile job destroying prison and Gestapo files. Even the Commissariat didn't know precise numbers involved because the Germans wouldn't supply figures of detainees in their section of the gaol, nor admit to what extent they were also using French cells, because of overcrowding. Only the Germans knew how seriously they had been hurt.

The left wing of the gaol, where the Germans were quartered, was completely demolished; a bomb had directly hit the guardroom; the German Kommandant was dead; German military and civilian casualties were high; two Milice (French Gestapo) had been killed at the gaol – the official German casualty toll kept mounting every minute.

Pint-sized Raymond Dewas was a tower of strength, leading the Defense Passive forces which imprisoned Captain Tempez had commanded when free.

Dewas was busy at his family's weaving business in rue Jules Barni when the bombs dropped. As an assistant to the mayor, passive defence was a responsibility which weighed more heavily on him since the imprisonment of Captain Tempez. Automatically assuming the station and railway yards were the target, as they usually were, he ordered the duty car to head for the station, then realised the bombing was further north. Nearing the German-occupied Hospice St. Victor, he saw the dust pall over the gaol.

Scrambling over the smashed front wall, he ran straight into Captain Tempez, already digging injured from the ruins with a volunteer team of prisoners.

'Save yourself, Captain Tempez! – Please take care of your life – without it you're dead!' Dewas begged, but, like Dr. Mans, Tempez insisted on continuing aiding others even though he accepted he was due to face a firing squad if he stayed.

'Everyone dies, but not everyone lives,' was all he replied. Before leaving home, Dewas telephoned for rescue workers, firemen, and back-up technical and medical teams, including Dr. Odile Regnault, a Public Health Service assistant of Dr. Mans, and a member of his Intelligence organisation. Like Dewas, they also first headed for the station.

'Charles Julian,' chief technical adviser to Defense Passive services, went on the pillion of a friend's motorcycle to the area where he assessed bombs were falling. His assistant, monumental stonemason-funeral director Sosthène Denis, whose home and business premises were almost next door, soon joined him. 'Julian' was the pseudonym of engineer-building constructor Robert Pecquet. Leading a double life, Pecquet was a link in the highly specialised Intelligence network code-named ORA, which had only seven agents covering the entire Somme region. Via Paris, ORA fed top-level secret, highly technical and political information to Geneva, from where it reached Allen Dulles in Berne, and Washington and London. Sosthène Denis, second-in-command of Pecquet's eight-strong passive defence technical unit, surveyed the devastation with his chief and Raymond Dewas, then ordered rescue work reinforcement shifts to be sent every two hours. In below-freezing weather conditions, the task would be rough on everyone, and fresh help would be needed at regular intervals.

First aid units went about collecting dead and wounded, moving dead bodies into less spectacular positions, and comforting, as best as they could, those about to die.

Rescue teams, making do with only picks and shovels when winches and cranes were essential to shift outsize blocks of masonry and concrete, risked being crushed themselves by falling debris.

'Be careful how you move anything trapping someone,' Pecquet warned, 'because if we're too quick, we could bring even more muck down and kill them.' Little Raymond Dewas bustling everywhere, making decisions, dealing with technical difficulties, issued one instruction to Red Cross first aid helpers which had nothing to do with official passive defence responsibilities.

'Bandage even those not wounded who want to escape, and take them to the ambulances,' he ordered.

Many recovering too late from shock to run to safety, were stretcher-carried from the gaol, whisked away by ambulance, and either delivered to homes ready to open doors and provide shelter for them, or, if they preferred, permitted to go it alone when sufficiently distant from the main danger zone. Establishing first aid posts in the dining room of a nearby house, and in a café opposite the gaol, helped facilitate these evasions.

'It would also be advisable to remove prisoners' records from the offices, if they're still intact,' Dewas suggested.

The team which immediately went to what remained of the administration section, observed that there had been a fire in the office which had apparently burnt the files. Curiously, the office had only been partially damaged by fire, which appeared to have been localised and quickly burned itself out.

Lying flat on his stomach, struggling to dislodge a beam to reach someone, Robert Pecquet heard a voice behind him demand:

'Papers!'

He turned to look up into a muzzle of an automatic gun pointed at him by a German soldier. Too amazed at first to do anything about complying with the order, he simply stared at the soldier.

'Papers!'

Repetition of the demand triggered realisation that refusal to produce identification papers, or any attempted argument regarding blind insistence on official formalities, even amidst cries of injured and dying French and Germans, could result in him being shot.

Pointing at the stripes on his arm, Pecquet snapped: 'I'm an *Officer* of the Defense Passive!'

He could almost see the soldier's thoughts. Only after studying the stripes for almost a full minute, did he lower the gun slowly, then almost resentfully move on, leaving Pecquet thankful for the thoroughness with which the Germany army drilled respect for stripes and the word 'Officer' into its men.

As the soldier walked away, a young woman approached.

'I have a message and a request for you, Monsieur.'

Although he had never seen the woman before, he instinctively felt that this was important, and that she was genuine. Years of

236

living a lie himself had made him super-sensitive at recognising truth.

'There's a man trapped in one of the last cells on the left – I'll show you exactly where,' the woman continued. 'If you get him out, whatever state he is in – dead, or alive – put a sheet over him and send him to the morgue.

'Orders for this come from outside,' she added almost as an afterthought.

'Where outside?' Pecquet asked.

'From rue Gloriette,' the woman replied.

The street, the house, and the remarkable woman who lived in it, close to Amiens cathedral, told him all he needed to know. Whoever was in the cell, was very important – dangerous enough to be valuable even dead.

The woman left immediately after indicating the cell. Summoning help, Pecquet set to work shifting debris, and the prisoner was finally uncovered in one piece, apparently unconscious. As instructed, a sheet was draped over the body which was taken to the morgue without being medically checked. No indication had been given as to what the procedure would be once the body reached the morgue, and Pecquet hadn't asked for an explanation.

A little later, he found an excuse to visit the morgue. The body wasn't there.

Additional troops from other areas were summoned to reinforce Amiens – inside and outside the town. Reinforcements were also poured into the gaol, and with them the Gestapo, to spy on everyone – prisoners, staff, helpers. At such a time, friends of the Resistance and Allied sympathisers might expose feelings through emotional acts of humanity, and the Gestapo wanted to be around to catch them out.

Gestapo chief Braumann and his interpreter Lucienne reappeared. He was wearing fresh clothes because the bomb blast had almost totally stripped off the suit he had on when interrogating the French warden Brasseur. Lucienne, tearful, nervously agitated, covered in debris dust, was limping from a wound in her left side.

'The English pigs – look what they've done to us!' she cried, 'but those who've escaped, we will catch again.'

Braumann and Lucienne methodically began scrutinising every corpse extracted from the ruins before it was taken away on a stretcher. With Lucienne it didn't matter what she hated, as long as she hated something. Removing the cloth with which, out of respect for the dead, rescue workers covered each body, she tried to identify faces, whilst a Gestapo companion noted physical characteristics and took fingerprints from dead men and women.

'That bitch is getting all she can from this world, but she'll get what she deserves in the next,' said Gendarme Achille Langlet, shocked by the ghoulish scene.

Striving to reassert authority, Lucienne questioned prisoners hustled before her, toying all the time with a revolver she had brought from her pocket.

Braumann studied one of the corpses a long time, then turning to Dr. Odile Regnault and indicating the dead man, dramatically declared:

'This was the Sous-Préfet of Abbeville.'

Dr. Regnault made no comment.

Monseigneur Chanoine Duhamel, chaplain to the Defense Passive, who arrived to comfort the wounded and dying, was also anxious to assist in other ways. Carrying messages would be easier for him than anyone else, as he knew through years of working secretly for the same top-level ORA Intelligence organisation as Robert Pecquet. The Monsiegneur's speciality was supplying information milked from senior German and French officials.

As he tried to console the sobbing husband of a woman who had just died, the man pushed him away, protesting.

'If God is so all powerful and loves us so much, why does he allow so much evil in the world?'

'Your pain is in my heart,' the Monseigneur answered quietly, 'but you must understand that God doesn't exclude man from choosing evil or good. It is for man to choose his way.'

'But with so much inhumanity everywhere, what's the point in trusting God?' the man cried.

Putting his arm around the overwrought man's shoulders, Monseigneur Duhamel said:

'Through suffering we find strength. We have to trust Him in spite of doubts, which means believing nothing escapes Him. It means He can permit injustice, and the torture of the innocent or undefended. Above all, it means believing evil can only endure for a time, and that God's hour will surely come to restore justice, mercy, and peace.'

Rescue and first-aid efforts of Dewas' hundred-strong force, which included twenty girls, didn't halt even when unexploded bombs were located. A French bomb squad was summoned, and defused them.

Many suffocated under debris as under-equipped rescue workers beavered away. When the Clearing Officer notified that he was positive nobody else was alive beneath the ruins, Dewas commanded:

'Don't stop! – move *all* rubble until you can *see* there's no one living beneath it!'

Ten minutes later, someone shouted:

'There's somebody under this lot – and I can *hear* him!'

Tunnelling could only advance centimetre by centimetre, as it was obvious the merest disturbance of the balance of masonry and rubble would result in the trapped man being crushed. A rubber tube lowered through a gap in the masonry above him poured drink to him. As excavation slowly progressed, each section was propped up with wood, then rubbish removed from that section. Prop lengths were adjusted section by section. When a small hole was burrowed through almost to the man, tiny Raymond Dewas – no bigger than a small boy – wriggled into the tunnel to inspect whether it was secure enough to extend and widen. The man finally brought out was Dr. Gerard Perdu's missing friend – solicitor Maître Bellemere.

After examination, Dr. Odile Regnault concluded:

'He has no external injuries, nor any apparent sign of internal lesions, but is in a state of extreme weakness.'

Rescuers cheered, and as Robert Pecquet, who had directed the intricate tactics, gratefully watched Red Cross stretcher bearers take Bellemere to an ambulance, a stranger announced:

'My name's Gauntier, and I'm the brother of the bureau chief of the Somme Préfecture who was imprisoned here. Do you know where my brother is?'

'My brother Gauntier is alive,' Pecquet replied.

He's not *your* brother – he's mine!' the man protested.

'He's my brother too,' said smiling Pecquet – 'we belong to the same Masonic lodge.'

The Prefect of the Somme – Le Baube – notorious for pro-German collaboration, arrived, accompanied by an SS Officer friend. Le Baube was said to be more pro-Hitler than the Germans. It was certainly true of him that the evil many men do makes them eligible for nomination to office.

François and Raymonde Vignolle – Dr. Mans's two able young secretary-assistants in the Public Health Service division of the region – came to the gaol to check if he was safe. Seeing them arrive, Braumann's Lucienne said.

'Dr. Mans is here, and very courageous. He has been attending prisoners and our soldiers, and Captain Tempez has also been of great assistance. We will repay them later for their help. You'll find Dr. Mans somewhere inside.'

They went directly to his ground floor cell and medical treatment room, anticipating he might be using medical facilities there, but he was obviously busy elsewhere. Passing the adjoining cell they stopped on recognising a coat and hat on the floor. The familiar curled-brim hat lying upside down bore its owner's initials 'R.V.' on the inside band – Raymond Vivant.

*

'Halt! – or I'll shoot you!' Gendarme Robine yelled at another evader running through the streets. The man instantly stopped and held his hand high above his head in surrender.

Pressing the pistol against the small of the evader's back, Robine prodded him on. Too many eyes could be watching, and too many mouths talked to the Gestapo to permit him to let the man go openly so he kept pushing him along towards the military barracks at rue Jules Barni. As they drew alongside Madame Vignon's house, next to the barracks, he pushed the evader into her home and to safety, until he could be transferred to the caves hideout organised by Lieutenant Laverdure.

The German authorities also depended on Laverdure – their liaison officer at the Gendarmerie – to alert hospitals, Red Cross services, and Defense Passive French and German nurses were despatched from the French Hospital Nord, and German Hospice St. Victor, around the corner from the prison. Gendarme Lieutenant Laverdure, responsible for arrangements for the care of survivors, wounded, and dead bodies, made sure that wherever possible the dead were used to help live escapers.

'If they're unconscious but still breathing, put them if you can, among the dead,' Laverdure directed associates. 'Get the living out with the dead, and sort them out later.'

All wounded had to be declared to the Gendarmerie and logged by them, but injured known, or believed to be Resistants, were 'overlooked' by Laverdure and his friends, and not officially recorded.

Resistants in need of medical attention were also diverted to a private clinic in the heart of the town, close to its great cathedral, and directly at the back of the Palais de Justice courts of law. Although ambulances were mainly German, Laverdure saw to it that the drivers of most of them were his men. The opportunity to assist escapers with ambulances was too good to miss. Instead of hospital, they took some to the clinic of Dr. Jean Poulain and his son Pierre, in rue Victor Hugo, facing the Palais de Justice back entrance through which handcuffed accused were continuously shuttled under armed guard for trial.

Ambulances could conveniently disappear straight into the clinic's private courtyard to unload behind the big courtyard doors, out of sight of passers by, or anyone else.

It was only a small clinic with fifteen private wards, Sisters from the Order of the Bon Secours de Paris, two surgeons, and four general doctors in attendance, but the clinic had some not so obvious extra accommodation.

Earlier in the war, the doctors Poulain had hidden hunted Jews in secret cellar vaults of the clinic until they could be led to safety. Immediately prison bombing news reached the Poulains, Dr. Jean Poulain advised Mother Superior Marie de le Visitation, who was in charge of the clinic:

'I think we had better prepare the vaults for a probable overflow from the wards.'

It wasn't the first time the Poulains and their nursing nuns had offered sanctuary and medical care to Resistants wounded during expeditions, regardless of the risk of them being in the clinic, which was always liable to surprise official inspections.

Sister Monica, Sister Emanuelle and Sister Marie Jean Baptiste hurriedly got the vaults and wards ready for the influx of injured expected within minutes from the gaol. They set up extra beds in the small wards and vaults, which, dating from Roman times, were ventilated by a high grille directly opposite the Palais de Justice.

Dr. Pierre loved joking with Sister Marie Jean Baptiste about her background, because her French name camouflaged that she was Irish, from County Cork.

'It's amazing how at ease you are with us in spite of us French being so difficult for foreigners to understand. We're suspicious of foreigners and never make things simple for them, yet underneath we really have a lot in common.'

'Maybe you French are so frequently irritated by the Irish and the English because you recognise so much of yourselves in us,' Sister Marie Jean Baptiste gently replied.

'I am sure you forgive us for being so inconsistent about almost everything,' Dr, Pierre laughed. 'We're religious yet appallingly anti-clerical; distrust and detest authority, yet revel in civic or state office; are sceptical, yet expect so much; demand quality, yet excel in making something out of nothing.'

The entrance to the steep ancient stone steps leading down to the cellars, hidden under the main staircase of the clinic buildings, couldn't be found or opened without understanding the secret locking mechanism. To allay suspicion, a second inspectable basement area – below courtyard level – housed the morgue.

The clinic was private, but forty-eight-year old Dr. Jean and his doctor son Pierre treated rich and poor. Both had the gift of somehow retrieving something good from even the worst situations, and good-humouredly calmed the desperate and despairing.

'The time when patience is most needed is when it's exhausted,' Dr. Jean advised Sister Yves-Marie.

As soon as ambulances began to drive up to the twin-house red-brick clinic behind the high garden wall, injured men and women were swiftly disrobed from their prison clothes and dressed in bed gowns and pyjamas.

'To prevent identification, bandage them facially whether they need it or not, then good luck to police or Gestapo who decide to come and check us,' Dr. Jean told the Sisters. 'We've handled Gestapo this way before.'

The Gestapo did come. Four men.

'We wish to inspect your list of patients,' the one in charge challenged Dr. Jean.

'Certainly,' he replied, long accustomed to using politeness like an air cushion to ease bumps.

Mother Superior Marie de la Visitation disappeared an instant into the office and returned with the clinic register. The Gestapo leader scanned it carefully then, holding on to it, asked to be shown round the entire premises. The four, accompanied by Dr. Jean and the Mother Superior, moved from ward to ward. In each case, two Gestapo entered the room while two stood guard in the corridor. Two or three of the beds in each ward had patients. A couple of men's heads were swathed in bandages with only their noses visible.

'A road accident,' Dr. Jean explained.

'Why don't they use the public Hospital Nord?' the Gestapo leader queried.

'Because they can afford privacy,' said Dr. Jean.

Several patients were in traction, some with broken legs. Opening a maternity ward door, the Gestapo were confronted by three large mounds beneath the blankets of three beds.

'When are these women due?' the Gestapo asked.

'Probably at three o'clock tomorrow morning.' Dr. Jean replied.

'Why three o'clock?' asked the puzzled Gestapo.

'We're as mystified as you are, but obstetricians can never understand why most babies have to be born at three o'clock in the morning.'

The Gestapo stared at him blankly for a moment, then smiled, and Dr. Jean returned the smile.

Tension eased slightly after the medical humour interlude, and the inspection continued, taking in the morgue and the Sisters' private chapel.

When the Gestapo had gone, muffled laughter emerged from the bandages of several patients, and the three 'expectant mothers' patted and congratulated their cushion-stuffed bed gowns.

'You even joke at a time like that, doctor!' Sister Yves-Marie reproved affectionately.

'Finding something to laugh at when you're in trouble, helps make life more of a laughing matter,' explained Dr. Jean.

All gaolbreak 'patients' had been carefully rehearsed on what to answer if questioned about their 'ailments', but the Gestapo visitors didn't interrogate any of them.

The Poulains never shirked danger, because Jean Poulain always maintained that although he couldn't do anything about the length of his life, he could do something about its width and depth.

When the clinic could hold no more from the gaol, the Poulains arranged for many to be nursed in private houses. With Pierre covering for him at the clinic, Dr. Jean toured these 'emergency wards' with a nursing sister accompanying him in his car, and even operated on patients in some of them when there was no alternative.

'What shall we finally do about dispersal of our prison friends?' Dr. Jean considered the question with his son Pierre and the Mother Superior.

'We'll simply wait and see how things progress with the counter-measures the Abwehr and Gestapo will undoubtedly order, then we'll deal with the problem . . . Anyway problems are the price of progress.'

# 14 Of brothels and men

'Let's go to a brothel,' Victor suggested to Freddie as they walked from the Gestapo house at rue Jeanne d'Arc.

'I realise you haven't had any for a while,' Freddie responded, 'but surely our priority right now is getting out of Amiens, not getting into some girls?'

'Show me a better place than a brothel or maison de passe to spend an undisturbed night,' Victor challenged, but Freddie didn't need convincing – he already knew a bordel or maison de passe was safer than even the most insignificant hotel. Hotels were liable for inspection at any time of day or night, but the Germans didn't close brothels, nor the maisons de passe, which were usually sleazy rundown hotels where a man and a woman could rent a room for a few hours or a night without questions asked. This kind of accommodation was far too hard to control, because guests weren't asked to sign registers, which is why they were such useful places to get lost in.

'Tarts always lock bedroom doors when they're entertaining,' said Victor, somewhat wistfully. 'Not even police burst into a tart's locked bedroom, because in this country it's accepted that to disturb a man in the middle of fucking can cause psychological harm.'

'I'm glad to hear that,' said Freddie. 'I know this town well, but not its knocking shops – where are they?'

'Around the Boulevard du Port, where we're going. The Abwehr, Gestapo, Milice, French police – the lot – will be crawling over every road leading out of town, so we're better off not trying to get out yet.'

German soldiers and Gendarmes, striving to cover every main road, were interested in anything that moved – cars, bicycles, pedestrians – so Freddie wasn't arguing. Military trucks with troops, streamed past them heading for the gaol and, almost certainly to strategic points inside and outside the town.

'Look at the couple of characters across the street, Victor – the ones with the hats. If they're not plain-clothes police mixing with crowds watching for anyone clearly avoiding check-points, fingering them for German police, also in plain clothes, then my name really *is* Freddie,' said Freddie.

Hunters from the Abwehr and the Gestapo, reinforced by brigades of French collaborationists, were fast gathering their counter-measure forces together. Roadblock checking, for people they might recognise or recall observing in contact with Resistance suspects, was already tightening the grip on the town. Although Freddie and Victor had destroyed prison and Gestapo files, a few photographic records still existed in Amiens' Palais de Justice court dossiers, and remaining identifications were distributed among a group of expert physiognomists – men whose speciality was faces. Each was given several photographs to remember, and for double-checking, photos were stuck inside their hat sweatbands. Most of the memory men were former gambling casino employees accustomed to 'spotting' at casino entrances. On seeing someone whose face they recognised from 'undesirable' lists, they'd ring for assistance to remove the unwanted gambler. Now their memories were being recruited to 'spot' Amiens prison escapees.

Security police, who operated at rail stations, also set up road blocks for checking cars, and even Schutzkommando – camp security guards – had been drafted in to stop people at barriers, demanding:

'Ausweis!' – identity papers. But Freddie noted, for possible future reference, that cycling kids got through without hindrance.

Compelled to act in rare unison, Abwehr and Gestapo established a communications centre to monitor all search-and-recover actions, and, as far as possible, centrally to direct anti-escape operations. Almost as soon as the new communications controls were established, main telephone cables between Amiens and Paris were cut. Police Lieutenant Laverdure, responsible for Amiens Gendarmerie liaison with German forces, was ordered to institute enquiries into the cable cutting, which had already occurred in the village of St. Sofleur area over twenty previous times. Laverdure phoned Gendarme chief Lamont at St. Sofleur:

'The phone cables have been cut again somewhere in your district, so you're instructed to make top priority investigations, as maintenance of communications is essential to the rearrest of escapers from the gaol bombing.'

'Right, sir!' – Lamont curtly confirmed that the sabotage would receive immediate attention.

Replacing his telephone, Laverdure smiled, certain the escapees would have a free run for quite a while yet, without any efficient German communications nerve centre further diminishing their slim chances. Gendarme chief Lamont and his officers were unlikely to have much official success in preventing phone cable sabotage in their district as they, in fact, were the saboteurs and had therefore just been asked to investigate themselves!

Acting more by reflex than reason, Freddie and Victor could only extend their thoughts from moment to moment. It was pointless thinking too far ahead when only now mattered. Victor was suspicious of everything and trusted nobody – not even himself.

A passing suspicious-looking car pulled up a little ahead.

'It's a Gestapo car!' Freddie said evenly, yet suddenly gripping Victor's arm, practically propelling him towards the Citroen car. Victor felt his stomach go into a spasm as if stricken by a sudden attack of chronic indigestion. The overpowering pain of fear made him want to vomit. Seeing the fear, Freddie said softly:

'Whatever you're feeling, it happens to the best of us, so stop thinking about what *might* happen, and maybe it won't.' Their nerves were tensed for instant reactions, ready to dive for cover at the slightest indication of danger.

Four men in civilian clothes emerging from the car, with

revolvers drawn, seemed to be coming straight at them. Freddie, feeling Victor striving to pull away from him as if bursting to go in the opposite direction, urged him on with a firm grip, cutting short hesitation.

'Don't!' – Freddie snapped. 'If you run, we're dead. Hold on.'

As they were about to meet the four head on, two suddenly jumped a man just ahead of them, handcuffing and searching him at the same time. Pushing back excited passers-by, one of the others shouted:

'Anyone approaching the prisoner will be shot!'

The man was hustled to the Citroen, with its uniformed driver, shoved into the back seat with a Gestapo man on either side of him, and driven away, leaving Freddie and Victor drained and sweating. The street had become strangely quiet.

'Until you've passed through fire, you never know what it's like,' said Freddie, breaking the silence that temporarily enveloped everyone who witnessed the arrest.

'I recognised one of the men,' Victor almost whispered, still watching the disappearing Citroen. 'It was Pechon – chief of Amiens Milice – the collaborating bastard!'

They resumed their purposely unhurried progress towards the brothel quarter. Fate puts a special mark on some friendships. You meet someone totally new, and feel you've known them a lifetime. Victor couldn't resist any longer the feeling of trust and reassurance, so alien to his chronically suspicious nature, that Freddie was instilling into him.

They strolled beside the river Somme along Boulevard du Port, Port d'Aval, and the aptly named rue l'Aventure, taking stock of closed houses which were plainly bordels.

'The one on the corner with the Red Cross on the door looks interesting,' commented Victor. 'That must be the Germans' Service Sanitaire clinic, or pox checkpoint. The Red Cross door's on Boulevard du Port, but the house appears to be connected to one on Port d'Aval which has the brothel's main entrance. It's obviously mainly for the military, but you can bet Gestapo also get their pound of flesh there, so a couple more civilians at the knocking shop won't look unusual.'

Marching up to the door and ringing the bell, he used the same approach he had been ready to employ at the house adjoining the rue Jeanne d'Arc Gestapo headquarters.

'Is Madame Pasteau in?' he asked Louise as she peered through the spyhole.

'I'm sorry, you have the wrong place,' she replied.

'Can we speak to you a moment anyway?' Freddie pleaded. 'Even if Madame Pasteau isn't here, you might be able to help us – please open the door.' The spy panel shut and they waited.

Even a turtle gets nowhere until it sticks its neck out, thought Freddie, and this wasn't the moment to hope and wait for things simply to happen for them. They were more likely to come faster if they met them halfway.

The door opened.

They didn't realise how lucky they were that Madame Jacqueline and her husband were in Paris for a few days, because, although willing to let her husband give money to support Resistants, Jacqueline tried to avoid personal involvement, cautioning her husband Louis:

'As I'm running the brothel – not you – you can do what you want. If money's needed, give it; if something else is needed, give it, but I don't want you, me, or anyone else to get shot – we have to work far too closely with the Germans to take stupid risks. We have to be especially careful.'

Louise stood in the open door studying them at first in silence. Then, addressing Freddie she said:

'You speak excellent French, but you're not French.

People are never more frightening than when they are absolutely certain they are right, and her emphatic assessment shook Freddie and Victor; but worse was to come. She detonated a bigger bombshell when staring at Freddie she added:

'You're American.'

He was startled, but fascinated.

'How did you reach that conclusion?' he questioned, treading as warily as someone looking both ways before crossing a one way street.

'With my ears,' Louise answered. 'Whatever language is spoken, however fluent and apparently perfect, I can usually distinguish a person's mother tongue.'

Freddie and Victor stood motionless at the door, as though hypnotised.

'You'd better come in,' she suggested, unable to suppress a slight smile. They obeyed.

As she led them into Madame Jacqueline's empty office, she said:

'I think I can guess where you've just come from, but you tell me.'

'From the gaol, Madame,' Victor said with tiredness in his voice.

'We escaped during the bombing.'

'And you want somewhere to hide until you can figure how to get out of town?'

'Yes,' they answered as one.

She knew she was at risk. They could be a Gestapo plant, but she had to follow instinct, as always. Every tomorrow has to be faced, and until Madame Jacqueline returned tomorrow, she could provide shelter, food, and the opportunity to think. One day she might be running herself and need helping hands. The Madame would have a fit if she knew, because Germans were usually everywhere in the house, but she'd cover somehow, at least for twenty-four hours. The two houses, specially remodelled in anticipation of possible police raids, had secret exits and passages leading to adjacent buildings. As for the girls, she was confident they were patriotic enough to keep their mouths shut if they suspected a couple of evaders were being harboured in the place.

As she led them up to a room, one of the girls, as provocatively vulgar as a dirty postcard, passed on the stairs, and their heads turned to watch her descend. When she walked, eyes followed – she was that kind. She wasn't hard-pretty. She looked outwardly like a teenager, but her big blue eyes didn't belong to a little girl. They'd seen too much and lacked something: whore's eyes – cold but friendly, bold yet cautious.

'She's a great worker,' said Louise – 'Hardly gone before she's back again, shaking herself like a ruffled hen ready for the next one.' Opening the door of a room, she gave them a key and instructed that the door be locked from the inside.

'I have the only other key to the room,' she said, 'so if you hear a key in the lock, don't hit me over the head as I come in,' she added smiling.

'Did you eat before you left the gaol?' she inquired. They both laughed.

'The bombs reached us before the soup,' Victor explained.

'I'll bring you something.'

The shuttered room, smelling of cheap perfume, was dressed with frills, bric-a-brac, and lace curtains to add to its femininity. There was a brass bed, marble-topped dressing table, bedside cabinet, a single tapestry-upholstered armchair, wardrobe, and behind a tapestry screen, a wash basin and a bidet. The slightly threadbare Turkish-style carpet was reflected – as was the bed – in full length gilt-framed mirrors. Two army grey blankets looked as if they were German army issue, and almost certainly were.

'It's tatty, but home!' Freddie announced.

'I bet this bed's had its share of ups and downs,' Victor said enviously. 'Well, fools and their legs are soon parted.'

The meal was a feast to them.

'Fortunately, Madame gets heavy workers' ration cards for her girls, which is as it should be, because they are,' Louise explained. 'We and other local brothels also get a bit extra from farmers with whom we have special deals.' An elderly farmer who supplied weekly Black Market produce to Madame Eugene's brothel at 34, Boulevard du Port was one of the few civilians, apart from the Gestapo, to enjoy bordel facilities. Arranging part payment for his food in girls' services, he admitted regularly imbibing a recommended potion to boost his sex urge, but stopped when told the mixture was almost certainly made from the urine of pregnant mares.

'I'm not paying for horse piss when I can get as much as I want free from my own farm,' he protested.

Although never confirming whether or not he switched to home brew, he remained a brothel regular until he died in his late seventies.

Farmers' illicit trading deals with Madames were highly valued because some places liked to provide food, which could be as important an attraction as the girls provided for dessert. SS officers were particularly lavish spenders in meals-and-sex establishments.

Stretched out on the bed, Freddie and Victor wrestled with potential plans to get them away from Amiens.

'It'll soon be time for us to plan less and do more,' Freddie asserted ruefully, then they both jerked up at the sound of an appalling rumpus from downstairs.

'A raid?' Victor ventured nervously.

'Unlikely in a place as well supervised by the military as this,' Freddie reassured him.

Risking creeping to the head of the staircase, they gazed down on two massive soldiers pummelling the life out of each other, one already with a severe gash across an eye and blood streaming down his face.

'You know what they say?' Victor whispered – 'When words fail, try a punch on the jaw.'

Louise, almost as tall as Madame Jacqueline, and no lightweight herself, tried to break them up, but wasn't as experienced at stopping fights as her mistress. The alternative was to call for help. As she opened the front door, a Gendarme patrol policing the brothel quarter happened to be outside, and soon tore the two apart.

Staring at items of the battling men's uniforms scattered around the hallway, Victor grabbed Freddie's hand and dragged him back into their room.

'I've got the answer for us!' his voice rose excitedly. 'With so many undressed soldiers about the place, why don't we fit ourselves out with a couple of German uniforms and leave town that way?'

The idea appealed, but when they broached it with Louise she vetoed uniform stealing.

'It would be discovered as soon as the men you took them from finished with the girls.'

'But we'd be gone,' Victor pointed out.

'Yes, *you*'d be gone, but we'd be in it up to our necks for robbing soldiers, even though we protested our innocence.'

Fiddling pensively with a pencil on the dressing table, she became significantly silent.

'I know where I can lay hands on uniforms that may do,' she said softly, without looking up, 'and if they're the wrong sizes, there could be another source. Male nurses in the medical centre next door keep some spares around, in case of vomiting accidents, and a break-in of the medical room in a separate house wouldn't directly involve the bordel.' Her face brightened at a further inspiration, 'I can even get you stamped army papers from there, but what about your German?'

'I speak it fluently,' Freddie replied.

'I can get by,' said Victor, 'but will let Freddie do any talking that's necessary.'

After the house had closed for the night, she returned to their room with a bundle of clothes in her arms. She had even managed to get the right size pairs of boots and socks from somewhere, and greatcoats.

'Try these,' she said triumphantly. 'They should fit reasonably enough.'

Excitedly, they stripped, put on the uniforms, and examined themselves in the dressing table mirror. Victor was particularly pleased with himself – he'd never been in uniform before.

'What about our civilian clothes?' Victor asked.

'Take them with you in these knapsacks,' Louise proposed, having clearly thought of everything. 'You'll eventually want to dump the uniforms and get back into ordinary clothes once you're well away from Amiens.'

'Tell me something, Louise,' Freddie asked, inquisitively, not really expecting an answer:

'Why are you here?'

His eyes studied her face, dwelling on it. She looked away as her face flushed.

'For a variety of reasons, but also because the one place no one ever breaks their heart from love is a brothel, so I decided this was for me.'

*

It took the authorities several hours to recover from the shock and realise the intent of the attack, but once they assessed the general aim had been to free prisoners, the most massive single manhunt of the war was mounted, covering the whole of the Somme, and far beyond it.

The Germans defined a mass escape as one involving more than five prisoners. If the number was greater, it had to be reported to High Command and the search organised from Berlin.

After completely surrounding the prison with policemen, Gestapo, Abwehr, Millice, and all available military personnel were in the streets and raiding private homes within a wide radius of the gaol. Roofs, cellars – nowhere was overlooked. Everything and everyone was checked and questioned. Many, totally unconnected with the escape, were deliberately detained to spread fear and intimidate any attempt to aid evaders. The whole of Amiens was put into a net and people indiscriminately hauled in for interrogation. The conquerors wanted to remind the population that the all-seeing eyes of Nazi Germany were so often the watchful eyes of their own next-door neighbours.

Armoured cars with manned machine-guns slowly patrolled mile after mile of the Route d'Albert searching for suspects along the road, and ceaselessly scanning snow-covered fields beside the highway for tell-tale footprints.

Military patrols, reinforced with Alsatian tracker dogs, fanned across fields and through woodlands. Hearing dogs, three escapers climbed a tree and saw fifty soldiers fanning out and spraying bullets at intervals at random with automatic guns as they moved forward. The line of men, most with dogs at heel, steadily advanced, guns levelled straight at where the three were hiding. A collaborator, seeing them enter the woods, had told the military. Although the soldiers couldn't see their prey, they intended to flush them out like wild fowl. If the three panicked, they would be dead birds. The dogs would only attack if ordered to do so.

Without a word, the soldiers surrounded them, and the dejected trio had to accept capture.

Road blocks and identity checkpoints were hastily erected on main and minor roads, whilst extra military assistance was despatched to railway stations and scrutinised trains from Lille to Paris.

'Escaped prisoners! – Escaped prisoners! – Give yourselves up or your wives and families will pay for your temporary freedom!'

Loudspeaker cars, blaring our reprisal threats, slowly crawled through the streets of Amiens and nearby Albert, convoyed by soldier-filled transports followed by large empty trucks.

The faces of evaders who had managed to find brief refuge in local houses mirrored horror as the amplified voices brutally stabbed thoughts and emotions.

'Escaped prisoners! – we will arrest your wives and children as hostages – surrender now and save them!'

From side streets and back doors – never front doors, to avoid incriminating those who helped – hopeless dejected men and women, hands held high in surrender above their heads, drifted out beaten, unable to cope with the terrifying dilemma imposed by the threat to their families.

Triumphantly, soldiers accompanying loudspeaker cars prodded defeated prisoners with rifles, herding them like cattle into empty trucks.

Four women from one cell, led by evasion line courier Claire Normand, argued among themselves as the street warnings were monotonously repeated.

'Don't budge from this house yet,' Claire insisted. 'It's too early for reprisal threats to be anything but bluff.'

'How do you figure that?' challenged one of her companions.

'Because they can't know who escaped and who's still trapped under the piles of gaol rubble. It'll be days before they can clear it all, and even then many bodies will be unrecognisable, making it virtually impossible for them to be certain of anything.'

The point made sense.

'We've got time to take precautions and warn families,' she added. 'We can send couriers to our homes, and those of others we knew inside, and tell them what to do.'

Nervously answering a knock on the front door of her little terraced house in Albert, Madame Druon, with her little son and daughter clutching her skirt, opened it to a friend of her husband.

'You've heard about the prison bombing?'

'Yes.'

'Felix is free, uninjured, but in hiding. The Germans are threatening escapers' families and could use you and the children to blackmail Felix into surrendering, so you must leave here immediately.'

'Leave our home? Everything we possess is here.'

'Don't worry, just take a change of clothes for yourself and the children and come with me now.'

'Now!'

The caller had been instructed not to leave without them.

'You haven't far to go, and we'll bring the rest of your things for you.'

Madame Druon, sensible enough to do as she was told, was hustled along the street to a house only doors from her own.

'Here?' she asked, bewildered.

'Yes, Madame Bourdon and her family are going to move immediately into your house, and you'll stay in hers. Wherever possible, we're getting families to exchange homes temporarily to throw the enemy off course, and if necessary, after we get you different identity papers, we'll take you elsewhere.'

Claire Normand and her three evasion companions remained in their hideout, comforted by the knowledge that they were under the enemy's personal protection, as two Gestapo lodged in the house. This was why they were warned to talk softly and advised to walk about in stockinged feet so that they couldn't be heard downstairs.

'Having Gestapo billeted here makes my husband and I feel more secure than other resistance couples,' the wife explained, 'and a lot of our people, and shot down Allied airmen, have passed through this house.'

Her eight-year-old son regularly added his own personal contribution to family patriotism by spitting on the Gestapo men's shoes whenever they left them out for cleaning and polishing.

The escapers' greatest enemy, though, was the weather. In the open, they were all too visible moving black dots on a snow-white background, and, recognising this, the Abwehr asked the Luftwaffe to join the hunt.

Hedge-hopping *FW190*s from Amiens-Glisy, Abbeville, and Poix squadrons, streaked across fields and trees prisoner-spotting for ground hunters. Radioing results and directions for transmission from their air bases to armoured car patrols with mobile receivers, the combined plane-and-ground forces rounded up evaders like sheep, and those who hadn't found shelter or made sufficient progress before the full-scale manhunt hardly had a chance. In days when householders were wary of too readily assisting strangers in case they were being set up for a trap, the Germans weren't slow in scattering Milice traitors to infiltrate rescuers or entrap sympathetic local inhabitants.

'Use the same technique as false Allied aircrew operations,' the

Amiens Abwehr Commandant ordered. 'Put all your available fluent French-speaking men and women into prison uniforms and distribute them widely either to join up with others on the run, or trace routes.'

Abwehr already had plenty of practice at this game with their planting of fake airmen, speaking excellent English and wearing captured flying suits. Seeking help, plants would pass from one 'safe' house to another and eventually smash another escape network.

A group of survivors from adjoining cells agreed to stay on the run together, as one of them – a self-admitted railway sabotage specialist – knew a safe house close to the gaol. It was less than a kilometre away, and they were welcomed by a middle-aged couple.

'While my wife makes some coffee, I'll try and round up some clothes – especially overcoats – from friends,' the husband said before departing. He returned about twenty minutes later with two civilians and half-a-dozen uniformed SS men behind them. The 'rail saboteur prisoner' who joined them had been a Gestapo prison spy for three months.

It was 3 p.m. before counter-measures gathered full momentum. Fortunately for the evaders, this meant little remaining daylight for recapture operations, and especially for Luftwaffe, to stay effective. Again winter was the enemy's best ally. Frozen without overcoats, food, or safe contacts, and unable to beat ice and snow, many who had run in panic, or hope, began to trickle back to Amiens gaol or surrender to local police stations, preferring to give up rather than freeze to death in impossible weather conditions. Those with short-term sentences, who had only run in fright, decided it was wisest to return and finish reasonably brief imprisonment from which they would soon emerge legally free anyway. The majority of those who returned of their own choice were common criminals, but some, like high-ranking Préfecture official G.auntier, voluntarily gave up for fear of reprisals against their families.

Some fared better. Two recaptured prisoners, handcuffed together, were being marched to cars by Gestapo when as the first Gestapo man bent to get into the car, the last manacled man butted the officer accompanying him onto the pavement. The handcuffed pair ran, zig-zagging across the street, and by the time the surprised guards started wildly firing automatic guns in their direction, they had already vanished round a corner, and were not recaptured.

A horse-drawn van was halted at a Milice-manned road checkpoint by a guard, demanding:

'What's in your cart?'

'A half-dozen of the escaped Amiens prisoners,' the driver replied. 'You wouldn't believe I could get so many in such a little van, would you?'

'Don't be funny,' the Milice growled, his nostrils suddenly flaring at the scent of fresh bread from the van. 'Those bastards are nothing to joke about. Go on – get out before I make you sorry for your rotten joke.'

The driver, and his six prisoners hiding behind piles of bread inside, passed through the barrier and headed out of town.

By the time Pepe – René Chapelle – got back to Amiens at 5 p.m. the town was virtually shut tight – streets, station – blockage was complete. You could get in, but not out, unless thoroughly checked.

Dominique Ponchardier and Admiral Rivière, anticipating the enemy would react strongly, had long gone, having done all they could immediately following the attack. They hadn't in fact found the most important people they were looking for.

Touring several safe houses and contacts to get a rough estimate of results, Pepe was informed . . .

'Well over five hundred got away, including some of our men . . . Even the first official report admits four hundred and thirty-seven men and women prisoners managed to escape . . . Roger Beaurin was killed and Mama Beaurin, hit by a falling beam, taken to hospital with severe head injuries . . . There's no news, as yet, of Jean Beaurin or Maurice Holville – the only hopeful indication was that there were no corpses in their empty cells . . .'

'With no sentences having been passed on them, Jean Beaurin and his two cellmates, Louis and Gilbert, were still in their own clothes, but knew their debris-grimed grubbiness could attract attention. Gilbert, from Abbeville, whose wife had betrayed him to the police, obviously couldn't return to his family.

'Come with me, and I'll hide you with some friends of mine,' Jean offered.

'Let's go to my house first and get some money for you to buy train tickets out of here,' Louis suggested. 'I live near St. Roque Station, so you can take the train from there.'

As Amiens was Louis' town he was clearly the best to follow. On reaching his home, they didn't stop for anything except money. Louis dived inside, grabbed cash for himself and the others, then they split up.

'I'm obviously not sticking around here for the police to call,' said Louis. 'I'll lose myself in town until I can organise fresh papers and a new identity.'

Pointing Jean and Gilbert towards the local railway station, Louis wished them good luck, and left.

'Our best bet is to avoid main line trains, which are certain to get most attention from patrols searching for gaolbreakers,' Jean said.

'We'll take a secondary line train heading for Rouen, because that doesn't even involve us going to the station booking office as they collect fares on the train itself.'

Jean's intimate knowledge of everything connected with trains was coming in handy again – he knew time-tables by heart.

Neither was surprised by the curious glances of passengers. They realised they looked a rough, dishevelled pair on the run from somewhere, but nobody made any comment.

'Two to Beaucamp le Vieux,' Jean informed the conductor, digging into a pocket for the cash and shaken to discover he hadn't enough for the fares.

'Don't worry,' said the understanding conductor, 'I'll take your address and you can send on the balance.'

'Thank you,' Jean said, supplying a false name and address which the conductor scrawled in a notebook, all very correctly, although Jean knew that the procedure was for the benefit of others in the compartment. The conductor was helping them out of trouble.

Deviating through a wood at Beaucamp le Vieux to ensure they weren't being followed, Jean tripped and fell into a clump of stinging nettles. Incredibly, he didn't feel a thing until twenty minutes later when they finally got to the home of Armel – one of his Sosie action group colleagues, who didn't know the gaol had been bombed.

Cleaned up and fed, they moved to a safe house in the Amiens region, at Poix – under the noses of the Poix Luftwaffe base fighter pilots, flying spotter sorties in conjunction with land forces tracking escapers. They were advised to stay in the safe house until Armel could deliver new identity papers. Agreeing it would be prudent not to resume derailing trains, Jean decided to become a forged ration card supplier for people running from compulsory enemy slave labour service, and for Allied parachutists and agents.

Coincidentally, the Amiens suburban station of St. Roque also became Maurice Holville's jumping off point. Unsure of the security of his cell companions, he chose to go on his own. Pepe and Dominique Ponchardier's support teams were somewhere in the gaol vicinity, but he didn't intend losing time searching for them. He needed temporary refuge quickly.

'Madame Deloiseaux's the best bet!' he told himself, and began walking unhurriedly from the gaol. A housewife with no Resistance links, whose husband was in the same Hospital Nord ward as his brother, Madame Deloiseaux lived about two-and-a-half kilometres away.

He almost changed his mind en route, after considering whether it wouldn't be smarter to head immediately instead for his good friend Monsieur Bluet, the stationmaster of Amiens. Bluet had helped so much in the past and worked closely with him and OCM Intelligence directed by Dr. Mans.

With Amiens such a crucial railway centre, the enemy insisted on two stationmasters – one German and one French – not trusting the French to run the important key station alone. The stationmasters had separate offices and separate organisations.

The vast amount of military traffic was controlled by German stationmaster Spiet, whose poor French still made him heavily dependent on Bluet for running the system.

Holville didn't know it, but Monsieur Bluet was already handling five civilian-clothed gaolbreakers delivered to him by a guide, who had collected them outside the prison and got them, via back streets, to the station.

Instead of taking them through the station passenger entrance, they were led through the employees' entrance and handed official railway workers' armbands, brooms, mops, brushes, pans, and buckets.

'Make yourself busy around the station,' Bluet instructed.

'Sweep platforms and waiting rooms, clean toilets – let the German guards openly see you and accept you as auxiliary station employees. Your unfamiliar faces won't arouse suspicion because we're forever changing auxiliary help. Meanwhile we'll get you some papers and travel passes.'

The five dispersed about the station and began sweeping and cleaning right in front of guards checking incoming passengers.

Stationmaster Bluet regretted this couldn't be one of the normally efficient evasion operations frequently organised in association with the 'Curé of Montparnasse'. There was usually sufficient time to make a good job of false papers and identity cards, but for the five from the gaol, speed was more essential than thoroughness. To get away fast from Amiens, they would have to chance their arms with whatever reasonably suitable identity cards and travel papers he could draw from the stock permanently kept hidden in his office for emergencies. Distributing the identity cards and papers to the five, he advised them which trains to catch.

'As railway employees, you'll be able to join them without being stopped or questioned.'

The trains came in, and the five went out.

Monsieur Bluet was one of the few forewarned of the imminence of a mid-day gaolbreak. Rail exits from the town could be vital to many at the outset, before reinforcement of station barrier checkpoints and train searches had time to become more stringent.

Patrol cars already tearing along roads put Holville off central station thoughts. He would leave by train, when ready, but the minor St. Roque station would be a wiser departure point. First, he needed to discard the railwayman's uniform he was still wearing, then contact his family, which Madame Deloiseux could achieve for him.

Suddenly grateful for military and police vehicles on the way to the prison, or hunting evaders, for obligingly ploughing pathways through the snow to make road travel easier, he continued walking normally, drawing no attention to himself, and talking to no one.

The knock on the door of the house was answered by Madame Deloiseaux's six-year-old daughter.

'Maman! – it's the man from the hospital!' the child shouted.

'I have just escaped from the prison, Madame,' he announced bluntly, 'and would appreciate your help.'

As she made him some steaming hot ersatz coffee, he explained:

'I know my father and other brother are both in town today to visit my sick brother. If you go now to the hospital with your daughter, ostensibly on a normal visit to your husband, you can tell my brother to let my family know I'm sheltering here and need different clothes for my getaway. Unless I leave town by tonight, I'm sure the whole place will be sewn up for days.'

After making him the first decent meal he'd had in weeks, Madame Deloiseaux left for the hospital. An hour-and-a-half later, his father arrived with clothes, and at 6 p.m. – an hour following Pepe's return to Amiens – Maurice Holville and his father took the train to Mers from St. Roque station, cautiously switching compartments at every stop. Their destination was the farm home of his sister Madame Renée George, in a village some fifteen kilometres from Mers. Both realised Renée, who had a flock of children and regularly supplied fresh eggs to German military in the area, could only safely be a brief stop – she was too close a relative not to be traced eventually, and checked by the Gestapo.

There was a surprise waiting for them when they got to her

home. She was already hiding another evader in the house – an agent trying to get back to Britain.

'Everyone comes to me when they're escaping around here,' she said.

*

Warden Gaston Brasseur was in a bad way.

'He's got to go to hospital,' warned one of his warden colleagues, who came to the Brasseur home to enquire about him. 'It's too dangerous to let him lie here in bed – he could have internal injuries.'

'But the Gestapo could find him again there!' his wife protested.

'Don't worry,' his friend Julian reassured her. 'I'll get him by ambulance to the Hospital du Nord, make sure he's bandaged so that nobody will spot him, and have him admitted under another name.'

An ambulance arrived within half-an-hour, and some two hours later Braumann, touring the hospital looking for German section prisoners, actually stood at the foot of Brasseur's bed and didn't recognise him.

Visiting the hospital in the course of her Public Health Service department duties, Dr. Odile Regnault found Braumann and his interpreter Lucienne continuing interrogations at the bedside of the wounded. Seeing Dr. Regnault, he said:

'I have high regard for the professional ethics of doctors. For example, I much admire the heroic and selfless conduct of Dr. Mans during the bombing, and assure you that German authorities, who acknowledge and appreciate such courage, will certainly liberate him before long.'

Unfortunately, Mama Beaurin's head bandages didn't save her from identification, and the Germans wanted her elsewhere.

'If you shift her now, you could kill her,' the French doctor in charge said emphatically. 'She's too badly wounded to be moved, and should stay under observation for several more days.'

Anxious, at that moment, to foment public indignation against the Allies for attacking helpless prisoners, and wishing to divert attention from their customary inhumanity, the Gestapo conceded the point, and permitted Mama Beaurin to remain.

When Maurice Holville's brother, in the hospital's bronchial ward, heard of Mama Beaurin and what was likely to happen to her within a few days, he passed the news to his father and brothers.

'We've got to get her out the instant she's fit enough to walk,' Maurice Holville told his father. 'If they keep their hands on her, they'll have a weapon with which to force Jean's surrender.'

As nightfall eased for a while the manhunt pressure, common criminals were imprisoned temporarily in a local disused factory, and the fifty remaining 'politicals' sent to the ancient Citadelle fortress which King Henry IV ordered to be constructed in 1598, and which was completed in 1620. Everyone fit enough to walk was marched through the streets to the Citadelle, guarded by police and soldiers. Twenty, taken earlier for treatment to the nearby requisitioned Hospice St. Victor, were transported by truck to the fortress. A section of the Hospice had been demolished by a stray *Mosquito* bomb.

Dr. Mans and Captain Tempez, still attending the wounded, were driven later to the fortress gaol by the doctor's Préfecture assistant, François Vignolle, in his little Renault van, with, of course, a Gestapo escort.

The fifty were put in the unheated old cavalry barracks on the first floor of the fortress. The Red Cross brought soup, and the German guards locked the prisoners in.

Utterly exhausted, they all fell asleep, only to be woken by an explosion and the scream of a diving aircraft.

A voice in the darkness said;

'They're really determined to get us out.'

Flak spattered the roof, and the noise was deafening, but it proved to be a Luftwaffe fighter taking refuge in the shelter of its own anti-aircraft defences, on being chased by American night bombers.

Within twenty-four hours of the gaol attack, 231 were officially listed as 'recaptured', but the figure deceptively included those who stayed in the first place, those who returned voluntarily, the dead, and the injured in hospital.

The authorities were reluctant to admit to the hundreds more still at large.

In the morning, Dr. Mans took stock of his Citadelle companions. Tempez, Gendarme Achille Langlet, and Mans' former Intelligence liaison assistant, Marius Couq, were among them, but in one corner of the room, he heard three civilian-suited men talking quietly to each other in English, with American accents.

'They're American aviators,' one of the German guards informed Mans. 'At least, that's what they say, but the Gestapo have only just started on them.'

Regretting his inability to speak English, Mans made the only hands-across-the-sea gesture available to him – he whistled a melody he had learnt in the First World War – the United States'

Marines 'From the Halls of Montezuma'. The three Americans appreciatively returned the gesture with big grins and V for Victory signs.

*

That afternoon, when the daily traffic of uniformed men passing in and out of the house was in full swing, Freddie and Victor Pasteau, with officially stamped German papers declaring they had just used the bordel's services and were free from infection and fit to return to their units, departed through the front door. Louise had taken the precaution of filling them in on the location and background of local military units, so that they would have answers to possible questions en route.

As they thanked her for everything, she smiled and said:

'What are friends for?'

Striding from the busy brothel quarter, Victor asked:

'Why are men so much randier than women?'

'They're not really,' said Freddie, 'but just won't accept that there's only so much paste in a tube, and squeeze it out too fast.'

Spotting a German army truck rumbling their way, Freddie blatantly signalled for it to stop. It did, and the pair of them thumbed a lift to freedom.

*

Michel Dubois and Gendarme Edouard Robine picked up more than they bargained for.

As a Gendarme who had frequently deliberately imprisoned people on civil charges for their own protection, Robine was very conscious that dozens of men and women in tell-tale prison brown, frantically scurrying about the streets seeking shelter, were not all professional criminals. Even if they were crooks, he and many other Gendarmes and townsfolk believed that the convicts nevertheless deserved reprieve or consideration for having been bombed. Although remembering that man is made of pounds of muscle but only ounces of brain, thereby making it foolish to expect too much from human nature, Robine was certain many must feel as he did – that fleeing criminals and 'politicals' should be classified together simply as escapers in desperate need of helping hands. All human beings warranted human treatment.

Evaders guided to Robine, Dubois, and their associates by local people, swiftly swelled those taking sanctuary in the centuries-old quarry caves of St. Pierre to some *three hundred*!

The caves once provided a plentiful source of building stone, and in the 1914–18 World War, they were used as shelters for the civilian population, and for the same purpose in World War II. On

20 May 1940, and in June, during the battle for Amiens, five hundred civilians took refuge in them.

The extraordinary scene in the caves was suddenly transformed into a resemblance of a Biblical Court of Miracles. But one has to work very hard to achieve miracles. Adequately clothing as many as possible had already stripped bare the emergency wardrobes of Madame Vignon and Madame Barré. Food and drink were nightmares too. Desperation demanded desperate measures.

'When you get to the end of your rope, you've simply got to tie a knot and hang on,' said Michel Dubois to Robine, trying to find an answer to the crisis.

'The solution to our troubles is here, under your noses,' a voice interrupted. They turned to face a tall, gangling young man in his twenties, about six feet two inches tall, with shell-rimmed glasses, a neat black moustache, and a mane of black hair which gave him an intellectual look.

'Who are you?' asked Michel.

'They call me "The Joker", but my name's Sammy Izard.'

'The Joker?' Edouard Robine said sceptically.

'Yes – mostly because I often used to see how many smash-and-grab raids I could do in a day for a bet, and because I enjoy playing practical jokes. I was inside the gaol for the raids, not the jokes, of course.

'I'm never going back to smash-and-grab – you can too easily get stuck in ordinary traffic jams after you've got away with a nice load. If you can't plan for that kind of thing, what's the point in taking the risk?'

'We don't want to hear about your past troubles – what's the magic answer to our present problems?' Robine asked impatiently.

'Us,' Sammy replied, waving a hand towards clusters of characters gossiping in different sections of the caves. 'Sometimes it takes criminals to beat criminals, and you'd agree there are no bigger criminals in the world today than Hitler, Goering, Himmler and company. I'm sure Amiens is full of people who would willingly help if they could, but we're in no position to make door-to-door appeals right now. We've simply got to take what we need to stay alive and free, and a lot of people in here are expert at taking things.'

'Thieving!' Robine exclaimed.

'Yes – amongst other things,' Sammy admitted. 'I appreciate it goes against the grain for a policeman to accept such a suggestion, but in times like these we're all dishonest in some way, and anyhow, there's dishonesty and dishonesty. Some of us are crooked, but ladies and gentlemen in all other respects.

'Everyone's become dishonest these days when the choice is starvation rations or Black Market, and those who can't afford Black Market prices trade on the Grey Market, which is also illegal.'

(Grey Marketeers bartered or bought and sold goods with farmers and other food producers.)

'We've got all kinds of crooked talent available here today,' Sammy enthused – 'Shoplifters, pickpockets, housebreakers, Black Marketeers – the sort who know where to look and how to get what we need most. Only this time they'll be thieving and getting up to roguery in a good cause – not just lining their own pockets. And what I'd be asking them to do wouldn't be, as you know, without risk. Maybe helping others for a change as well as themselves will make them feel good. Armies often need to forage for food, or requisition supplies, and at this moment, we're the same as an army struggling for life. Nor is everyone here a crook – there are plenty of Resistants and freedom fighters among us.'

Robine and Dubois looked at each other and said nothing. In the circumstances the justification put forward seemed unanswerable.

'Don't worry,' Sammy added with a reassuring smile. 'People aren't arrested for stealing – they're only arrested for being caught at it.'

What any of them did, or didn't do, to help was of course entirely up to each individual. Robine and Dubois accepted that they couldn't really control the situation. All they and others could do was to provide temporary shelter and time for escapers to get their breath back in the caves, until sufficiently recovered to attempt to get further away from Amiens and reach friends and havens where they could more securely re-establish themselves. The size of the problem and sheer volume of escapers had overwhelmed and surprised everyone – including the prisoners.

Sammy Izard, retired smash-and-grab thief, asking nobody's permission, took charge of his own idea. But even if you are a decision maker, you need people to follow you – no one really achieves anything completely alone. Quietly and efficiently, Sammy began his recruiting campaign, and started with Violette Lambert. No one knew her real name. She was on record under a string of aliases and used so many identities that she had virtually forgotten her own. Violette hadn't been a delicate flower for a long time. Raised in a convent school, a crooked relative introduced her to the criminal fraternity and she operated a transport service for thieves, picking them or their loot up at robbery rendezvous points, thereby enabling them speedily to unload incriminating stolen goods or burglary equipment. She progressed to burglary herself –

unusual for a female – finally graduating with honours in shoplifting until she queened her own team. Although ruthless if orders weren't meticulously carried out, she was generally kind, loyal, and even had principles, though they were somewhat twisted. It was, in fact, someone else's slack discipline which landed Violette and three members of her shoplifting gang in Amiens gaol. Now they were enjoying their first real reunion in many months in a corner of the St. Pierre caves.

When Sammy moved across to explain to them the problem, Violette's laughter echoed through the caves. The idea of becoming a Good Samaritan hugely appealed, but helping meant careful planning. Violette never ad libbed jobs. Detailed plans had to be carried out with military precision. She selected assistants only after long investigation and testing. If someone worked for her, you could be reasonably sure they didn't drink, didn't talk, and obeyed orders. She kept the team in line not with threats, but with gentle admonitions that if they didn't stick to rules and instructions, they'd be out. Violette and her trio – professionals with a considerable respect for their calling and a strong bond of affection uniting them – were caught because even the most efficient can't anticipate everything.

Two men and three other women shoplifters in the caves volunteered to join Violette, but she didn't like working with people she didn't know or didn't totally command.

Violette nodded thoughtfully as the five stood around her, instinctively gravitating towards her as leader.

'We need all the help we can get, but you know me – I like things my way – feel safer, you understand?' she said soothingly. 'Let's prepare things together – share shopping lists so that we each go for specific things and don't overlap nor waste effort, but let's go our separate ways. My team's doing the biggest department store in town, which doesn't mean you shouldn't go there – where you shop is up to you.'

They saw the sense. All had a healthy regard for Violette, who they knew could put away three fur coats and a roll of cloth in the time it took most of her girls to lift a set of underwear.

The three women and one of the men were strangers to Violette, but she knew Joseph Metz was a good thief. He was a high-grade respectable type who went off to work every day like an efficient business man, without his neighbours having the faintest idea that he was anything than he appeared to be. He never brought 'work' home, so he didn't have to worry about his place being turned over by police because they would never discover anything incriminating there. He was an ex-bank robber turned shoplifter.

'My wife would hate police cars appearing at all hours outside the house – what would the neighbours think?' he gossiped to Violette as they scribbled lists of types and sizes of clothes required for those still in prison uniforms.

'When I was in banking, we even had a bank manager as our neighbour who was forever talking about bank raiders. I was tempted to show him how they operated – at his bank – but didn't want to shit so close to my own doorstep. I keep my business well away from my home life.'

Little Adolphe, a Belgian cattle thief and Black Marketeer, was next on Sammy's recruitment list.

'We need food – as much as you can get – and I'm told you were a big man in the food Black Market,' Sammy complimented him flatteringly.

Little Adolphe drew his five feet up to their full extent to confirm:

'I *was* big in business. Physical size isn't everything. If Napoleon was alive today he wouldn't be able to get a job as a doorman. I know all the local smugglers and Black Market operators working for the better restaurants as well as the smallest bistros, so leave food to me. You know I even used to blackmail Germans for extra supplies by threatening to expose how much they were themselves involved with regular traffic of Black Market stuff.' Perky little Adolphe was an expert Black Market go-between – beef, ducklings, peaches, salmon, Chablis, champagne – you name it, Adolphe traded in it.

'I also had an excellent reputation in the Black Market,' chubby faced Sophie Glasser, with the butter-wouldn't-melt-in-her-mouth look, volunteered as the news of The Joker's requirements spread around the caves. 'Cute' described Sophie, with her brown hair and retroussé nose – cute enough to persuade German soldiers to carry her heavy Black Market-filled suitcases at railway stations, the cases frequently stuffed full of pig.

'Thank you for helping me with my heavy case,' she would coyly murmur, opening her big brown eyes at the nice kind soldiers.

'A pleasure, Mademoiselle,' they'd say, and she'd repay with an even wider smile.

Sophie would be quite a catch for some man – apart from policemen, for in addition to being a shrewd business woman she was a Cordon Bleu cook and made superb pâté and pork savouries. She knew all there was to know about getting the best out of a pig. Ham and gammon portions of a pig's carcase she cured for forty days in a bath of brine, then hung them in cheese cloth to dry. Every Friday night brine was ladled from the bath and the carcase removed to permit Sophie and the rest of her family to have their regular hot soak, after which the brine was poured back into the bath.

Regrettably, one of Sophie's suitcases burst at the seams while being lugged through the streets by an obliging soldier, which is how Sophie found herself in Amiens gaol.

Sophie offered to supplement Little Adolphe's results with cooked meats.

'I'll tour some of my former food shop accounts, slip through their side doors, and come out with my Black Market foods camouflaged with ordinary vegetables. I'm sure my clients will be generous to me for old time's sake and also,' she added coyly, 'for future goodwill.'

'What about bread? – we need bread – lots of it,' plump Georges Danielou, with the flat-brushed black hair, interjected. 'I could tap local tobacconists I used to supply with forged bread coupons to loan me some of my own work. I'll promise to replace coupons – with bonuses – later!'

Georges, who could counterfeit almost anything – from ration cards and identity papers to banknotes – proudly asserted that at least his wife never complained he didn't make enough money.

'I know honesty is supposed to pay, but it never paid enough to suit me,' Georges confessed.

Bread cards were lucrative for Georges because the traffic in bread cards was massive. Counterfeit and genuine cards were sold by people who had their own sources of wheat and were therefore able to make their own bread. The trick was knowing who had real cards, or false cards.

Camille Druon, a handbag thief, whose speciality was ladies' toilets, suggested that as there was hardly a franc between the lot of them, having come straight from gaol, a little cash would be handy for financing some of them when they finally started running.

'We're not stealing from ordinary women's purses!' Sammy protested contemptuously.

'Of course not!' Camille agreed. 'I'll only rob purses of women or girls accompanying German soldiers, or anyone German.'

'That's different,' Sammy enthused approvingly.

Violette chimed in that a cash float was essential for shoplifting operations.

'We have to buy *some* things,' she explained, 'otherwise hovering around counters, never dipping into your own purse for anything can arouse suspicion, so we need a float – can't start without it.'

Assistance in this direction came from some Resistants who had friends in the St. Pierre district on whom they could call to raise some money quickly. Several immediately left the caves to collect cash, and where available clothes, for others. Overhearing Camille, two middle-aged, maternal, very respectable-looking women made a further proposal:

'We could add to cash reserves on the same principle of hurting collaborators only. Collaborators should be hit where it pains them most – in their pockets. They make money out of everything – famine, rations, tobacco, soap, toilet paper, and selling people to the Gestapo.'

Observing both the women almost unconsciously massaging and pulling at their unusually long first and middle fingers, Sammy instantly identified them as pickpockets. It was interesting, he noted, how the normally shorter first finger had been deliberately developed by constant pulling until it extended almost to the length of its neighbour – important because the 'fork' movement, in which the first and middle fingers are used like a pair of scissors, is the surest way to lift a wallet.

Marguerite Miller and Madeleine Gillis, who specialised in lifting wallets, extracting currency, then returning the wallet without the victim even knowing, also kept their sensitive fingers supple with exercises, rather like loosening a new pair of gloves.

'I'll miss not working with my lovely signet ring which is still in the gaol prisoners' valuables safe,' Marguerite said sorrowfully. 'I had a sharp knife blade made small enough to fit inside that ring, because the blade made it so much easier to slash right through overcoat or suit material to reach wallets.'

During winter, men wearing tightly buttoned overcoats made hip or inside jacket pockets virtually inaccessible for pick-pockets, but women carrying bags always offered opportunities.

'It never occurs to most men that they haven't just lost their wallet – that it's been lifted,' Madeleine claimed. 'A little preliminary pocket-patting usually tells us all we need to know.'

The pair of them categorised every pocket:

Back trousers, easy to dip into, as are breast and side jacket pockets. Not so easy, but still good pickings, inside jacket and trousers front pockets. Safest, waistcoat pockets.

'What about me lending a hand? – I'm sure I can quickly lay my hands on a few Francs,' a lanky, dark-haired twenty-year-old offered. 'It's Friday – pay day – so there'll be more money about.'

Sammy knew that Bernard Bouville in a temper, was unpredictable. He looked the Boy Scout type, but was a vicious thug who would beat up any woman, no matter how old, simply to rob her.

He would be incapable of sticking to stealing from collaborators, and robbery alone never satisfied him. He habitually got a sordid sex kick by mauling victims and having a feel whilst he robbed them of cash or valuables. He had started this game at the age of fourteen when he had, in fact, been a Boy Scout. He also went in for store hold-ups and was a one-man crime wave until thrown into Amiens gaol.

Sammy realised handling Bernard called for diplomacy, which meant he needed to think twice before saying nothing, and tactfully making a point without making an enemy.

'Thanks, Bernard,' Sammy began gently, 'but what we need now isn't really your speciality because we mostly want to thieve without anyone knowing they've been turned over – we can't afford creating attention that could lead the dogs to the rest of us.'

Bernard stared at him with sullen mistrust, until Sammy, contemptuous of strongarm methods, placatingly added:

'You're good at rough stuff, so you'd be more valuable here if police or Gestapo turn up.'

Recognition of his brutality appeared to satisfy Bernard, who ambled back into the shadows of the cave.

'Find me a white walking stick, and we're in business!' Denis Lazard exclaimed, without offering any explanation.

Denis was the kind of criminal who, as Rabelais says, has sixty-three ways of getting money, the most common and the most honourable ones being stealing, thieving and robbing. As the only male pickpocket in the caves, he was eager to contribute his talents, but advised that he couldn't do so until the essential piece of equipment was rustled up from somewhere – a white stick.

'Has anyone got a newspaper?' Denis inquired.

'A newspaper and a stick. – That's a strange working combination,' Violette ventured.

'The newspaper's nothing to do with the stick,' Denis said testily. 'I want to see if there's a horoscope section in the paper because I like looking at my horoscope before I go thieving. Anytime it says the day isn't good for business, I don't do any.'

There was no paper; the walking stick arrived, and Denis departed.

Violette Lambert and her shoplifting team also had special requirements. Minus equipment such as false-bottomed boxes they could place over goods to pick them up, and clothes made specifically for shoplifting purposes, they requested safety pins, needles and thread, material remnants, and handbag mirrors.

'Pieces of old bed sheets, curtains, or pillowcases will do,'

Violette instructed the scrounger being despatched to fill the order.

When the items arrived, the women set about creating massive inside pockets in their coats and dresses, stitching them very strongly into position.

'If a couple of cars could be with us we'd bring back bigger single loads,' Violette added.

Cars were arranged.

The targets were to be mainly sweaters, blouses, skirts and dresses, as 'Wardrobe Mistresses' Madame Vignon and Madame Barré, seldom called on extensively for such items, were consequently well understocked in these lines.

A jaunty, teasingly flirtatious heavy-breasted blonde, with jiggling buttocks, approached Sammy Izard from the rear of the cave.

'Maybe I could help too?' she suggested. 'My name's Florence . . .'

'What can you do, Florence?' Sammy hastily asked, noting that her obviously well-matured years hadn't diminished her pinchable qualities.

'As I was saying before you interrupted me,' she responded irritably, 'my name's Florence Valentine – whores have last names like anyone else – and I'm willing to contribute what I do best to raise money for the cause.'

'It'll take too long to make it worthwhile,' Sammy replied half smiling, anxious to avoid hurting Florence's feelings.

'That's what you think,' said Florence – 'You don't know me. Anyway, I like working, and stuffing wads of notes in a bra is the best way of improving the figure.'

Sammy couldn't tell her or anyone what to do or not to do – no one could. All were free to help as they pleased. Even Gendarme Robine couldn't stop them. Of their own choice, they were putting their freedom at stake on behalf of everyone in the caves.

They left – Florence included – singly and in pairs, and then, like a locust plague, descended on the town. Violette and her team were last to leave due to the preparations they needed to complete.

It was some of the black sheep's way of saying:

'Thank you for our lives.'

\*

As Violette and her gang headed in style for the town in chauffeured cars put at their disposal, she noticed a man, tapping along the boulevard with a white stick, bump into a black-uniformed SS officer who raised his arms to stop him falling.

'It's Denis!' Violette cried – 'So that's what the white walking cane was for!' she laughed as she tried to spot the 'blind' pickpocket helping himself to the SS man's wallet, and God knows what else.

Entering the busy department store, Violette's foursome fanned out in different directions. With the small fund they'd managed to collect before leaving the caves, each spent a fair time selecting one item, which they paid for. During this time they memorised the complete lay-out of the place. Violette had the thorough and conscientious attention to detail of a well-rehearsed actress. When she cased a job, it was something like chess, as she matched her skill against the protective devices and moves of opponents.

Gradually, they edged towards each other until a couple of them began holding up lengths of material as a screen against inquisitive eyes while the others busily pushed clothing into the enormous pockets they had sewn inside their own clothes. It was amazing where they put it all. Several times they left the store, unloaded into the car waiting nearby, then shot back into the store again like an army of worker ants. You couldn't even see bulges under their coats.

Two of the other women headed for different nearby stores, but the third woman and two men, mainly working the men's wear section of Violette's target, also dived outside a few times to stock up the second car. The men first entered the store with their overcoats casually draped over their shoulders, after which they carried them over their arms. Closed at the ends with safety pins, the coat sleeves had been converted into convenient receptacles into which goods could be stuffed.

At different times, Violette and her team utilised the ladies' toilets. Within the cubicles they removed their coats, put on more dresses on top of their own garments, and finished off by wearing several blouses. Reappearing fatter than they went in, they were making their final haul when Violette spotted Joseph Metz being eyed suspiciously by a saleswoman. He hadn't observed he was being watched. Danger signs were up.

Like police who chase them, criminals act instinctively. When there's little or no time to think, they depend upon trained reflexes.

'My bag's been stolen!' Violette promptly yelled.

All eyes switched to her, and Joseph, instantly identifying the significance of her diversion, aborted his last attempted theft and left.

As the cars sped back to the caves, Violette and a woman in the other car, holding handbag mirrors up like periscopes, kept scanning through the rear windows to spot 'tails'. None appeared, and the nine made the return astride massive bundles of clothes.

*

Camille Druon, the handbag specialist, hung around cafés watching for women or girls with Luftwaffe, Abwehr, or SS officers. She went for officers' girlfriends or mistresses because they were likelier to be well heeled.

The technique was the same every time. She would go into the toilet, supposedly to have a pee, then dally around washing her hands or freshening her make-up or hair until a well-dressed woman or girl she had marked stepped into a cubicle. When the handbag was either hung on a coathook on the inside of the door, or placed on the floor, Camille waited until she heard the toilet flush, which meant the occupier was now busy dressing herself, then reached over or under the door, grabbed the bag, and ran like hell.

*

The caves, filled with undisciplined solidarity, became excited changing rooms when Violette and the lifting teams returned. Wherever you turned, people were stripping, trying on garments, and dressing, leaving piles of discarded brown prison uniforms scattered on the floor. Their minds were their strongest weapons, and with the arrival of more clothes, food, drink, and false identity papers, hope was added to their armoury.

Many intended to take refuge with friends in the Somme, but even greater numbers were anxious to put maximum mileage between themselves and the region. Few of them could equal the extensive previous experience of being on the run of a French-speaking shot-down American pilot in civilian clothes who introduced himself simply as 'Martin'. He looked an ordinary sort of individual, but his eyes showed he wasn't. Lean, medium height, with hair cut so close to his scalp that from a distance he appeared bald, he was a mixture of aggressiveness and reserve.

Martin had learned not only to profit from rough times, having been an escaper before, but even more important, to recover from them. He started a survival school in the caves for those planning long-distance escapes. He lectured:

'Plenty of drinking water is essential if you're forced to live off the land. We can do without food for days, but not without water, nor can the body work properly by restricting water. Always drink more water than your thirst demands. With enough water you can eat almost anything, but if you've only less than a pint of water a day, stick to eating biscuits.

'If you're dubious as to the safety of any wild animal or plant, eat a little and wait six to eight hours. If you don't vomit or have pains and the runs, then eat another spoonful or so and wait another six to eight hours. If there's still no ill effect; then reasonable amounts can be safely eaten, and if your bowels won't move regularly, don't let it scare you.

'Half of what we eat and drink keeps us alive, and the other half kills us, but hunger and thirst should be taken with *something*.

'Hunt for anything that crawls, creeps or flies because with few exceptions, all the animals in Europe are edible, and animal food gives the most food value per kilo. Old prejudices don't matter when you are hungry enough to eat anything you can lay your hands on, and you'll discover that many despised and neglected animals are good tasty food once prejudice is forgotten, but Sophie is our meat expert, so I'll hand this part of the lesson over to her.'

Cordon Bleu cook Sophie Glasser, the baby-faced Black Marketeer, took over:

'All animals may be eaten raw or cooked, but be careful the meat hasn't putrified, and eat animals soon after killing them to ensure this. Dead animals, such as run-over dogs, or horses killed in action, should only be eaten if still warm when found.

'Animal food is actually more digestible when eaten raw than when cooked, but you have to have the right frame of mind from the outset, otherwise you're likely to spew the lot up.

'Because they have a higher food value than most vegetable foods, small animals, even two or three snails or some frogs' legs, are worth collecting for adding to a meal of boiled leaves or roots.'

After pausing an instant, Cordon Bleu Sophie advised with authority:

'Rats and mice are very palatable. Rats cooked in a stew could be taken for chicken. Skin, gut and boil them in a tin – rats for about ten minutes, mice for five. Either can be cooked with dandelion leaves for a stew, and be sure to include the livers.

'All birds are edible, and their eggs too, if not rotten. Eat unspoiled eggs even if there's an embryo inside.

'To skin rats, mice and birds, cut off the heads, make a skin deep incision down the centre of the breast and abdomen, then peel off the skin from centre to sides. Pull the skin off the back from above downwards, cut open the belly and draw out the guts, leaving the liver behind.'

There was little Sophie could do to dress up the bare facts and drape the naked truth.

'Take care to skin frogs as some have poisonous skin glands. As most of you know, the flesh of all frogs is delicate and wholesome,

272

with most of the meat on the hind legs. Snails are of course a delicacy either raw, or by dropping them in boiling water for five minutes.

'To eat grass snakes and lizards, cut off the heads. Skin and boil for ten minutes. Liver is the best part of dogs and cats, and both animals, stewed with edible leaves, can provide delicious meals.'

From expressions of distaste on so many faces, she realised she had just kicked them in their stomachs, but if they didn't look after their stomachs, they soon wouldn't look after anything.

'Sophie!' – someone interjected – 'Did your Black Market paté come from dogs' and cats' livers?'

Smiling coyly, Sophie countered: 'You can't expect me to give away trade secrets.'

She advised that squirrel flesh was tastier and tenderer than chicken, and that a hedgehog could be a particularly lucky find.

'Turn it on its back, and tickle the body lightly with a stick or the fingers. It'll poke out its head and neck, then kill it with a knife. Skin and cook it the same as dogs and cats.'

Pilot Martin interrupted: 'I'd better warn you that if you hunt birds, an improvised catapult can be a dangerous giveaway weapon, especially if it's used at dusk or at night when silhouetted birds can be observed in bushes and trees. And, if you want to make a smokeless cooking fire, bore two rows of holes through the sides of a tin, close to the bottom. You can do this with the spike of a clasp knife, or something similar. Holes should be nearly big enough to admit the end of the little finger, and its important to bore them close together right at the bottom of the tin. This forms a miniature blast furnace, with the upper part of the tin acting as a chimney to create a draught which enters through the holes when the fire is lit. Twigs from dead branches of spruces or other conifers are ideal fuel, but dry twigs collected from beneath hedges, even in wet or snowy weather, like today, will also do nicely.

'Start a fire with a small piece of paper over which sprinkle a few thin dry twigs. As soon as these are alight, add more twigs, and if the twigs are dry, there'll be no smoke. Big advantage of this kind of fire is that the tin can be placed on the ground in wet weather and the fire will burn as well as in dry weather. The tin could also be used for storing stuff, or kept ready-filled with dry twigs.'

Sophie went on to cover recognition of wild vegetables such as stinging nettles which, after six minutes' boiling, made a tasty wholesome vegetable like spinach. One minute's boiling entirely removes the sting. The fleshy leaf of clover could be chewed and rapidly swallowed, and most pastures contain lumps of it.

Tender-boiled bracken roots are rich food, as are dandelions which, Sophie stressed, are one of the most important wild vegetable foods.

'Don't worry about pissenlit (the appropriate French name for dandelion) making you pee buckets,' Sophie laughed, 'they're really good for you. And anyway, peeing is one of life's greatest pleasures, as anyone bursting to go will tell you afterwards.

'Like most of you, I think the most enjoyable way to follow a vegetable diet is to let the cow eat it. I take mine in steaks, but although many of us live to eat, in present circumstances we have to eat whatever we can to live.'

As Sophie completed her living-rough lessons, light-fingered Marguerite and Madeleine returned from their pickpocketing. Both were very satisfied with results and their financial contributions to survival funds. They were particularly delighted and amused by a bonus in a wallet lifted from a Luftwaffe officer. Marguerite translated the find – a German poem, hand-written on a sheet of writing paper, which read:

TEN LITTLE GRUMBLERS

Ten little grumblers sat down to dine
One imitated Goebbels, then there were nine.

Nine little grumblers got hold of a bright idea,
One of them was spotted, only eight got clear.

Eight little grumblers wrote something on the wall,
One was discovered, leaving seven now in all.

Seven little grumblers were asked how they liked their fare,
One answered 'fit for pigs', then only six were there.

Six little grumblers complained of the Nazi leader,
One called him a lousy hound, louder than he need'a.

Five little grumblers sat down round an upright grand,
One started playing Mendelssohn, then they were a four-man band.

Four little grumblers made cracks about Ley.
One was too insistent, so they carted him away.

Three little grumblers said the Aryan myth was muck,
But Rosenberg was listening and snaffled two for luck.

The last one was careless, dropped this poem on the floor,
They took him off to Dachau's halls, where they were ten once more.

'If Luftwaffe officers are writing like this, there's reason for us all to be more hopeful about the future,' Marguerite happily forecast. For Marguerite, the spotlight the verse threw on Luftwaffe morale as

Allied invasion day drew nearer, was revealing. A tea kettle when up to its neck in hot water, sings, and the Luftwaffe was obviously starting to change its tune.

For centuries, abandoned quarries, forgotten underground passages and natural caverns beneath areas of Amiens – even under a cemetery – were havens for fugitives guided to them for temporary shelter. Accesses, including well-disguised deep stone stairways of thirty or more steps, in gardens, courtyards or within buildings, led to incredible sprawling subterranean labrynths. One set of quarried galleries, some four kilometres long, comprising two levels with smooth walls and ceilings, have giant pillar-supported circular chambers equipped with stone furniture. Crevices, cut into walls at regular distances, still bear traces of oil lamps that burned in them hundreds of years ago. Pottery relics and coins dating back to the reign of King Henry IV were also found. Some caverns were utilised for commercial mushroom growing, but many entrances, blocked since the 16th century, were only reopened during World War II.

At one time, St. Pierre caves could be reached from beneath ramparts of the medieval Citadelle fortress now holding Dr. Mans, Captain Tempez and other recaptured 'politicals' from the bombed prison.

The thought of literally hiding under the feet of the enemy was somehow satisfying to gaol escapers in the caves.


# 15 Pick-a-back nightmare


'I am the wife of the Sous-Préfet of Abbeville, and I wish to see the Kommandant!' Jane Vivant demanded.

All the phones in the Amiens Kommandatur headquarters were ringing at the same time when she stormed in soon after hearing of the attack on the gaol.

Years of untangling red tape had taught her how to cut through official jargon so she wouldn't be fobbed off, or allow authorities to claim conveniently they had no authority, as they often do when it suits them. Refusal to discuss the reason for her visit with anyone but the Kommandant, finally opened doors.

'It's a disgrace that arms should have been stored in the prison, because this is obviously why they bombed it,' she angrily criticised.

'It wasn't because of arms that they bombed,' the Kommandant furiously protested, 'but because we had seventeen English and French agents in there they wanted to release!'

The statement shook her, though she felt that the most surprising thing about it was that there were still some things that could surprise her.

'I want you to send an officer to search for my husband,' she insisted.

The Kommandant nearly burst a blood vessel.

'An officer! – An officer! – I haven't even got a single *soldier* left anymore!'

Realising there was panic everywhere, she suggested that as he had no one available to make enquiries, he should issue a pass permitting access to the prison, the fortress, and the hospital, allowing her to look for her husband.

'Without a permit I wouldn't get in anywhere as these places are forbidden to civilians,' she reminded him.

Without another word, he wrote out a pass, stamped it, and handed it to her.

Waiting outside in the chauffeur-driven Sous-Préfecture car were her ten-year-old daughter Claudine, and her male secretary. They drove first to the prison where she asked person after person –

'Have you seen my husband – Raymond Vivant?'

Nobody had.

She went next to the Citadelle – the ancient fortress which often temporarily housed special military prisoners and was sometimes used for firing squad executions. She inspected every part of the fortress. She saw dead and wounded from the gaol in the hospital, but found no trace, no word of her husband.

That evening, she was arrested at the Sous-Préfecture by a military police squad commanded by two officers.

Somehow, she had expected it. An imprisoned wife could be a vital lever in compelling a husband on the run to surrender.

'I have a ten-year-old daughter and I cannot leave her alone. I must take her to prison with me,' she said adamantly.

The request caught the two officers off balance because it wasn't according to the book.

'We are not barbarians – we don't put children in prison,' they insisted.

'Give me time enough to arrange for my mother-in-law to come, and I will give her my daughter,' she suggested.

One of the arresting officers telephoned headquarters at Amiens to discuss the problem with their chief.

'It is agreed for you to stay in the Sous-Préfecture until your mother-in-law arrives, after which you will go to prison,' she was informed, 'but you must promise to advise us if your husband attempts to get in touch with you, and must consider yourself a prisoner.'

Although guards were left outside, no instructions were issued concerning the Sous-Préfecture's official car, and therefore no restrictions were placed on it.

As soon as the officers departed, she phoned the family's doctor, Dr. Jacques Dezoteux, asking him to come. Dezoteux and Henri Maire, a journalist on the region's newspaper, the *Courrier Picard*, were all that remained of OCM Intelligence in Abbeville. She needed their advice, needed time to discover what had happened to her husband, and knew Dezoteux, who aided Allied parachutists to escape, also employed cute dodges to keep people out of enemy hands, such as placing sponges dipped in chalk behind a patient's body to produce X-ray photographs giving the impression of faulty lungs.

'Say I have a contagious illness, doctor,' she pressed, but he felt it would be miraculous if they swallowed this without sending for a second opinion.

'They'll suspect we're trying to fool them, and since the prison bombing, even doctors are forbidden to venture outside their medical practice areas.'

There had to be another route.

'Tenaillon!' they both exclaimed together.

Tenaillon, the local wholesale grocer who supplied the Sous-Préfecture, had since her husband's arrest called daily with his car to offer whatever help he could.

'If you need to get away – tell me, Madame, and I'll find an answer,' Tenaillon promised.

'He's a man of great courage,' said Jane Vivant.

'And smart!' Dr. Dezoteaux added. 'I'll contact him.'

\*

The roast chicken airing itself on the window sill of Pierre Bracquart's cell looked beautiful until bomb blast splattered it against the door at the other end of the cell.

Pierre's mother had just brought him the ready-to-eat chicken which now lay in pieces on the floor, covered with dirt, but appetites disappeared as bombs continued to fall. All five of his cell's inmates huddled in a corner for safety, remembering that wall angles could effectively protect from debris.

When the attack stopped, using their hefty chair like a battering ram, Pierre and his friend Gratien Bocquet smashed the door base panel.

Scrambling in turn through the hole, they saw prisoners pouring from cells with doors blown open or completely off their frames.

'Maybe the blast has broken the exercise courtyard gate too,' Gratien shouted – 'LET'S TRY IT!'

Scurrying to the end of the corridor, two of them hurled themselves at the big gate leading to the courtyard, but it wouldn't budge. Without a word, a guard, unlocking it with his key, deliberately left it open. Rushing into the courtyard, the four clambered through main prison wall bomb gaps to emerge onto the Route d'Albert.

Pierre Bracquart wasn't with them – he had gone to the women's quarters to search for his fiancée, Dr. Mans's nurse, Elaine Guillemont.

When he found her – face streaked with dust, clothes blood-stained – she looked so ashen that he thought she was dead. She didn't appear to be breathing. Trying to stifle the panic he felt but scared to waste moments attempting closer examination, survival and the desire to put the gaol as far behind them as possible, suddenly cleared his thinking. He was committed to flight, and the knowledge increased his speed. His execution was already overdue. If they shot him, and if, miraculously Elaine was alive, she would almost certainly be shot too, despite her value as a nurse in Dr. Mans's prison surgery.

Lifting her deadweight, he positioned her on his back and carried her into the front courtyard. Cradled in his arms, he put her through a perimeter wall bomb hole onto the street pavement outside, then crawling through himself, began to pick-a-back her along the Route d'Albert. Both were in civilian clothes, but without coats. The cold cut into him like a razor.

He knew Gratien Bocquet and his three other cell companions were making for the nearby town of Albert, but that was far too distant and dangerous for him. As an Amienois, knowing all the little back streets, he decided to take the easily reachable not so busy Route de Corbie.

Breathlessly he reached the Corbie road and felt his heart pumping heavily from the strain, but his mind goaded his body forward, forcing it on beyond apparent limits. Resting a moment to catch breath, he realised they were escaping from gaol but not from bleak reality. They had just been nearer death than ever before, and he was still unsure whether she was dead or alive.

Elaine suddenly shuddered violently.

He wanted to cry out for help, but cautiously his mind stilled his voice, accepting this wasn't a time for trusting strangers. There was no way of knowing who would help and who would betray. Exhaustion made him vulnerable to anonymous fears he could have resisted if stronger and refreshed, but at least he knew now that she wasn't dead.

Blood seeping from her head wounds was soaking his suit, leaving a crimson trail on the snow behind them. He needed assistance, yet incredibly, the street was utterly deserted. With sinking heart he realised there could be many kilometres to go, so there was no alternative. He had to take chances.

He knocked on the nearest door. Nobody answered, so he tried the next house. At first there was no answer so he knocked again, and the door inched open a little, just about enabling him to glimpse the nervous face of a middle-aged woman. She studied them, then opened the door wide and said:

'Come in.'

Asking no questions – not even names – she led him into a small room with a settee.

'Lay her on that – it doesn't matter about the blood. Stay with her while I go for a doctor. I don't have a phone, but I can call from a café close by.'

The doctor was out. Explaining to his wife that it was an emergency, she asked him to come urgently. As the woman was returning, she saw the doctor's familiar car coming towards her. Standing in the road, she waved it to a halt.

'I'm sorry, I can't go with you now,' the doctor apologised. 'My brother's been hurt in the prison bombing and I must help him first.'

Bathing Elaine's face with a warm-water-soaked serviette, the woman advised Pierre:

'We'll have to do the best we can ourselves, for the moment.'

Just water could work miracles. Elaine stirred, groaned, and opened her eyes. They were glazed and unfocused.

Pierre bent to her eagerly, putting a glass of cordial-flavoured drink to her lips. As she sipped it, slowly and gratefully, her eyes became more alert.

She was drained, but the sense of relief at escaping from the enemy revived her.

Raising her head from settee cushions to face Pierre squarely, she whispered:

'We'll make it.'

Shakily, she pushed herself upright, leaning against a table to steady herself.

'It's too dangerous to stay here, Elaine,' he said uneasily. 'Patrols are certain to be swarming everywhere soon. I want to carry you to my parents' place.'

'I'll walk.'

'No!'

'Yes,' she said, in a voice which had made up its mind, revealing determination had put her past the point of worrying about pain and punishment.

'All right,' he said resignedly.

They were bound to each other by the same spirit – love, and comradeship in adversity – a unity which brought from deep recesses unexpected fortitude.

Suddenly she was trembling. Gripping her arm, he steered her towards the door knowing it was futile attempting to dissuade her. She couldn't walk very well, but at least she was on her feet.

Thanking the woman who had so unstintingly offered sanctuary, they left. With his right arm firmly supporting her, they slowly made their way through the back street until the remnants of her strength gave out, and without protest, she allowed herself to be carried again.

As they approached the footbridge behind the main Amiens station, they were confronted by a trio of German soldiers ahead.

Pierre swallowed hard, his scalp tightened, and he felt a solid dread creep into his bones along with the bitter cold of the afternoon. Neither of them feared death – they had lived with it daily for years – but it would be tragic if they lost out now when the help they needed was so agonizingly close.

Moving towards the patrol, he weighed words.

'Where've you come from?' the patrol leader demanded with the merciless accent of a born bully.

Standing defensively before them, Pierre's compressing torment mingled with seething outrage, felt anger rise in his throat, but answered in a voice that struggled to stay reasonable.

'My fiancée has just been injured by a bomb at the station, and I want to get her to a doctor.'

Diversionary *Mosquito* action in the station area made this feasible and she was obviously badly hurt.

After what seemed an interminable interval, the patrol leader said:

'Pass!'

They continued toward his parents' house just beyond the station. He knew the Gestapo had the address, but was gambling they wouldn't think him mad enough to head straight for his own home in Amiens.

'Let's hope the bad dream's almost over,' Elaine murmured.

Pushing on, he felt a wave of giddy incomprehensible certainty that they would win through. By the time they finally reached the house, he was emotionally exhausted.

Pierre's mother washed Elaine and rendered first aid, while his father phoned for Dr. Beauvillain, their family doctor, who came at once and diagnosed shock and severe head wounds, including a fractured temple. Hearing how she had been injured, he attended her like a goddess.

'We daren't stay long as the Gestapo have this address,' Pierre reminded them. 'It's best we split up and hide at different friends' places on the other side of town.'

'Well, she can't walk, and you can't carry her that far on your back or you'll drop dead,' Dr. Beauvillain advised. 'I'll organise a stretcher and you'll have to manhandle her through the streets – using transport would be too dangerous. They're stopping everything on four wheels.'

'We must do it tonight – after curfew,' said Pierre's father. 'We know it's risky, but there's no other way.'

The clock speedily threw minutes into the room as Pierre carefully mapped the route they would take. He was familiar with the regular barriers and checkpoints but needed to plot where additional roadblocks were likely to have been erected since the gaol attack. Having detailed the proposed routes, a friend reconnoitred the streets involved to ascertain new diversions and patrol points.

They left at 11 p.m. – two hours after curfew. It was forbidden even to be out. Pierre, his father, and the friend took turns carrying Elaine on the stretcher, with one of them always walking slightly ahead on the lookout for patrols.

Elaine felt as if she could sleep forever, but was afraid that if she let herself sleep, she was sure to wake up in prison. She was determined to remain awake throughout the journey, to be ready for any emergency, knowing the enemy were in the habit of suddenly cordoning off a street, after which they would check everyone caught in the trap. She felt terrible, ached all over, but was alive, still free, and with Pierre.

Viciously cold, the night seemed never ending, and the silence magnified every sound.

At one stage they could make out ahead silhouettes of guards lounging about, smoking and gossiping in tired, subdued voices. Patrols were everywhere, but their noisily stamping feet in the bitter evening, and the rattling of their equipment, made it easier to locate them.

A loud scream tore the silence, followed by sudden pandemonium. Pierre, his father, their friends, and even Elaine, exchanged smiles, sure that the shriek was from a victim claimed by 'silent minefields' sewn by Resistance friends by removing sewer gratings in the dark. As the Germans and their collaborators were the only ones allowed out after curfew, it was of no consequence which of them broke bones falling into sewers. Pierre and company had been forewarned where not to tread.

Altering course to an optional route, the stretcher party didn't encounter any more patrols. Providence, sound-cushioning snow, and open drains were their allies.

*

Pierre Bracquart's four cellmates knew it was insane, but couldn't help themselves – all wanted to go home, feeling they would be securer among friends and familiar surroundings, even though their Péronne region was 55 snow-bound enemy-exposed kilometres distant, and Gestapo would be breathing down the necks of everyone in any way associated with them.

As the sole possessor among them of identity papers and some cash, thirty-year-old dairy director Gratien Bocquet had a distinct advantage over the others, as his identity card would permit freer movement. His wife had managed to smuggle the papers and money in to him only the previous day.

The ability of the eldest of the four, insurance agent Emile Malezieux, to endure the strain of the journey was worrying Gratien. Although, like café proprietor Alexander Grisentello, Malezieux was still in his fifties, his health had badly deteriorated in gaol.

'I'll make it – I'll make it,' he kept repeating, 'and rest when I get to my son in Péronne.'

Twenty-year-old Leon Rat was the youngest.

Like Pierre Bracquart, they also headed for the Corbie area, close to the prison, but kept well away from main roads.

'The Golden Virgin's our signpost, no matter how far off the beaten track we're forced to travel,' said Gratien. 'If for some reason we get split up, make for the Golden Virgin and we'll meet up again in the church.'

Glittering high above the horizon on top of the church at Albert, the statue of the Golden Virgin offering her infant Son to His Father in heaven could be seen for miles from surrounding countryside. Albert was a front-line town in the 1914–18 war, and every one of the millions who fought on the Somme knew the legend of the Golden Virgin. Soldiers superstitiously believed that when she fell, the war would end. The church was said to have been struck by some two thousand shells, yet the statue miraculously stayed aloft, and a French engineer even climbed the tower to support the semi-toppling statue with thick steel wires.

When Albert was taken by the Germans in March 1918, the British, determined to prevent the tower's use for artillery observation as they themselves had done for so long, destroyed it with heavy guns and the Golden Virgin finally crashed into the square below. Within months, the Virgin legend became true with the war's end. Years later, an exact replica was constructed of the old church; and the Golden Virgin, once more dominating the Somme, offered a welcome landmark to travellers – and escapers such as Gratien Bocquet and his friends.

The stinging snow almost blinding them was falling thicker and thicker as they stumbled on, with the cold icily cutting through their light clothes, chilling their bones. None had coats.

They longed to stay with roads and signs of life, but knew it would be safer to stick to open country and isolated tracks. They were hunted, so needed foxes' instinctive cunning.

They hadn't travelled all that far and yet already, Malezieux was almost choking as his lungs snatched for breath. Thankfully, they reached the cover of a small woodland, and Malezieux fell into a deep snow drift and lay there awhile struggling for strength.

Extensive dense woodlands and small copses were the countryside feature, but between the woods and numerous villages, the chalk downland, mainly covered with rich wheat and sugar-beet-growing soil, was very open, with almost no hedges and few trees. In these areas, natural cover was non-existent. Along the roads from Amiens, countless metal canisters of unexploded mustard gas lying under the soil since World War I made it difficult to plant straight rows of trees. Somme fields and meadows have an underlay of army boots, canisters, and British, German and American shells which were used to fill up the holes made by other shells. Most people tend to think of the Somme as a river, but the entire region forms part of the old province of Picardy and includes the ancient battlefields of Crécy and Agincourt.

Gratien knew that little Albert was a good place to make for if they were in desperate trouble, because this town of a mere few thousand inhabitants had an abnormally high proportion of potential sympathisers. Many of its families had British origins through the British ex-World War I soldiers who had married local girls and settled permanently in Albert and surrounding villages.

'The village of Daours is about four or five kilometres from here,' Gratien estimated. 'I've a friend there, and with a bit of luck could try and contact him to help.'

'You're the only one who knows his way around these parts – we're lost if you go,' Grisentello said uncomfortably.

'I'll be back,' he promised. 'I've got papers, so I have a better chance of passing any checkpoints. One of us has to risk looking for assistance.'

They were unhappy about him leaving, but accepted the sense of his decision.

His dusty dishevelled appearance was an absolute give-away, because a man and woman in a horse-drawn cart halted beside him. He stopped abruptly, breathing heavily, staring at the couple with puzzled eyes.

'Do you know what happened to the people in Cell 24 at the gaol?' the woman asked.

He suddenly felt tired, as if all strength had ebbed from his body.

Seeing his reaction, the woman anxiously assured him:

'I only want to know if you have news of my brother in Cell 24. I'm sorry if I scared you stupidly.'

'I understand,' he said sympathetically, 'but we didn't stay long enough to discover about anyone else.'

'Quick! – get into the cart with us!' the man briskly ordered.

'What?' Gratien cried in astonishment.

'I think there's a Gestapo car coming towards us – for God's sake get in!'

The danger registered and he dived into the cart next to the woman. The approaching car slowed as it neared them, but didn't stop.

'Thank you!' Gratien said, 'It was lucky you saw the car in time – they did look like Gestapo.'

He was about to ask whether they could get him to Daours when he had second thoughts. It wouldn't be fair – the woman was desperate for news of her brother and would be anxious to reach the gaol as fast as possible.

'I'm going to Daours – thank you again – and I hope you have good news of your brother,' he said as he dismounted, and then trudged on, knowing every time he faced fear, he gained strength and confidence. Inexplicably he recalled a comment of Don Quixote's:

'Until death it is all life.'

He waited interminably at the little Daours post office trying to telephone his friend, but lines were either constantly engaged or out of order. Everyone in the post office was discussing the bombing, and eyes kept glancing curiously at him. A man came across and said quietly:

'There are German patrols in the village – you ought to get out of here.'

'Thank you – if I'm that obvious I'd better leave,' he replied.

Returning in the direction he had just come, he crossed fields instead of roads. Footprints in the snow were a dead give-away, and dead could well be the word because anyone could follow tracks, so he jumped around to create untrodden snow gaps, laid false trails, and even doubled back on himself to create more footprint confusion.

The wind whipped across the fields, snow blurred his vision, and freezing mist stung him, but there was no fear in his face – only determination.

A startled rabbit scurrying out to safety made him feel safer too because if he had shaken the rabbit then it was unlikely there was anyone else about.

His numbed fumbling fingers carefully withdrew some broken biscuit pieces from a pocket. Gratefully sucking them for the sweetness, he washed them down by scooping a handful of snow and licking the moisture.

The long shadows of sunset were reaching across the country-side when he reached his companions, and was disappointed to observe from their attitude that they had given up on him, believing he had deserted them.

'You know, there still should be a little bit of trust left in the world,' he said reprovingly. 'I never intended to go it alone, especially knowing your total unfamiliarity with this district.'

'What news?' Grisentello asked fretfully, his voice heavy with impatience and weariness.

They were hungry, frozen, their clothes already stiff as boards, so he knew his reply wouldn't be much comfort.

'It looks like we'll have to spend the night here.'

They were starting to huddle together to give each other some warmth when he saw the little cart that had helped him out of trouble earlier, travelling along a path beside the wood, obviously returning from the gaol. He startled the others as he shot to his feet.

'They're people who were helpful on the way to Daours,' he

explained. 'They're locals, so maybe they can give us all a hand, or at least some useful advice.'

'It's dangerous,' cautioned Leon Rat.

'I know, but I'd rather take a chance on them than risk dying of cold.'

Running to the cart, he stopped them.

'It's you again!' the woman exclaimed.

'Did you find your brother?'

'No. There's so much confusion there that nobody knows answers to anything yet.'

'I'm hiding in the woods with some of my cell companions, and we'll freeze to death if we don't get somewhere warm fast,' he told them. 'Have you any ideas?'

'Yes,' the man in the cart instantly answered. 'I work on the railways. Wait until it's a little darker, then go to Daours station and I'll make it my business to put you all into a compartment of a northbound train. A railway guard friend of mine, who I'm sure will agree to help, will get you into a train for Péronne once you reach Albert.'

With a flush of goodwill, the man reached across and shook Gratien's hand to wish him safe journey.

He kept his word. There were moments of panic transferring to another train on the completely dark platform at Albert, but once en route again, being cold and soaked somehow didn't matter as much. Now they were finally on the line for Péronne and home.

A railway employee at one of the numerous tiny stations, slowly inspecting the little suburban train, holding aloft an oil lamp, stopped beside their carriage and cried out:

'Alexander! – What are you doing here?'

He was a regular customer at Grisentello's café, so Grisentello explained.

'Don't go as far as Péronne station,' the railwayman warned. 'Jump off when the train slows at a countryside halt a few kilometres from the town. There are too many Boche hanging around Péronne station, especially at this time of night.'

It was almost ten o'clock when they leapt from the train.

'As we're back on familiar ground, I think it best for us to split up now,' Gratien suggested. 'I'm only stopping long enough to reassure my wife and family.'

They said au revoir and Gratien made for his parents-in-law's home, about three kilometres from where they jumped the train. It took him almost two hours to cover the short distance, because of necessary caution after curfew. The moon wading through clouds gave unwelcome illumination at intervals, like an enemy searchlight putting him starkly on the spot. He was also compelled to dive into snowdrifts whenever car headlamps questioned the night, for night cars could only be the enemy.

Spotting some soldiers, he flattened to the ground, camouflaging himself with snow and leaves until they passed.

Even relieving the bowels could be dangerous when travelling. He had no intention of being trapped with his pants down, like one Resistance colleague who, caught bending, hadn't time to pull up his pants and repeatedly stumbled over his trousers until he felt a soldier's rifle prodding his bare backside.

Gratien, whose long experience of dodging the enemy made him cautious about everything, including answering bodily calls, was unlikely to forget that his friend Pierre Bracquart had been arrested in a toilet.

A cat pouring itself through a fence startled him, although fear, that earlier inevitably crept into his body and brain, had gone. Time was the strengthener. Sometimes tasks ahead seemed impossible and courage died, until time strengthened our backs and breathed fresh hope and spirit into us.

'Blessed is Time that heals,' he said to himself.

All the long hours of tension and suffering were worth it when the door of his parents-in-law's home opened, and he found his wife there. Hearing of the prison bombing, she had no means of learning whether he was dead or alive.

'With you again, I'm very much alive, thank God!' he said, realising the reunion would need to be brief as it would be wisest to keep well away from his family.

'Go to my uncle,' his wife advised, 'he's got a perfect place for a hide-out.'

Uncle, who lived on the other side of Péronne, was a fish farmer who owned a pool only accessible by boat, with a canal on one side, and the Somme river on the other. Between the two were a vast network of rivulets, marshes, and artificial pools. To get there, the demarcation zone between occupied and unoccupied France had to be crossed. The night was going to be sleepless.

The snow shone ghostly in the starlight when at 3.30 a.m., Gratien set off with his mother-in-law as his guide. She knew all the short cuts and solid paths through the marshes along the Somme to an unguarded canal lock which led to the other zone. The sound pattern of croaking frogs and occasional duck calls was suddenly broken by angry cackling of disturbed ducks. Gratien and his mother-in-law stopped. Was it a patrol, or were they the sole intruders? Listening for other movement sounds around them, but hearing none, they continued.

Once across the unguarded lock, they followed the canal path until after two hours pushing through deep snow, they reached the rendezvous where uncle was waiting with a rowboat with muffled oars.

Well before dawn, Gratien was comfortably installed with ample food and fuel, in a hunting hut on a little island discreetly hidden by large trees and tall rushes.

*

Washing his hands to the accompaniment of the roar of low-flying planes and then a tremendous explosion, Raymond Vivant thought a Luftwaffe plane had crashed, until more explosions followed and he crouched for protection in the corner of his cell as the window shattered.

The left cell wall suddenly gaped open. As dust clouds cleared a little, he saw the cell door torn from its hinges, and the rubble-strewn outside corridor. Buildings on the right appeared intact, but to the left the way was wide open to the countryside.

He couldn't find his hat or overcoat, but it was pointless hanging about looking for them. Scrambling over debris and bomb craters, he reached a breach in the rear wall together with four other prisoners. They ran into the fields to avoid being spotted on the road where German soldiers were already searching for escapers.

He sucked the crisply fresh freezing air into his lungs, exchanging it for the choking corrupt dust breathed in gaol. Thanking God for the pure air, he knew that only his tired body was holding down his spirit which wanted to fly like a bird.

Heading away from town, he alternatively ran fifty yards, then walked fifty, to conserve strength, and as he walked sucked one of the sugar lumps he'd saved in his pocket. One of the prisoners kept pace with him.

'What were you in for?' Vivant asked.

'Black Market – I was fiddling petrol.'

'Have you got somewhere to hide?'

'I've friends in Albert – stick with me and they'll look after you too.'

'Thanks.'

Being conspicuous without coat and hat in that weather was bad enough, but the fields were impossible – they were knee-deep in snow and freezing.

The white ermine cloak of snow on the ground looked exquisitely luxurious, but was a nightmare to cross.

288

'If we don't get out of these fields, we'll either freeze to death or get pneumonia,' Vivant said. 'We'd be better off going where we are unlikely to be expected – into Amiens itself. Sticking to the road may be chancier, but worth trying.'

'I don't fancy the idea,' said his companion.

They had covered little more than a couple of kilometres when Vivant saw six field-grey uniforms flitting like ghosts through the snow.

'There are German soldiers in the field ahead,' he warned, 'and if we go on, we'll run smack into them. There's nowhere around here to hide and wait for nightfall, apart from which, I guarantee there'll soon be police dogs after us. I'm turning back to Amiens.'

'Not me – I still think you'll be safer in Albert.'

Vivant disagreed, so wishing each other 'Bon voyage!' the Sous-Préfet and the Black Marketeer parted company.

Optimistically, Raymond Vivant felt the Gestapo non-appearance that morning for the daily interrogation session, had to be a good omen. Miraculously, they hadn't come, otherwise he would have been at their headquarters when the gaol was bombed.

Walking along the main road, three laughing chattering teenage girls stopped dead on seeing him, then Vivant realised why – he was covered from head to foot in grey dust.

Approaching them, he asked:

'Would you be kind enough to brush me down?'

They obliged. Passing opposite the prison, he saw rescue teams and soldiers scurrying about before a gaping crowd. He was congratulating himself on making excellent progress when a car abruptly halted beside him and a young woman jumped out – it was Braumann's Lucienne!

Jubilantly, in German, she screamed: 'Vivant! – the Sous-Préfet!'

He remained motionless, stalemated, remembering the traditional Resistance advice:

'If you run, they shoot.'

The automatic rifles of three soldiers pointed at him and he was marched back the way he had come. As he couldn't be returned to the wrecked gaol, he was taken to a nearby factory where he found himself with several others recaptured after brief freedom. One came across.

'Monsieur, the Sous-Préfet of Abbeville?'

The face seemed vaguely familiar, but Vivant couldn't place it.

'Don't you remember me?' the stranger asked. 'I'm the secretary of the police superintendent at Abbeville.'

Vivant recalled the arrest several months previous, though the man had got much thinner and grown a beard.

'What are you doing here, Monsieur le Sous-Préfet?'

Vivant smiled at the innocence of the question.

'Simple – I've also been arrested, and tried to escape.'

Overhearing the conversation, dark-haired young girl asked:

'You're the Sous-Préfet of Abbeville?'

'Yes, Mademoiselle.'

'Is there anything I can do for you?'

He was touched by her obviously sympathetic concern.

'I would like to rinse my hands.'

He had just noticed his left hand had been slightly injured.

Turning to a German guard, she explained, then asked Vivant to follow her. The guard, in turn, followed them, but as they entered the main factory building, Vivant shut the door in his face, leaving him outside, waiting.

Whilst he bathed his hand, the girl introduced herself:

'My name is Christiane Lecaillet. If there's anything you would like me to do – anything – please ask.'

'There is, Mademoiselle. I should like to get a message to my wife as, if she is still in Abbeville, she will probably be interrogated soon. I should also like to escape.'

'All the doors are guarded, but the courtyard wall at the back is unguarded, and with so few soldiers here as yet, I'm sure they can be distracted long enough for you to get over the wall.'

She gave him the addresses of a friend living nearby, and of her parents.

'Tell them you're a friend of Christiane's, and they'll shelter you.'

Removing his wedding ring, he handed it to her.

'Go to the Préfecture in Amiens and give this to the Préfet's secretary, Mademoiselle Caillé. The ring will confirm you have seen me, then tell her everything.'

The backyard wall was fairly high, but as Christiane had forecast, there wasn't a guard in sight, so Vivant jumped and nearly landed on a surprised passer-by on the other side.

Seeing a man talking to a little five-year-old boy on his doorstep, Vivant stopped.

'Will you help me? – I've just escaped from the prison and they're after me. I could do with a little bit of disguise – would you give me your cap?'

'But it's a new cap,' the man replied. Then, realising how this must have sounded, handed it over, saying: 'Hang on a minute.'

Opening the front door of the house, he shouted:

'Where's my old cap?'

A woman answered:

'I don't know where you put it.'

Turning back to Vivant, who was clutching the new cap, he said:

'Keep it.'

Thanking him, Vivant pulled the cap down on his head and was walking away when he heard running footsteps behind him. He wasn't frightened or startled, but his mouth was suddenly dry with the taste of tension. Unable to restrain himself any longer, he swivelled round abruptly to face his follower. It was the little boy clutching another cap.

'We found the old one, so my father says will you take this cap and give him back his new one?'

They swapped hats.

There were few people about when he knocked on the door of Christiane's home. Her parents had just finished lunch in the kitchen.

'Christiane sent me,' he announced immediately. 'I'm an escaped prisoner, wanted by the Germans.'

'Come in and have something to eat and drink,' was the only reaction from the motherly woman who opened the door, and he felt instantly at home.

'I'm not hungry, but could do with an old overcoat and help in getting to the centre of Amiens without using any of the main roads.'

'My old coat would never fit you,' Christiane's slightly-built father said almost apologising, 'but we'll think of something. It wouldn't be wise for you to remain here – we're too close to the gaol, but we have friends in Amiens who would give you accommodation.'

'And I know the answer to your overcoat problem,' exclaimed Madame Lecaillet, looking very pleased with herself as she vanished through the front door. Within minutes she returned with her brother who was carrying a black coat on his arm which he offered to Vivant:

'I hope this fits.'

'But what about papers?' cried Madame Lecaillet, anxious not to overlook anything.

Producing his wallet, the brother said:

'Take my identity card. The photo isn't exactly like you, but you might be able to get away with it.'

Unhappy with the battered old cap, feeling it wasn't in character with the rest of his clothes, Monsieur Lecaillet gave him a more suitable black hat.

Vivant was glad he had stuffed the battered old cap in his coat pocket when he saw a road block in the distance.

'Take back your good hat for the moment, Monsieur Lecaillet, and I should be grateful if you would loan me your bicycle until after we pass that German barrier ahead.'

Christiane's father had been wheeling the bicycle beside him, having only taken it for the return journey.

Calculating guards wouldn't expect one of the gaolbreakers to be cycling casually about, with the old cap pulled down on his head. Looking typically like a factory worker heading home for lunch, he went straight for the barrier. As he fumbled inside his coat for the identity card, the officer in charge waved him through without bothering to examine papers, but Monsieur Lecaillet had to produce his.

On arriving at the home of Monsieur Lecaillet's friend, Vivant asked the man's wife to remove the 'R.V.' embroidered initials on his handkerchief and shirt.

Less than an hour later, Christiane's mother turned up.

'We're unhappy about a young woman who was here earlier and saw you,' she said anxiously. 'She gossips too much, and nowadays, we all know gossiping can cost lives, so I'm taking you somewhere else.'

They left immediately, and as they walked arm in arm through the streets like a young married couple, she explained:

'The Boutvillains, where we're going now, are good people who hate the enemy – you'll be safe with them.'

On showing Boutvillain, the carpenter, his borrowed identity card, he was promised:

'We'll get your own photograph on it.'

Within the hour it was done by a neighbour, and a few hours later he had new identity papers, signed and rubber stamped.

They were as false as the scalding hot ersatz coffee he had just swallowed, but they would do.

'We have a relative staying with us tonight,' the Boutvillains advised him, 'so we'll say you're an old regimental friend of ours. You'll use our bedroom, and he'll take the other room.'

Having observed that the tiny house only had two rooms, Vivant protested:

'But where will you sleep?'

'Don't worry – we've put a mattress on the landing. You're the one who needs a good night's sleep – make yourself comfortable in our room.'

They wouldn't listen to his objections, but he cautioned that the Germans would undoubtedly be making widespread dawn raids on houses all over town in the hope of netting some escapers.

'I haven't forgotten the '14–'18 war, so I'm ready for them,' Boutvillain laughed. 'I'll wake you at the crack of dawn, and you'll see my special arrangements. Sleep well!'

*

The night was sleepless for almost everyone at Hunsdon and Mongewell Park. There was often waiting and hoping after a raid, and hopes were frequently fulfilled, but in the evening, when there was still no news of either Pickard or McRitchie's aircraft, the phone rang in Dorothy Pickard's home at Selsey, in Sussex. It was Sculthorpe air base.

'Can you come immediately?' Pick's former second-in-command pleaded. 'Ming's terribly ill.'

'Have you called a vet?' she asked.

'Two vets, and both agree there's nothing organically wrong with the dog, yet she's obviously ill, and won't eat.'

Dorothy ploughed through snow-deep roads and swirling blizzards driving to Sculthorpe.

Ming lay on the floor vomiting blood, and Dorothy's comforting whispered words to her produced no reaction. The dog remained prostrate.

'Pick is dead,' Dorothy said.

'How can you say that?' the shocked officer reacted. 'You *can't* read such significance from a pining dog! – With no news there's always a chance – you know that.'

But Pick *was* dead. She knew it, and Ming already knew it. There was something between the dog and Pick beyond anyone's comprehension.

Basil Embry ordered reconnaissance planes to overfly Amiens and all other areas the raiders had crossed for wreckage signs of the missing *Mosquito*s.

Without concrete proof of the men's deaths, optimism was still possible. The anticipated worst had been wrong so many times before, but Ming continued to lie in a stupor, only kept alive by Dorothy's devoted nursing.

Several of the crews were convinced that, seeing Ian McRitchie hit by flak and about either to crash or forced-land, Pick had followed to check if the crew escaped.

'Typical of Pick to leave the formation to follow up one of his own lame ducks,' everyone agreed.

Even Senior Air Staff Officer David Atcherley, in a note to his chief, Embry, agreed with Intelligence summaries and wrote:

I surmise he broke away from the escort and main formation in order to investigate closely McRitchie's and Sammy's crash. He must have been well aware that in doing so he was taking a chance on enemy fighters. Whilst pre-occupied watching the ground for survivors of the first crash, he was probably bounced.

It wasn't true, but the legend grew, was eventually officially logged and issued for publication, and persisted thereafter. It didn't happen like that.

*

Pick always took chances with himself. This time he took one chance too many – he shouldn't have hung around Amiens gaol waiting for bomb smoke and debris dust to settle more to enable him to get a clearer assessment of the results. In his wish to get it right he committed the worst wrong – broke the golden rule – 'Get the hell out and home.'

It's ever the same in life. A man does miraculous things, and people continue to expect him to perform miracles.

But an airman is never safe from surprises.

As the Luftwaffe opponent Pick respected most as a 'clean fighter' – Adolf Galland – commented to Pick's friend, Wing Commander Douglas Bader:

'Errors have the habit of being timeless and are invariably repeated. And,' he added, 'every soldier knows that during a war it is not always the odds that count – a great deal depends on luck.'

The odds proved to be two to one – two of Galland's Abbeville *190*s versus 'F' for Freddie, and Pick and Broadley's luck was out.

Pick had only just finally decided to make a bee-line back to his squadrons when the two *Fockes* dived, realising this tactic offered the greatest opportunity for 'bouncing' what was obviously the prison attack's leader. Luftwaffe pilots knew to their cost that the twin-engined *De Havillands* had a speed no German fighter could approach, so diving from a far greater height, thereby temporarily achieving advantageous extra speed, was the best hope of catching a *Mosquito*. This was why *190*s usually waited well above Mossies running for home, looking to pick them off if the chance arose.

Now they had a solitary *Mosquito* to deal with, and no escort *Typhoon*s to interfere. Cannon fire told Pick and Broadley there was to be no scot-free ride back to Hunsdon.

Pick reacted by accelerating away with a diving turn and cork-screw movement down to the left and up to the right, upsetting his opponents' aim.

They were travelling northwards from Amiens, and all ack-ack batteries held off, leaving the sky to the trio's dogfight.

The pair took it in turn to try and blast Pick out of the air with their four 20mm. cannons and two machine guns apiece, but every time the smoke streaming from their gunports was answered by long blasts from the Mossie's cannon. Pick knew that unless a fighter was allowed to get nearer than 1,000 yards, the *Mosquito* would have no trouble in gaining cloud cover.

Changing tactics, they came at him simultaneously from different directions making it impossible for him to concentrate on one or the other at the same time, and in aerial combat, unguarded seconds are potentially the most fatal. For the *Mosquito*, over-violent acrobatics, spinning, and sudden superhigh accelerations weren't recommended. High acceleration forces were a must to avoid, as the upright position of the crew reduced the amount of 'g' they could withstand without blacking out, and this was no time to be blacking out.

One of the *Fockes* repeatedly tried coming up from under, but never managed to get within range of the *Mosquito's* level, because spotting him each time, Pick smartly kept beyond range by accelerating quickly. Then, on a climbing turn made only a brief distance from the underbelly attacker, Pick and Broadley managed to get in a cannon broadside, ripping the wings and right side of the *Focke's* fuselage. Hurt and realising it couldn't out-turn the *Mosquito*, the *190* dived for the cover of some lower cloud, and then, in obvious serious trouble, banked and abandoned the fight, heading towards Abbeville.

The second pilot instantly dived from above, but seeing this in time, Pick accelerated away at low level. With the excellent forward view the Mossie provided, flying low-evasive manoeuvres could be carried out at high speed far more effectively than at altitude. Even so, a fighter in close range could be presented with a fairly easy shot, and as Pick yanked his aircraft into a vertical turn, dropping its nose steeply, the remaining Abbeville pilot countered by wrenching his stick towards himself with both hands and achieving the correct firing angle. The Luftwaffe pilot moved his index finger a millimetre on the gun trigger, and bullets battered 'F' for Freddie's tail. The whole sequence took seconds, but it only takes seconds to die.

The tail of the wooden *Mosquito* splintered into pieces like a matchbox and fell out. The plane shuddered, flipped over on its back, and in a final death convulsion, dived, shattering and scattering pieces far and wide.

The *190* circled its 'kill' and returned to base.

The few who witnessed the fight from the ground, ran and cycled to the crash area. Using long sticks, hastily cut from a nearby wood, several tried to extricate the bodies but hurriedly withdrew when unspent ammunition started exploding in all directions. Finally dragging the bodies from the flames – the engines were still burning – they laid them on salvaged struts of wood and a young girl wrapped them in their parachutes. Before doing so she cut away the RAF wings and ribbon decorations from the remnants of one of the uniforms to hamper German identification. The other man's uniform was almost in ashes.

Finding Broadley's maps, one man at the scene threw them into the flames to destroy them before the authorities could get their hands on them. Another found a box of French currency – the crew's emergency cash in case of forced landing; a third located a camera with film in it. Running to the nearby wood, he hid the camera and film in a rabbit burrow, retrieving them only after official inquiries into the crash, and interrogation of everyone at the scene had been completed. Months later, when the Allies invaded, he was to hand that camera and film to an army officer and get a receipt for it.

Gagnard Pinket, son of the mayor of St. Gratien – a village of a couple of hundred inhabitants, eight miles from Amiens – who found the bodies, had them carried to his father's house. The villagers wanted to bury them. The Germans wouldn't allow it, so young Gagnard Pinket managed to mark Alan Broadley's oak coffin with four deep scratches to ensure that, should the Germans be careless with the burial of the two airmen, relatives would some day be able to establish their remains.

*

The gaol morgue wasn't large enough. It was full, so the Salle de Bal – a dance hall some four hundred metres along the road from the prison, also used for festivals and school functions – was requisitioned as an overflow morgue.

Bodies were lying all over the dance floor when twenty-year-old Pierre Gruel came to try and identify a corpse believed to be his father, who had so effectively aided the fight for freedom by supplying genuine Préfecture identity papers to so many on the run, including American and British agents and shot-down aircrews.

The body on the floor, next to Dr. Robert Beaumont, was unrecognisable, yet Pierre was somehow certain it was his father.

'Are you sure it's him?' Raymond Dewas asked.

'Yes,' Pierre unhesitatingly replied, 'but take off his wedding ring and the confirmation should be there.'

The ring was removed. Inside it was his father's initials and the date of his marriage – April 21, 1921. At that instant, Braumann and Lucienne marched in.

'Gruel! – Gruel! – Where is Gruel?' Braumann angrily shouted, cheated of someone from whom he had hoped to learn much through systematic beatings and torture.

After identification, the bodies were taken to a large high-ceilinged room in a building in rue Jean Masset – just behind the Gruel family's home. The freezing cold room was suitable for keeping corpses until coffins were made, and funerals arranged. Prisoners' families silently moved in and out of the room, identifying, where necessary, or simply seeing them for the last time. Prayers didn't need to be voiced to be said.

As so many had been awaiting execution anyway, perhaps the one consolation relatives and friends had as they filed past, was that now at least, the men and women lying on the floor were free from thoughts of death.

\*

'Once we're out of here, put your foot down hard on the accelerator, and keep it down – even if they start shooting at us.'

Jane Vivant wanted her chauffeur to understand clearly what was expected of him. She still wasn't certain whether her husband was dead or alive, but at least she knew the corpse Gestapo chief Braumann thought was her husband's, wasn't. She couldn't risk the enemy using her and their child as hostages to force him back, should they discover he was alive and free.

'Get the car ready; open the main courtyard doors; draw up close to the house and leave the car doors open. Claudine and I will slip into the back of the car at the first opportunity, then we can go. As no restrictions have been put on the car, the guards probably won't take particular notice of you – you're already part of the scenery, as far as they are concerned.'

'What if they do stop me?' the chauffeur asked.

'Then we'll stop crouching at the back before they get around to it, and I'll simply tell them I'm going to see the Préfet.'

'The Préfet?' the chauffeur said disbelievingly.

'Yes, because that's exactly where we *are* going, so if they follow, let them.'

They moved off without a hitch, and the car sped at 100 kilometres an hour towards Amiens, which was really pushing it for a Gazogene car.

Before entering the Préfecture building, she issued final instructions.

'We had better say goodbye now, because we won't be coming out again – anyway, not to you, but continue to wait in the car outside the Préfecture,' she explained to the bewildered chauffeur.

'After a couple of hours, go in and inquire for me, but they won't be able to trace me. Return to Abbeville and go to the Gestapo'.

'No, Madame, I don't want to do that,' he said uncomfortably.

'You must – for your own safety. Tell them you brought me to the Préfecture, waited hours, then when I didn't return, wondered if I had been arrested. They'll do nothing to you.'

She went to the office of the despised collaborator Le Baube, Préfet of the Somme.

'You always boast the Germans arrest no one without your permission,' she accused. 'Does this mean you authorised my husband's detention?'

'No.'

'So much for your powers!' she said contemptuously. 'The least you can do is to assist in any way you can – just help me find him!'

Storming out, she stopped an instant to hand an envelope to the Préfet's secretary, Solange Caillé – her husband's OCM spy contact in the Préfet's office.

'It's money . . . for him, in case he manages to reach you,' she whispered, then disappeared hand in hand with Claudine.

They couldn't go to friends because the Gestapo had taken family address books when they raided her home, and would undoubtedly check them all, but she recalled one friend whose new Paris address she hadn't yet entered in the address books, so she chose Paris.

They walked in the direction of the station, and at a rendezvous point, Tenaillon's grocery delivery van was waiting. The van drove straight through Amiens station goods yard and unloaded into Tenaillon's own railway wagon groceries, sacks of potatoes, flour, Jane Vivant, and Claudine.

\*

As promised, it was dawn when Boutvillain, the carpenter, tapped on Vivant's bedroom door and led him across the yard to the carpentry workshop. In the attic it was impossible to detect the hiding place only reachable by a mobile ladder. It was uncomfortable, you couldn't stand upright in it, and it was as cold as ice despite layers of straw, a blanket, and a canvas tent into which he rolled himself. Every couple of hours, Boutvillain supplied a hot drink and books, but Vivant didn't feel like reading. His body was icy so he curled himself into a ball for warmth. It didn't really help.

He could feel all his muscles twitching with fatigue.

He was grateful when it was late enough in the morning for him to move the leaden weight of his body and return to the house. It was torture to open his lips, but as he gulped down the hot acorn coffee he began to thaw, and colour returned to his skin.

During the morning, Christiane brought news from Mademoiselle Caillé at the Préfecture, and he received the money his wife had left for him.

'She's gone to Paris,' he was told, 'to stay with your friend Madame Ducombeau and wants you to join her as soon as possible.'

'That's all very well,' said Vivant, 'but there's the problem of getting a railway ticket with a special slip showing the journey's necessary.'

'We'll take care of that too,' Boutvillain confidently assured him.

That evening, a plumber friend who was due to travel to Paris the following morning for the funeral of a relative killed in an air raid, explained:

'You're going to be part of the family delegation of mourners. Six of us were going, and you'll replace the sixth – a cousin of the dead woman.'

They filled him in on family background, just in case the knowledge was required at some point.

'I'd better alter my appearance a little more,' Vivant suggested, 'and the first thing to change are my hands – they don't go with a grubby cap and the rest of me now.'

Madame Boutvillain provided a bowl of old fat, and Vivant plunged his lily-white 'desk' hands into the fat, rubbed ashes into them and broke a few nails. A not-so-smart outfit together with one of Boutvillain's caps and a pair of steel-rimmed spectacles completed the picture.

At 6.30 a.m., the five mourners called for him. At the station, the telegram notifying the family of the funeral was examined and third class tickets issued. The train was due to depart at 7.30 a.m., but the time passed and there was no sign of a train as German military police patrolled platforms, on guard to prevent escapers leaving town.

A Gendarme and a soldier picked people at random, examining their papers. It was plainly a matter of luck – several wouldn't even be questioned, then one would be singled out. It was like Russian roulette.

They were still there at 9 o'clock when they heard the railway sheds had been machine-gun strafed by Allied aircraft. The delay was due to the station administration endeavouring to find an engine in working order.

As a Sous-Préfet, he had for years philosophically learned to bear and handle with equanimity the misfortunes of others. Now he needed all his professional composure to deal with his own troubles. If he went too fast, he was liable to catch up with misfortune, and if too slow, misfortune was likely to catch up with him. Patience was best – it helped you wait faster.

At 9.15 they left.

Two more passengers joined the compartment at Beauvais, and while Vivant's group were eating a packed snack, the new passengers gossiped about the gaol attack.

'The Sous-Préfet of Abbeville was killed,' they announced. 'They found his body under the debris, and he's already been buried in the military cemetery.'

Vivant pretended to sleep while they discussed him, but found the gossip an entertaining diversion.

A few kilometres beyond Beauvais, the train halted – the Resistance had blown up the track. The train was compelled to reverse, and the extensive detour lost them hours. They didn't reach the Paris Gare du Nord until 4.30 p.m. Once through the barrier, Vivant thanked his 'family', said goodbye, and took a cycle-taxi to Resistance friend, Madam Claude Salvy.

'What do you want?' she asked suspiciously.

'To say hello and find my wife,' he replied, and she instantly recognised his voice, though she hadn't recognised him.

'The first thing I'm going to do before you go anywhere else, is run you a hot bath!' she laughed.

Raymond Vivant grew a moustache, and totally altered his appearance and his wife dyed her hair blonde and also substantially changed her looks. They sent their daughter to the centre of France, with a new identity, to be looked after by a friend. It was too dangerous for the three of them to remain together.

The Vivants took over a first floor apartment owned by an American who evacuated just before the Nazis marched into Paris. The American had left the keys in the safe-keeping of one of the Vivants' friends. The apartment was in Avenue Wagram, two hundred metres from the Arc de Triomphe, opposite the 'For Germans Only' Empire Cinema.

The Gestapo were three doors from them, and the Vivants felt safer under their noses, knowing the Gestapo were more likely to be sticking them into other people's businesses elsewhere.

\*

The day after the attack, the first official report supplied to German and French controlling Ministers, headed: 'Information Report' stated:

On the 18th of February 1944, towards mid-day, some aeroplanes – 'Allied' – bombed part of the north of the town of Amiens, completely destroying the prison situated on the route d'Albert, the numbers 15 to 17 of the rue Voltaire, consequently the Hospital Saint Victor had to be turned into a 'quarantine' by the German authorities.

They appear to have recaptured many from the prison and dug out thirty. The prison had held approximately 640 prisoners of communal rights, and 180 prisoners gaoled by the German authorities. It has not as yet been possible to make an exact census of prisoners as the archives were destroyed.

The count is:

37 dead, killed by rubble including Doctors Goyot, of Bray-sur-Somme; Beaumont, of Warloy-Baillon. So far, we have only been able to identify six or seven.

92 injured have been taken to the hospital and various clinics.

M. Bellemere, Solicitor Attorney at Amiens, was gravely injured and recaptured the same day at 1 o'clock.

A large number of prisoners have benefitted from the bombing by escaping. But apart from these, 231 have been recaptured by the French and German police services who know:

163 prisoners of communal rights provisionally "cut off" in the Lebel factory at Faubourg de Hen;

50 prisoners held by the German authorities, shut in the Citadelle;

18 women at the Dury and at the New Hospital.

Clearing and salvage work was carried out day and night by the firemen equipped for passive defence, and some factory workers. One presumes that a number of important prisoners are under the enormous mounds of material lying about, thirty certainly.

On the other hand, a woman has been killed at her home in the rue Voltaire. The total victims at the Saint Victor hospital is still unknown.

The number of prisoners who evaded recapture is still to be exactly determined, but there are certainly many. M. Vivant, the Sous-Préfet of Abbeville, has disappeared. He had been detained by the German authorities for several days.

The police services carried out identification of victims, and also actively continued to search day and night to try and find escaped prisoners.

I should signify the exemplary behaviour of certain prisoners who, after the event, co-operated actively with some of the other prisoners. Among them, particularly Doctor Mans, Tempez, and Gendarme Langlet, of the Nesle brigade.'

M. Heannot, Divisional Commissioner.

The figures given were deliberately understated, apart from the fact that the French authorities didn't realise the extent to which the civil criminal sections of the gaol were being used to house the overflow of German detained 'politicals'.

The report confirmed the destruction of archives, then falsely stated Maître Bellemere was 'recaptured' an hour after the bombing when, in fact, Bellemere was trapped at the time under debris and not rescued until the early hours of the following morning.

It also notified the disappearance of Raymond Vivant, although Braumann, of Gestapo, insisted Vivant was dead.

# 16 It's safer in gaol

'Come on you lot – you're being transferred.'

The three recaptured prisoners held for three days in the little Gendarmerie at St. Sofleur knew they weren't going back to the now uninhabitable Amiens gaol and expected to be sent to one of the major prisons at St. Quentin or Lille.

It had been cramped in the local police cell, but they had been well treated and reasonably fed since surrendering through total exhaustion. One of them was coming down with chills and fever.

Tough, humorous, forthright Julien Michel, a saboteur who loved his wife, religion, beer, and wine, in that order, was undisputed leader of the three who had been imminently scheduled for an Amiens firing squad. From Julien's creased face you could judge him to be anything from thirty to sixty. Henri Foy – rough and coarse, like the scrub known as Maquis, from which the military movement took its name – was a Maquis soldier. A born grumbler, Henri ceaselessly complained about everything, but even while complaining, could become a ruthless fighting machine. Bushy-eyebrowed Roland Caron was an evasion line operator and guide, mainly acting for MISX – American counterpart of Britain's MI9 evasion Intelligence and organisation department.

After Gendarmerie chief Lamont informed them of the transfer, they were handcuffed and individually locked in the mini-cells of a Black Maria, watched by a small crowd of villagers.

The transport had been travelling for some thirty minutes when there was a loud report and they skidded to a halt. The rear door was opened and each cell unlocked.

'A tyre's burst,' Gendarme Lamont announced, 'so get your weight out of there, and you can also help change the tyre.'

The prisoners expected to see a military escort because of their classification as 'political' detainees, but there was only Lamont, the police driver, and a single Gendarme motor cyclist.

Observing the surprised expressions, Lamont smiled as he freed their handcuffs.

'If you're thinking of making a run for it, don't bother,' he advised.

Looking at the revolvers in the police holsters, they didn't relish dodging bullets, especially in the middle of open country-side, without cover or a house in sight.

'Just change the tyre quickly before a German patrol turns up – we're with you,' Lamont said.

At the last words, the prisoners' heads jolted up almost in unison, and three pairs of confused eyes intently studied Lamont.

'What do you mean, you're with us?' Julien inquired warily.

Lamont grinned at the other two Gendarmes as if sharing a secret.

'Why do you think we kept you in our Gendarmerie for a few days while things were so hot? Because you were safer in than out, and the cell was the one place the Gestapo were unlikeliest to look. Apart from which, one of you had time to recover from fever, and you all had a chance to get your strength back – so change the tyre and let's move on.'

'Where to?'

'Close to Lille where we've arranged to pass you along an evasion line – you never know, you might even end up in London!'

'But what about our families?'

'All in safe hands,' Lamont promised as he handed them each new identity cards.

'So that's why you took our photographs again when you recaptured us!' Julien said appreciatively.

Jubilant, smiling Julien, Henri, and Roland changed the tyre double-fast, then went back to their Black Maria cells, in case a military patrol stopped them at some point. Gendarme chief Lamont returned with his driver to the cab, and the Black Maria with solo motorcycle police escort roared down the road towards Lille.

Finally halting on the outskirts, the Gendarmes released the three. Waiting for them was a large butcher's van and Joel – a big fat bustling local pig merchant who, as an important pork supplier to German forces, was among the few freely allowed to operate transport over a wide area. Joel, who knew everyone in Lille, also delivered false papers, identity cards, and frequently evaders, with pork to customers.

'I love the idea of using pigs to outwit pigs,' he laughed. Indicating a concealed compartment under the pork, he ordered:

'Wriggle in there – you'll be out before you have time to suffocate,' he laughed again, thoroughly enjoying it all.

'What do we do if the van's searched – grunt?' Julien asked, and the three Gendarmes relished the remark as much as Joel, who said confidently:

'They never search my van – everybody knows me. Under their uniforms they're just like anyone else – vulnerable.'

When Joel vanished for an instant to the front of the van, Gendarme Lamont said quietly to the three:

'Don't let the easy-going jollity fool you – he's as tough as they come. I know for a fact that he once threw an SS officer, who came to requisition meat and treated him like dirt, into his cold storage and let him freeze to death.'

Thanking Lamont and his colleagues, Julien, Henri and Roland crawled into the back of the van and settled down as best as they could for the uncomfortable ride into Lille.

Formerly the capital of French Flanders, and now of the Department of the Nord, the industrial and textile centre of Lille, having been occupied by the Germans for most of the 1914–18 war, was well experienced in the art of resistance. The blowing up by Nazis of a marble memorial erected in one of the main streets in honour of local resistants caught and shot in the First World War, so angered residents that they retaliated by wrecking German graves in a cemetery. The Nazis punished by imposing a crippling fine on Lille, but people hit back by hiding and aiding hundreds of escapers, despite substantial rewards offered to anyone betraying evaders or their helpers.

Unloading the Amiens trio in a secluded courtyard, Joel pointed at two schoolgirls playing with a hoop and skipping rope in the street just outside the courtyard.

'They're your next guides – follow them.'

Julien showed surprise, but Henri and Roland, accustomed to evasion line tactics, immediately started walking towards the girls who were, in fact, a few years older than they looked. Deliberately dressing themselves to appear younger, they pranced along streets – one hitting her hoop with a stick, and the other skipping beside her, until they stopped outside a large house and continued to play near the front door.

'That's obviously the safe house,' said Henri, and as a very fat woman opened the door to his knock, the two schoolgirls pranced away down the street having completed their assignment. The fat woman clearly expected them. She was magnificently ugly, with a cigarette in a holder clenched between her teeth.

'Monsieur Joel sent us,' Julien said.

'I thought so – I'm Madame Samiez, come in.'

Joel hadn't told them anything about the safe house, but the instant they entered the three of them knew that somewhere, roly poly Joel was laughing himself silly, because Madame Samiez's place was a brothel.

That wasn't the only surprise. There were three American aircrew evaders being hidden in the house at the same time.

Leading Julien, Henri, and Roland up to a bedroom, Madame Samiez, eyes gleaming with pleasure said:

'Financing escapes with money Nazis spend here is one of my greatest pleasures – the other is killing them.'

She meant what she said, for they learned that whenever she waddled out shopping, she always had four German stick grenades suspended under her skirt from her underwear, and grenades in her shopping bag. She either dropped them from a bridge over the main Lille railway line or rolled them under parked enemy cars or military transports.

Disappearing to greet new clients for her girls and to arrange food for Julien and company, she swiftly returned to inform them delightedly:

'We've got some Abwehr customers taking an unofficial break from hunting Amiens gaolbreakers. Dictators can control everything, except feelings. I'm going to put them with girls in rooms either side of you to make a tasty Amiens gaol sandwich!'

She had instructed the girls to tap the Abwehr for information about the hunt.

'It's useful to know what they're up to, and I normally manage to find out whatever I want to know by greasing the right parts – wheels don't turn so well unless they're well greased.'

It was all part of the slow corruption of conquest.

'Also,' added Madame Samiez smugly, 'When a man's flies are open, so's his mouth.'

The following morning she produced sets of travel papers for all of them.

'The best way is to let the enemy get you there by rail. We've had dozens of evaders pass through this house, and most got away by train. Railways are less dangerous than roads. Our Abwehr visitors last night admitted they'd recaptured a lot of your prison friends all over the Somme, but none, so far, at stations or on trains.

'You've got good new identity cards, but should you need to switch cards in an emergency, I'll give you some blanks, extra photos of yourselves and a hard-boiled egg can help do the rest.'

'An egg?' Roland probed, intrigued by a wrinkle he had never previously come across.

'Yes. The biggest problem is, of course, getting cards officially stamped. If you gently roll a shelled, cold hard-boiled egg over the ink stamp of a genuine card, then roll the imprint this leaves on the egg over a false identity card with a fresh photograph, you get a reasonably usable result. But this should only be a temporary measure. It might not resist too close scrutiny. You know what they say – every official form or piece of paper in France today is a mousetrap.'

Madame Samiez advised them that they would soon be leaving with a courier as it was considered best for them to quit the Somme for a time.

'My three American visitors are departing in the same direction as you. Though you won't be starting out together, I'll briefly introduce you so that you'll recognise one another and, if necessary, help each other should any of you get into trouble during the journey.'

She left the room, and in seconds their reopened doorway was filled by a big friendly-looking character in civilian clothes whose outsize frame hid the short curly-haired Italian-looking airman behind him. The third, as tall as the first, combined rosy cheeks with the blue-black shadow of a potentially heavy beard, and Madame Samiez waddled in after him. They shook hands warmly, but not even first names were exchanged. Language difficulties made the moment awkward, but all six valued the purpose of the introduction. They were comrades on the run.

Producing a bottle of wine and six glasses, Madame Samiez poured for everyone, including herself, and they wished each other 'Good health, and bon voyage!'

Madame Samiez added another toast:

'To Liberation!'

Madame Samiez sent them to Lille station in style with two expensively hired cars run on Black Market petrol. She had reserved a first class compartment for the six. An evasion party of six usually comprised five evaders and a convoy guide, but because of Roland Caron's experience in the work, he was deputed to look after the compartment, and their convoy guide – an attractive young girl – was to be in the next compartment.

The platform was thick with soldiers humping kitbags and civilians with suitcases or packs. When their papers passed barrier inspection, the Americans separated from Julien's trio, and the girl also stood apart from them.

As two German soldiers approached, Julien cautioned quick-tempered Henri, who he was sure would compensate feeling cornered with anger:

'Hold on! – Don't assume the worst.'

Confronting the three, one of the soldiers asked:

'Do you know the destination of the next train?'

'Paris,' Julien replied.

Two SS guards with sub-machine guns passed by occasionally – the increased security resulting from the Amiens gaolbreak wasn't being relaxed.

Further sporadic identity checks started on the platform, and as guards approached two men, one suddenly jumped onto the track and ran, putting distance between himself and the station.

'Halt!' an SS guard shouted, immediately alerting everyone, but the man stumbled on as guards from both sides of the tracks splattered machine-gun bullets around him. He didn't dodge or weave – simply ran straight ahead making for sidings with a number of trucks on them, and then for a goods train heading in his direction. Tearing across the rails, he grabbed one of the fast-moving wagons, and swung himself aboard.

A soldier was levelling a gun at the companion abandoned in panic. The man lifted his arms in surrender and was marched off with a gun in his back.

In a cloud of steam, the Paris train rolled alongside the platform, brakes squealing, couplings clanking. As it screeched to a stop, military guards resumed checking identities. Two were about to speak to the Americans when, seeing the danger, the girl courier pulled a timely faint with a piercing scream that even penetrated the platform bedlam. Forgetting about identity inspections, one of the guards yelled at people crowding around the prostrate body on the platform:

'Keep back! – Give her air!'

The Americans and Julien's party boarded the train.

Extracting travel documents from the girl's handbag, a guard carried her onto the train and gently put her into a corner of her compartment. The rest of the seats were occupied by German army officers.

'Don't worry,' they assured the guard, 'we'll look after her.'

From Paris they were directed to Toulouse, in south-west

France, and petite, rough-voiced, grey-haired sixty-one-year-old Françoise Dissart, who lived in an apartment facing the local Gestapo headquarters, and owned and ran a nearby dress shop.

She always wore black; kept a black wooden cigarette holder almost permanently in her mouth; practically existed on black coffee, and had a fat black cat named Mifouf constantly at her side.

Sharp-mannered Françoise – outwardly brusque, but with a soft centre for fugitives from the Nazis whom she hated – established her own evasion line with a personal group of guides who took agents, airmen, and other evaders across the Pyrenees mountains to Spain. On occasions, she escorted escapers personally, although even for younger, fit persons the journey could be an exhausting nightmare.

Delivery of fugitives to the rear entrance of her apartment always coincided with the Gestapo's lunch break.

The three Americans from Lille she successfully got to Spain. Roland joined her evasion line, and she found homes and also put to use the fighting talents of Julien and Henri, who were the first of many Amiens *Mosquito* raid escapers whom she helped.

'Take a lesson from the *Mosquito*,' she advised Julien. 'It never waits for an opening – it makes one.'

\*

Joe Balfe, who had supplied many of the hundreds moved to safety along the Toulouse evasion line, followed up Louise's receipt of Julien Michel, Henri, and Roland, with more Amiens gaolbreakers.

They weren't his customary clients. His regular speciality were American and British aircrew, but overwhelmed by sheer weight of numbers and the enormity of what his brainchild had unleashed, René Chapelle – Pepe – asked for Joe's expertise, and got it.

'Reaction to the attack is so intense that hundreds who escaped need to disappear from the Somme; cut themselves off from their families, and from all previous contacts for months. Or at least until the Allies invade,' Pepe told Joe, adding:

'Safe houses in these parts may not be safe much longer. With so many running, tongues are liable to be free too. We're having to use our own safe houses to look after evaders unconnected with our action groups, so we must move them – fast!'

From the day of the bombing, the manhunt never let up and massive rewards were offered for information leading to rearrests. Direct orders from Berlin sent unending streams of armoured vehicles, tanks, car and motorcycle patrols, and troop-packed transports pouring all over the region and well beyond it. Officers and NCOs in the convoys reconnoitred every woodland. To maintain terror pressure on the population, Berlin authorised widespread random raids on houses and entire streets, with searchers combing houses from top to bottom, not even missing tool sheds nor waste bins.

At farmhouses every bale and sack was bayonet-prodded. Soldiers bullet-sprayed barns, riddled haystacks with machinegun fire, and set many ablaze. All the Somme and surrounding areas were far too hot for gaol evaders. Joe Balfe, who had served a spell in Amiens prison himself and had one of the best escape lines and safe house networks in northern France, did more than his share of getting out as many as possible.

Throughout the war he lived thirty kilometres from Amiens in the village of Hornoy, but was born in Manchester of a Dublin-Irish family. Like his two sons – Joe junior and John – he worked for the British and Americans to rid his adopted country and the world of Hitler and the Nazis.

Choosing the army as his career before the outbreak of the 1914 world war, and lying about his age, Joe, whose father was a Manchester city police Inspector, joined the Irish Guards when only sixteen. Well over six foot, he was big for his years and looked older. With brain as well as hefty brawn, he rose through the ranks to become Regimental Sergeant Major. His appointment to the post was recognition of leadership qualities, for anyone able to rule the justly famous fighting Irish Guards had to be outstanding.

When World War I began, his was one of the first battalions to land in France and he became a highly decorated World War I hero. His bravery awards included the Military Medal. During a rest break from the battle front, towering Joe met tiny Madeleine Gaudière in the little Somme village of Hornoy. The same age, and even born the same month as him, Madeleine, who didn't even reach five feet, gave Joe something to live for through horrors that turned his hair silver-grey by the time he was twenty.

As with so many soldiers, he married and brought back the girl he found over there. His loud bark began to echo around the parade ground at the Guards' barracks at Birdcage Walk where he trained officers and did his share of duty at Buckingham Palace, across the road.

Leaving the Guards, he joined his sister in Manchester where, in 1919, his first son John was born. Nostalgically hankering for a taste of his Irish background upon the arrival of Joe junior two years later, the family moved to Dublin only to soon find themselves surrounded by the Irish troubles and bitterness with the British.

309

'We've had enough war, Joe,' Madeleine said, 'let's go home to France.'

Returning to Hornoy, they finally settled in the port town of Dunkirk where Joe, contriving to keep a foot in his wife's world and his own, worked for the cross-Channel ferry service between Dunkirk and Gravesend, becoming a Purser and a Chief Steward.

Their third son died at three months, but within a few years there were also two daughters – Madeleine and Marie Thérèse.

Employed by a French shipping line and faced with the loss of work during depression times when, understandably, the principle was 'French jobs first', Joe became a naturalised Frenchman to keep his job.

Joe junior was in the French Air Force when Hitler's forces overran France. With no cross-Channel work to provide a living, the Balfe family moved back to Hornoy to run the twelve-roomed hotel owned by Madeleine's mother.

It was, perhaps, somewhat unfortunate that locals took to calling Joe senior 'Winston Churchill', due to his facial likeness to Churchill. So, in some respects, the Gestapo really did Joe a favour when they threw him into Amiens prison in 1941 for the arrest brought the nationality issue into the open. Joe's World War I army career and British origin were no secret, and it was admitted that the sole detention basis was:

'You are British born.'

They hadn't reckoned on arousing Joe's Irish blood, nor his Irish shrewdness.

'Everyone has always known where I was born, but also knew I became a naturalised Frenchman before the war. My wife's French, our children and everything we possess are in this country, so why would we jeopardise it all for a land that is no longer mine and hasn't been my home since 1918?'

Joe then threw in a Blarney touch:

'You're forgetting something else. I come from Dublin-Irish stock – that's where my roots are – and we've both got a lot of friends in Dublin. If you start on me, you start on them, and when they hear Germany imprisons people just for their origins, the Führer's liable to lose sympathisers he needs in Ireland.'

That did it. Joe was released. Pressure on him eased, but he remained cautious.

When Joe junior was demobilised from the air force in unoccupied France and rejoined the family, Joe senior, together with his wife and two sons, organised their own secret war.

From the beginning of the occupation, the country north of the

Somme was made forbidden territory and the river's banks heavily guarded. The demarcation line between occupied and unoccupied France ran through Amiens across the Bovillier bridge which leads to the cemetery of St. Acheul, and fugitives learned to make good use of this. Imposing, but fake, funeral processions often disappeared as soon as they reached the other side.

'Escaping prisoners of war, shot down pilots, and bomber crews, are certain to come looking increasingly for help,' Joe senior told Joe junior. 'Our hotel gives us an ideal safe house cover for accommodating strangers, but we ought to fish around and organise a chain of safe houses with people we can totally trust whom we've known for years.'

With John working for a transport company, they had precious wheels to help move evaders, and as Joe senior was still the conspicuous former 'British-Irish Tommy', he felt it diplomatic for Joe junior to do most of the contacting and liaison with links in the escape chain. The Balfes initiated the crucial French branch of the famous Comet Line – a largely Belgian-run operation in the hands of a Madame Degreese, and the elderly, beautiful Madame de Jongh, known to the line as 'Auntie Alice', her husband Frederic, and daughter Andrée, known as Dédée.

For every airman who escaped after being taken prisoner, and reached home, there were some ninety evasions by those shot down when operating over Europe. It became known throughout Allied air forces that anyone landing in France had at least a fifty-fifty chance of getting home. A captured evader became a prisoner of war, but those who helped were tortured and shot, and often along with their whole family. The greatest danger was the informer. The Gestapo loved using elderly mild-mannered men to do shadowing, rather than sinister-looking toughs, rightly assessing grey-haired nondescript characters were less likely to arouse suspicion.

Wherever possible, married couples were recruited as general helpers or safe house hosts. The husband or wife collected evaders from an organisation member and hid them in their own house or apartment, drawing on clothing stocks stored at strategic points along evasion lines. False identity and food cards, and even bicycles, were supplied when necessary.

Escapers usually walked shoeless in houses to cut noise, especially when the man of the house was at work. Nor were they permitted to peer from windows or move curtains.

Having to provide for hotel guests as a matter of course, made things somewhat easier for the Balfes, especially in respect of shopping for food and other supplies. A safe house wife normally feeding two would be noticed when buying more. In country districts farmers usually managed a little extra produce for special customers, but the Balfes had another advantageous cover – SS and Tank Corps troops were billeted in part of the hotel.

The requisitioned section was partitioned off, except for the courtyard, in which the Germans established a canteen, using a trailer for cooking, and an outhouse for supplies and as a covered area in severe weather. Companies came and went, and the SS certainly would never have believed anyone to be insane enough to hide evaders beside them, but that is precisely what the Balfes did.

Joe senior also kept a large cage in the courtyard for holding and breeding pigeons he frequently caught for food, although pigeons in a little cage within the cage were never eaten – they were British, dropped by the RAF in cylindrical containers. The parachuted pigeons, supplied because of the Balfes' inability to have a radio transmitter, flew home to London with emergency messages.

Just having these pigeons was sufficient to warrant a firing squad without trial.

American and British airmen briefly residing in the hotel loved the idea of black-uniformed SS feeding the Cockney birds.

'They're very tasty with pommes frites and peas,' Joe said to an SS officer making friendly noises to the pigeons.

In July 1943, Joe junior disappeared, and shortly afterwards, so did his brother John. According to their parents, Joe had run because his life had been threatened by the husband of a woman with whom he was alleged to have been having an affair. John was said to have subsequently gone to find him. Now neither could be traced. Amazingly, the story was accepted. In truth, both had been warned they were about to be shipped to Germany as slave labourers. Also, Comet Line security had been breached in Belgium. Madame de Jongh and her husband Frederic were being interrogated, and their daughter Dédée had vanished.

With the compulsory labour threat and the possibility of Comet security crumbling under their feet, thereby endangering the whole family, Joe junior used his own evasion line routes. From Paris he reached Bordeaux, Madrid, and Gibraltar, where he met one of the Intelligence chiefs for whom he had been working for so long – Donald Darling, of the MI9 division of Britain's secret services, specialising in evasion. While John Balfe remained in France, Joe junior came to London and joined Airey Neave and Lieutenant-Colonel Jimmy Langley in the Westminster headquarters of MI9.

Despite the SS and other military personnel swarming about the hotel, Joe and Madeleine regularly listened to the illegal BBC

Overseas Service broadcasts, and knew Joe junior was safely in London when an announcer said:

'The words are silver, but silence is golden.'

It was the prearranged message they had chosen with Joe junior, prior to his departure.

In Hornoy, Joe senior continued the fight by constructing an alternative organisation to the Comet connection, to handle shot-down airmen carrying out the stepped up, pre-invasion missions against northern France. The new network was integrated into what became known as the Burgundy Line, and it was Joe's new set-up that René Chapelle called on to assist Amiens gaolbreakers. In addition to her courier work, Maria Chapelle was also very active in evasion operations.

MI9 and America's MISX depended on volunteers to contact men and hide them until they could be got out. The function of MI9 was to supply money, communications, equipment, food and 'pickups' by aircraft or naval evacuations from the coasts of France. Evaders were still being smuggled into Spain via the Pyrenees, though it seemed crazy to go all that way when northern France was across the Channel from Britain. But stealing a boat and trying to get across could be even madder.

Trucks were risking collecting evaders from farms and houses by daylight to minimise curfew problems, carrying as many as twenty evaders at a time. To ease the enormous strain on safe houses and evasion lines, motor torpedo boats known as 'Shelburnes' or 'boat trains' started to pick up 'parcels', as evaders were called, from Channel beaches. The craft were about 128 feet long, powered by three high-speed diesel engines. Cruising at 33 knots, they had a crew of 36, a six-pounder gun aft, twin turrets on each side and aft of the bridge, and a two-pounder forward gun. A typical load of nineteen evaders included 13 American airmen, 4 RAF, and 2 Frenchmen wanting to join Allied forces.

Joe senior went on using Rolande Witon – his son's best courier contact in northern France – and safe house reliables such as René, the white Russian in the Corbie district of Amiens, and the talkative Amiens hairdresser who knew everyone's business, but kept his mouth shut about his own double life. There was also an English Mother Superior of a convent in Normandy, and two elderly ladies – one of whom always wore a red hat for luck when acting as a guide. They collected evader parties from safe houses, assembled them in Paris parks such as the Luxembourg Gardens, then either led them to railway terminals or convoyed them personally to Spain. And, of course, there was Madame Irène and her associate, Madame

Paulette, who ran the brothel catering exclusively for Luftwaffe pilots and ground staff at Poix fighter base. One night, when a bunch of drunk airfield workers attempted to break the brothel's 'For Germans Only' rule, military police brutally beat up several and even shot a couple as a hands-off example to any future would-be intruders.

'Madame Irène and Madame Paulette are getting a great kick out of hiding four of the Amiens prisoners their Luftwaffe clients are out hunting,' Pepe told Joe Balfe, 'but it's time the escapers were shifted.'

Joe was also enjoying the thought of two guests comfortably settled in his hotel, and three more distributed among neighbouring farmhouses while SS and Tank Corps forces daily fanned out from Hornoy, running themselves into the ground trying to locate escapers they were billeted beside.

One of Joe's guests reached him via a wine cask. In most of France, wine vendors were a common sight pushing outsize wooden casks mounted on a two-wheeled trolley with shafts and a crossbar, or with their casks on horse-drawn carts. Selling direct to the public, wine was drawn as required from a bung hole at the bottom of the cask. Divider partitions inserted into many such casks retained the bottom half for wine, but left the upper section dry and large enough to hold a travelling radio operator and transmitter. The oak lid couldn't be opened from the outside, and if a radio detection van was spotted in range, transmissions stopped. A cask hideout could also provide a useful getaway transport for a gaol evader.

Another of Joe's guests came from a fortifications construction work camp. Desperate for rest and warmth from the cold, the man, who had run from the gaol bombing alone, smuggled himself into a work camp for a night's shelter and a meal. This he did by tacking himself onto a work party, counting on the enemy not noticing one too many, nor expecting anyone to consign himself voluntarily to one of their camps. The next morning the uninvited labourer left with the work party and slipped away.

Joe put all his evasion facilities and know-how at Pepe's disposal and promised to come up with something to ease the situation at the Poix brothel. What the bordel's Luftwaffe clients didn't know about the voluptuously tall, blonde, heavily made up Madame Irène, who was in her early thirties, was that her fiancé was a French pilot serving with the RAF in England. Irène loved helping evaders, and loved her business, constantly badgering public health officials whenever one of her girls was removed for hospital treatment.

Visiting Dr. Mans's office to dispute the loss of a girl, she demanded:

'You must release her quickly, otherwise I'm going to lose so much money. She gets through seventy a day.'

Now she was seeking Pepe's assistance for a less selfish, more patriotic cause. She wanted to get the group of prison fugitives away from the region.

'I normally use my own evasion line which operated through Péronne, but there's been arrests, so I've got to abandon it for the moment,' she told him. Her Péronne connection had been a British Intelligence agent.

Joe and Pepe found the answer. The bordel four left the house at Poix and the Somme, in stolen uniforms – dressed as Gendarmes.

Briefing them, Joe said:

'If anyone asks, just say you're following up information on a group of prison evaders.'

A police uniform was a handy outfit to be dressed in when trying to escape the police, but on reaching the first town, they encountered an appalling traffic jam. As they were the first Gendarmes to appear, people shouted at them to do something about it. There was no alternative. Two of them stepped into the middle of the road, commenced untangling and directing traffic, and couldn't leave until it was sorted out.

*

Two days after the initial official attack assessment, a more detailed report was forwarded to the authorities in Paris. Repeating some of the information of the February 19 report it added:

Anglo-American aircraft, flying at low altitude, bombed, and their objective appears to have been the prison, which has been completely destroyed. Thirty houses situated in the neighbourhood of this establishment suffered equally severe damage; two apartments partially damaged. In another section, the pavilion of the monastery Saint Victor, which was being used as a hospital for occupation troops, was partially damaged. Two of the attacking planes were shot down following aerial combat.

Up to the present, 77 dead bodies have been dug out of the demolition, and 78 have been hospitalised, many gravely wounded, but all these are prisoners. The personnel of the prison have not been hurt. Nevertheless, these numbers are provisional as the clearing of demolition immediately following the raid has not been completed.

Among officials who have been arrested by the German authorities, and found dead in the courtyard after the bombardment, was Monsieur Gruel, Chief of the Prefect's office, who had been imprisoned since November 11, 1943.' Repeating notification of Vivant's disappearance, the report added:

M. Vivant has been seen safe and sound some time after the bombing.

The authorities have retaken 192 detainees who were imprisoned by the French; 54 prisoners of the German authorities, and 20 women equally arrested by the occupation authorities. The number of escaped prisoners still cannot be precisely determined. Prisoners are being guarded by urban peace corps in an old factory which offers no guarantee against invasion.

Proceedings have been taken against some authorities.

The claim that prison personnel were unharmed, was, of course, totally untrue. It was estimated that 20 Germans were killed at the gaol, and 70 wounded, but no casualties whatsoever were officially admitted. The Divisional Commissioner then updated the bombing aftermath situation.

*Before the bombing*

| | | |
|---|---:|---:|
| French quarters . . . (men) | | 448 |
| French quarters . . . (women) | | 72 |
| | | 520 |
| German quarters (men and women) | | 180 |
| | Total | 700 |

*After bombing*

| | | |
|---|---:|---:|
| Recaptured: | | 182 |
| Held at 52 rue de la République (women) | | 26 |
| German quarters at Dury (women) | | 8 |
| Citadelle (men) | | 48 |
| At the hospital (injured) | | 74 |
| In the care of the Chief Guard | | 20 |
| Killed | | 87 |
| | Total | 445 |

In effect, from 700 persons, 255 are missing.

The above were official statistics, but, according to Gendarme Achille Langlet, an unofficial count he organised whilst imprisoned himself in the gaol produced a very different pre-bombing picture. Whilst confirming the 180 in the German quarters, the so-called criminal quarters, which also housed a considerable number of official and unofficial 'politicals', showed a total of 640 detainees – 120 more than the figure issued by the Divisional Commissioner.

Even more significant and authoritative was a written report from the Prefect of Police of the Somme at the time, stating:

The prison held about 840 civil or political prisoners and 180 locked up by order of the Germans.

Those figures, plainly well in exess of the Divisional Commissioner's figures, placed on record prove the extent of the deliberate clouding of the prison's true population size, and prove that the number of those who actually escaped were unquestionably far more than admitted at the time.

*

'You can camouflage something, but seldom cover it up for long, so the sooner we get them out of the St. Pierre caves, the safer they'll be,' Marceau Laverdure was telling Gendarmerie colleague Edouard Robine, when the telephone on his desk suddenly joined in with the alarm bells ringing in his head.

As he listened to the phone message, he stared at Robine, replaced the receiver, and said:

'It's Enfeld's office – there's an immediate conference. I don't know why, but I think it's the caves.'

Robin threw up his hands.

'Why do you assume that? – It could be anything.'

'Too many are in on it now,' Laverdure insisted with sharp anxiety. 'Someone's bound to talk sometime, and gossip eventually reaches the wrong ears – probably those attached to that traitorous shirtmaker Pieri's head.'

'You're only guessing.'

'We've both made a comfortable living for years from guessing,' Robine said as he left the room.

There was cause to be concerned about Lucien Pieri because Pieri was himself very troubled by the mass escape. He had good reason to be concerned, for many who had got away could exact retribution on his network. Far too many would now have the opportunity to compare arrest circumstances and identify some of his undercover agents, who were working through him with the Gestapo. Treacherous activities could be stopped – by bullets. 'Mouton' collaborators working under cover in the cells as fake 'prisoners' were similarly in danger. As far as the Resistance was concerned, eliminating traitors and 'Moutons' would be simply prevention.

Kommandant Enfeld, German chief at the Amiens Gendarmerie; Braumann from the Gestapo; Milice Chief Pechon; the Kommandant of the Peace Guards Corps whose name Laverdure never could remember; and Kommandant Mullot were at the meeting. Only Mullot wasn't a threat as he was an undercover Resistant operating under Laverdure's direction.

'We suspect the old caves at St. Pierre are being used to hide evaders, so we'll surround them tomorrow,' Enfeld announced.

Laverdure kicked himself for being right at the wrong time.

Enfeld was one of those who positively enjoy war – get drunk on it. War transforms ordinary men into something totally foreign to their natures.

Laverdure's thoughts were jolted to attention on hearing himself directly addressed by Enfeld:

'Lieutenant Laverdure, I want thorough co-ordination between the Wehrmacht, Milice, and Peace Corps,' Enfeld commanded. As main liaison officer between German and French military and civil forces, the efficiency of the raid was Laverdure's responsibility.

'Certainly, Kommandant,' Laverdure barked, in the manner expected of him, and took leave to progress the order.

Robine was still waiting in his office.

Laverdure strode in, closed the door and said:

'Unfortunately, I was right, and the raid is early tomorrow morning. Tell Michel. It's up to you two to get them out fast!'

Michel Dubois and Edouard Robine went to the caves immediately after dusk to break the news. Michel told them:

'You've had time to recover; have fresh warm clothes; new identity papers; even a little money – now it's up to you all to lose yourselves however and wherever you can. And leave nothing behind – not a trace that you've been here.'

'That bastard Hitler! – to think that one man's ego could kill us all,' said stocky tough Resistant Roger Delassus, who had escaped once before from another gaol. 'But he won't defeat us. He thinks he's right about everything and there's something diabolically wrong with a man who thinks he's always right.'

'I'm scared,' confessed ex-bank thief Joseph Metz. Finally confronted with it, he realised how much any task one is afraid of tackling becomes a nightmare.

'It takes a lot of courage for a man to admit he hasn't any,' Delassus said, making Metz feel a lot better.

'In spite of the horrors Hitler and his gang have brought, in spite of imprisonment, the arrest of my whole family and treachery of so many, I'm still optimistic about the world and those in it. We've always known people can become beasts to their fellow men, but there are plenty of good human beings, so I'll stay optimistic,' Delassus added.

The time that the incredible mass of evaders could continue securely hidden and fed in the caves was obviously running out, so it was as well for them to disperse now. Anticipating the necessity of having to evacuate soon, many had already planned intended destinations, and a considerable proportion had arranged to travel in pairs to help each other. Pairs were safest because seeing even three people together was enough to make the Germans suspicious. The thought of being forced to begin their journeys in below-zero weather at night, when almost the only people about were alert patrols, appealed to nobody.

'Well, I'm not roaming the streets nor the countryside tonight, that's for sure,' a slim, medium-height, clean-shaven, distinguished-looking character announced. Phillippe Clement's brown hair was greying at the sides, and he had a violinist's hands.

'I'll tell you what I am going to do, and I would advise most of you to do the same – I'm going to find myself a modest little hotel. We're wearing the right clothes; some of you have acquired empty but suitably impressive cases, and we have brand new identities and papers to go with them. We know hotel lists are checked by the Germans every morning, so just be sure to leave nice and early.'

'He seems to know all the tricks,' someone remarked.

'So he should. He's a professional card sharper, among other things,' said another.

Philippe wasn't the type to win medals for bravery, but was always game to try and talk his way out of trouble, and well-upholstered curvy blonde Florence Valentine liked his approach for their first night away from the caves.

'He's got the right style!' she said approvingly, 'except I'll find myself a client to foot my hotel bill.' Florence's beautiful eyes and deep husky voice had a peculiar appeal, but the loveliest flowers frequently fade the fastest, and it was already obvious that by the time she was forty, she would, as they say, almost certainly spread like a bale of hay after its retaining wires are cut.

'I'd like to get myself a local farmer – they're usually loaded from all the Black Market food they sell,' Florence continued, virtually talking to herself. 'Mind you, most farmers treat us like horses, and always expect to get a bloody good ride.'

For most in the caves, the thought of departure made it one of those occasions when you wondered why you wanted so much to stay in the world. It was marvellous to be free again, but the trick now would be to remain free.

The caves suddenly echoed with 'advisers' offering last-minute counsel to clusters of evaders about to take their chances again. Resistants and criminals exchanged dodges and techniques:

'It often takes one to beat one,' someone said mockingly.

Particular attention was paid to forger Georges Danielou, as much relied on the variety of official papers everyone needed to comply with endless police and rationing regulations, all of which were subject to continuous change.

Use of fictitious identities was an elementary common denominator among 'political criminals' and common criminals.

'If for some reason you need to alter or add to the false papers you already have, there are essential things to remember,' Danielou warned:

'Stick to your real christian name, then you'll be less likely to slip up. But don't forget to add one or two other christian names as a single christian name is rare in France. Whatever you do, don't use a name that could possibly be of Jewish origin.

'Keep to your real date of birth; choose a genuine street from the phone directory or local street guide and preferably a village or area where you know records were destroyed by bombing. Never use Paris or any major city as your birthplace because quick checking is usually simpler in cities.

'Descriptions must be accurate, and take care to use only terms employed in police or mayoral offices. And according to civil service rules, black eyes don't exist. If you can't get the mayor's signature or have it forged, you need an illegible signature with 'p.p.' added. The date must be after 1940 when identity cards became compulsory, and never a Sunday or public holiday as no mayor deals with papers on those days,' Danielou concluded.

Bulletins on the condition of wounded comrades and ex-cellmates had been brought daily to the caves by a messenger, who collected information from the Hospital Nord's doctors and nurses. The courier arrived for the last time as they were preparing to leave.

'Maître Bellemere, who was so incredibly rescued after hours of tunneling, and brought out without apparent serious injury, has died.'

Reading from a scribbled note, the messenger explained:

'He became ill with a toxic syndrome, with hypothermia and anuresis, which are symptoms similar to those found in people who have been severely burned.'

Violette Lambert, queen of the shoplifters, who had provided clothes for so many around her, fingered her rosary, thinking how often life turned out to be a dead-end street. By the time you learned to make the most of it, most of it was gone. In the darkness of the caves, she stared momentarily into the depths of her past years with vague disquiet in her mind.

'What a tragedy life can be,' she said softly, then, after pausing pensively, continued: 'For Bellemere to do all he did, and come through all he did without appearing to be seriously hurt, and then die. Fate was fatal – but that's life.'

The shot-down American pilot, Martin, who organised the caves' survival school, gave his pupils a parting warning:

'I should have told you before that if you're living off the land, never touch deadly nightshade (belladonna). They can be easily recognised by the bright black hue of the berries, and grow tomato-like, half covered by thin short leaves.

'And one more thing – nothing to do with food,' he added abruptly, but smiling – 'Never look back, because someone may be catching up.'

Everyone under fire becomes the brother and sister of whoever is in the same plight.

Normally, the only time retired smash-and-grab specialist Sammy Izard was on the level was when he was sleeping, but this was one occasion when he sincerely meant every word. As they started to move out of the caves he shouted:

'When you're at the end of your rope, that's the moment to tie a knot and hang on.'

All realised that without cover, they would be like animals, moving by instinct alone, but fear could create courage. You can fear for your life so much until you can be afraid no more.

Many sadly said goodbye to each other. War is always rough on goodbyes.

'Don't worry,' exclaimed Father Janin, who had escaped from Raymond Bonpas' cell – 'God is on our side!'

'I don't care whose side He's on,' Sammy Izard replied, 'as long as I'm on His side.'

*

Dozens of transports carrying Gendarmes, Milice, Peace Corps guards, accompanied by Wehrmacht and police staff cars, converged on the St. Pierre district, and hundreds of officers and men quietly took up positions until the caves were completely encircled.

At 4 a.m., heavily armed units raided while others covered all possible exits from the area to stop anyone slipping through. They found no one, nor any indication of the caves having been recently occupied.

Summoning an immediate middle-of-the-night conference of the original five raid planners, Kommandant Enfeld exploded:

'There's a traitor among us!'

'How's that possible?' Kommandant Mullot answered. 'I can guarantee Laverdure.'

'And I can guarantee my men too!' Milice's Pechon said firmly.

'If I say I *know* escaped prisoners – many of them – were there, Laverdure,' Enfeld said significantly, turning to him with a disarming candour which instantly put him on guard, 'wouldn't you agree that *somebody* must have sold the secret of the raid and tipped them off in time?'

'Not necessarily, Kommandant,' Laverdure said, looking straight at him, shrewd enough not to quarrel with an angry man, and by answering calmly, frustrating him more than ever.

'If they *were* there briefly,' he went on, 'they could have gone days ago, realising the best chance of getting out of Amiens would be within twenty-four hours of the bombing when counter-measures would still be gathering strength and therefore not be at their most effective.'

'There's a traitor somewhere – I'm positive!' Enfeld raged on, accusing everyone at the meeting, but anger achieved nothing, despite it being only one letter short of danger.

*

'Mama Beaurin's progressing well – the doctors won't be able to keep the Gestapo away from her much longer,' Maurice Holville's father reported after returning from visiting his son at the Hospital du Nord.

'Then we've got to get her out now,' Maurice said. 'Get one of our nursing staff contacts to tell her what we intend and check whether she feels strong enough for the journey.'

'But with her head bandaged so heavily, she'll be an easy patient to spot in the streets, and you never know with the Milice or Gestapo – they could be stopping *anyone* with bandages,' said Holville senior.

'Then she'll have to be moved at night, when she won't be so visible,' Maurice replied.

This wouldn't be much simpler, because after nine at night German patrols were liable to shoot anyone about, but with the co-operation of sympathetic hospital staff she was smuggled out at night and hidden in a house close to the gaol until well enough to travel to the village of Beaucamp le Vieux. There she was cared for in the Armel family house in which her son Jean first stayed after his escape.

Warden Brasseur also decided it would be safer to discharge himself from hospital. Although suffering intense pain from a back injury, he knew he dared not stretch good fortune too far. At any time, Braumann, or his side-kick Lucienne, were liable to recognise him, so his wife, and fourteen-year-old daughter Yvette, brought a set of civilian clothes and three bicycles to the hospital, and he just walked out.

'There's no alternative,' he told his wife, 'I'd rather go through hell with my back cycling out of Amiens, than find myself going through even greater hell again with Braumann.'

Gaston Brasseur, his wife, and schoolgirl daughter, cycled away from the hospital, heading for his mother's home at Fouencamps, near Boves – well beyond Amiens. It was a long ride, but they couldn't return to their own home. Exhaustion was like a leech drawing blood and strength from his body. Several times, he almost passed out through the excruciating pain in his back, but whenever he reached the boundary of patience and pain, summoning his will, he somehow pedalled on, and out of Amiens.

*

Pierre Bracquart was unable to organise false papers for Elaine Guillemont and himself, so, when after several days she was declared medically fit to travel, his only uncle came from Paris to escort them out of Amiens.

As Principal Controller of the railways, uncle was entitled to an exclusively reserved train compartment wherever he travelled – a useful privilege when anxious to avoid unwelcome curiosity.

Elaine's two black eyes and bandaged head would undoubtedly have attracted attention and enquiries, but uncle arrived in his suitably impressive uniform to instal Elaine and Pierre in his private compartment. The military patrol checking the majority of the train's passengers didn't intrude on the reserved compartment, so Elaine and Pierre travelled in style to Paris, to vanish in the city until able to reappear with new identities.

*

In his personal official report, Le Baube, the collaborationist Prefect of the Somme, accused a high official, the imprisoned Captain André Tempez, and others, of pre-knowledge of the attack. Le Baube's report stated:

The police services and the gendarmeries of my department have carried out active searches with a view to putting their hands on prisoners who profited from the bombing by escaping. In the hour that followed, they arrested 165 prisoners, of which 22 were apprehended by police at Amiens, Péronne, Villers-Bretonneux, and in other localities.

Police security detectives arrested 18 prisoners, 9 during the day, and 9 in the night. Moreover, 56 prisoners who had been imprisoned by the Germans were recaptured by French police. Several of these prisoners were women.

The total of prisoners retaken was 284, and this figure increased unceasingly as various prisoners' homes were known to the police and other services.

I consider that the possibility of bombardment and its consequences were known to M. Melin, in charge of the mission to the regional Préfecture, as he had been forewarned by about 14 hours by the director of the department of passive defence of the Somme.

In other areas, security police concerned with general enquiries were generally alerting regional services, and the Paris gendarmerie was warning all associated departments.

\*

Early morning light was still hanging on to the night's coat tails when Georges Danielou emerged from the cheap little hotel in which he had chosen to spend the evening after evacuating the St. Pierre Caves. Walking along the street, he turned the corner, then stopped and began feeling in his pockets for an item he obviously couldn't find. Appearing to have forgotten something, he immediately headed back to the hotel, noting on the way everyone on both pavements. Re-entering the hotel, he reappeared some five minutes later and, upon satisfying himself that none of the faces previously observed on the street were still around, strode confidently in the direction of Place Parmentier and the floating market which he hoped would drift him, and two of his former cave companions, from the town.

Tuesdays, Thursdays, and Saturdays – Amiens' floating market days – were the best mornings to be out and about in the early hours, because even the Germans shopped then on treelined Place Parmentier, by the river, for fresh vegetables and fruit direct from the famous market gardens of the Somme.

On the three market days, processions of large flat-bottomed boats glided through the three arches of Pont Baraban into the basin-like area alongside Place Parmentier, laden with salads, onions, potatoes, cauliflower, carrots, radishes, and fruits freshly plucked from the Hortillons meadow lands of the Somme's fertile swamp zones. The 'Hortillonages' – a complex of little market gardens bounded by 'rieux' (narrow waterways) – were largely traversed by shallow skiffs. Virtually impossible to security patrol effectively, they were ideal for hiding or getting lost. The many minor tributaries of the great river Somme and much smaller river Ancre, flowing through Albert into the wide marshy valley, provided traditional transport routes for farm produce offered first to wholesalers, from 4 a.m. on the three weekly market days, and to the public from 5.30 a.m.

As a professional forger, Georges was well accustomed to considering the extent to which time factors could benefit him, as well as calculating the probable strength of opposing forces. Considering everything, he assessed road and rail risks, then focused on the region's extensive rivers and canals. The river Somme runs due west to the sea. The original river ran in lazy loops in a valley it had cut for itself in the chalk uplands, but deepened sections had been straightened to form a canal, leaving the original course as a wide marshy area. The Canal de la Somme, linking the small port of St. Valèry-sur-Somme with the Canal de St. Quentin at St. Simon, using the river bed for almost forty-five miles, and an independent channel for about fifty-two miles, carried well-guarded barge consignments of goods such as building and road materials, coal and wood from the north. But Georges was also aware of the important local unguarded traffic in sugar beet – the prime Somme valley product, after general market garden produce. Largely because of navigational difficulties, especially at Amiens, where there are several bridges, main traffic concentrated on the section from Amiens to St. Simon. The entire area's waterway system was based on navigable rivers, forming a link between the waterways of Belgium and those of the Paris basin.

Weighing options, Georges unhesitatingly plumped for waterborne exit from the town. Leaving on a market day vegetable barge was likely to be the best way out. He realised canoe patrols sporadically crossed the river at various points, but river patrols were easier to dodge than roadblocks and land forces. The trick would be convincing an understandably wary market gardener to take them aboard his barge for the outward journey, but Georges was gambling on the persuasiveness and local knowledge of the two Resistance escape mates due to rejoin him at the rendezvous. Both had been saboteurs, and fortunately, as a former market gardener, Roland Avy knew some of the river market farmers. Roland's local knowledge had been the final decisive factor for Georges.

Tall, slender, in his mid-thirties, with neatly combed blonde hair and a thin expressive pock-marked face, Roland Avy's speciality had been breaking armoured vehicles' front axles with small bombs. Having placed a plastic charge, he only had to select a time pencil with a suitable delay, press it into the primer, then activate it. For more ambitious efforts, he sometimes used a couple of kilos of plastic explosive positioned six feet further apart than the wheelbase of the train engine he was to derail.

Towering over Georges and Roland, heavy, built like a bear, Vincent Miller looked ponderous, yet spoke at near machinegun speed. His sensitive fingers knew precisely how to destroy telephone junction boxes swiftly, or exchanges and also how to rearrange cables to cause continuous wrong numbers. Cutting wires, which could too easily be traced and repaired, wasn't enough.

Vincent's lively eyes and fast-changing expressions contradicted his apparent physical cumbersomeness.

Thinking of the two characters he was joining, whom he had first encountered in the caves, even though they had been imprisoned at the same time and same place for months, Georges found himself concluding that under dictatorships, those in gaol are usually superior to those who put them there.

Stopping to look into a shop window to check if he was being followed, watching reflections of passers by in the window, he noticed a couple of civilian-clothed men staring into a nearby shop. Were they Gestapo or Abwehr counter-Intelligence agents playing him along, hoping he would lead them to others?

Striding away, he cut down a side street and slightly quickened pace, but could hear shoes pounding behind drawing nearer until they were on top of him.

'Identity card!' one of them demanded.

Tugging his forged identity card from a pocket, he handed it to them and awaited inevitably questions as it was inspected. While one shone a torch onto the card to study it carefully, the second stepped forward and started frisking him, looking for arms.

'Where are you headed so early – Are you on early work shift?' the frisker asked.

'No, I'm going to Place Parmentier to buy food – It's a Somme market day.'

'Oh, of course!' the card checker exclaimed.

'Early birds get the best quality,' Georges reminded them.

Returning the identity card, they waved him on.

The riverside market was crowded with shoppers – mostly women. Georges observed them all, wondering which were genuine civilians, and which possibly secret police? As he moved among the displays of fruit and vegetables, ostensibly comparing choice and prices, he spotted Roland and Vincent already there, also contemplating goods, and possibilities.

There it was! – the flag – the predetermined signal denoting successful contact achieved. Roland was buying a lettuce and sharing a joke with the seller. He had found a friend. It was time to make motions of purchasing a few things, then move on to the second rendezvous to learn Roland's arrangements.

'We're to return to the market by nine o'clock, when my friend will be packing up for the day,' Roland informed Georges and Vincent as they sat sipping steaming acorn coffee at a café within easy distance of Place Parmentier.

Roland sat with his back to a wall to prevent anyone coming up behind, whilst Vincent kept ears and eyes alert for any Germans, Gestapo, or their Milicien French equivalent, and noted every possible emergency exit, such as windows and the staff entrance to the kitchen. The three continued chattering about nothing in particular for as long as they remained at the table. Keeping silent was liable to attract attention.

As they sat in the café with its rows of neat tables each side, other customers also conversed in low voices, inspecting them at the same time over drinks or plates of food.

When it was about time to depart, Roland quietly confided:

'I've a gut feeling we'll make it together.'

'So have I,' agreed Georges, 'and when we do, I'll put you both in ample funds with cash I've stashed away. It will help keep you and finance fighting the bastards until you're able to link up again with your friends. I love the idea of using some of their own forged banknotes against them.'

Likewise appreciating the thought, Vincent grinned:

'As money's the root of all evil, it'll be nice retribution hurting them with it.

'It isn't the root of evil, you know,' Georges the forger asserted. 'No money is.'

'But it can be a curse,' Roland insisted.

'Well, there's always someone ready to take the curse off you,' Georges countered, as he paid for the coffees.

As the horde of fruit and vegetable barges slowly evacuated Place Parmentier, Roland was aboard one, Vincent on another. Georges was lying flat under empty potato sacks on Vincent's boat, as the farmers felt one visible extra passenger per vessel was the maximum advisable.

Slicing through iced-up tributaries, the market fleet headed back to swamp-land landing stages far beyond the town. At one point, the river section was so frozen that they all had to get out to manhandle the boats, sliding them to an open channel.

The boats' home bases had been the trio's originally intended disembarkation point, but reconsideration deemed it wiser to part company sooner in case enemy security patrols happened to be hovering around the landing stages. Roland's familiarity with the locality and the marshlands was their most valuable asset. He would be their guide.

As the boats scraped against the deep snowdrifts on the riverside, Georges, Roland, and Vincent scrambled up the icy bank and waved silent thanks to the market gardeners as the boats floated on.

Pushing against freezing winds, they repeatedly slipped and fell on treacherous icy paths. When they stepped from the paths they were instantly sucked down to the waist by mud and hung on for life to reeds, grass tufts – anything – until reassured by Roland that they had reached bottom.

Wading almost up to his neck in muck, Georges, fumbling to open his flies, dying to pee, started laughing uncontrollably. Roland and Vincent looked anxiously across, concerned whether the ordeal of moving wearily from swamp to swamp was driving Georges crazy.

'Here we are up to our necks in all this crap, and I'm struggling to get my flies open to do a piss! – What the bloody hell for?' Georges explained almost hysterically as he happily peed his trousers, revelling in the sudden warmth of his own urine as a welcome change from the ice-cold swamp waters.

On reaching firm ground, they rolled themselves over and over in the clean white snow to help remove some of the swamp muck; washed their faces with handfuls of snow; then, breaking off bush branches, used them as clothes brushes to clean themselves up a little more.

Removing boots and socks, they squeezed water from the socks, drained the boots, then put them on again. They were almost too shattered to go on, and for awhile lay on the ground struggling to catch their breath and swearing at everything and anything. Hands and feet were so numb that they practically couldn't feel them anymore. Only by lying down in the snow for a few moments were they able to restore sufficient strength to continue, and to raise circulation they even tried simple physical jerks from time to time – touching toes, jogging on one spot, and swinging arms – anything to stop freezing to death. They needed somewhere dry and warm – fast – to thaw out and rest.

Suddenly digging deep into the snow and earth beneath it, Roland came up with three sugar beets. Cleaning the beets with snow, then sharing them out, he said:

'They'll taste vile, but are full of sugar, and we need all the energy we can get.'

Somehow, they chewed and managed to swallow the raw beets, helping them down by sucking handfuls of snow.

Pressing on, they at last reached a road and signpost. Roland and Vincent instantly speeded ahead at a cracking pace.

'Hey! – Slow down!' shouted Georges, who was exhausted and trailing well behind.

Halting, they turned to gaze sympathetically back at him staggering breathlessly on very wobbly legs.

'Going too fast could make us conspicuous,' Georges gasped. 'How often do you see men in such a hurry to get to work?'

Roland and Vincent laughed, but acknowledged the remark's shrewdness.

Some distance ahead, off the road, they could see the silhouette of a farmhouse and large barn. Cutting diagonally through trees, slipping behind one tree to the next, scurrying, half crouching, to a better vantage point, they were almost on top of the house when Vincent suggested making for the barn.

'In the state we're in, we need more shelter than a freezing barn or we'll die of pneumonia,' said Georges, who had neither the stamina nor the resilience of his tougher companions. I'd rather risk the house.'

Their knock on the front door was answered by a man in his sixties. Without beating about the bush, Georges announced:

'We're on the run from Amiens gaol – can you help us?'

Grinning, the old man beckoned them into the blessed warmth of the living room and its log-burning stove. A grey-haired woman rose from a rocking chair, and without a word automatically poured three cups of piping hot ersatz coffee and handed them bread and cheese.

'You can bed down for the night here, and my wife will make you some soup and a meal.'

'Remove your things and I'll dry them by the fire,' the woman ordered, instantly disappearing into an adjoining room and re-emerging clutching three blankets.

As they stripped and wrapped themselves in the blankets, she draped their frozen mud-caked clothes over the backs of three wooden chairs which she stood before the roaring stove.

It was incredible to be accepted at face value and offered aid without question. They could have been Gestapo decoys, but the old couple were plainly delighted with the opportunity to be of use.

Because they hadn't asked whether the trio were escaping common criminals, Resistants, or whatever, Roland decided to tell them he had forsaken farming to become an explosives saboteur and had been due to be shot for his sabotage activities. He thought knowing this would make them feel they were making a truly valuable contribution to the fight for freedom.

The couple smiled.

'Why are you both smiling?' Roland inquired, somewhat puzzled by the reaction to the admission.

'You're the second in that line we've assisted,' the woman said. 'The hunchback of Notre Dame was the first.'

'The hunchback!' Vincent exclaimed, astonished and suddenly concerned about the couple's mental condition.

329

'Yes – well, he's not a genuine hunchback – he turned himself into one, and thoroughly enjoys polite enemy soldiers sometimes giving up their seats to him in the Metro or buses. He's very careful about that hump – he carries explosives in it.'

Georges, Roland, and Vincent enjoyed the thought too.

'We've sheltered many evaders in our home,' the old man declared proudly. 'We may be a bit decrepit, but we can still hit back in our own way.'

Georges watched the quiet dignified woman as she served supper, and was sure her meek and mild appearance was deceptive. An undercurrent in her manner and words indicated she could be as fierce and courageous as a lion, and the feeling was reinforced by the way she related an incident.

'SS and army units were crawling all over the area chasing four gaol-breakers they were convinced were being hidden by locals,' she explained.

'After turning over farms and the village and finding nothing, the SS collected a dozen children, lined them up in the village square with a tripod machine-gun facing them, and announced they would shoot them all if the escapers weren't surrendered.

'Everyone stood silently in the square expecting the threat to be carried out. Not a child moved or cried.

'Although the SS commanding officer ranted and raved for ages, nobody broke. Faced with mass-murdering the children before an entire village of witnesses, it was the officer's nerve that cracked. He ordered the children's release and then even more intensive house-to-house searches which again produced nothing. None of us – not even children – are afraid of death anymore after that experience.'

Georges found himself contemplating what it would be like to die. We come from nowhere and go back again. There's as much oblivion about our first hours as our last, so it was pointless worrying about death or afterlife because we eventually meet whatever is waiting for us.

Thinking of the thousands of men outside searching for them, and the hundreds of others who had fled the prison, Georges knew what the hunters would do to this wonderful selfless couple if they were discovered in their home. Then, succumbing to the warmth and comfort, his stomach satisfactorily full, his mind drifted from reality, convinced they'd be awakened by Gestapo shaking them. But he slept. He was too tired to care.

They breakfasted well, but as they were about to leave, the old man – a dairy farmer – gave them each a gift: a long white cotton dairy farm coat.

'You won't need them travelling on the roads or through villages, but if you have to cross snow-covered fields, they'll be good camouflage. You'll practically merge with the snow and won't be spotted so easily.'

'Brilliant!' Georges exclaimed with grateful unstinting admiration. The forger – a genius at spotting flaws in anything – couldn't fault the idea. Then, embarrassed by the generosity, he hesitated.

'We can't take such valuable working clothes from you, they must be so hard to come by nowadays.'

'There's plenty more where they came from,' the farmer assured them.

'Plenty?'

'We have a friend who works in a hospital occupied by the Germans. She steals cotton coats for us from the doctors' supplies, so take them – they'll make marvellous cover in this weather. They could even save your lives.'

They did.

Wearing the stark white cotton coats, they crossed safely some seven kilometres of snow-blanketed countryside, passing almost under the noses of several patrols, but were now confronted with the largest yet – a convoy of a dozen German army trucks drawn up at a roadside.

'They could be an outsize anti-evasion unit, or just a military convoy in transit,' commented Vincent. 'Either way, we'd better get out of sight.'

Making effective use of their white coats, they crawled along the snow, skirted around the trucks, and reached a barn where they dug themselves deep into the tops of straw stacks, well away from the barn ladder.

The sound of barking dogs finally identified the convoy.

'They *are* hunters,' Georges whispered, 'which means I'm due for a pee.'

Getting up, he made straight for the barn door and proceeded to unload his bladder against it.

'My God! – What a moment to pick for a pee!' Roland said, his voice rising with anger and exasperation. 'A patrol with dogs almost on top of us and you're pissing against the wind.'

Smiling broadly, continuing to pee, and turning his head, Georges explained with an air of superiority:

'Apart from the urgent necessity of needing to relieve my bursting bladder, your commando, or whatever training, didn't teach you all the dodges, because I'm also pissing with a tactical purpose. In the course of my profession, it was necessary, at times, to break into printing works to steal suitable paper supplies for my forgeries, and whenever I came across a place with a guard dog, I used this trick. My waterworks will make the hounds want to piss too, and that usually puts them off the scent.'

'If you're right, I'll never complain about your weak bladder again,' Roland promised.

Georges dived back into the straw and they waited. As forecast, when the soldiers and dogs arrived, each animal in turn took a hefty sniff at the barn door, cocked up a leg and added to Georges' effort. Sniffing around the barn afterwards, none uttered a bark and they were lugged out by their handlers.

Georges' stock rose considerably higher in Roland and Vincent's estimation after that near miss.

About forty miles south of Paris, travelling through the picturesque woodlands close to the village of La Brosse Monceau, Georges advised his companions:

'We're almost there.'

'Almost where?' inquired Roland.

'Where my money is, and where we can find well organised help,' explained Georges.

Within minutes they were walking into the spacious grounds of the virtually self-supporting seminary of the Order of 'Les Oblates', whose ninety priests – mainly students training for missionary work – grew their own wheat and vegetables, and tended the seminary dairy herd and poultry farm.

'I heard of this place from someone in gaol, so arranged for a friend to stash some of my forged cash here for a fresh start in case I ever managed to escape or get released.'

'A *fresh* start - with forged notes?' Roland said drily.

'At least it's a start,' Georges grinned, 'and we have to begin somewhere. And in any case, most of the stuff was forged by the Germans in concentration camps, so using their own false money to help our getaway and for fighting back is a sweet touch.

'But the seminary's much more than just the hiding place for my money. I'm told all the priests here are ready to help any escapers, and that the Bursar and several other priests even hoard sizeable stocks of arms for evaders, for emergencies.'

The Nazis made a tremendous error in attacking religion, for they made enemies of the Church.

Although the trio requested to see the Father Superior, the Bursar appeared instead.

'My name is Georges Danielou, father. Some months ago a friend left a package here which you kindly agreed to keep in the hope that

I might be able to collect it in person. The three of us have just escaped during the bombing of Amiens gaol, and the package contains money to help finance new lives for us.'

The Bursar invited them in.

'One of my old middlemen brought the cash here,' Georges informed Roland and Vincent. 'No coiner or counterfeiter distributes his own false money. It's supplied to a middleman who spreads it to distributors, which is why we usually manage to stay out of gaol longer than most crooks. I know a coiner who made counterfeit money for thirty years and wasn't copped once. And do you know there even used to be counterfeit money shops in Barcelona and Seville openly selling French and Italian money?'

The seminary's Father Superior knew everything that went on in the place, but carefully distanced himself from subversive activities to avoid compromising his position in the event of enemy investigations.

'Watch your language,' Georges whispered to Vincent as they were led along stone corridors to three single rooms containing beds.

'Sleep here tonight until we finalise arrangements for you,' said the Bursar. Soon after his departure, a housekeeper brought hot vegetable soup with bread and cheese, a brown paper parcel tied with string, and three monks' habits.

'The habits are for your journey tomorrow,' they were simply told without further explanation.

Roland and Vincent gasped when Georges opened the package. It held millions of francs of all denomination, plus a money belt stuffed with a half a million more francs.

As efficiently as a bank clerk, Georges briskly counted notes, methodically licking his finger and thumbs as he flicked through the wads. After dividing the cash into four piles, he handed a quarter to Roland, an equal amount to Vincent, keeping a third share and the money belt for himself. The fourth share he offered the Bursar the following morning.

'It's money forged by the Germans,' he explained. 'Spend it on seminary requirements in places you know are run by German collaborators – they deserve to be paid with fake money manufactured by their Nazi friends.'

'Surely you need it more?' the Bursar insisted, reluctant to accept the thick wad of banknotes.

'I've always had more trouble in taking care of money than getting it, father. Please use it.'

'God bless you, my son,' the Bursar said, pocketing the cash. 'It will help us with the Lord's work.

'If you want to know what God thinks of money, look at some of the people he gives it to,' Georges added.

'It's time to change your clothes,' the Bursar advised, and as soon as they had donned the habits, led them to the chapel.

'Would you kneel and pray with me for guidance for your safe journey?'

Georges couldn't remember when he had last been to church or prayed, but fell to his knees alongside the others, clasped his hands, and was suddenly amazed to find himself asking for God's help. The atmosphere was getting to him.

As the Bursar ushered them back through the stone corridors, he explained:

'You will be passed along an escape route run entirely by a Holy Order, and moved from monastery to monastery across France, accompanied by genuine monks or priests. Even the Gestapo are wary of stripping and searching monks. Two of our priests will guide you on the first stage.'

'What about papers?' Georges inquired.

'You presumably have documents obtained in Amiens?'

'Yes, but they won't match our monks' habits.'

'Hopefully, your holy attire will lessen the risk of you being questioned.'

'Why take unnecessary chances when we can give ourselves extra cover with appropriate papers?'

'But you're due to leave this morning – everything's arranged – so there's no time to obtain new forged documents.'

Georges smiled.

'You forget, father, forgery is my profession and I always believe in forging ahead. If you provide me with inks and some simple equipment, I'll amend our current papers to suit future circumstances. They won't be as good as totally alternative sets, but they'll do.

'There's hardly any ink that can't be removed from paper by some form of bleaching agent. This isn't the problem. You've got to "wash" a document so that little damage is done to the paper, otherwise if injured too much, writing on it can produce a blotting effect, or alterations spotted if light falls obliquely on them. Strong, good quality paper is ideal for forgery. Poor paper is hard to manipulate.'

Georges was clearly enjoying the moment.

'For tracing, father, I need a piece of glass about the size of a sheet

334

of average typing paper, and something with which to fix the glass at a convenient sloping angle for writing, with a strong light beneath it. I also want whatever bleaches you have, several pens, all the inks you stock, and say a little prayer for one of the inks to match.'

The Bursar immediately disappeared to fulfill the requirements.

'I only use tracing as a guide, but never precisely follow it,' Georges continued to expound to the fascinated Roger and Vincent. 'You have to capture some of the spontaneity of the original writing, and that can be a swine to achieve, often being a battle between the forger's own handwriting and the hand he's trying to counterfeit. One of the best tricks is simply adding one letter or cipher, but even this isn't as easy as it sounds.'

The Bursar returned with a cardboard box containing an assortment of items, and they all left Georges alone in his room to concentrate on the task. Less than an hour later, he emerged smiling triumphantly, clutching the altered identity documents.

'I'm a little rusty, but haven't lost my touch! These will see us through very nicely, I think, and we'll worry about substitute sets of papers when we get to wherever we're going.'

As Georges the forger, and Roland and Vincent the saboteurs, strode from the seminary in their monk's attire, the Bursar called after them:

'God be with you!'

# 17 Requiem mass

To demonstrate spectacularly the inhumanity of the Allies and their callous senseless killing of defenceless imprisoned men and women, the authorities ordered a municipal Requiem Mass service at Amiens' Notre Dame Cathedral – the magnificent first cathedral of France – deservedly called the Parthenon of Gothic Architecture.

Amiens is to other Gothic churches what St. Peter's at Rome is to ecclesiastical edifices of Greek architecture. Its roof towers 208 feet from the pavement – ninety-six feet higher than that of St. Paul's Cathedral in London. In the eyes of the Germans, such Gothic grandeur made a perfect setting for a public propaganda condemnation of the British and Americans.

Nothing more beautiful than the cathedral has ever been cut from the trees of the world. To create the great church, oak, as sound as it was centuries ago, had been cut like clay. Under carvers' hands, it had been persuaded to fold like silk, grow like living branches, leap like living flame. Canopy crowning canopy, pinnacle piercing pinnacle, the entire square mass of building, varied by a slightly elevated West tower and slender centrally rising spire, was fashioned to shoot and wreathe itself into an enchanted glade, fuller of leafage than any forest, and fuller of story than any book. No nails were used. Everything was morticed so perfectly that even after centuries, joints are imperceptible. Reinforced with blocks of chalk from Somme cliffs, the beautifully enriched, yet not ostentatiously ornamental sculptured external walls were formed into an alphabet and epitome of faith.

By associating the uplifting of Amiens cathedral with the depths and shock of the gaol attack, France's Nazi conquerors were seeking to manipulate emotions and beliefs just as their predecessors, the Roman conquerors, had done 1642 years previously. In the year of Christ 301, there had come to a hillside of Amiens on the 6th day of the Ides of October, the messenger of a new life named Firmin who, apparently coming from nowhere, was received by the pagan Amienois with surprised welcome. Firmin preached, and baptised so many that, after only forty days, priests of Jupiter and Mercury accused him of 'turning the world upside down,' and the Roman governor had him beheaded.

Called Ambianum by the Romans, being encompassed with water, Amiens was acknowledged by Caesar as a city that vigorously resisted his legions, and Firmin, its first Christian missionary, became its first Saint.

A Roman senator buried Firmin in his own garden, and built a little oratory over the grave. The senator's son constructed a church, dedicated to Our Lady of Martyrs, to replace the oratory and established it as an episcopal seat – the first in France. On that site the building of the cathedral was begun in 1308, completed fourteen years later, and Amiens became the first capital of France.

Near the cathedral site stood the ancient Roman gate of the Twins, where Romulus and Remus were suckled by the wolf, and out of which, one bitter winter's day in the year 332, a Roman soldier, wrapped in his horseman's cloak, rode among people dying of cold in the streets. Just beyond the city gate, the Roman was met by a shivering naked beggar, and seeing no other way to offer him shelter, drew his sword, dividing his cloak in two, and gave the beggar half of it.

The people of Amiens never forget St. Firmin, who gave his life to bring them faith; and in remembering the compassionate warrior who wanted to help a citizen facing death, remembered how many of their countrymen and women, and Allies, were also awaiting death inside the prison before bombers brought them the opportunity of freedom and life. Paying homage to the dead, and the living, throughout the night of 23 February 1944, a guard of honour drawn from the Red Cross stood beside sixty-eight victims' plain wooden coffins in a large school room transformed into a funeral chamber, as hundreds of local inhabitants filed silently by.

In the morning, assisted by firemen and volunteers from Defense Passive services, the Red Cross escort loaded the coffins onto a procession of eight single horse-drawn coal carts waiting outside the school. Platforms had been fixed on the carts so that each cart could carry six or seven coffins.

Normally, mourners followed hearses to church services, but this time the custom was omitted as the sixty-eight corpses from the school were required early at the cathedral for positioning in the transept – the transverse arms extending north and south of the cruciform church – with nineteen other bodies brought from different morgues, including the hospital.

The eighty-seven wooden boxes were borne through the cathedral's great central door with its decorative quatrefoil tracery depicting the Massacre of the Innocents.

Day after day, newspapers had raged, debated, and questioned motives for the attack. The Nazi-intimidated French press heightened public concern with stories and bitter editorials denouncing the bombing.

Beneath the headline: 'The Liberators Have Passed' and referring to the *Mosquito* squadrons as 'Bandits of the air', the opinion column of the *Journal d'Amiens* sarcastically declared:

It is the war, say some wooden-headed Anglophiles.

The war? For what? The Germans? How can destruction and death hasten the end of the war? It is the war, yes, but a savage and barbaric one on the civilian population.

Why the prison? Was this to deliver some kind of disorder? Were the best assistants of England inside? It's possible, but the attackers let loose more than intended. Was it not a distraction?

The liberators have passed. They brought the only freedom they could give.

Under the heading: 'The English as Liberators', another journal, taking a similar line, asked:

What secret reason dictated this order? If the purpose was liberation en masse, the numerous bodies lying covered in blood under the rubble confirm in a tragic way the complete success of such a cynical enterprise.

Cried the newspaper, *Le Progrès de la Somme*:

A prison is not a military objective, and at first sight one does not understand the plane attack against such an establishment. One understands it even less because many detainees in that place were partisans of the people who carried out the raid.

Was the object to create confusion to allow several of the detainees to flee? If this was the aim, it is far from having been reached because most of the people who should have been liberated this way, found death.

The cathedral was filled with the rustle of people.

Laid on the white stone paving of the transept in six rows averaging fifteen per row, the coffins were all alike exept two draped with French flags. The tricolour-decorated coffins held Milice - French Gestapo – killed at the prison. As far as the Germans were concerned, they were the only true patriots.

Each family of mourners had been allotted a reserved place in the cathedral, but hundreds more came, and well before 11 a.m., when the service was to start, the vast 442 feet long church interior was full.

Father Janin and sixteen other uninvited mourners emerged from different cathedral chapels enclosed behind gilded iron palisades – including the chapel of St. John the Baptist, founded in 1642, in which the actual frontal head bone and upper jaw of the Saint is still carefully preserved for annual exposure to the veneration of the faithful on June 24th, the festival of the Saint, and during the novena prayer period.

Five of the uninvited worshippers, coming from the direction of the St. John the baptist chapel, were unobtrusively ushered into the main cathedral and dispersed by Father Janin, who, as soon as he heard of the memorial service arrangements conceived the idea of using the occasion for faciliating departures from the town and suggested it to fellow escapers in the St.Pierre caves.

'We can take brief sanctuary in cathedral chapels; lose ourselves among the Requiem Mass congregation, then try joining the funeral cortèges to get out of Amiens he proposed.

'If we can't stay long enough in the chapels, we may be able to hide in the cathedral vault. It's enormous, half as high again as the roof of Westminster Abbey in London. We'll wait there, or in the chapels, until the right moment – it always takes patience to achieve victory.'

Sammy Izard, the thief, and several other cave dwellers listened and were prepared to follow, acknowledging the advantage of Father Janin's intimacy with cathedral and funeral service procedures.

'Doesn't a man like you have any conscience about using the dead for our selfish ends?' Sammy laughed.

'Not at all – the purpose is a good one, so my conscience is clear,' Father Janin smiled, 'and I can assure you that a man with a clear conscience feels as good as a criminal with no conscience at all.'

When sixteen agreed to make their individual ways to the cathedral and join him, Father Janin suggested they all take a good look at the cathedral front depicting the Apostles and Prophets.

'Thinking about those, particularly in the next few days, could help sustain you,' he advised, specifically referring to the apostles with their special virtues, standing in opposite ranks, and the virtues answering each other:

Courage to Faith
Patience to Hope
Kindness to Charity
Love to Chastity
Obedience to Wisdom
Perseverance to Humility

The sixteen with Father Janin in the cathedral included French-speaking American pilot Martin; baby-faced Black Marketeer Sophie Glasser; Resistant Roger Delassus; ex-bank raider Joseph Metz; shoplifting queen Violette Lambert and her supporting trio, and, of course, Sammy Izard. The women wore head scarves, and Father Janin slipped an ordinary coat over his clerical attire. Only 'politicals' could be spotted by Gestapo.

'I've never been religious,' Sammy whispered to Violette, 'but suddenly here, I feel like praying.'

Ordering a low profile for themselves, the military barred soldiers from attending the Requiem Mass, determined to retain the appearance of total civilian mourning, involvement and condemnation. But civilian-clothed Gestapo, including notorious Braumann, mingled in force with the congregation. Unable to enter, thousands of local people lined the snow-thick streets outside.

Those who didn't already have old black garments in their wardrobes had to settle for black ties, armbands, or black badges, and the women wore black veils over their hats or black head scarves. Shortages made new clothes impossible for the occasion.

As the congregation entered, they saw the altar devoid of relics, as required for Requiem Mass. There were no images of the saints and no flowers. Six candles of unbleached wax stood in plain candlesticks. The altar steps and sanctuary were uncovered, but a black carpet lay on the footpace, and the sedile – the canopied stone seats on the south side of the chancel for the priest, deacon, and subdeacon – were also covered in black.

On the credence table, the chalice had been prepared as usual. As Absolution was to follow the Mass, a black cape and aspersory vessel for sprinkling holy water were ready, and the processional cross placed on its stand near the credence table. Only black vestments would be used, and albs – the surplices with close sleeves worn by priests when celebrating Mass – worn without lace or other ornaments.

The eighty-seven coffins had been placed so that the feet of the bodies were nearest the altar, and six candles of unbleached wax encircled the coffins.

Even the colossal figures of worshipping angels and saints, bending forward at the bases of the lofty majestic solid piers supporting the cathedral's enormous height and oak and chestnut roof, added sentiment and homage to the scene.

Clergy grouped themselves around the coffins, standing not directly before them, but a little to the side to avoid turning their backs on the high altar. Instead of customary name plates, the coffins had cardboard squares stuck on them, bearing the name, if identified, and cemetery in which it was to be buried.

\*

The sisters from the Order of the Bon Secours de Paris, staffing the nearby Poulain Clinic, had already attended morning Mass in their private chapel, and thereafter been preoccupied with their contribution to the funeral for prison victims.

In charge, Mother Superior Marie de la Visitation supervised her own particular funeral arrangements. Hidden gaolbreakers were brought from the clinic's secret vaults beneath the main staircase, fed, and fitted out with suitable clothing.

Sisters Monica, Emanuelle, and Marie Jean Baptiste unwrapped heavily bandaged occupants of some of the private wards and provided them, and the three former 'expectant mothers', with sets of fresh clothes.

Dr. Jean Poulain and his son Pierre were personally in attendance to say farewell to the escapees for whom they had risked their own liberty and lives by offering sanctuary.

Almost immediately upon their arrival at the clinic, individual photographs had been taken of the ex-prisoners. Now, as they were about to leave, Dr. Jean handed each of them false official papers with the essential affixed photograph 'authoritatively' stamped. Always thorough, the Poulains thought of everything.

Surrounded by the devoted sisters, and aware of the Poulains' deeply religious convictions, one of the women escapers, clasping both Dr. Jean's hands to express thanks, added self-consciously:

'You've done so much for us that you make me feel guilty for not having prayed or gone to church since I was a child, and for all the years I've been a thief.'

Looking at the pain and discomfort so clearly exposed in the woman's face, Dr. Jean murmured softly, with a wistful smile:

'Many who don't go to church say they can't because they're not good enough, but people don't worship in church because they're good. The church is a sinner centre. The only difference between sinners on the inside and those outside is that those inside are trying to do something about their sin.'

The clinic's gaol 'patients' still couldn't accept the fact that they were free, and expected to be caught at any moment. Reassuring them, Dr. Jean said comfortingly:

'The massive funeral has answered our prayers in a larger way than we asked for. Do as we advise, and you will soon leave Amiens far behind. Remember – rolling stones gather momentum.'

*

As the hands of the church clock set in the circular stained glass window above the nave called 'The Rose of the Sea', with its dolphins, sea shells, and varied flowers, joined at eleven o'clock, Madame Ponchel, seated at the giant pipe organ just below the clock, sounded the opening notes for the Latin words of the Gregorian chants of the Requiem Mass.

Simply and softly, Madame Ponchel accompanied the choir of 113 men, women and boys in the 32 high stalls and 26 lower stalls behind the stone screen with large central iron gates, and although the Gregorian chants actually required no accompaniment as by their very nature they are self-sufficient, the organ served as restrained background to the light, constantly moving melody and text. The great organ sustained, but never overpowered, the Latin cadences that recalled memories to so many present. The chants engulfed the congregation.

Acolytes carried their lighted candles in procession to and from the altar, and the candles on the credence table, alight through the Mass, wavered uncertainly at times in the cold air.

The silver bells sounded for the Consecration and the Elevation, and the sea of heads bent.

At the close of the Mass, Monseigneur Martin, Bishop of Amiens, wearing only a simple cassock and cloak, ascended to the black-draped pulpit to address the congregation:

'Brothers, once again our city is mourning. A catastrophe has fallen upon her. Never in our cathedral have been gathered so many dead and so many families in tears. How right are the Holy books to warn us that death comes like a thief, and to tell us to be ready for it. This advice had never been so true, nor so well timed.

'Too often, unfortunately, during the first war, I was called to give the last duties to my comrades in arms all lined up in immense trenches. I had a broken heart, yes, but this was the rule of war. They had been fighting, so they had run the risk of battle; but why must this all become more and more inhuman and hit peaceful and defenceless people? So the tragic event of last Friday has provoked intense emotion in the town of Amiens, and throughout Picardy.

'Before giving final benediction to these innocent victims, I give them a supreme farewell. I pray God will grant them the compensation of eternal life – a life in peace after so many afflictions; a life of happiness after so much suffering. Lastly, speaking to the families and friends shedding tears for them I express, in the name of the Church, my deepest compassion. I invite them to find in their faith the courage to carry this heavy cross weighing on their shoulders, and remind them what the poet said:

"You who are crying, come to God because He is crying too." '

Removing vestments, the Celebrant donned the black cape for the Absolution, and as chanters and clergy commenced the text of the Absolution 'Libera me' prayer, the suddenly striking topicality of the ancient words stunned everyone . . .

'Deliver me O Lord, from death everlasting, in that day of doom and terror: When the heavens shaken shall be and likewise earth: While Thou comest to judge the world by fire. Trembling am I, and fearful, until the judgement comes, and Thy sure anger. When the heavens shaken shall be and the earth. Day of doom, day of anger, of calamity and of misery, day momentous and bitter exceedingly. While Thou comest to judge the world by fire. Rest eternal grant to them O Lord: and light perpetual shine upon them.'

The Deacon walked along the right side of the coffins sprinkling them with holy water three times without pausing, sprinkling first the end nearest the altar. Passing along the left side of the coffins, he similarly sprinkled them again three times.

The hour-long service had been a superbly mounted performance, and as it concluded Dr. Odile Regnault, Dr. Mans's Public Health Service and Intelligence network assistant, looked across at her Préfecture chief, Le Baube, resplendent in full uniform to pay public homage to victims of the Allies, and thought – the creature chooses to forget that many of the bodies on the floor are members of the Resistance. Too many of the best never survive to build the future bought with lives.

Red Cross, Defense Passive Corps and other volunteers, carried the coffins from the cathedral through the central door to the accompaniment of the choir's . . .

'Into paradise conducted be thou by Angels: upon thy arrival received be thou by the Martyrs . . .'

Coffins were loaded onto the coal carts standing in the adjoining spacious Place St. Michel, with its statue of Christ holding a cross aloft in the centre of the square.

As Pierre Gruel followed his father's body, he halted an instant beside one of the great stone columns upon which was a tablet inscribed:

'In memory of the Sixth Regiment United States Engineers who gave their lives in defence of Amiens March 1918.'

So many had come from so many lands so many times before to fight for Amiens, and the freedom for which his father had also given his life. Watching the Gestapo's Braumann departing, he recalled his father's battered bruised face that last time he had seen him alive in gaol, and like so many others in the congregation, knew where true responsibility for the tragedy of the eighty-seven coffins lay.

Pierre Gruel's sister requested Gestapo consent for the collection of their father's body after the service. Permission was granted, and a funeral society van took the body to their home, then on to a little cemetery twenty-five kilometres from Amiens, where the Gruel family had a country residence.

Liliane Beaumont and her sister-in-law Madeleine Gandon also asked for permission to bury Dr. Robert Beaumont in his home village. At first, the Gestapo refused, still afraid of some deceit with the body, but when they finally agreed, the contemptible Pieri insisted on opening the coffin to check the corpse. It was the second occasion that it had been reopened to verify that the body was genuinely Robert Beaumont.

Outside the cathedral, as families and friends gathered behind each cart earmarked for specific cemeteries, Father Janin and the sixteen, mainly splitting into two and threes, marshalled alongside different groups of mourners. Nobody asked questions because, as so often happens, many people only meet at funerals or weddings.

The procession of carts moved slowly off along the rue Robert de Lazarches – named after the cathedral's architect. As it passed the Palais de Justice, several men and women slipped from the pavement crowds, further increasing the numbers following the coffins on foot. For protection against the biting cold, many wore scarves around their mouths, but scarves, hats, caps, and berets also camouflaged identities.

Doctors Jean and Pierre Poulain, with sisters of the Poulain clinic opposite the Palais de Justice, watched the sudden reinforcement of the mourning groups, and knew several of their clinic wards and vaults had just satisfactorily discharged 'patients' admitted after the gaol attack. Their charges had joined the mourners to walk out of Amiens.

Turning to his son Pierre, Dr. Jean said:

'To the unbeliever, death is the end, but to the believer, it's the beginning.'

As no cars or transport were permitted for any mourners, the long straggling processions of men, women, and children – from the very old to the very young – trudged ankle-deep through snow for up to an hour to reach cemeteries inside and outside the town, as thousands, paying their respects, lined the roads. All along cortège routes, people stood stiffly silent and stony faced as uncomprehending children huddled into mothers' skirts and faces crowded against window panes of overlooking houses.

Cortèges headed for cemeteries at St. Pierre, St. Acheul and de la Madeleine, within the town boundaries, and Petit St. Jean on the outskirts. Beyond Amiens, they made for Montières, Longpré, and various little villages with their own very personal local cemeteries.

'It's sad that the only way to heaven is in a hearse,' said Sammy Izard to Father Janin, walking beside him.

No one interfered with the procession of mourners – no police or soldiers stopped them to demand identity papers.

Well beyond the town limits, a relieved Father Janin, smiling at Sammy Izard, said:

'I think the men and women in those coffins would appreciate going this way – even in death, still helping the living fight for freedom. They would have liked that.'

*

Sammy Izard had never slept in a cemetery before and thought it would have been a great spot to rest in peace if it hadn't been so cold.

Little more than two miles south-west of Bois des Fourcaux –

'High Wood' to 1914-1918 troops – which formed part of the main German defence line during the first Battle of the Somme, is a narrow ribbon of woodland shaped like a looping caterpillar, known as 'Caterpillar Wood'. In the deep, chalky valley below it, on the road from Albert to Longueval, is the entrance to the square-shaped Caterpillar Valley Cemetery – permanent resting place of 1,584 United Kingdom fighting men, 55 Australians, 125 New Zealanders, 7 South Africans, 1 Southern Rhodesian, with 3,796 unidentified bodies; and temporary resting place of Father Janin, former smash-and-grab specialist Sammy Izard, Resistant Roger Delassus, Intelligence agent Richard Joliot, saboteur Guy Bayard, and ex-bank raider Joseph Metz.

It was orginally a small burial ground containing only 25 graves. After the Armistice, it was enlarged to take over 5,500 originally in other cemeteries or found on Somme battlefields.

Emerging from the convent in the heart of Amiens where they had been hidden by nuns since the prison bombing, Richard Joliot and Guy Bayard mingled with one of the cathedral coal cart cortèges to walk out of the town among a procession of mourners, and found themselves trudging alongside Father Janin, Sammy, Delassus, and Joseph Metz.

Father Janin's extensive knowledge of evasion line links made him automatic leader of the six. For security, it was agreed to travel in pairs. Caterpillar Valley Cemetery was chosen as the initial hideout.

'Cemeteries are valuable rendezvous,' Father Janin advised. 'I've often slept in them, using a marble gravestone scroll as a cushion. They're a bit hard, but at least I've never been disturbed, and found the old custom of sometimes adding photographs of the deceased to graves puts faces on stones and gives me people, not just corpses, to think about. War graveyards of British, Empire, and American forces don't have photos.'

It was down this windswept fertile valley that the caterpillar tracks of tanks first lumbered into action on 15 September 1916.

The cemetery's classically designed stone shelter, with square piers and slender columns, standing amid groups of red horse-chestnut trees sturdy enough to resist the exposed valley's fierce winds, had been Father Janin's suggestion for a first halting and assembly point. The shelter's 'well' roof collects rain, then stores it in sunken tanks for watering the cemetery.

Most war grave cemeteries have shelters or entrance buildings where visitors can rest or consult registers of the dead who lie buried there. Caterpillar Valley Cemetery was so named because when burial grounds come to be given permanent names, the Imperial War Graves Commission kept, where possible, those that the soldiers had used, and the most original belong to three cemeteries which were once alongside Casualty Clearing Stations. The cemeteries are called Bandaghem, Dozinghem, and Mendinghem. (Bandage 'em, Dosing 'em, and Mending 'em were the war-time names of the Casualty Stations.)

'Our target is Bapaume or Arras,' Father Janin announced as soon as all six had arrived at the cemetery.

'I have evasion connections in both places which, unless lines have been broken since my imprisonment, could get us well away. If the Abwehr or Gestapo have destroyed this safe house chain, we'll revert to the basic evasion principle of approaching at dusk any small isolated farm. If we fail to obtain assistance, we keep going towards unoccupied France, repeating the process until we do succeed, then follow instructions without question. A helper may not be in direct contact with an organisation, but would have friends, or friends of friends who are. After checking our bona fides in the Somme or with London, and possibly equipping us with different clothes and papers, arrangements can either be made to establish us elsewhere in the country, or even get us to England by sea, or overland via Spain or Gibraltar.'

'And if none of those angles works out?' Richard Joliot questioned.

'We'll head for Normandy where I know an elderly delightful English Mother Superior whose convent would provide sanctuary, and who I'm confident would ingeniously come up with an alternative escape avenue. You've got to have faith.

'I remember an old peasant I once saw seated alone in the pew of a church. The service was over, so I asked what he was waiting for. The peasant simply replied:

' "I am looking at Him, and He is looking at me."

'That's what I mean by trusting in the Lord. Because God is the only being who doesn't even have to exist to be all powerful, a priest's job is very difficult. We have to create belief in so many extraordinary things.'

Staring at the white outlines of the headstones, Roger Delassus, feeling all time and space enclosed within the hushed grounds, mused:

There's a lot of people in cemeteries who thought the world couldn't get along without them.'

'Personally, I'd rather have nothing to do with death yet,' Sammy ventured.

346

Father Janin looked at the strangely assorted quintet with whom he had joined forces, then across at the Stone of Remembrance with a Lombardy poplar each side, and the great Cross of Sacrifice on the opposite boundary.

Two memorials to common sacrifice mark the cemetery – the tall stone cross set upon an octagonal base and bearing upon its shaft a crusader's sword of bronze; then mounted on three steps, the great altar-like stone carved with the words from the Book of Ecclesiasticus: 'Their names liveth for evermore'. The two monuments have come to be known as the 'Cross of Sacrifice' and 'Stone of Remembrance', the latter being acceptable to all faiths.

'Would you join me in brief prayer before the Cross of Sacrifice for those who fought in the past for freedom, and those who have died for the same cause in this war?'

As one, they moved along the paved terrace to the Cross and stood, heads bowed, as Father Janin spoke.

'An English soldier poet named Alec Waugh, wrote these telling lines of the First World War battlefields from Albert to Bapaume . . .

Lonely and bare and desolate,
Stretches of muddy filtered green.
A silence half articulate
Of all that those dumb eyes have seen.
A battered trench, a tree with boughs
Smutted and black with smoke and fire.
A solitary ruined house,
A crumpled mass of rusty wire.
And scarlet by each ragged fen
Long scattered ranks of poppies lay,
As though the blood of the dead men
Had not been wholly washed away.

After pausing an instant, Father Janin continued:

'Prayer isn't just a lot of words repeated from a book. We may wonder why the world seems to need the unnaturalness of war from time to time to help us accept the natural, but God has reasons for all His actions. Man can only rely on God, if God can rely on man.

'If we think we can live without others we're mistaken, but thinking others cannot live without us, is an even greater mistake.

'The last thing a man wants to do is the last thing he does – die.

'Lord, let us not live to be useless.'

As they walked from the Cross of Sacrifice, Joseph Metz whispered to Sammy:

'By the time we get to the grave, most of us have had plenty of time to prepare for it.'

As they arrived back at the stone shelter, Sammy abruptly stopped.

'Someone's here!' he warned softly. 'We've a visitor, or visitors.'

Metz stood transfixed, mouth open with astonishment. All remained motionless, listening, concentrating.

The sun went cold on Sammy's face. Roger Delassus clenched and unclenched his fist around the handle of a sheath knife he had acquired, as Guy Bayard, lips compressed, brow stern, shot him a piercing look, sensing Roger's surfacing violence. Richard Joliot just pushed his specatacles higher on his nose, while Father Janin crossed himself.

As yet, they only heard sounds, rather than saw movement.

Roger Delassus looked shocked for a moment, then acted with cat-like speed.

'Let me tackle that one alone, and you lot stay here in case there's more,' he insisted, creeping away, his hand now openly gripping the knife.

Sammy shifted uneasily, straining his eyes to follow Delassus, who had already virtually vanished. Metz suddenly jumped, startled by birds arrowing from tree to tree. Closing his eyes, in despair, Metz waited for German voices to cry out, expecting to find rifles pointing at them, at any moment.

Having second thoughts about the knife, Delassus returned it to the sheath, not daring the risk of even a dying warning scream to others from the victim. Strangulation was less likely to shatter the silence.

Almost on top of the shadowy figure which seemed to be bending or hiding between a row of headstones, he leapt for the throat to throttle and stifle any sound. Wrapping his arm around the windpipe, he pressed until the flailing kicking body struggled no more and slumped unconscious, only releasing pressure seconds before he would have choked the life from the girl he had grabbed.

As she dropped to the ground, he assessed she was in her mid-twenties, but wasn't overcome by any sense of guilt at having nearly strangled to death a girl. Why should he? They could be as dangerous as men. The Gestapo used them, so did the despicable Milice. A male or female enemy could be equally vicious, he thought, recalling vividly Braumann's sadistic mistress Lucienne relishing Gestapo torture sessions she witnessed in the prison's interrogation room.

Crouching over the body of the girl he had just throttled, he waited to see if the very brief commotion had drawn the attention of possible companions. When, after long moments, nothing stirred, he lifted the body in his arms and carried her to the shelter.

'A girl!' Father Janin exclaimed, shocked, 'You killed her?'

'No. Simply put her out. And don't start feeling sorry for her – she could be the forward eyes of a patrol – anything. We'll see what we can get out of her when she comes round. Meanwhile, stay alert for others.'

Roger Delassus looked down at the prostrate figure he had almost killed. The cherry red overcoat was open revealing the matching red dress beneath. Her dark brown hair was wrapped in a chignon at the back of her head, and she wore no make-up, although her rosy complexion didn't need any. He noted her long nicely-shaped legs, narrow waist, and fulsome breasts straining against her dress. She was very attractive. It would be a pity if she did prove to be an enemy. If she was, they couldn't afford to let her go and he would definitely have to finish expelling the breath from her pretty young body.

Her eyelids fluttered, then opened, gazing up at the six faces staring down at her. Saying nothing with her lips, she let the bewilderment in her eyes speak for her.

Watching consciousness fully return, and vision clear, Father Janin, solicitous and worried, asked:

'Who are you, and what were you doing in the cemetery?'

When she didn't respond, he persisted:

'Either give us a satisfactory answer, and proof, or you leave us no alternative.'

He didn't spell out 'no alternative'.

Massaging her bruised throat, she finally managed to speak, though every word seemed painful to utter.

'I was visiting my father's grave. I come here regularly.'

'But this cemetery is for British and British Empire soldiers,' Father Janin pointed out, 'and you are definitely French.'

'My father was English, and my mother a local girl. He was killed only weeks before the Armistice.'

Fumbling in her overcoat pocket, she withdrew an identity card and handing it to Father Janin, challenged:

'Come with me to the grave and you will see that my surname and the name on his headstone are the same.'

Suspicious of his reflections but respecting his reflexes, Roger Delassus helped her up. Leaning heavily on the arm that had almost pressed life out of her, she slowly led them all to the spot where she had been attacked, halting before a gravestone.

The identity card surname and that on the stone were identical.

Roger's nails cut so deeply into the flesh of his palm that he had to clench his fists with the terrible tension he felt, but his bitterness against himself was unjustified.

'I'm sorry,' he apologised.

Seeing the remorse on the faces surrounding her, she said consolingly:

'Please – I understand. If you are Resistants, or evaders, you had no option. You couldn't take chances. I'm a Retriever myself, so I really do understand.'

'You're a *Retriever*!' Father Janin exclaimed.

'What's that?' Sammy asked.

'Retrievers are women evasion line assistants who help guide evaders to safe houses or pick-up points,' Father Janin said excitedly.

'If you're local, Mademoiselle . . .'

'Call me Claire,' she interposed.

'Then maybe you connect with houses in Bapaume and Arras, which were our destination, and could make contact on our behalf. All of us escaped during the bombing of Amiens gaol.'

'You're from the prison!' she said quickly, instantly understanding so much more.

'I can lead you to a place close by where they'll feed you and you can stay briefly until I reach our Bapaume friends.'

All suspicions gone, they were ready to trust their freedom to her.

'I must warn you, though – before you throttle me again,' she laughed, her dark eyes looking straight into Roger's. The farmhouse we're first heading for is also a German soldiers' billet, so follow me in pairs, and if after I knock at the door I remove my beret before entering, it means there are soldiers about. Stay outside, wait for me, and I'll only be a few minutes.

'There are patrols everywhere, but they're so busy searching houses that they're taking scant notice of ordinary pedestrians passing them in the streets.'

'There's nothing safer than being bloody ordinary,' commented Sammy, who was anxious to get going as his stomach was already screaming for food.

When the farmhouse front door opened and Claire's scarlet beret remained on her head, the six moved swiftly forward, entered the house, and were immediately led upstairs by the farmer's wife.

'Stay very quiet and don't put a foot outside this room unless I say you can,' she warned. 'I'll bring something to eat and hot coffee, but I'm also shortly due to feed the dozen soldiers billeted on us.

Fortunately, we get extra food rations because of them. And don't worry – they won't come up. They'll feed their faces and go. Hopefully, Claire will be back soon with news, then you can move on to somewhere safer.'

A military truck drew up outside, they heard raised voices of soldiers descending from the truck, then the clump of their boots in the house. Soon afterwards, as they listened to them chattering in German, noisily stuffing themselves in the kitchen, they silently did likewise, happily tucking into bread, cheese, pâté, and coffee.

The soldiers left, and Claire returned.

'Our Bapaume friends are ready for you,' she informed Father Janin. 'You'll be split between three houses until we can arrange the next stage of your journey. All the houses will be using the flower pot signal.'

'Flower pots?' Roger questioned.

As he returned Claire's smile, he was conscious of a soothing atmosphere about her.

'Housewives hosting evaders sometimes place a flower pot on a small window table to indicate everything's clear to a caller. If the pot isn't there, we know the house is under surveillance or being searched.'

Claire departed first, arm in arm with Roger as though he were her boyfriend. Roger didn't object.

Following a brief distance behind with Father Janin, Sammy studied the backs of Claire and Roger, and reminisced:

'Women never brought me luck, father. If all you go for is big brown eyes and a luscious shape, you deserve all you get, and may Heaven help you!'

Father Janin laughed.

'I should think right now, with his arm around the girl he almost destroyed with his big hands, Roger is feeling very grateful for Heaven's help.'

'You've got a point there, father,' Sammy grinned.

Whenever a patrol approached, Sammy's heart pounded and he desperately felt in need of a drink of water.

Claire and Roger were stopped once, but satisfied the soldiers with their papers.

Father Janin and Sammy were suddenly aware that Richard Joliot, Guy Bayard and Joseph Metz were passing them. As they did so, without turning his head in their direction, Joliot said:

'There are too many patrols for our liking. There's a good cross-country cut from here that can keep us off the roads almost to Bapaume, so we're taking it. We'll move up and let Roger and

Claire know what we're doing, and you can follow us.'

Quickening pace, they overtook Claire and Roger, repeating the message then moving ahead.

Not having been in the heavy militarised Pas de Calais for months, they were unaware how much had changed since their imprisonment. The build-up of missile launching sites, with protective fortifications, had been massive, and all manner of invasion defences were also under ceaseless construction or reconstruction.

Even though a local girl, Claire was equally unfamiliar with secret countryside alterations, as it was too dangerous and conspicuous for a lone girl to traverse largely uninhabited or forbidden areas.

Joliot, Bayard, and Metz were well in front when they froze as a loudspeaker-amplified German voice commanded:

'Halt! – Halt!'

Roger pushed Claire to the ground, lying flat beside her, and Father Janin and Sammy followed their example, watching Juliot, Bayard, and Metz swivelling about trying to locate forces apparently encircling them, although there wasn't a soldier in sight. The silence was again shattered by the blaring:

'Halt! – Halt!'

When the threatened three chose to run for it, the invisible enemy struck – by remote control.

Sheets of flame shot towards them, and they found themselves running the gauntlet of strategically placed automatic flame throwers that could shrivel a target to nothing from sixty-five yards.

They had accidentally walked into a newly fortified zone with remotely operated batteries of flame throwers installed as anti-invasion traps. Wherever the trio scurried, five to ten second bursts of blazing jets roared into life, playing with them. Suddenly they saw Richard Joliot defiantly gesturing a two fingered V for Victory sign and heard him distantly but distinctly shouting –

'May Hitler rot in hell!'

It was the last sound he made. A devastating battery of fiery bursts totally enveloped him, and when the flames died, Richard, Guy Bayard, and Joseph Metz were all no more – burnt to cinders. It was their Armageddon.

'Dear God in Heaven – Why?' Father Janin agonisingly cried, stunned by the horror of the spectacle, his normally gentle face turning steely. Tears burned, then flooded Sammy's eyes. He had been taught prayers as a child but hadn't mouthed the words since. Now they sprang to his lips.

Aghast, Roger protectively clutched shocked Claire, who closed her eyes, but when everything started whirling in her mind, opened them again. This wasn't a moment to faint.

Crawling slowly backwards, the surviving four evacuated the death zone, preferring to face roads and patrols than uncertain fortified fields and woodlands. Drained and weak, they began to half walk, half jog away, stopping after a while to catch breath, then alternately walking and running. Despite the intense cold, all were sweating and trembling, and, as what they had just witnessed sank in, they felt even more sickened, and overwhelmed by the tragedy.

Flower pot 'All Clears' were awaiting them in Bapaume safe house downstairs windows, but now there were only three to hide.

\*

Victor Pasteau and Freddie had hardly been more than a few hours in the German army uniforms provided by Louise, the brothel chambermaid, when they decided they were due for promotion.

'We'd get a lot further as officers,' Freddie suggested. 'No matter how strict the orders, ordinary ranks are more scared of challenging officers.'

Marching boldly into a German camp, they stole two officers' uniforms, greatcoats, and hats. After quickly changing, they made for the exit, smartly returning the salute of a sentry snapping to attention as they marched out again.

'That's better!' Freddie said approvingly.

Being blatant would be the best defence, and Freddie knew precisely where they were headed.

'If you've got to go wrong, then do it with confidence – that's my creed,' he quipped.

They almost saluted their arms off acknowledging soldiers in passing armoured vehicles and on foot.

'I'm not so sure about this officer stuff – it's too much like hard work and my arm's already aching,' Victor complained.

Smiling indulgently, Freddie said:

'You can rest it at our next stop – not too far from here. There we can locate suitable evasion connections to get us completely away from the Somme. Our uniforms could create a slight problem – I hope they don't frighten the pants off my friends or make them trigger happy before they have the chance to recognise me.'

'Recognise you?'

Victor looked at him questioningly.

'Yes. I've been there before.'

With ever increasing curiosity, Victor puzzled more and more about his companion, but was thankful to be partnering him.

Passing a barbed wire enclosed field, they spotted mechanics, servicing tanks and armoured vehicles.

'My feet are killing me, so how about stealing a tank, or anything with wheels?' Victor proposed.

The thought appealed.

'I'd love to try a Tiger tank,' Freddie enthused.

It wasn't worth straining their officers' uniform luck too far and attempting openly to flout the servicing park's sentry, who kept patrolling within a few feet of where they were lying. Staying absolutely still, they avoided hurried movements for fear of being overheard.

As it was almost dusk and mechanics were quitting for the night, Freddie coolly crept towards the tanks while Victor, holding his breath, already regretted impulsively making the suggestion.

Lying flat on his stomach, arms stretched full length, Freddie inched his body under the barbed wire. It took ages, and in spite of care, barbs ripped his uniform and into his flesh. Wriggling on, he suddenly felt his right ankle gripped. An army patrol dog's teeth were grasping him firmly without actually biting. He struggled to free himself, but the dog wouldn't let go.

Victor looked anxiously at the nearby sentry. As yet, he'd heard nothing. Any second, Victor expected the animal to start growling, barking, drawing attention. He felt the muscles of his chest tightening.

Turning on his side, searching for anything that might make a useful equaliser weapon, he spotted a hefty lump of wood, probably kept handy for levering stuck vehicle wheels out of mud. Although doubting whether he had the brute strength to wield it, he snatched at it.

The guard lowered his rifle an instant and that was long enough. There wasn't time for hesitation or doubts. Jerking up abruptly, Victor jumped him, smashing the lump of wood on to his skull, knocking him unconscious.

The effort of the attack left him almost as wrecked as his victim. His ears were ringing, eyes couldn't focus properly, neck was stiff. He was utterly spent – but satisfied that, despite not being the physical type, he had contributed his bit and proven you should always do the thing you think you can't do. Nobody knows what they are capable of until they try – you can do anything you have to, Victor thought, congratulating himself as he stood panting over the sentry lying at his feet. Mopping sweat from his brow with his coat sleeve, he breathed deeply, sucking in new energy.

Still fighting the tenacious hound, Freddie, noticing a tree branch on the ground beside him, grabbed it, shoved it between the dog's jaws, then ramming the branch right down its throat, choked it to death.

With the sentry out of action, Freddie crawled on his stomach across a hundred or so metres of totally exposed ground to the tanks, in full view of anyone else who might appear. Climbing into a Tiger, he studied the controls, switched on without starting the engine, observed the fuel gauge registering empty, and clambered out again.

Returning to Victor he advised:

'I could handle the tank, but it isn't worth risking starting the engine of a tank or any other vehicle here because, like the one I just looked at, the fuel tanks could have been emptied, or practically dried out for servicing, so your feet will have to hold out a bit longer. I only wish we had some plastic explosive and fuses to blow the lot up. Tigers are one of the finest armoured weapons they've got. The best points for putting them out of action are the side of the hull, the bogies, the rear, and the soft underbelly. You can't take the front because the armour there's a foot thick, so shots at it either ricochet or stick. Only another tank, or well placed plastic explosive can do it.

'By the way, you made a good job of that sentry.'

'When it's them or us and down to self preservation, it's amazing the extra strength you suddenly find in yourself,' Victor said casually, feeling very pleased with himself.

As they pushed on in the failing light, from time to time they saw the glow of sentries' cigarettes, though the soldiers themselves were usually swallowed by shadows. One sentry seemed on the point of asking for passes, but clearly thought better of it. Freddie wasn't over worried by camps they might have to get past, because at many places guards patrolled in floodlight circles which, in fact, made it more difficult to sight anyone beyond the illumination patches.

At one stage noisy motor engines hit their eardrums like sound shock waves, as lorry loads of soldiers appeared on the road. Not wanting to put their now somewhat dilapidated looking uniforms to the test, they hurled themselves into roadside bushes. Lying there, they watched the passing convoy, stuffed with soldiers gripping sub-machine guns or rifles with fixed bayonets. It was almost certainly an escaper-hunting unit.

When they finally knocked at a house door, it was opened cautiously, then fully by a freckle-faced thickset character with a boxer's battered nose who, reaching slowly for a cigarette perched behind his ear, and sticking it between his lips, demanded:

'What do you want?'

'We would like to know whether you agree that Germans either lick your boots or shove their naked backsides in your face?'

Victor was almost as startled by the question as freckle face, whose eyes opened wide. Flinging his arms around Freddie he cried:

'You bastard! – Where the hell have you been?'

'In gaol,' Freddie replied, and roared with laughter.

Victor felt as if he was intruding into a family reunion as he followed into the house. There was a Cocker spaniel asleep in a puddle of ears in front of a roaring fire, and a trim, pretty teenage girl in a pastel-green peasant-style dress. Instantly recognising Freddie, she hurled herself at him in a frenzy of virtually non-stop hugging, kissing, and weeping.

'Why the tears, Catherine?' he chided.

'Oh, she cries for the slightest reason,' smiled freckle face, 'but those tears of hers have more hidden power in them than any waterfall.'

In their excitement, nobody knew where to start the endless questions needing answers.

'We notified London weeks ago that you had to be presumed dead.'

'Well you were close, Alain,' Freddie said quietly. 'I would have been dead in days if the RAF hadn't bombed the prison.'

'So you were in that lot.'

'Yes, and oh, I'm sorry – this is my friend Victor who was responsible for loads of people getting out, and staying out. He's been a great help.'

'Were you in for your Resistance work, Victor?' Catherine inquired.

'No, for thieving.'

Freddie grinned.

'He'll take anything, except a hint, but he's earned honourable spurs now.'

The compliment paid was plainly appreciated by Victor, even though he couldn't cash it.

'We need a fast route out of northern France and fresh clothes, so make the connection,' Freddie said.

'What about papers?'

'We've still got false civilian sets we can use. And by the way, I'd better reclaim the piece I deposited with you.'

Alain disappeared upstairs, returning within minutes, to hand a gun to Freddie. Noting the surprise on Victor's face, Freddie said:

356

'It's a .32 Colt automatic pistol – a great weapon, and my favourite. I suppose you've never seen one before?'

'No. Never in this country.'

'You can't even get them in England. They're not official issue, although I brought this one with me from London.'

'How did you get it?'

'An American liaison officer cabled Washington to ask the Mayor of Chicago to appeal to their gangsters for .32 Colt donations for the war, and he got three hundred!'

'So you've got patriotic crooks too,' Victor grinned. 'But what was all that guff at the front door when we arrived about boots and backsides?'

'Oh, that!' Freddie responded. 'Alain and I have our own personal recognition code phrases. That choice one was based on one of Winston Churchill's cracks. I could have been disguised as Hitler and Alain would have known it was me.'

Catherine, who was the woman of the house – her mother died at the outbreak of the war – had efficiently kept home for her father since a schoolgirl. In next to no time, she whipped up an excellent meal for the visitors.

'Anyone who can make food as tasty as this from what's available nowadays, would be a fabulous cook in less restricted times. I ought to marry you, Catherine,' Freddie laughed.

Blushing, but staring straight into his eyes, she said gently:

'I'm willing.'

'Let's get the war behind us first,' Alain smiled.

Discarding the uniforms, they switched back to civilian clothes and didn't budge from the house for two days while arrangements were made.

'We have to satisfy evasion line people that you're genuine,' Alain explained to Victor who was anxious to get going.

'We can't ruin our chances for a centime's-worth of impatience,' Freddie cautioned.

'How do you people know who is genuine?' Victor asked.

'Lots of ways,' Alain explained. 'For example, London supplies a list of questions by which we're able to tell a real Allied airman from a fake enemy-planted one. Airmen are supposed only to give their name, rank, and number, but couldn't refuse to tell us their height or weight. An Englishman will reply without hesitation, but a German will start struggling to convert his weight into stones and pounds.'

Seeing the Cocker spaniel scratching at the door, Catherine crossed to open it.

'Liberty wants to do her business,' she smiled, patting the dog. 'She's a very clean girl.'

'The dog's name is Liberté?' Victor queried.

'Yes, and spelled English style, or the French Liberté, it means the same,' Catherine explained. 'It was Freddie's idea to call her that as it gives us a great excuse for being able to walk the streets shouting Liberty! – without getting arrested for using the word.'

When she had taken the dog out, Victor remarked appreciatively to Alain:

'You're very fortunate to have such a wonderful daughter. She's delightful – like a lovely delicate rose.'

'Not so delicate!' Freddie laughed. 'I've been in action with her and seen how she disposes of SS troops with a tommy gun.'

Like most pleasures, it ended all too quickly. When it was time for 'Au revoir', Alain and Catherine in turn warmly embraced Freddie without speaking. Catherine's embrace was the longest, and as they released each other, Freddie kissed her on the forehead.

Shaking hands with Victor, they wished him 'Safe journey', and like rolling stones gathering momentum, Victor and Freddie moved on – this time by bicycle, which pleased Victor's feet.

Cycling by day to avoid the greater risk of being spotted at night, they still couldn't accept the fact of their freedom and expected to be caught at any moment. They had their cover stories ready and were going well when an armoured scout car appeared over a hill heading straight for them, and coming fast.

'It might be a patrol, or simply a military transport,' Freddie shouted to Victor pedalling alongside. Whatever it was, they couldn't switch directions and had to continue towards the oncoming vehicle.

When it halted commandingly in the centre of the road, a little ahead, they braked their bicycles and dismounted. Slowly they wheeled their bikes towards the two soldiers who had got out of the car and were waiting for them.

'Papers!'

At the expected demand, they tugged forged identity cards and 'Ausweis' travel permit papers from their pockets. As one soldier studied these, the other stepped up to Victor and began frisking him, looking for arms.

This was it. The .32 Colt inside Freddie's coat, and the ammunition, were all they needed. Tightly gripping the pistol in his pocket, he eased the safety catch.

As the frisker came to him, Freddie jokingly commented:

'These body searches always make me feel like a Chicago gangster being frisked for his Colt gun.'

Freddie caught the look in Victor's eyes. He'd got the message.

Turning to the soldier still preoccupied with their papers, Victor tensed.

'Unbutton your coat, then hands high!' the frisker barked.

Freddie responded by pumping three bullets through his coat pocket point blank into the frisker's stomach.

With every action having its reaction, the sound of the first shot was the starter pistol signal that launched Victor at the paper-examining soldier. Hitting him on the chin with a straight left, an uppercut to the temple, he followed with a piledriver punch into the solar plexus which put him down. For good measure, Freddie clubbed him with the pistol butt,

'Come on!' he yelled. 'There could be more.'

There were. Military trucks were already tearing down the hill as they pedalled furiously back the way they had come. The shots must have been heard, and the scout car and bodies would spell out the rest.

Victor felt a knot in his gut.

'Let's make for the cover of the woodland ahead and dump the bikes because they'll have to go on foot in there too,' Freddie ordered.

Abandoning the bicycles, they ran into the woodland traveling as fast as undergrowth allowed. Welcoming the giant shadows cast by trees, they were suddenly conscious how noisy a woodland could be – creaking branches, wind howling through trees, rustling leaves. But it got a whole lot noisier when machine-guns started spewing bullets, exploding snow, earth, and air all around them. Zig-zagging to reduce the chance of being hit, they sped on, half crouching, positive they couldn't actually be seen. The hunters, knowing they were in there, somewhere, had obviously decided to shoot at everything. It sounded like a couple of dozen men advancing, firing, and cursing.

'Victor! – where are you?' Freddie shouted, surprised to suddenly find his companion had disappeared.

'Here!' came the reply from a deep hollow into which Victor had stumbled. Momentarily he considered remaining right where he had fallen in the faint hope that the enemy might miss him. It was one thing to lie in a hollow letting bullets fly overhead, but another risking standing up and getting a slug in your belly. Orange flashing grenades exploding around them changed his mind.

Intermittently, the streams of machine-gun bullets were replaced by jarring cracks of heavy rifle fire also trying to cut them down. Ignoring the hail of ammunition whiplashing them, they rushed on, ran a fair distance, then stopped and looked back. Firing several rounds at dark shapes he could just about discern moving forward, Freddie looked satisfied when a cry indicated that one of his shots had found a mark.

'Harassing shots will force them to keep their heads down so that they won't be able to sight their guns,' Freddie said. 'It'll give them something to think about and slow them a little.'

Pushing on, ignoring branches viciously stabbing at their faces, they realised the situation had to change soon, although change didn't necessarily mean for the better.

Steady streams of tracer bullets flashed like fireflies through the shadows of the woods, then mortars opened up, crunching down too close for comfort, plastering trees and bushes. They were throwing the lot at them, but all that mattered was getting through.

Questions whirled like sparks in Freddie's mind. They had no clear awareness of direction. Then something punched him in the shoulder. He felt no pain, just a numbness, and knew he'd been hit. Blood from the shoulder wound was already soaking his shirt.

'I've copped a bullet – not seriously,' he calmly informed Victor, who was immediately crestfallen. 'Knot a handkerchief tightly around my left arm.'

Victor gulped and did it. Freddie's hand went cold due to the impeded circulation, but the bleeding was controlled. There wasn't time to check the extent of the muscle damage.

Coming across narrow cart tracks, they followed them and emerged into dazzling daylight on an open hillside to find, of all things, a group of laughing schoolboys, totally oblivious of the woodland battle, enjoying winter sports with toboggans.

Most of the toboggans were crude home-made types fashioned from boxes, with wooden runners with metal strips along the edges. Riders either sat feet forward, holding a rope or strap fixed to the front, or lay face downwards, steering by digging one foot in the snow. But Freddie, who had experienced the famous mile-long ice-covered Swiss Cresta Run track, with its 450-feet fall and share of sharp corners, immediately noted that two of the toboggans were very professional-looking jobs with grooved steel runners about eighteen inches apart and four feet long, fixed to a platform with a sliding seat. On these, tobogganers could lie face down on the seat, which slid forward while going straight, and slid back to transfer weight to the rear when taking a corner, forcing the front part round curves.

'We're going to borrow a couple of toboggans,' he announced to Victor – 'one for you, and one for me.'

Victor gaped at him, mouth open, wagging his head from side to side, unable to suspend disbelief.

'Are you kidding?' he bawled. '*Me* – on a *toboggan*?'

Compressing his lips and replying firmly, Freddie insisted stubbornly:

'Make the choice now! – Risk breaking your neck on a toboggan, or wait for that lot to burst out of the woodland and shoot you down. After what we did to their kamerads they're unlikely to take us prisoners.'

Groaning, but recognising the simple truth, Victor helplessly accepted the situation.

'Tell me what to do,' he pleaded.

Briskly expounding fundamental tobogganing facts, Freddie pointed to a main road at the foot of the slope.

'That's our target. We'll be well beyond firing range, and the patrol are now a long way from their transports, so they'll be less mobile than we are.'

'Where do we go when we get down there?' Victor asked despondently.

'Let's get there first and worry about that afterwards.'

He was sorry for poor Victor, understandably terrified at the thought of manoeuvring a toboggan, but there was no other way. They didn't have crash helmets, padded clothing or the spiked boots to help steering and braking – any safety paraphernalia – but this wasn't St. Moritz winter sports, and the only prize at the end of the run was possibly saving their own lives.

Freddie was already talking to the boys with the super toboggans.

'Can we borrow them for one run? – We're escaping from a patrol who'll be coming through those woods any moment now. If they ask, just say we stole your toboggans.'

Unhesitatingly, the boys agreed.

Settling Victor face down on to a toboggan, Freddie then mounted his, and the boys gave them both a strong push.

He who hesitates is pushed, Victor thought.

Feeling suddenly older than his arteries, he hurtled at ever-increasing speed down the steep slope until, surprisingly, the exhilaration of the ride got him. Unable to restrain the pulse of excitement in his chest, he found himself laughing and actually enjoying it. Life was never anything to laugh at, unless you could laugh at trouble.

Hearing delighted shrieks of kids behind him – they considered it a great lark – he kept right on laughing until he saw something at the foot of the slope which wiped the smile off his face – two motorcycle patrol Gendarmes standing beside their machines, watching the toboggans streaking towards them.

They'd had it! He felt utter despair, and the sight of the police filled Freddie with bitterness too. For the first time he was aware of the pain in his injured shoulder. There would be no chance to draw the Colt and counter-attack. The Gendarmes would be on him the instant the toboggan slewed to a stop.

Slithering on, braking from time to time with his foot, Victor swept past the Gendarmes and vanished completely into a snow-drift. By the time he'd dug himself out, he was confronted by two grinning armed policemen, with Freddie already standing quietly beside them. It was over, he thought. Then, confused, he noticed with curiosity that Freddie hadn't as yet been handcuffed.

'Quickly! – Get on the pillion behind me!' one of the Gendarmes ordered.

'Where are you taking us?' Victor asked dejectedly.

'To where we were going in the first place,' Freddie replied, smiling broadly. 'I told them what we're running from, and they're giving us a lift. We're going to make it after all – but with a police escort!'

Staring at him in astonishment, feeling as if he had just been reprieved from the guillotine, Victor was elated with the news, and with discovering that he could play his part in spite of his fears.

Freddie smiled, then laughed aloud.

Mounting the pillion seats, clutching the Gendarmes tightly around the waist, the noise of the starter pedals being kicked and engines roaring were the sweetest music they'd heard in years. As they tore along the road, the German patrol emerged from the woodland.

Agreeing it would be imprudent to be delivered by police to the very doorstep they wanted, they dismounted on the outskirts of their destination village, and thanked the Gendarmes.

If people stopped to think more, they would thank more, Freddie told himself.

After walking only a brief distance, they entered the lobby of a little hotel.

'The two guests we've been expecting have just arrived, Madeleine,' Joe Balfe called out to his wife.

*

The lorry that picked them up was stacked with sacks of potatoes.

'Climb over the sacks and hide behind them,' the driver

instructed Victor and Freddie. 'You'll find you've got company.'

As they clambered over the sacks, a voice said:

'Welcome to the club!'

Amazed, Victor cried:

'Sammy!'

Camouflaged by the mounds of potato sacks were Sammy Izard, Father Janin, still in his priest's garb, Roger Delassus, and five American airmen whom Freddie greeted like long lost brothers, although they had never met before.

Neither Victor nor Freddie had ever seen Father Janin or Roger in the gaol, but Sammy and Victor had been acquainted since happier days in Paris.

Two of the aircrew had also been housed in Hornoy by Joe Balfe, who arranged daylight collection of evaders from hiding places, deeming it wisest to move them by day and observe curfew at night.

'I don't know what we're really doing among this bunch of heroes,' Sammy murmured to Victor, 'but they say I've earned freedom and deserve a second chance, mainly for my efforts in the St. Pierre caves.'

At night – especially at night – Victor and Freddie had talked of the future, recognising that what the future has in store largely depends on what we place in store for it.

'Don't worry,' Freddie said confidently. 'We'll adapt your talents somehow to honest employment, wherever we end up. The lives you saved by making prison skeleton keys, and the destruction of gaol and Gestapo records, entitle you to a new beginning.'

The greatest torment in life is not knowing what you want out of it, but for the first time Victor Pasteau knew he wanted to try starting over again. Realising our limited years makes them more precious.

'I'm sad quitting France, but not sorry to be leaving the Nazis,' Roger Delassus said as the truck left main roads and commenced jolting and jarring across more obscure tracks. They were obviously nearing the final stage.

'The sun wasn't created for creatures such as the Nazis,' Father Janin commented quietly, with unaccustomed hatred in his voice. 'Might doesn't make right, but unfortunately, it never gives up trying. Millions of people forget the basic truth that every human being gets his fundamental rights from God, not from the State.'

More 'Parcels' or 'Bodies,' as they were called by escape line personnel, joined them when at last they reached the rendezvous point. They were an assortment of escapers and evaders. Strictly speaking, men and women on the run were officially classified into two categories. Escapers were those who had been in enemy hands, whilst evaders hadn't.

Two American pilots arrived on bicycles, guided by an eighteen-year-old girl.

The pathway to the mine-free beach was steep as they proceeded single file. In accordance with orders, they all lay flat as they hit the sand, eyes scanning the darkness of the sea for Morse signals from the rescue ship.

There was still imminent danger of discovery or a beach raid, for it was known that the Abwehr's military counter-espionage service had recently revised policy. They'd stopped arresting everyone who helped Allied airmen, having found it better to keep an eye on evasion lines they knew, rather than be confronted with locating replacement lines employing different methods.

Britain's MI9 and America's MISX divisions fully integrated staff to co-ordinate and carry out rescue functions, although Joe Balfe also reported and acted individually for both departments.

The Morse letter 'B' was flashed with a masked torch every two minutes from a cliff position, whilst a blue light was shone on the beach below.

'Trying to look at the bright side of things is giving me eyestrain,' Sammy complained to Victor. 'There's as much sign of a boat as butter on your arse.'

'Absolute silence!' a voice warned.

Sammy hated suffering in silence because that took all the pleasure out of it. In any case, it sometimes helped to be flippant in moments of crisis.

On several occasions, the men flattened on the sand thought they saw something . . . until suddenly at last glimmers of light winked from the Channel's darkness. The evacuation controller answered with his masked torch, and rubber rowing boats manned by crews with blackened faces appeared from nowhere.

Somewhere out there, more than a mile from the shore, beyond the range of coastal searchlights, a motor vessel drifted silently.

Wading into the surf, the American airmen and five Amiens gaolbreakers were assisted into the rubber boats, then ferried to the craft waiting to take them to England.

# 18 The cycling assassin

Killing a man wasn't like sabotage. It wasn't the same at all. It was a cold calculating thing to do, thought Jean Cayeux, as he waited to murder someone he had never met or spoken to, wondering whether he had any right to try and take the man's life.

A secret Anglo-American-French 'court' in London had pronounced sentence for treachery, and for suffering and deaths caused. Transmitted by radio to France, the verdict declared that an executioner be appointed to carry out sentence 'as soon as convenient', as an example of Allied justice and retribution.

Bespectacled Jean Cayeux, a shy schoolmaster in his early twenties, volunteered to do the assassination during school holidays, and so write an end to the story of the *Mosquito* attack on Amiens gaol.

Lucien Pieri, who had imprisoned so many and cost countless lives, had largely started it all. Now Jean Cayeux knew the final chapter was up to him, and the gun in his pocket.

As he sat on the bench in the little public garden of Place René Goblet, apparently reading a book, but observing the hosiery shop opposite, Jean realised that others, far more experienced than him, had tried and failed to kill Pieri. Only recently in Dulon, an entire group had shot at him, and missed. There were some jobs best tackled single-handed, and maybe this was one of them. It was something he had to do alone, but then he was used to fighting alone. Since 1940, when he had helped prisoners of war held in Amiens' Hospice St. Victor to freedom, he'd waged a one-man battle; provided escapers with clothes; got them across the river Somme at night. Some could swim, some couldn't, but all had made it somehow. Then there were the telephone lines and transports he had sabotaged, fighting his own little war whenever opportunity arose to hurt the enemy in some way. Happily there were lots of opportunities.

In the summer months, the Germans drove transports with bonnet sides slightly raised to help cool engines and prevent over-heating. If they happened to stop, as they often did, Jean was ready with little sachets of sand. Each sachet was closed by a little thread. All he had to do was pull the thread, open it for action, and pour the sand into the oil intake. Everything had gone fine until that Thursday when, dressed in workman's blue overalls, carrying a shoulder bag of sand supplies, he approached a large military convoy halted by an accident. When guards and drivers left their lorries to sort out the problem, Jean moved from bonnet to bonnet with sand until he walked straight into the arms of two Gendarmes who wanted to know why he was hanging around. A French-speaking German officer arrived to take him under guard to a house for questioning.

'I'm done for, this time,' Jean thought, unable to spot any avenue of escape.

Three German officers routinely opened the interrogation:

'Who are your superiors? . . . We're sure you are not acting alone . . .'

Jean didn't answer, but when one of the officers slapped him across the face, his instant reflex was to defend himself. Automatically putting up his fists, Jean landed a punch on the officer's jaw that sent him flying over the desk, delivering him head down with legs spreadeaged in the air like a V sign. The astonished faces of the other officers were worth what he was sure his reaction was about to cost him.

Locked in a tiny room with a small barred window, he could hear the sentry in the corridor. He was obviously in a temporary cell for the newly-arrested. Opening the window to let some air in, he was amazed to find that the bars weren't firmly fixed, as in so many old French mud-built houses. It was easy. Pushing back the bars, he squeezed with difficulty through the square window, thanking God for making him thin and lanky. Then he ran like hell until he hadn't breath to run anymore.

Luck had remained his friend, just as it had when he evaded the Obligatory Service for call-up. He asked his family doctor to help out with a false certificate stating he suffered from a bad heart.

'Take two of these pills, they'll give you palpitations when you're examined,' his doctor said, handing him some pills in an envelope.

Confidently, Jean presented himself for the medical, having taken more than the prescribed two pills, for added precaution. As the doctor tested him, his heart beat quietly at sixty a minute.

'Good – you're very strong – you go to work in Germany,' wasn't the decision Jean had hoped to hear. On leaving to retrieve his clothes from the adjoining room, he was handed a form which was instantly collected from him and added to a pile of similar forms on a desk, beside which stood a giant pot with a large plant. Although there were 'grey mice' (German military grey uniforms) everywhere, Jean saw possible salvation in the potted plant. Stumbling, he hit the desk, knocking over the plant. Grabbing at the desk to stop the fall, he scattered the pile of medical papers over the floor.

'Clumsy bastard!' an officer screamed, kicking Jean in the rear, 'you'll pay for that smashed pot.'

Apologetically, he paid up, considering the cost a bargain for the medical form now safely in his pocket. Call-up authorities never bothered him again. Nobody wanted to go; some managed not to.

For years he continued his one-man resistance, for, being a country teacher in an isolated village, it was better for him to act on his own. If he had been in a city or town, not in a virtually cut-off community, it would have been simpler, but everything changed when Jean fell in love and became engaged to a petite Amiens girl living in the St. Pierre quarter close to the prison.

Teaching in a mixed school at Molliens Vidame, Jean devoted as many outside classroom hours as he could to extra-curricular activities of which he told his fiancée nothing. He could have taken her into his confidence – even taken her with him, because she was fearless – but he was afraid for her in case he was caught or arrested on suspicion. Now that he had legitimate cover for spending more time in town courting his girl, the way was clear to link with other freedom fighters. But how? Walking up to someone to inquire:

'Are you in the Resistance? . . . I want to join,' could bring an instant invitation to visit Gestapo headquarters.

The bookseller! – Monsieur Poiret-Choquet – that was it! We've known each other a long time. I would trust him, and I'm sure he'd trust me. It's dangerous, foolish, but worth the risk. If my judgement of the man is that wrong, I'll deserve whatever happens.

Hurrying to the little Amiens bookshop for some pencils and a book he had ordered, he started, as always, chatting to gentle, ever helpful M. Poiret-Choquet who knew almost everyone and everything in town.

'You know me, know my background – I want to get into the Resistance – can you help me?'

The elderly bookseller studied Jean for a moment, then replied:

'I think I could introduce you to someone tonight, come to my home at eight.'

Monsieur Poiret-Choquet had offered the hospitality of his home to another of his regular clients – Lieutenant Marceau Laverdure of the Amiens police. The Lieutenant and his friends had, in fact, been using his house for some time as a rendezvous, although he was aware that they switched meetings elsewhere from time to time. There was Laverdure's gendarme colleague Edouard Robine,

Robine's wife, and Michel Dubois. Monsieur Poiret-Choquet smiled whenever he mentally pictured the evening he had first said to Laverdure:

'You're from the Resistance, aren't you?'

'No! no!' Laverdure protested, 'I'm against it!'

The truth remained unspoken, but the bookseller permitted the meetings he never attended to continue in his home. No one referred to the reasons for them until the Lieutenant arrived at the house to find a tall, slim young man, wearing spectacles, waiting for him.

The normally shy Jean instantly challenged:

'You're in the Resistance.'

'No,' Laverdure insisted.

'You are – I know you are.'

'You've the wrong information,' said Laverdure, wondering if the Gestapo were on to him at last, and whether reinforcements were outside ready to raid.

At that point, Monsieur Poiret-Choquet emerged from a room to reassure:

'I told him – I've known him a long time – trust him.' Laverdure was furious at not having been consulted before the introduction. The stranger could be an infiltrator, but the damage was done. The only way now was to investigate the would-be recruit.

'I'm fed up – I want to do more against the enemy than I've managed to do so far on my own,' frustrated Jean explained. 'I'm alone – my only relative is my mother. I'll do anything. All I ask is that you take care of her if anything happens to me.'

'I'll think about it,' Laverdure cautiously promised. 'Come back in a couple of days.'

Someone was always on guard outside the house when a Laverdure group meeting was in progress inside, and as Jean Cayeux left, one of the guards shadowed him wherever he went for two days, until he returned to the Poiret-Choquet home. Meanwhile, Laverdure's police sources also checked Jean.

'Do you mind risking your life?' he asked. 'I've an important job for you, but you may be killed in the process.'

'It doesn't matter, I'll do it, Commandant,' Jean replied, making Laverdure suddenly very conscious of his immediate use of the word 'Commandant'.

'We have in Amiens one of the most dangerous men in the country, with spies working for him everywhere – amongst Resistants, and almost certainly amongst us too. We must eliminate him – kill him – but it won't be easy. Many have already tried and failed.

Nor is the decision to assassinate him mine – the death sentence was actually passed on him in London. We've been ordered to carry it out as fast as possible.

'The dossier on him is vast, the evidence of guilt overwhelming. More than any other single individual, he was responsible for destroying freedom armies built in readiness for the invasion; and he, more than anyone, helped fill Amiens, Abbeville, and other gaols, putting hundreds in front of firing squads or sending them to concentration camps. We learnt a great deal more of the extent of his activities as a direct result of the Amiens prison bombing, from evidence we obtained after it, and from information supplied by freed prisoners.

'You say you want to do something really important. Well, shoot this man.'

Laverdure handed him a photograph.

'Pieri the shirtmaker!' Jean Cayeux almost whispered. 'I know who you mean, know his shop, know where he lives. His house is in rue Victor Hugo, just behind the Palais de Justice.'

As he said this, it struck him how ironic it was for this man to be living behind the façade of the region's centre of so-called law and justice.

'He did all you said?' asked Jean.

'Far more. We don't know all the damage he's done, but we know enough.

'That he was judged and condemned in London for his actions, shows how serious a threat he's considered to be,' Michel Dubois affirmed. 'He's classified vitally dangerous to invasion support plans and to victory itself.'

'How do I do it?' the determined but somewhat shaken Jean Cayeaux asked, nearly regretting his haste in volunteering. Only now did the full force of the fact hit him that he would have to kill methodically and callously.

To murder a man was no small business, he thought, it always affects you. Perhaps he had decided too hastily, because he knew how hard it would be to commit cold-blooded slaughter. It wasn't him – wasn't his character. But he'd volunteered and wouldn't renege on the job.

One of his closest friends had been betrayed and was in Amiens prison when it was bombed. Luckily, he escaped, and stayed free.

'The only way we'll ever get him is to find a chink in his security armour,' Laverdure advised. 'You must watch all his comings and goings for two or three weeks. We'll arrange a daily rendezvous so you can regularly report progress or problems to me.'

'I'll need a bike if I have to follow him around checking all his movements and habits - the Germans requisitioned mine some time ago.'

'Steal another one.'

'*Steal*!' Jean exclaimed, shocked, 'I couldn't steal a bike, or anything – it's against my nature.'

'Well, it's probably against your nature to murder someone, but you've agreed to do it, so you'd better get used to the idea of stealing too,' Laverdure smiled sympathetically. 'Have you got a revolver?'

When Jean produced his own gun for inspection, Laverdure laughed.

'It's a toy - too small, too lightweight. You need something powerful enough to finish him when you finally get him.'

Michel Dubois offered a heavier calibre weapon.

'This will do it,' he said confidently. 'Knock him down properly with this piece, and he'll stay down.'

'Before you go, Jean, two more things,' Laverdure concluded. 'If you're caught, commit suicide, or they're certain to make you give us all away. We, perhaps, don't matter so much, but what we have to do, does.

'Finally, welcome to the Charles de Gaulle group – you're one of us now.'

They all shook hands with him, and the schoolteacher assassin left to begin the toughest, most ruthless task of his life, only to find within twenty-four hours that he couldn't force himself to achieve even the essential initial stage of the assignment. He just couldn't steal a bike.

As he headed for the pre-arranged emergency rendezvous point – the little Moulin du Roi café on the market place behind the old Amiens central Post Office – he met Michel Dubois in the street.

'Why are you here already? What's the matter?'

'I can't do it, Michel.'

'Can't do what?'

'Can't steal a bike. I don't think I'll ever be able to make it. I'd kill an evil man like Pieri but can't bring myself to steal an innocent person's bike.'

'Don't worry, I understand. We'll do something about it,' Michel promised.

Later that day a bike was delivered to his home, and he didn't ask where it had come from.

Jean Cayeaux took to sitting frequently on a bench in the Place René Goblet garden, reading a book or newspaper and, at the same time, detailing in a little notebook Pieri's comings and goings.

For over a month he watched and followed, often continuously day and night, keeping tabs even on the almost daily visits to Gestapo headquarters at rue Jeanne d'Arc. Conveniently, his school was shut, so he was free to continue without worrying about classes and unauthorised school absences arousing suspicion. To avoid attracting further curiosity, he had also taken to changing clothes and his entire appearance several times a day. Sometimes he didn't wear glasses; sometimes switched to different style spectacles; wore a cap, a hat, or nothing at all on his head; or altered the way he combed his hair.

About ten o'clock one morning, standing beside the little flower stall near the hosiery shop, Jean observed two black Citroens with eight passengers draw up in front of the shop. Last out was Pieri, who was immediately surrounded and sheltered by the others, taking no risks with their valuable Lucien. Jean spotted them looking suspiciously in his direction and quickly departed for home.

'It's hot, Mama,' he said, reappearing from his room with a bathing costume and towel. 'I'm going to the swimming pool to cool off.'

As he strolled out, he saw a motorcycle being pushed by two mechanics, and recognised the registration number. It was Pieri's, and he watched them push it into a little garage on the Route de Corbie, only a hundred metres from his home. The garage had obviously been taken over by the Gestapo, because he always noticed them hanging around there. Trying to shoot Pieri down in that garage would be too close to home for comfort. His idea had long been to kill the traitor in front of his house in the rue Victor Hugo – executing him by the Palais de Justice seemed a nice touch – and he had organised the getaway with this approach in mind. But he couldn't now resist following the motorcycle. Pieri wasn't at the garage so Jean settled on a boulevard bench and waited, certain he would turn up for the bike during the day, hopefully with fewer or perhaps no guards. As Laverdure had said: 'Everyone gets careless sometime.'

At half past one, Pieri arrived, alone. Jean almost didn't recognise him because he was wearing an unfamiliar new brown suit. Fortunately, he couldn't change his broken boxer's nose, and there was no mistaking that face. Jean wondered if the moment had arrived. The barrel of his big military revolver, so cold at times, tucked beneath his belt and inside his trousers, felt cool and comforting. It was a beautiful piece of well-oiled machinery which he knew would do its part well, if given the chance, unless rust affected it. He had been sweating more than usual on this job, and his constantly wet shirt was liable to get rust into the gun – it already had rust marks from being so much next to the soaking shirt.

As he watched, someone waved to him from across the road, smack next door to the garage Pieri had just entered.

Oh, God! It was his mother's nurse. She lived next to the garage and frequently gossiped to him about Pieri and the Gestapo garage when she came to give his mother morphine injections to ease her cancer pains. He couldn't shoot if she, or any other innocent bystander, was around to be hit by stray or ricochet bullets.

Unavoidably, he crossed the road to say 'Hello'.

'Isn't that Pieri's motorcycle over there?' he asked imprudently, wishing he could have bitten off his tongue the second the words were out of his mouth.

'Yes, but why do you ask?'

'For no particular reason – just curious.'

He returned to his own cycle strategically propped against a wall a short distance away, pretended to fiddle with it, then realised there was another factor he hadn't taken into account – the military occupied Hospice St. Victor on the opposite side of the street. On top of the wall, each side of the Hospice main gates, German sentry look-out posts had an uninterrupted view of the surrounding area.

Pieri appeared with the garage owner, his back to Jean, but the idea of shooting him in the back didn't appeal. Turning his bike on the road, about seven metres from Pieri, he drew his revolver. Pieri saw it, and the terror on his face as he stared at his executioner, said everything. Running to the garage, he tried to put the garage proprietor between himself and the gun. Hesitating, helplessly realising he was losing precious seconds, Jean again questioned whether he had the right to kill a man who might never have been condemned to death by any normal court of law. But he had learned so much about him and the network he controlled. Their indisputable menace to invasion success, victory, freedom, and the future, had grown in him a terrible hatred of Pieri and all he stood for. If he didn't destroy him, he would continue destroying others.

Jean fired – one shot. The brand new jacket suddenly looked as if it had been pressed in at a point close to the heart. Blood spurted down his arm as he fell.

He was sure he had killed him.

Cycling away, still pointing the revolver at the garage in case opposition appeared. Forgetting about sentries on the Hospice walls, he was on the point of jabbing the revolver back in his belt when he looked up and saw a soldier's rifle trying to get a line on his moving bicycle. Seeing Jean whip out his revolver again to take aim, the sentry ducked, then fired, too late.

Women seated gossiping to each other on their doorsteps in the warm afternoon sun saw the revolver clatter to the ground as a road pot hole tipped him from the cycle. Snatching up the gun and remounting, he found the whole street completely deserted.

Reaching home, he changed clothes, made a bundle of those he had worn at the garage and told his young sister to take them to his mother-in-law-to-be and ask her to hide them.

Telling his mother that he was going to his school to meet someone, and pedalling away towards Molliens Vidame, he almost crashed into Pieri's Citroen car speeding to the scene of the shooting. Inside was a woman and men from the Gestapo headquarters.

He escaped Amiens only just in time, because the Gestapo, police, and military turned the place inside out searching for clues to the assassin, even scouring the swampy marshes of the area.

Michel Dubois had arranged for him to hide in a girls' school at Molliens Vidame. Trustworthy Madame Bertin, the headmistress, cautioned Jean to stay out of sight, but he was worried.

'It was so close to my home, and I stupidly talked too much to my mother's nurse, even asking her to identify Pieri's motorcycle,' Jean admitted anxiously to Madame Bertin.

'If for some reason – even unintentionally – she says too much, they'll know it's me and arrest my mother. I've got to go home.'

'You can't, Jean!' Madame Bertin warned. 'Let me send someone who knows nothing about your involvement in the affair to your home to get some books for you. It's a good excuse, then we'll soon know if everything's alright.'

Reluctantly, he agreed.

The friend returned, and reported that Jean's mother was well looked after, adding:

'What a business it was getting through to Amiens at all. I can't count how many times I had to show my identity papers and how many times I was searched. It was even worse leaving.'

The next day, to allay Jean's concern, Madam Bertin sent someone else to check his home again, then Michel Dubois arrived.

'Pieri's all but finished. They rushed him into the Hospice St. Victor – the only French civilian they'd let into that place – and operated on him. He's in intensive care, but I'm glad to tell you, in a very bad way.

'Your bullet actually went right through him and landed in the lap of that fat, placid little 85-year-old woman who sits summer and winter on a chair outside her doorstep. She found it in her blue apron.'

'Jesus!' was all Jean could say at first, until he recovered enough to add:

'If I'd thought he wasn't dead, I would have put another bullet into him!'

'Don't worry, Laverdure knows everything that goes on in that hospice, and according to latest information, the medical officers hold out little hope for him.'

Day after day they waited for news of Pieri's death, but it didn't come.

Laverdure decided to make arrangements to finish the job somehow in the hospital itself. There were friends – some of the sisters – who could help.

On the fifth day after the shooting, Laverdure fixed a rendezvous with one of the nursing nuns.

'How is your special patient today?' he enquired.

The sister raised her eyes to the sky, and with a saintly devout look on her face, replied:

'The good Lord will surely call him in a few hours.'

And He did.

# Postscript

When D-Day was launched on June 4, fifteen weeks after the prison attack, Gestapo and Abwehr-mauled underground forces were sufficiently recovered, regrouped, and revitalised to give effective support to General Dwight D. Eisenhower's invasion. The importance of the contribution Amiens zone resisters were expected to make was clearly set out in an official document headed: 'Instructions Concerning The Employment Of The Resistance Movement Within The Framework Of The Military Plan Of Operations For Liberating Continental France.' Instructions stated:

From the beginning to the end of the operations of liberation in Continental France, the northern area should be characterised more than any other by:
(a) the collection of information;
(b) activity against communications by a series of either localised or general reprisals, neutralisation activities (sabotage of railroads, various installations and material, seditious activities and finally stoppages of work), and by acts of destruction of a limited duration carried out by armed groups.

Only in the northern area would localised acts of armed aggression against specific objectives take place throughout the entire duration of the operations.

Neutralisation of big-scale supply movements by temporarily knocking out all power cranes, railroad turntables, steam locomotives, feederlines of electromotive power at their source and in the distribution from power stations, transformer stations and sub-stations. Interruption of communication wires.

The measures were designated to be carried out for a period of 15 days over the whole of France, with the main effort concentrated in predetermined areas.

The job was done by men and women reinforced and heartened by the freeing of colleagues from Amiens prison and strengthened by the consequent deflection and disruption of enemy counter actions.

'It turned out more successful than I hoped, and your people are to be congratulated on the wonderful job they did,' Air Marshall Sir Trafford Leigh-Mallory wrote to Air Vice-Marshal Basil Embry some time after the raid, adding: 'As an operation it certainly was an epic. It was a tragedy that we lost Pickard, but I hope that we may see him before long.'

Dominique Ponchardier, Admiral Rivière, and Pepe, didn't have the slightest idea of the true results of the raid, but based on the knowledge that they did have, Dominique sent a message to London, in March 1944.

I thank you in the name of our comrades for the bombardment of the prison. We were not able to save all. Thanks to the admirable precision of the attack the first bomb blew in nearly all the doors and 150 prisoners escaped with the help of the civilian populations. Of these, 12 were to have been shot on the 19th February. In addition, 37 prisoners were killed, some of them by German machine-guns, and 50 Germans were also killed.

To sum up, the operation was a success, although the bombing was too violent. No aircraft were shot down over Amiens, but we are searching for pilots of missing aircraft.

When he sent that note, Dominique Ponchardier didn't realise how inaccurate and undervalued his figures were. Neither he, nor 'Pepe' – René Chapelle – knew the incredible sequence of events they set in motion, nor their actual outcome. Thanks also went to Allen Dulles and Bill Donovan in Washington.

A second message in March, expressing someone else's appreciation, was forwarded to Basil Embry and No. 2 Group of the Tactical Air Force. The letter, marked 'MOST SECRET', said:

I have been asked by 'C' to express his gratitude and the gratitude of his officers for the attack carried out on Amiens prison on 18th February, and also their sympathy for the relatives and comrades of the air-crews who were unfortunately lost.

Before writing I wished to ascertain what the result of the attack had been. This has taken some time; however, we have now received certain messages from France . . . I should be grateful if you would pass the above 'Highly Secret' information to Air Vice-Marshal Embry.

Replying to Leigh-Mallory's congratulations Embry wrote:

It is most satisfactory that we should have released so many.

The rescue attempt, vivid proof that no one's sacrifice would be overlooked or forgotten, instilled new courage into surviving Resistance ranks and gave fresh heart to invasion support.

There was another immensely valuable side benefit. Escaped 'political' prisoners identified more than sixty of the Gestapo agents and collaborators responsible for their imprisonment. Enemy counter-Intelligence in the entire region was consequently disastrously undermined, and countless Gestapo arrests avoided.

Escaped criminals who didn't return of their own free will to complete sentences, or weren't caught by the Germans, were unofficially allowed a clean start. After a brief period, French police stopped looking for them.

376

'Our reason for discontinuing the search,' a senior Prison authority confirmed, 'was that they were never sentenced to be bombed. We therefore considered they had been punished enough and deserved another chance.'

For months, everyone was inexplicably certain Pickard would turn up somewhere, and it was decided that immediately the Allies invaded an Intelligence officer should be specifically assigned the task of going to Amiens and discovering the truth – as far as it could be ascertained – of what finally happened to Pickard and Broadley. He found many answers: located, marked and photographed the graves, and submitted the report, together with some of the actual *FW 190* shell cases that shot down 'F' for Freddie, to David Atcherley, Basil Embry's Senior Air Staff Officer. The shells were retrieved and kept as mementos by the local villagers who rescued the bodies from the burning plane.

Largely relying on Amiens Préfecture files and information from local people involved, this initial RAF on-the-spot assessment, made by Intelligence Officer, Squadron Leader Edwin Houghton, indicated that of 700 officially alleged to have been imprisoned in the gaol at the time of the attack, 258 successfully escaped. It stated that the final death toll of prisoners killed in the bombing was 102 – very few of whom were political prisoners.

This RAF investigation was misled by inaccurate and insufficient records on German arrested prisoners, and the numbers of 'politicals' actually detained in both the German and French quarters without official French knowledge.

The report admits:

It was not possible to discover the reason for the detention of the Political prisoners arrested by the Germans because in all the records, the reason was stated to be unknown, nor were the French ever told when the Germans intended to execute the Political prisoners.

The report then adds:

One point was clear – that the most important prisoner to escape was a Monsieur Vivant, the Sous Préfet of Abbeville, who was arrested by the Gestapo on the 14th February, 1944.

Monsieur Vivant is now in the Ministry of the Interior, in General de Gaulle's Government.

I think it probable that we were asked to carry out the attack mainly to effect his escape. Monsieur Vivant was a key member of the Resistance at Abbeville and probably had in his possession important secrets of the Resistance Organisation.

From all sources it was clear that the population of Amiens had wondered why the attack had been carried out, more particularly since the section of the prison occupied by Political prisoners was the most seriously damaged; but that within a few days, when it became known that Monsieur Vivant had escaped, together with so many other Political prisoners, the attack was generally applauded.

Dr. Marchoire, the former Amiens Chief of the French Forces of the Interior Resistance Organisation, assuring Squadron Leader Houghton that he had not personally been in any way connected with the request for the attack, nor had advance knowledge of it as underground forces worked in water-tight compartments. Nevertheless, he agreed with the report conclusion, which stated:

It was probable that the request had come from within the prison through our agents.

In the winter of 1944, censored versions of the raid, and apparent reasons for it, were finally published in the world's Press, and on December 5th, at St. Martin-in-the-Fields church in London, a memorial service was held for Pickard and Broadley – commencing precisely at noon.

Giselle Cage – the young girl who cut the wings and decorations off Pickard's uniform – eventually sent them to Dorothy Pickard. They *were* his.

Local people constantly laid flowers on the graves and months afterwards, removed the German markings and placed their own crosses on them. The cross on Pickard's grave was inscribed:

'Group Captain P. C. Pickard, VC, DSO, DFC, Bar.'

They got the bars wrong, and the VC – Pick was never awarded Britain's highest medal for heroism – but the French clearly thought, and hinted, that he should have been.

The village of Warloy-Baillon also honoured a victim of the raid by renaming a public square – 'Place Robert Beaumont' – in memory of the local doctor who died as an English spy in the gaol; and Canadian Robert Vannier, one of the soldiers he saved, was at the commemorative street christening ceremony. Squadron Leader Ian McRitchie's navigator, Flight Lieutenant R. W. 'Sammy' Sampson, from Waipukurau, Hawke's Bay, New Zealand, was buried at Poix de la Somme churchyard.

Shot down Ian McRitchie found himself in hospital around the corner from the prison he had bombed, then was transferred to a prison camp where he was kept in solitary confinement for forty two days. He was threatened with Gestapo 'treatment' in addition to medical treatment unless he revealed how the RAF and underground had planned the raid. He said nothing.

His technical know-how resulted in his becoming 'production manager' of the prison camp's escapers' 'factory'. Until the end of the war he applied the McRitchie brand of ingenuity, which contributed so significantly to the gaol bombing effectiveness, to fashioning such useful items as barbed wire cutters – POW escapers, for the use of – from Red Cross ice skates.

For propaganda purposes, eleven days after the bombing, a handful of prisoners who helped rescue wounded comrades were pardoned and released. Gendarme Achille Langlet and Raymond Bonpas, who shared a cell with Father Janin, were among them.

Amiens Gestapo chief Braumann asserted that the self-sacrifice and devotion to duty of Dr. Mans and Captain Tempez in saving German and French lives would be officially recognised and rewarded. It was. Dr. Mans was deported to slave labour in Germany and only rescued when American forces freed the camp in May 1945. In October 1944, outside the Somme town of Arras, a mass grave was uncovered with the remains of 260 bodies. Among them was Captain Tempez who was shot only a few weeks after the gaol raid.

Braumann's notorious Amiens Gestapo headquarters house on the corner of rue Jeanne d'Arc and rue Dhavernas now bears a commemorative tablet inscribed:

En Souvenir des Resistants Torturés
dans cette maison par les Nazis.
1942–1944

In Abbeville cemetery, an inscription at the foot of a stone cross at one time read:

RAYMOND VIVANT SOUS-PRÉFET D'ABBEVILLE MORT 18 FÉVRIER 1944

As long as the Germans were in occupation, Vivant's friends frequently visited the grave to lay flowers. One of them, their family doctor, Jacques Dezoteux, who assisted Madame Vivant's escape, looking sceptically at the grave, remarked to his wife:

'They give only the bare facts – just the name and the date, and even a gravestone usually says something good about a man when he's down.'

After Liberation, the cross was removed. The coffin only contained Vivant's overcoat and Homburg hat. The German authorities preferred locals to think he had died, rather than escaped.

'I don't know if they put anyone else in the grave,' said Vivant. 'I simply know it wasn't me.'

With his new identity in Paris, Vivant, who registered as a

'Wholesale Fruit and Vegetable Merchant', left home at regular hours to go to work, but the work had nothing to do with fruit and veg. – only Intelligence.

Although in the Somme Raymond Vivant was officially declared 'dead', at Castres, in Central France, the Gestapo arrested his father-in-law, 57-year-old lawyer Lucien Coudert, and put him in St. Michel prison, in Toulouse. They let it be known that he would only be released if the Vivant family surrendered. The father got word to his daughter and son-in-law to remain in hiding, and even sent funds to them. Lucien Coudert wasn't freed until after the Allies liberated France.

As for Vivant's courageous friend Courvoisier, the one-time Paris pimp, he not only survived the war, but was actually placed in Charge of German prisons *in Germany* – a genuine case of poacher turning gamekeeper: the ex-criminal, a prison director!

Louise, the remarkable chambermaid spy in the brothel at Boulevard du Port, was reunited with her Canadian soldier husband when Canadian forces re-entered Amiens. Soon afterwards, she was officially reassigned with him to a post in Paris.

The one-legged British spy chained to a wall in one of the prison's dungeon cells surfaced again years later as a civilian-clothed top-ranking officer of British security services on the island of Cyprus.

Forger Georges Danielou invested in a lithographic and printing business (legitimate).

Victor Pasteau and Sammy Izard went into partnership. Applying their thieving expertise, they became commercial and domestic security specialists, protecting citizens against criminals.

Brothel keeper Madame Jacqueline continued catering for the public but turned her attention to eating instead of sexual tastes. She purchased and ran the Pavillon Bleu, one of Amiens' most popular top-class restaurants, until she sold it and retired.

Former navy pilot, Pierre Ponchardier, Dominique's brother, became an Admiral after the war, and died in a plane crash.

Teenager Jean Beaurin, whose wartime speciality was the destruction of trains and railways, developed into a highly successful specialist in the metal construction industry, whilst René-Chapelle was content to return to repairing bikes and being in charge of maintenance at a cycle racing track. When he died in January 1978, Jean Beaurin and Maurice Holville, the 'Curé of Montparnasse', were amongst the mourners at the graveside. René's son Jean – the child who provided the alibis for Maria Chapelle's courier journeys – was also at the funeral. Young Jean, who became an army paratrooper, served in Algeria and took part in the operation against

Suez in 1956, is now responsible for security at Radio Paris broadcasting house.

Maria was arrested with little Jean in April 1944 and driven to the Palace of Justice in Paris where the Gestapo repeatedly beat Maria and the boy in front of each other to make her reveal René's whereabouts and name associates. She was interrogated for a month, but didn't break. The child was sent to the German-controlled 'Children's Centre' – the official term for what was in fact a prison, or detention centre for children. Maria was imprisoned in the notorious Fresnes gaol and afterwards in concentration camps in Germany. She was freed in May, 1945, almost blind through maltreatment.

Allen Dulles became the first Director of the Central Intelligence Agency which emerged from the foundations of the OSS, and David Bruce, who was in charge of London-based OSS operations, was appointed United States ambassador to Britain, France, and West Germany.

Claude Dansey, whose judgement significantly influenced final Amiens raid decisions, was knighted in 1943, and further honoured by Britain, America, France, and Belgium after the war. His American Citation for the Legion of Merit commends Colonel Sir Claude E. M. Dansey, KCMG, most highly for his never flagging determination, and his superior diplomacy to ensure complete success in special and vitally important Anglo-American Operations in the defeat of Nazi Germany.

Basil Embry was knighted in 1945, and as Air Chief Marshal commanded Allied Air Forces Central Europe from 1953 until his retirement in 1956, when he returned to Western Australia. He died in December 1977.

Many associated with the Amiens action were honoured after the war. Maria Chapelle, for example, received the highest awards of America, Britain, and France. Her husband, René was similarly honoured. Dominique Ponchardier received the MBE from Britain, and was appointed an ambassador for his country.

Joe Balfe senior and his wife continued running the hotel in Hornoy, and he also resumed his pre-war cross-Channel ferry job, whilst Joe junior emulated him in reverse by marrying an English girl, settling in Britain and taking British nationality. Both he and his father were honoured for their evasion organisation activities. The United States' Medal of Freedom was awarded to both Joes, whilst Britain gave Joe senior the Order of the British Empire, and France, the Croix de Guerre. But hundreds, who were also part of the prison bombing story, remained unrecognised.

Pickard wrote his own postscript to the event. He had always been a notorious non-letter writer – even when working in Kenya for years before the war, his letters home were largely:

Dear Mum and Dad,
How are you? I am very well.
Love,
Boy.

Always a fatalist, he wrote two letters for delivery, should he be posted missing or dead – one for his wife, the second for his mother. He handed them to his adjutant in a blank sealed envelope, directing they be delivered to his friend Lord Londonderry, whom he had often piloted on Air Ministry missions. One morning, Lord Londonderry visited Dorothy Pickard to hand her an envelope with an undated letter in it which read:

Dear Lord Londonderry,
I am writing this short letter to you and handing it in a sealed blank envelope to my adjutant, to be opened and delivered to you if I should fail to return from a sortie.

For nearly two years now I have had a feeling that one day or night I shall be knocked down, and although I myself am not afraid, I do feel my responsibilities.

The morning you tried to persuade me to take you on a raid, I decided at that moment, that when my son was born, I should invite you to be his godfather, as I felt confident that you would do all in your power to help and advise Dorothy as to my son's future.

Financially Dorothy is safe. Although I have no money, my pension plus the small income Dorothy has will be sufficient to look after them both. Anyhow it is my wish that Dorothy should marry again, in which case she will have nothing to worry about. My other wish is that Nicholas be educated at my old school 'Framlingham College' or some other similar college, which is not considered expensive. On leaving school at no more than 17½ years, he should be sent abroad for a period of at least three years, with an allowance sufficient only to keep him, if that is necessary, no more than £100 per year. At the end of that period, I should like him to return to this country, and join the Royal Air Force and endeavour to obtain a permanent commission. Under no circumstances should his hand be forced. If he wishes to remain overseas for good, he may do so, but he is to be given no financial assistance whatsoever, and after reaching 21 years of age his allowance shall cease.

I am not informing Dorothy of my intention regarding Nicholas, but should like you to communicate with her immediately I am posted as missing.

My adjutant has instructions to communicate with you should this occur and he also has instructions to open the sealed envelope and will find this addressed to you. Should, on the other hand, I be taken prisoner, I would like you to do all you can for Dorothy and the baby, but under no circumstances are you to help financially. Dorothy has instructions regarding this matter.

My chances of being taken alive are remote as I always carry a revolver and intend fighting it out. If you hear I am a prisoner it will be either because I am too badly injured to fight, or because I funked it.

In conclusion, I should like to thank you for what you have done for me, and also to inform you that I have every confidence in your carrying out my instructions. Finally, I cannot speak too highly of bomber command, particularly the men who are least mentioned, the wireless ops, and the gunners, their risks are greater than anyone's, yet they are the least rewarded.

Good Luck,

Charles Pickard.

To his mother he wrote:

I'm beginning to see the red light. I feel that my number is up, but under no circumstances are you to fret for me. So many of my friends have gone, and if it happens to me too, I shall not be unhappy to join them, and want you to know this.

I apologise for anything I have done in my life that upset you, and if at any time you have felt I have been a bad son, I didn't mean to be. You have always been a wonderful mother.

The letter from a son who loved his mother deeply, but felt that possibly, he hadn't shown his love enough, wasn't given to her until he was officially declared dead on 24 September, 1944.

Lord Londonderry wrote to Pick's sister, Lady Hardwicke:

Dear Lady Hardwicke,

Your wonderful brother and I had a delightful alliance. Years of difference in our ages, but those seemed to disappear. I would like to talk to you about it because it has been one of the brightest interludes in what is now getting into a long life. I could not hold on to him and he always told me that if I succeeded he would never forgive me, so one has to feel that he would have been restless in the post-war world.

Yours sincerely,

Londonderry.

Three weeks before the official announcement of the Amiens raid and deaths of Pickard and his navigator Alan Broadley, Helena Hardwicke – 'Pixie' to her family and closest friends – received another letter. Dated 9 October 1944, the letter from Pick's wife Dorothy read:

Dearest Pixie,

Thank you so much for your sweet letter. It helps me a lot to know that you think Boy was happy with me, and that I helped him as much as was possible. No one will ever know how much I miss him. He was my whole world. I don't grieve for him because we know he had a wonderful life, full of happiness; also he achieved something that is only given to very few, to be the example and inspiration of thousands. And I think it is fitting, that as it had to be, that he lost his life after doing something that will be remembered here and in France for always.

I feel sure that wherever he is now, that he is supremely happy, otherwise why should he have been killed at the very height of his career. It is only the people who love him and are left alone without him that are unhappy. Therefore I try not to cry and be sad, because it is only for my own heartbreak that I weep . . .

A few years later, Dorothy Pickard, who moved to Rhodesia, was awakened one night by a whimper from Ming. Putting on her dressing gown, she went to let Ming out into the garden, and as she did so, heard four sharp whistle blasts – exactly like those Pick used to make with his fingers when signalling Ming to join him.

Dorothy went into the garden and walked around calling out repeatedly: 'Is anyone there?'

Returning to the house she found Ming, who had been ill for months and too weak even to stand, back on her haunches looking up, her head moving slowly from left to right – just as she had done years before whenever waiting for her master to return from combat missions. Ming howled to the sky, and Dorothy was sure she was speaking to 'Boy.'

Suddenly, Dorothy again heard the four distinctive, unforgettably familiar whistle blasts. Ming raised her head higher, stared straight upwards for several seconds, then fell to the floor, dead.

Opening her newspaper next morning, Dorothy Pickard was startled by the date – February 19, 1952.

It had been the night of February the 18th when Ming's whimpers had awoken her, those two sets of finger-whistle signals sounded from nowhere, and Ming – the pup Pick had given her as a wedding present – had followed her master.

*And it shall come to pass, that when they make*
*a long blast with the ram's horn, and when ye*
*hear the sound of the trumpet, all the people*
*shall shout with a great shout; and the wall*
*of the city shall fall down flat, and the people*
*shall ascend up every man straight before him*
*(Joshua.)*

# THE MOSQUITO SQUADRONS
## OF THE FEB. 18 AMIENS RAID

### 487 Squadron

*Pilot*

| | |
|---|---|
| W/C Smith D.F.C. | F/L Barnes D.F.M. |
| F/S Jennings | W/O Nichols |
| P/O Sparkes | P/O Dunlop |
| P/O Darrell | P/O Stevenson |
| P/O Fowler | W/O Wilkins |
| F/L Hanafin | P/O Redgrave |

### 464 Squadron

| | |
|---|---|
| W/C Iredale D.F.C. | F/L McCaul D.F.C. |
| S/L Sugden | F/O Bridger |
| F/O Monaghan D.F.M. | F/L Dean D.F.M. |
| F/L McPhee D.F.M. | F/L Atkins |
| S/L McRitchie | F/L Samson |
| G/C Pickard D.S.O., D.F.C. | F/L Broadley D.S.O., D.F.C., D.F.M. |

### 21 Squadron

| | |
|---|---|
| W/C Dale | F/O Gabites |
| F/L Benn D.F.C. | F/O Roe |
| F/L Wheeler D.F.C. | F/O Redington |
| F/L Taylor D.F.C. | S/L Livry D.F.C. |
| F/L Hogan | F/S Crowfoot |
| F/S Steadman | P/O Reynolds |

# Author's notes and acknowledgements

I am certain that every one of the many who helped make this book possible will appreciate why I wish to acknowledge first the contribution of Airey Neave, DSO, MC – the Member of Parliament assassinated by terrorists with a car bomb within the precincts of the House of Commons.

He was the first British officer to escape successfully from the notorious Colditz Castle – the punishment centre for inveterate escapers – returning to organise the escapes of thousands of Allied fighting men and women. From the outset of my researches for this book, he gave me the benefit of his guidance, requested others to assist, and pointed me towards several fruitful directions.

For his work as Officer-in-Charge of British rescue operations, directing and co-ordinating escapes from occupied countries in association with his American opposite number, Major James Thornton, Airey Neave was decorated with America's Bronze Star, France's Croix de Guerre, and Holland's Order of Orange Nassau. His generosity towards me was typical of the man. He lived to help others.

*

Every incident depicted in this book happened. Although the interpretations of events are mine, they are based on the recollections of hundreds of people directly involved; unpublished sources including private letters; official records, and hitherto secret but recently declassified documents and correspondence.

All events, scenes, and quotations stem from the testimony of eyewitnesses and documents. I did not blindly accept participants' accounts without exhaustive personal cross-examination and cross-checking. Even official archives were often contradictory and confused, as readers will have seen in the course of the book.

Unstintingly, Service personnel, former Intelligence directors, ex-airmen, soldiers, and secret agents gave their time in interviews, showed me over the places concerned, supplied diaries, letters, preserved action reports, plans, drawings, and photographs. I used memories and material to reconstruct in detail the entire story and underlying reasons for countless previously unknown incidents which became pieces of the whole.

To guard against fallible memories, every statement or quote in the book was reinforced by the corroboration of others who either directly participated or witnessed, or by factual evidence. Hearsay and rumours were discarded. If a story couldn't be supported, I didn't use it.

It has taken me almost four years to uncover, investigate, and present the fateful decisions made, the intrigues, motives, treachery, errors, parts played by the principal actors, techniques of organising the air attack and supportive ground actions, with all the incredible ramifications and repercussions.

Inevitably, some will dispute my interpretations, but I solely sought clarity and depth in order not merely to portray a single outstanding event, but above all, to picture thousands of people – largely unknown to each other – yet all drawn into, and having significant roles linked with something which was of far greater importance than almost anyone involved realised. Theirs was a series of acts which added up to a great triumph.

I avoided political entanglements and rivalries so prevalent during those Occupied Europe years, and concentrated essentially on personal human aspects. I took some liberties. The first was in the use of names. Almost all are genuine, but pseudonyms were substituted for comparatively few for continuing security reasons, or at the specific request of individuals. In respect of several ex-criminals, my concern was for their families and new lives. In some instances I used wartime operational names which hid identities.

I strove to achieve an understanding of the thinking and personalities of the major people concerned, and to maintain narrative continuity. Due to the vastness of the subject, the story, at times, appears episodic, but this reflects events described.

Whilst determined to give a true comprehensive picture, I nevertheless avoided compromising certain security factors, but am confident that accuracy is in no way unbalanced by omissions and tactful changes I considered necessary.

In all records and testimony there are bound to be contradictions, and I have contradicted much of what has already been printed or discussed on the subject. The fullest previously published account was written in France immediately after the war by that distinguished Intelligence officer, Gilbert Renault-Roulier, DSO, OBE, known as 'Colonel Remy', but he was severely restricted by what was revealable at the time. There was no access whatsoever to secret files. On learning that I was seeking the real story, Remy generously offered co-operation, hopeful that I would succeed in finally finding the truth.

I am deeply indebted to him, and so many others. I cannot name them all, but my sincere appreciation is due to everyone who co-operated, advised, and in particular to those who so vividly detailed RAF aspects – from Air Chief Marshal Sir Basil Embry, GCB, KBE, DSO (3 Bars), DFC, AFC, and Lady Hope Embry, to his navigator Peter Clapham. Thanks are equally expressed for air material to Air Vice Marshal L. W. Cannon; Charles H. Foster; Air Marshal Sir Thomas Elmhirst, KBE, CB, AFC: Squadron Leader Edwin Houghton; Wing Commander R. W. Iredale, DFC, Squadron Leader Livry-Level, DFC; Air Vice Marshal G. R. Magill, CBE, DFC; John McCaul; Squadron Leader A. I. McRitchie; Patrick Shallard; Air Commodore Edward B. Sismore, DSO, DFC, AFC; Group Captain I. S. Smith; Squadron Leader W. Turner Lord and his son Simon. I am also grateful for the assistance of Group Captain E. B. Haslam and E. B. Turner of the Ministry of Defence Air Historical Branch, and F. S. Lovie of the Australian Department of Defence.

For the very personal memories of Pickard, my gratitude goes to his wife Dorothy, son Nicholas, sisters Marjorie Woods and Nancy Tibbet, and proudly helpful nephews, Michael J. Woods, and Edward Hardwicke, the actor son of Sir Cedric Hardwicke.

I owe the Intelligence development of the story to many former Intelligence service directors and agents, and am indebted for recollections, background, or guidance to Joe Balfe; David K. Bruce; Colonel Maurice J. Buckmaster, who headed Special Operations Executive: Commander Kenneth Cohen, CB, CMG, RN; Andre Dewavrin; Donald Darling; Colonel Georges A. Groussard; Marie Madeleine Fourcade, OBE; John Haskell; Lt. Col. James F. Langley, MBE, MC; Andre Manuel; Professor Justin O'Brien; Colonel Paul Paillole; Colonel G. H. Pourchot; Vice-Admiral Edouard Rivière; Philippe Schneidair, DSO; Sir Kenneth Strong, KBE – Eisenhower's Chief of Intelligence; Mrs. Frances G. Suter (formerly Lady Dansey, the widow of Sir Claude Dansey); and Francois Thierry Mieg. I also wish to acknowledge Jean Claude Beloeil, an ex-soldier who met the Amiens prison one-legged spy in Cyprus years after the war.

For assistance on criminal aspects, thanks are due to Gaston and Alice Brasseur-Royer; Maurice Durand-Barthez and Patrice Maynial of the French Ministry of Justice; M. Dupertuys, Magistrate in charge of France's Penitentiaries Secretariat; and to Sammy Izard; Violette Lambert; Victor Pasteau; Sophie Glasser; Gendarme Achille Langlet; and former Gendarme Lieutenant Marceau Laverdure, who also corroborated the account personally related to me by Jean Cayeux, of the assassination of traitor Pieri.

I appreciated Madame Jacqueline's frankness on the wartime

brothels of Amiens. Although retired, she still lives in the Somme. And the same subject was graphically elaborated by Dr. Albert Gerault who, among other duties, supervised the brothels, and today runs the largest maternity clinic in Amiens. Additional information on the theme was provided by Mademoiselle Annick Baudot, in charge of medical records at Amiens' Hospital Nord.

Mademoiselle Baudot's uncle, Marcel Baudot, Inspector General of the Archives of France, was also of immense help, as were Claude Levy of the office of France's Prime Minister, and his associate, Henri Michel, with their unique knowledge of Second World War documents. For inquiries in Brussels, help came from J. Vanwelkenhuyzen, Director in charge of Belgian war historical records. German archives assistance was supplied by Herr Noack of the Bundesarchiv in Freiburg, and I also owe acknowledgements to former Luftwaffe General Adolf Galland, who led the 'Abbeville boys'.

I welcomed the co-operation of Alain Ode, present Sous-Préfet of Abbeville, and his daughter Catherine, who interpreted for me at several interviews, and also of Sister Monica, Sister Emmanuelle, and of Sister Marie Jean Baptiste, back in her native County Cork, for recollections of the Clinic Poulain, now the Clinic de Bon Secours in Amiens. My thanks also to Monseigneur Chanoine Duhamel; Father Guerville of St. Pierre; Jean Binard, M. Gauthier and Jacques A. Lesnard of the Prefecture of the Somme; Max Lejeune, deputy mayor of Abbeville, and Rene Lamps, deputy mayor of Amiens. The distinguished newspaper *Le Courrier Picard* gave me access to their wartime files, and I am grateful for the assistance and guidance of Editors M. Collet and Bernard Bocquillon, as well as staff journalist Robert Glaudel.

For Dr. Antonin Mans's story my appreciation goes to Doctor and Madame Mans; to his associate Professor Francis Raveau of the Faculty of Medicine at the Academy of Medicine in Paris and to Francois and Raymonde Vignolle – Dr. Mans' wartime assistants in the Somme.

Now residing in south-east France, Raymond Vivant and his wife were startled to learn of my official evidence establishing that he was a key factor in the prison attack. Both he and his wife related their experiences, as well as providing answers affecting many others. He acted as best man at the wedding of Christiane Lecaillet, the young secretary who helped him escape, and Christiane told me her story too, as did Dr. Jacques Dezoteux, who aided Madame Vivant's exit from Abbeville.

The very security conscious Dominique Ponchardier, always

reticent to discuss in detail his magnificent role in the epic, only relented on viewing copies of official, previously secret, documents which I brought to his home outside Nice. My gratitude and admiration are expressed to him and four of his leading associates who also personally assisted me so much:

Jean Pierre Beaurin; René Chapelle, his wife Maria Benitas Chapelle, and Maurice Holville.

Of the many directly involved, I am also particularly grateful to Raymond Bonpas; Liliane Beaumont; Gratien Bocquet; Pierre Bracquart; Jean Cayeux; Anne Marie Chedeville; Raymond Dewas; Sosthène Denis and his son Michel; Pierre Gruel; Madeleine Gandon (Dr. Robert Beaumont's sister); Resistance Commandant André Loisy-Jarniere; Henri Moisan; Robert Pecquet; Dr. Gerard Perdu; Dr. Odile Catherine Regnault.

For technical guidance on Amiens buildings and locations, acknowledgements are due to Pierre Sellier and architect Francois Vasselle, and for assistance in locating people, to Micheline Agache-Lecat of Abbeville's Municipal Library, Didier Faure-Beaulieu, and Max Ferenc.

Finally, of course, there is my indebtedness to my wife, Lilian, who accompanied me on countless interview recording sessions. Contributing, where necessary, her French, which is better than mine, she helped create comfortable confidence for many who might otherwise have been less forthcoming.

# Bibliography

Darling, Donald, *Secret Sunday* (William Kimber)
Dulles, Allen W., *The Craft of Intelligence* (Weidenfeld & Nicolson)
Embry, Sir Basil, *Mission Completed* (Methuen)
Galland, Adolf, *First and Last* (Methuen)
Groussard, Georges A., *Service Secret* (La Table Ronde)
Hamilton, Alexander, *Wings of Night* (William Kimber)
Langley, J. M., *Fight Another Day* (Collins)
Neave, Airey, *Saturday at M.I.9.* (Hodder & Stoughton)
Paillole, Paul, *Services Speciaux* (Robert Laffont)
Ruskin, John, *Our Fathers Have Told Us* (George Allen)
The poem, 'From Albert to Bapaume', from 'Resentment', by Alec
Waugh, reprinted by permission of A. D. Peters Ltd.

# Illustrations

For illustrations in the book I am indebted to:

Madame Liliane Beaumont; Jean Beaurin; the Central Intelligence Agency in Washington; Maria Chapelle; the French Government Tourist Office; Edward Hardwicke; the Imperial War Museum; *Le Courrier Picard* newspaper and editorial executive Georges Ducrocq; Madame Antonin Mans; Sister Marie-Luce of the Clinique Du Bon Secours (formerly the Poulain Clinic); Dominique Ponchardier; the Popperphoto agency; Vice-Admiral Edouard Rivière; Mrs. Frances G. Suter (formerly Lady Dansey); and Madame Raymond Vivant.

# Dedication

This book is dedicated to someone who is never mentioned within its narrative, yet is present throughout, in spirit.

Tiny, eighty-four-year-old Mademoiselle Jeanne Fourmentraux appeared to be a frail slip of a woman in the years when she was a Somme schools inspectress, but she resolutely refused to accept dictatorship and oppression. Recognising that nothing can save a nation if it will not save itself, she established, with vision and resourcefulness, the first organised Intelligence and Resistance operation in northern France, setting the example for all the Second World War networks to come.

When Amiens prison was bombed, she was no longer free, but endured everything the Gestapo and SS inflicted on her in various prisons and concentration camps.

Her knowledge of resistance was important to me, so I sought her advice at Saint Charles retirement home, in Amiens. Her mind was still razor-sharp.

When my wife and I were about to leave, she insisted not only on courteously accompanying us to the main exit, but walking with us outside the building. Head high, with dignity and stature far taller than her physical size, she ignored the freezing cold wintry day and wore no jacket or coat, merely a thin dress.

We begged her not to risk the biting icy winds. She replied:

'Don't worry. You got used to the cold in Ravensbruck.'

My wife and I wept unashamed as we walked away from her. She made us feel humble, but proud and privileged to have known her even briefly.

Jeanne Fourmentraux extracted from the heart of suffering and sacrifice the means of inspiration and survival, typifying those who, understanding the high causes in human fortunes at stake, rose above the debasers and above fear, instilling into millions courage, strength, and hope.

Jack Fishman

# Index

Abwehr 16, 17, 19, 20, 54, 61, 68, 243, 244, 245, 251, 253, 305, 326, 375

Arnold, General 42, 89, 197

Atcherley, D. 42, 72, 73, 77, 293, 377

Avy, R. 325–35 *passim*

BCRA (Bureau Central de Renseignements et d'Action) 31, 91, 92, 108

Bader, D. 196, 294

Balfe, J 308–15, 362, 364, 381

Balfe, J. (jr.) 309–13 *passim*, 381

Barré, Mme 144, 215, 262, 269

Le Baube (Prefect of the Somme), 239, 298, 323, 343

Bayard, G. 345, 348, 351, 352

Beaumont, R. 178–80, 233, 296, 301, 343, 378, 390

Beaurin, Mme 82–9 *passim*, 142, 209, 255, 259, 322

Beaurin, J. 54, 79, 85–9, 142, 151, 155, 200, 209, 213, 255–6, 259, 322, 380, 390

Beaurin, R. 54, 79, 85, 87, 88, 209, 255

Bellemere, J. 233, 239, 301, 302, 320

Black Market 53–67 *passim*, 170, 215, 249, 263, 265, 289, 306, 319

Bluet 80, 257

Bocquet, G. 278, 282–8 *passim*, 390

Bonpas, R. 199, 321, 379, 390

Boutvillain 292, 298

Bracquart, P. 153, 154, 155, 277–82 *passim*, 287, 323, 390

Bradshaw-Jones, Squadron Leader 161, 231

Brasseur, G. 191–3, 200, 237, 259, 322–3, 388

Braumann (Amiens Gestapo chief)

15–21 *passim*, 32, 61–3, 82, 152, 171, 172, 180, 191, 200–1, 237–8, 259, 297, 302, 317, 322, 339, 379

Broadley, A. 14, 37, 39, 41, 162–8 *passim*, 182, 205, 221, 294–6, 377, 378, 383, 385

Bruce, D. 24, 26, 29, 45, 381, 390

Brunel, H. 121–2, 126–7

Burgundy Line 313

'C' *see* Menzies, Sir S.

Canfield, S. 192

Cannon, L. W. 72, 388

Caron, R. 302–8 *passim*

Carpentier, Abbé 57, 119–20

Cayeux, J. 365–74, 388, 390

Chapelle, M.-B. 81–5 *passim*, 313, 380–1, 390

Chapelle, R. 81–7 *passim*, 142–51 *passim*, 213, 217–18, 255, 258, 308, 313–15 *passim*, 376, 380, 381, 390

Chedeville, A.-M. 119–23

Churchill, W. S. 29, 35, 44, 108

Clapham, P. 72, 78–9, 388

Cohen, K. 31, 91, 92, 388

Comet Line 311–13

Communist FTPF 83

Coningham, Sir A. 48–53 *passim*, 112, 117, 129, 159

Courvoisier ('Napoleon') 94–6, 98, 107, 380

'Crossbow' 42

Cummings, J. 79, 116, 118, 141

Dale, Wing Commander 'Daddy' 118, 119, 138, 155, 167, 181, 182, 204, 205, 385

Danielou, G. 65–8, 209, 266, 319–35 *passim*, 380

Dansey, Sir C. 31, 32–5, 89–93

*passim*, 100, 107–8, 381, 390

Darras, V. 57, 68, 209

De Gaulle, C. 29, 31, 91, 97, 106, 108, 377

Delassus, R. 318, 339, 345–52 *passim*, 363

Deloiseaux, Mme 256, 258

Den, L. 55, 191, 237–9 *passim*, 259, 289, 297, 322, 348

Dewas, R. 234–9 *passim*, 296, 390

Dewavrin, A. ('Passy') 29, 61, 91, 100, 388

Dezoteux, J. 277, 379, 389

Donovan, W. J. 22–35 *passim*, 43–6 *passim*, 89–91, 100, 108, 376

Druon, C. 266, 271

Dubois, M. 144, 215–17, 261–3, 318, 368–73 *passim*

Dulles, A. W. 22–32 *passim*, 44, 46, 84, 85, 91, 112, 143, 235, 376, 381

Dumant, S. 54, 64–8 *passim*, 193, 209

Dumay, J. 54–7, 68, 209

Durand, A. 121, 122

Dupont, F. 122, 125

Eisenhower, D. D. 20, 21, 42, 46, 49, 100, 108, 375

Elmhirst, T. 388

Embry, Sir B. 35–53 *passim*, 70–79 *passim*, 108–19 *passim*, 129–40 *passim*, 158–9, 183, 197, 221, 229, 232, 376, 381, 388

Enfeld, Kommandant 317, 318, 321–2

Farjon, R. 62, 97–8, 107

Farnborough Research Establishment 115, 140

'Freddie' 211–12, 222–7, 234, 243–50, 261, 353–63

Free France *see* De Gaulle, C., BCRA

FW 190s 194, 195, 197, 218–20, 227, 230, 253, 294–6, 377

Galland, A. 76, 186–97 *passim*, 218–9, 389 *see also* Luftwaffe

Gerault, Dr. 169–70, 173–8 *passim*, 389

Gestapo 15–21 *passim*, 28, 32, 41, 43, 53, 54, 57, 61–2, 68, 82, 84, 91, 98, 100, 100–7 *passim*, 120, 123, 127, 128, 147, 150, 151, 152, 171–2, 180, 192, 199, 223–4, 237, 242, 244, 245, 253, 254, 259, 311, 339, 343, 348, 375, 376 and *passim*

'Gilbert, Colonel' *see* Groussard, G. A.

Gillis, M. 267, 274

Glasser, S. 265–6, 272–4, 339, 388

Goering, H 195–6, 221

Grisentello, A. 282–6 *passim*

Groussard, G. A. 27, 28, 29, 44, 85, 92, 112, 388

Gruel, M. 147, 207, 297, 315, 343

Guillemont E. 63, 152, 278–82, 323

Hanafin, Flight Lieutenant 188–91, 198, 229, 335

Harriman, A. 89

Harris, Sir A. 47, 160

Haskell, J. 43–5

Heinemann, Lt. Gen. E. 99

Hill, Air Marshal Sir R. 52

Hitler, A. 17, 19, 20, 24, 29, 33, 43, 98, 108, 127, 128, 196, 262

Holville, M. 54, 56–7, 69, 70, 80–84, 142, 151, 154, 209, 213, 255–9 *passim*, 322, 380, 390

Houghton, E. 72, 109, 377, 388

Iredale, R. W. 118, 119, 139, 167, 180, 182, 188, 202, 203, 204, 206, 218, 385, 388

Izard, S. 262–9 *passim*, 321, 339, 344–52 *passim*, 363, 364, 380, 388

Jacqueline, Mme. 169–78, 247,

248, 280

Janin, Father 321, 338, 339, 343–52 *passim*, 363, 379

'Jens Dons' Ring 34

Joliot, R. 345, 346, 351, 352

Kauert, Dr. 63, 175, 177

Koenig, General 108

Lambert, V. 263–71 *passim*, 320, 339, 388

Lamont 170, 245, 303, 304

Langlet, A. 192, 208, 214, 234, 238, 260, 301, 316, 379, 388

Langley, J. 89, 312, 380

Laverdure, M. 21, 27, 144, 170, 215, 240, 245, 317–18, 321–2, 367–74 *passim*, 388

Lecaillet, C. 213, 290, 291, 292, 389

Leigh-Mallory, Sir T. 46–51 *passim*, 112, 117, 159, 229, 375, 376

Leopold, A. 65, 209

Livry-Level, Colonel 115, 129, 388

'Louise' 169–78 *passim*, 246–50 *passim*, 261, 308, 353, 380

Lucienne *see* Den. L.

Luftwaffe, 42, 47, 48, 59, 76, 99, 128, 158, 177, 185–8, 193–7, 227, 228, 230, 231, 253, 256, 294, 295 *see also* FW 190s, Galland, A.

Magill, Wing Commander 71, 73, 79, 111, 183, 229, 232, 388

Malezieux, E. 282, 283

Mans, A. 53, 59–63, 96, 98, 99, 101, 107, 142, 146, 147, 152, 173, 180, 207–9, 231–5, 239, 257, 259, 260, 301, 343, 379, 389

Manuel, A. ('Maxwell') 91–3, 108, 388

'Martin' 271, 273, 320–21, 339

McCaul, J. 118, 181, 202–6, 218, 231, 385, 388

McRitchie, I. 115–16, 119, 140, 184–5, 201, 204–5, 221, 232, 293, 379, 385, 388

Menzies, Major General Sir S. 30–35 *passim*, 108

Metz, J. 264, 270, 318, 345, 347, 351–2

MI5 91

MI6 22, 30–34, 50, 89, 91, 92

MI9 90, 302, 312–13

MISX 90, 302, 312

Michel, J. 302–8

Milice (French Gestapo) 82, 96, 234, 244, 246, 251, 254–5, 317–18, 321, 338, 348

Miller, M. 267, 274

Miller, V. 325–35 *passim*

Moisan, H. 58, 59, 60, 210

Montgomery, Gen. B. 50

'Napoleon' *see* Courvoisier

Neave, A. 89, 312, 386

'Noah's Ark Alliance' 31, 146

O'Brien, J. 89, 90, 388

Office of Strategic Services (OSS) 22–34 *passim*, 45, 89, 91, 381

ORA network 235, 238

Organisation Civile et Militaire (OCM) 54, 61, 93–100, 107, 257, 277, 298

Organization 'Z' 34

'Overlord' Operation 20, 31, 42, 45, 49, 117

Passy, Colonel *see* Dewavrin, A.

Pasteau, V. 148–51, 210–12, 222–7, 234, 243–50, 261, 353–64, 380, 388

Pecquet, R. 235–9 *passim*, 390

Pepe *see* Chapelle, R.

Perdu 233, 234, 239, 390

Pickard, P. C. 12–14, 35–41, 72, 112–19, 129–42 *passim*, 155–68 *passim*, 181, 182, 183, 197, 202, 204–6, 221, 232, 293–6, 375,

377, 378, 382–4, 385, 388

Pickard, D. 36–9, 114, 293, 378, 382–4, 388

Pickard, N. 13, 114, 382, 388

Pieri, L. 15–21, 27, 32, 82, 152, 180, 317, 343, 365–74 *passim*, 388

Ponchardier, D. 27–32 *passim*, 44, 45, 80–86 *passim*, 91, 92, 98, 112, 143, 147, 151, 155, 200, 213, 255, 256, 375, 376, 380, 381, 389

Ponchardier, P. 27, 28, 91, 98, 380

Poulain, J. 240–43, 340–41, 344

Poulain, P. 240–43, 340–41, 344

Pourchot, G. 388

Pullen, J. 73, 78

Regnault, O. 235, 238, 239, 259, 343, 390

Renault-Roulier, G. ('Remy'), 31, 387

Riviere, Admiral E. 85, 112, 143, 147, 151, 155, 213, 255, 375, 388

Robine, E. 144, 170, 215, 240, 261–3, 269, 317–18, 367

von Roenne, Colonel A. 98

Roosevelt, F. D. 22, 24, 50

Royal Air Force (2 Group of Bomber Command) 40–41, 52, 74, 158 *see also* 2nd Tactical Air Force

Sampson, Flight Lieutenant 'Sammy' 185, 204–5, 222, 232, 294, 378, 385

2nd Tactical Air Force 35, 41, 42, 50, 51, 70, 89, 90, 99, 376

Squadron 21 118, 131, 138, 139, 182, 183, 204, 205, 206

Squadron 174 181

Squadron 198 181

Squadron 245 181

Squadron 464 118, 131, 139, 167, 199, 202

Squadron 487 118, 131, 139, 167, 168, 203

   *see also* Royal Air Force, United States

'Serge' 81–2

Shallard, P. 388

Sismore, E. 72, 76, 77, 110, 111, 130, 135–6, 139, 140, 158, 159, 388

Smith, I. S. 118, 119, 167, 168, 188, 190, 198, 201, 203, 385, 388

Sosies 21, 81, 84, 98, 142, 143, 151

Spaatz, General C. 47

Sparkes, Pilot Officer 162, 167, 199, 227–30, 385

Sperrle, General 47

Stimson, H. 33

Sugden, R. 182, 232, 385

Tempez, A. 61, 96, 97, 98, 101, 207, 209, 210, 234, 235, 239, 260, 301, 379

Thierry Mieg, F. 92, 388

Turner-Lloyd, W. 71, 388

United States
  8th Air Force 48, 99
  21st Army 50

Valentine, F. 269, 319

'Vandreuil, Colonel' *see* Thierry Mieg, F.

Vannier, R. 179, 378

Vignolle, F. 63, 239, 260, 389

Vignolle, F. and R. 63, 239, 389

Vignon, Mme. 143, 144, 215, 240, 262, 269

Vivant, J. 93, 98, 99, 102, 275–7, 297–8, 300, 379, 389

Vivant, R. 93–108 *passim*, 151, 208, 276, 288–92, 298–302, 315, 377, 379, 388

Wickham, A. 131, 133, 138, 168, 181, 184, 205

## Fiction

| | | |
|---|---|---|
| ❑ **Options** | Freda Bright | £1.50p |
| ❑ **The Thirty-nine Steps** | John Buchan | £1.50p |
| ❑ **Secret of Blackoaks** | Ashley Carter | £1.50p |
| ❑ **The Sittaford Mystery** | Agatha Christie | £1.00p |
| ❑ **Dupe** | Liza Cody | £1.25p |
| ❑ **Lovers and Gamblers** | Jackie Collins | £2.50p |
| ❑ **Sphinx** | Robin Cook | £1.25p |
| ❑ **Ragtime** | E. L. Doctorow | £1.50p |
| ❑ **The Rendezvous** | Daphne du Maurier | £1.50p |
| ❑ **Flashman** | George Macdonald Fraser | £1.50p |
| ❑ **The Moneychangers** | Arthur Hailey | £2.25p |
| ❑ **Secrets** | Unity Hall | £1.50p |
| ❑ **Simon the Coldheart** | Georgette Heyer | 95p |
| ❑ **The Eagle Has Landed** | Jack Higgins | £1.95p |
| ❑ **Sins of the Fathers** | Susan Howatch | £2.50p |
| ❑ **The Master Sniper** | Stephen Hunter | £1.50p |
| ❑ **Smiley's People** | John le Carré | £1.95p |
| ❑ **To Kill a Mockingbird** | Harper Lee | £1.75p |
| ❑ **Ghosts** | Ed McBain | £1.25p |
| ❑ **Gone with the Wind** | Margaret Mitchell | £2.95p |
| ❑ **The Totem** | David Morrell | £1.25p |
| ❑ **Platinum Logic** | Tony Parsons | £1.75p |
| ❑ **Wilt** | Tom Sharpe | £1.50p |
| ❑ **Rage of Angels** | Sidney Sheldon | £1.75p |
| ❑ **The Unborn** | David Shobin | £1.50p |
| ❑ **A Town Like Alice** | Nevile Shute | £1.75p |
| ❑ **A Falcon Flies** | Wilbur Smith | £1.95p |
| ❑ **The Deep Well at Noon** | Jessica Stirling | £1.95p |
| ❑ **The Ironmaster** | Jean Stubbs | £1.75p |
| ❑ **The Music Makers** | E. V. Thompson | £1.75p |

## Non-fiction

| | | |
|---|---|---|
| ❑ **Extraterrestrial Civilizations** | Isaac Asimov | £1.50p |
| ❑ **Pregnancy** | Gordon Bourne | £2.95p |
| ❑ **Jogging from Memory** | Rob Buckman | £1.25p |
| ❑ **The 35mm Photographer's Handbook** | Julian Calder and John Garrett | £5.95p |
| ❑ **Travellers' Britain** | Arthur Eperon | £2.95p |
| ❑ **Travellers' Italy** | | £2.50p |
| ❑ **The Complete Calorie Counter** | Eileen Fowler | 75p |

| | | | |
|---|---|---|---|
| ☐ | **The Diary of Anne Frank** | Anne Frank | £1.50p |
| ☐ | **Linda Goodman's Sun Signs** | Linda Goodman | £2.50p |
| ☐ | **Mountbatten** | Richard Hough | £2.50p |
| ☐ | **How to be a Gifted Parent** | David Lewis | £1.95p |
| ☐ | **Symptoms** | Sigmund Stephen Miller | £2.50p |
| ☐ | **Book of Worries** | Robert Morley | £1.50p |
| ☐ | **The Hangover Handbook** | David Outerbridge | £1.25p |
| ☐ | **The Alternative Holiday Catalogue** | edited by Harriet Peacock | £1.95p |
| ☐ | **The Pan Book of Card Games** | Hubert Phillips | £1.75p |
| ☐ | **Food for All the Family** | Magnus Pyke | £1.50p |
| ☐ | **Everything Your Doctor Would Tell You If He Had the Time** | Claire Rayner | £4.95p |
| ☐ | **Just Off for the Weekend** | John Slater | £2.50p |
| ☐ | **An Unfinished History of the World** | Hugh Thomas | £3.95p |
| ☐ | **The Third Wave** | Alvin Toffler | £1.95p |
| ☐ | **The Flier's Handbook** | | £5.95p |

All these books are available at your local bookshop or newsagent, or can be ordered direct from the publisher. Indicate the number of copies required and fill in the form below                                                                    7

Name_____
(Block letters please)

Address_____

Send to Pan Books (CS Department), Cavaye Place, London SW10 9PG
Please enclose remittance to the value of the cover price plus:
35p for the first book plus 15p per copy for each additional book ordered
to a maximum charge of £1.25 to cover postage and packing
Applicable only in the UK

While every effort is made to keep prices low, it is sometimes
necessary to increase prices at short notice. Pan Books reserve
the right to show on covers and charge new retail prices which
may differ from those advertised in the text or elsewhere